Why is Everyone So Cranky?

Why is Everyone So Cranky?

THE TEN TRENDS

COMPLICATING OUR LIVES

AND

WHAT WE CAN DO

ABOUT THEM

C. LESLIE CHARLES

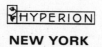

NEW YORK

To Rob Carr, my partner in life, love, and business,
who listens to me.

Copyright © 1999 C. Leslie Charles

Library of Congress Cataloging-in-Publication Data

Charles, C. Leslie.
Why is everyone so cranky? : the ten trends complicating our lives and what we can do about them / C. Leslie Charles. —1st ed.
    p.   cm.
ISBN 0-7868-6525-3 (hardcover)
1. Stress (Psychology) 2. Civilization, Modern—Psychological aspects. 3. Social change—Psychological aspects. 4. Life change events. 5. Stress management. 6. Anger. 7. Peace of mind.
I. Title.
BF575.S75C437 1999
158—dc21   99–22118
CIP

Trade paperback ISBN 0-7868-8443-6

FIRST PAPERBACK EDITION

Book Designer Vicki Fischman

10 9 8 7 6 5 4 3 2 1

Acknowledgments

Though I didn't know it at the time, this book began taking shape well over a decade ago, the result of deep observation and long conversations. When I began presenting the ideas to my audiences, their reactions were wildly enthusiastic. But it was Rob who said it should be a book. One week later I began writing the proposal.

It was my friend and mentor, Sam Horn, who suggested I attend the Maui Writers Conference, where I met my talented, insightful literary agent, Patti Breitman, who both saw value in this idea and shared my enthusiasm. I will always be grateful for Patti's patience, vision, and tutoring. It has also been a joy working with my keen-eyed editor, Leigh Haber, who helped enhance my ideas and add scope to this book. I feel fortunate to have such a competent team at Hyperion who did their utmost to make this book all it could be.

Thanks to Mary Bradshaw for always being there to take one more look at the manuscript, Dr. Carol Mase for her excellent feedback and examples and Mark Williams for his excellent research skills. I owe a debt to my friends and colleagues, Chris Clarke-Epstein, Eileen McDargh, Susan Heathfield, Barbara Braham, Marilynn Semonick, and Mary Jane Mapes for sending me articles, information, gifts, and nonstop encouragement. Thanks also to Terry Brock, Dr. Dale Anderson, psychologist Kate Hull, Rob Peck, Kathy Wagner, JoAnn Sckerl, Mary LoVerde, Tara Nofziger, Joan Nelson, Linda Rands, Jane Porter, Jeanette Heath, Jane Rhoades, Lori Randall, Bob Hamet, Tom Hackbardt, Judy Snow, Nada Gruber, Sharyl Kidd, Chris Wahl, Bev O'Malia, Carol Barker, Alan Zimmerman, Barbara Foose, Jay Kusma, Denise Barton, Wendi Alder, Pamela Butler, Michelle Davis, Sarah Marsh, Jane Handley, Susan Edlinger, Fred Merry, Jim Heywood, Dave Treinis, Kim Kauffman, Ed Bonnen, and Tom and Linda Dufelmeier, and the customer service "tag team": Patti Keefe, Darshelle Pierce, and Cheri Bower.

I especially appreciate my family's willingness to withstand my long absences as I withdrew to my writing space so I could complete this book: my parents, Bob and Julie Allen, my son, Ron Kuripla, my daughter, Cathy Patterson, and my grandchildren, Elissa, Samantha, Ashley, and Kris Jr. Thank you all for your patience, encouragement, and unconditional support. And finally, I'd like to express my gratitude to every one of my clients and audience members over the last four years who truly "got" the message in this book.

Contents

Introduction

As a society, we are in the grasp of an alarming series of trends that have systematically infiltrated our existence; and whether we know it or not, we've been influenced, individually and collectively. As a result, we've been thrust into an emotional tailspin that promises to change the quality of your life and mine permanently unless we take immediate action. It's America's "anger epidemic."

We're a nation whose collective mood has gone sour. On our streets and highways, in our workplaces, and even in our homes, we've abandoned common courtesy. Maybe at first your experience was like mine. You couldn't quite put your finger on it, but eventually you got it: People aren't as nice as they used to be. They're impatient, rude, and demanding. They're in a huff and in a hurry. They don't want to wait in line, they don't want to cooperate, and they don't want to be inconvenienced by anyone or anything. They want their way and they want it *now*, like a bunch of spoiled kids, demanding the lion's share of whatever there is to be had.

It's not simply a lack of manners, it's an open hostility. You've noticed the symptoms, just as I have. That's why you opened this book. People are cranky! Maybe you are, too. It seems our self-control has been replaced with scorn and none of us are immune. Kids, adults, politicians, businesspeople, and even some community and religious leaders are lashing out. *Never have so many, with so much, been so unhappy*.

There's a reason we're cranky. Actually, there are ten, and when you see the list in chapter 1, I guarantee you'll relate. Some of what you read will confirm your suspicions about what's going on. But it will also explain how you, too, have been unwittingly infected by the anger epidemic.

This book describes the serious nature of our cultural crisis but does so at a personal level. If you're reeling under the pressure of today's hurry-worry lifestyle you'll appreciate knowing that better choices exist, and they are accessible. We don't need to be so at odds with ourselves; we don't need to hurt so much. By taking steps to heal ourselves we help heal our society. These ideas will help you reflect, rebalance, and rebound; you can liberate yourself from unnecessary pressure and stress and carve out a more satisfying life.

Maybe you've wondered when our mood began to decline. The first incident that got my attention involved, of all things, Cabbage Patch Kids. It was Christmas season, 1983. I remember the flurry of panic shopping once word got out that supplies would be limited for the season. Shoppers held all-night vigils and stormed department stores as they opened. Clerks were stampeded and injured. High stakes negotiations and even fights ensued as shoppers desperately clamored to get their share of a limited commodity. The once simple act of acquiring a child's toy had become an obsession.

We turned a corner that holiday season: all of a sudden, giving became secondary to *getting*. Like the canary in a mine shaft, this display of bizarre buyer behavior warned of an insidious shift in our society—a slip in our cultural character. It wasn't the first social canary, nor was it the last.

Since then, the commercial aspect of holiday shopping has become more predatory. Harried parents stretch their time, patience, and budgets to afford the latest trendy gift their kids can't live without. Toys and games are becoming increasingly more high tech, more expensive, and even more imperative: just watch the backlash if parents can't locate the latest "must-have" holiday gift and the at-all-cost lengths to which they will go to get their hands on the prize. It's déjà vu all over again!

Of course, the problem isn't in the specific item we might purchase. It's the desperate, compulsive Big Game Hunt mentality we need to examine; the feeling that everyone's holiday will be ruined and worthless unless this year's trophy gift can be bagged so we can outdo whatever we did last year. The 1998 holiday season featured more gifts over one hundred dollars than any previous one: some psychologists suggest that parents are spending more to compensate for a lack of quality time. Intellectually, most of us know we can't replace real *presence* with a stack of presents, but at a gut level, we might make an effort to fill the void.

Let's briefly track another trend we're all familiar with: "road rage." It took some years for it to migrate from L.A. to the rest of the country, but I'm convinced there were small, scattered forces at work that helped propel this peril across our continent. In the late eighties one of my friends attached a tiny toy phaser gun to her car keys. It made cute little outer space noises as she pretended to "disappear" irritating drivers. This seemed harmless at the time but it was a hostile act. Did seemingly innocent individual expressions of hostility such as this eventually give way to open aggression? Do we think we actually *own* that piece of road our car occupies when we're in it?

You and I have witnessed increasingly sensational news reports and talk shows; graphic violence as entertainment. We're bombarded with noise from our television, computer games, power tools, convenience items, and even other people's booming car radios. Small wonder our levels of personal aggression have intensified. Stress has swept its way across the continent as if it were the common cold. We're all tense and irritable, but our dour disposition is not the cause; it's merely symptomatic of a larger problem.

In 1994 while I was consulting with a local insurance company, an employee said she had just received a death threat from one of her insureds. This was a first for me. A death threat in one of my client offices. In my hometown, yet. Even though the policy holder obviously didn't mean it (after all, his name, address, and phone number were on file) this kind of behavior was once unheard of. Somewhere, somehow, someone had upped the ante of what an angry customer could get away with.

So far we've discussed other people. Let's get personal for a moment. Dare I ask how you're faring under the pressures of your daily demands? Are you, like many others, living with chronic frustration or disillusionment over your job? We're all aware of the high divorce rate in the United States, and I'm alarmed at the number of people I meet who suffer unhappy, fragmented family relationships. Call it overworked and undernurtured: Our money concerns and job uncertainty cause many of us to work extended hours for no extra pay because we know if we don't, someone else will. Most of us compulsively overschedule the few free hours we have, so we end up feeling busy, burdened, or burned out. Despite the continual promise of more leisure time, we're mired in daily demands that hold little significance to the whole of our lives. And there's more.

Nonstop change, spiraling costs, market competition, elevated customer expectations, and workforce cutbacks influence how we treat one another. Technological acceleration, media domination, the pressure to keep up, the expanding gap between the haves and the have-nots, and the specialized needs of an aging society add to this challenging and complicated climate.

This is our culture today; we are describing your life and mine. We've been promised a lot but there's a serious shortfall. In our attempts to have it all, many of us are losing out and we're mad as hell about it. We know something is wrong but what exactly is it? Who has time to stop and figure it out, and what can we do about the problem? This book answers these questions and more, including the one nagging most people today, and maybe you, as well: *Why is everyone so cranky?*

In this book you'll find numerous depictions of the disagreeableness so common in our culture today and descriptions of the many conflicts we're experiencing. Be advised: you might discover *yourself* in some of the cranky examples! But that's the point. Not only will you isolate some of the spots in your existence that are sore or tender, you'll also find a wealth of practical options and anti-cranky solutions to complement the lifestyle you're trying to create.

Please keep a pen and notepad handy so you can write down insights or good ideas as they come to you. In fact, I recommend you buy a special notepad and keep a written record of page numbers where an idea "speaks to you" or any phrase resonates. What you read here is going to trigger a series of insights and for a while, you'll look at our society and your own behavior differently. I'd like to help make that a lasting, rather than temporary process, and your active participation will make it happen.

Because we're discussing a social epidemic, I thought it would be a good idea if we begin with a brief Self-Exam so you can establish a baseline. Just as your doctor conducts an annual screening to determine your state of health, you want to conduct occasional interpersonal screenings to check your state of mind and spirit. You have some knowledge of your personal patterns and the areas in your life that are the most compromised. The question is, Are you willing to: (1) admit to it, and (2) do something about it?

If so, with the help of this book, you can diagnose your current state of being and decide how to improve upon it.

Level One Screening

All good checkups begin with a few questions and that's where we'll begin:

- Are you feeling continually rushed and pressed for time?
- Has it been a while since you did anything fun or had time for relaxation?
- Have you become more irritable or impatient over the last couple of years?
- Are you neglecting your health in any way?
- Do you feel dissatisfied or discontent with the past year of your life?
- Do you feel at all apprehensive about this year?
- Is there a pending change in your life you've been resisting or avoiding?
- Is there a relationship in your life that needs attention?
- Are you working more and enjoying it less?
- Are you plagued with the nagging sensation that something is missing in your life?

Maybe you said "yes" to only one or two of these questions. If so, your condition is not extreme and you may only need minor adjustments in your routine. But wait, there's more. Before you go off on your own, here's the Level Two Screening where you can check for high-risk indicators.

Level Two Screening

Are you regularly experiencing any of the following (please check any that apply):

____ headaches
____ anxiety
____ shortness of breath
____ muscular tension

___ sleep problems
___ upset stomach
___ compulsive spending
___ overeating or loss of appetite
___ adrenaline surges
___ irritability
___ an inability to relax when you have a chance to unwind
___ tight, clenched jaw
___ difficult relationships
___ constant worries about money and debt
___ chronic distraction: an inability to focus on one thing at a time
___ building resentment toward work or family
___ a desire to strike out when people do something you dislike

If, by any chance, you're experiencing three or more of these symptoms with any regularity, heads up! That's an early warning. Like a low-grade infection, sometimes it takes a while before we recognize the severity of our condition. Treat yourself now by reading this book before your symptoms get worse, and you become one of those cranky people you've been complaining about.

Urgent Care Available

If you're suffering from most or all of the above symptoms, you need urgent care! If that's the case, don't read this book chapter by chapter. Take the triage approach as they do in emergency medicine and address the areas that require immediate attention while they're still treatable. After reading chapter 1, scan the table of contents and turn to the chapter or chapters you consider most relevant. Trust your intuition; there's a part of you that knows exactly what you need to read first. You can take one Cranky Quiz at a time or all of them at once (your scores will be a good indicator of where you should begin).

If you're too cranky and impatient to read a full chapter and only want to address a specific topic, go to the sections that coincide with the specific Cranky Quiz items you consider the most problematic. Then read the anti-cranky strategies and review the section entitled "A Dose of Reality" at the end of the chapter.

This book contains a lot of information but it's designed for busy readers. You can read one small section at a time and begin mapping out an immediate course of action. There will be parts of this book you'll want to revisit. List them in your companion notebook. Mark the quizzes and log your scores. Date them so you can compare today's scores with future ones. Let these pages and the notes you make become living documents to measure your growth and success. Highlight or underline the sections. Dogear the pages you consider worth revisiting. Read this book with your spouse or partner so the two of you can work through the material together. You'll both grow individually, and as a couple.

Take the Cranky Quizzes

The Cranky Quizzes are designed to help you zero in on the attitudes and behaviors that contribute to your crankiness and establish a baseline.

I feel compelled to make a few comments about the Cranky Quizzes. There are no trick questions nor is there any intent on my part to entrap you. I figure if you're going to read this book you may as well get as much out of it as possible, and that's why I created the quizzes. They'll help you isolate what ails you, and if you rationalize or justify any question too much (which could be interpreted as a cranky tactic) you'll end up cheating yourself and defeating the purpose.

So I invite you to be as honest as possible, not splitting hairs or giving yourself too large a helping of the benefit of a doubt. You'll be rewarded. I've found in my own life that self-awareness has taken all the fun out of lying to myself. However, what I get out of riding herd on my behavior has rewards too numerous to mention.

And last, not all of the Cranky Quiz items represent an area of cranky dysfunction. A few of them reflect the concern and disquiet anyone with a semblance of self-awareness would feel about some of the things we see happening in our world. Just think of the quizzes as the first step in your personal crankiness prevention program.

When All Else Fails

If you ever have an absolutely rotten day where you feel "rode hard and put away wet" and your spirit needs a quick dose of nurturing or self-renewal, go to chapter 13, entitled The Emergency Department. There you'll find a list of affirming ideas and calming statements to help you regain your equilibrium. You'll notice these items are organized by chapter, with each individual affirmation corresponding with its Cranky Quiz item. As your doctor might say, take as needed.

Why I Wrote This Book: Support for Sagging Spirits

In the course of my twenty years as a workplace consultant and professional speaker I've met a multitude of wounded, hurting people; far more than I could have imagined. Of course, emotional injuries are less obvious than physical ones, but the symptoms are clear: They show up as a lack of enthusiasm, high stress, poor health, negative attitude, a lack of team spirit, resistance to change, low pride in work, and conflicted relationships, to name a few.

Many, many people are hurting in our society today. Despite their families, good jobs, health, and numerous possessions, they feel isolated, alienated, and ignored. Some have been chronically angry for so long they don't know how to let go of it, *and they're afraid of what might happen if they do*. Too many people are living on the edge today, stretched beyond their means, mentally, physically, and financially. My mission is to help resuscitate the spirits of as many people as I can. That's why I wrote this book.

And now it's time to discover why others—and perhaps even you—are so cranky. I hope reading this book will make a difference in your life. After you're finished maybe you'll take some small but significant steps to help turn the tide from chronic crankiness toward a more civil society. You can be assured I'm doing my part.

The Whining Turns to a Roar

THE AGE OF MISSED MANNERS
AND DISSED RESPECT

It's hard to find a friendly, inviting face these days, and if we do see one we get suspicious. Even our language reflects our surly attitude: Once upon a time we would murmur a genuine "Excuse me" or "Sorry" if we accidentally brushed against or got in someone's way. Today, people snarl these same words, while forcing their way into line or pushing others aside, as a means of dismissing their absent manners. We may have gotten physically closer to one another with our in-your-face attitude, but we're more emotionally distanced than ever.

Even if you're not an active agent in spreading our anger epidemic, you're certainly suffering its consequences. The symptoms exist in your community and mine, from isolated aggressive acts to general surliness: someone arguing with a clerk, swearing, victoriously stealing your parking place, or littering the streets with trash. Take any of these incidents and isolate them: hey, no big deal; maybe somebody's having a bad day. But make them commonplace, a way of life, and it is a very big deal!

The most insidious aspect of our cranky culture is how dulled we've become to civil and social misdeeds. We mutely turn away from a stranger's hostile act, our combined fear and insecurity stopping us from speaking out. Yet when celebrities, political leaders, or sports figures misbehave, we're both curious and cynical because they seem to have it all, and their conduct often becomes the topic du jour at work and home. The point is that a lot of people are getting away with irresponsible acts and they need to be held accountable. Ignoring these acts—or tolerating them—only condemns us to more.

HOW DID WE GET HERE?

Before we can address the issue of cultural crankiness we need to explore where it came from, and I find the progression almost as intriguing as a novel. If you've ever enjoyed a good mystery, you remember watching a series of incidents stack up against one another like dominoes, one by one, ready to collapse at the slightest nudge. As the story approached the crisis, you could see it coming, but the characters couldn't. They were too swept up in the circumstances that would later set their fate. That's exactly what's happened to us.

We've been too close to comprehend the significance of singular incidents as they unfolded and upheaved our social landscape into a climate of anger and rage. The more we've been influenced, the busier and more self-absorbed we've become, unable (and in some cases, unwilling) to grasp what's happening to us. We can see it in others, but not ourselves.

IT'S BEEN A LONG TIME COMING

You've probably spent considerable time wondering how we got so angry as a nation. Well, just as a debilitating illness incubates for years before its symptoms become evident, our anger epidemic has followed the same slow, insidious pattern. The hopeful news is that just as an illness has a course of treatment and recovery, so does our cranky condition, but first we must understand the nature of what ails us.

Over the past half century, ten powerful trends have been influencing how we live, work, and look at the world. We've witnessed these events and the media have reported them, but only in isolation. We haven't fully grasped the extent to which they have become interconnected and entwined into the fabric of our society, or our lives.

Here are the Ten Trends complicating your life and mine:

1. Compressed Time
2. Communication Overload
3. Dis-Connectedness

4. Cost
5. Competition
6. Customer Contact
7. Computers
8. Change
9. Coming of Age
10. Complexity

Your life has been shaped by these trends and you'll know intuitively which are most severely affecting you. But before I explain the Ten Trends in the chapters to come, there's a quick side trip we need to take.

A BRIEF HISTORY OF TIME

We need an historical perspective on incidents from our past that seemed initially insignificant yet left a lasting imprint on our culture. Many of my own insights came after the fact, but eight years without a TV gave me a special vantage point and so did the nature of my work. As a business consultant, clients hire me to identify the "invisible"— policies, methods, and practices that interfere with productivity and complicate work relationships. Basically, I get paid to ferret out problems and bottlenecks everyone else overlooks, and this is the process I've used to analyze the last five decades.

The Fabricated Fifties: Birth of a Dream

The fifties were a time of promise and paradox. Promise if you were a member of the white, emerging middle class; paradox if you were a person of color. In the postwar era, many of our heroes were from the military. We respected and looked up to our leaders and teachers without question. Life was structured and boundaries were clear: Monday through Friday were business or school days. Saturday we shopped and did domestic chores, and Sunday was a day off for most of us. Technology led the field of dreams, with numerous new convenience items for homemakers, a revolution in car designs, and best of all, television, the miracle invention that promised quality entertainment, education, and access to information.

We knew our neighbors. People went for strolls at night and felt free to drop in on one another. We sat on our porches. Locked doors were a rarity. The introduction of our superhighway system offered us unprecedented mobility and a new unity from coast to coast. Little did we realize these same arteries also signaled the birth of today's dis-connectedness, fragmenting our neighborhoods, communities, and culture in ways we never dreamed possible.

The Skeptical Sixties: Tattered Dreams and Disillusionment

The pendulum took a wide swing in the sixties. Television was now entrenched in our daily lives. We reached our dream of landing on the moon but loosened our foothold here on earth. Witnessing the assassination of President John F. Kennedy on the screen brought our nation to a standstill. The later assassinations of his brother Robert and Dr. Martin Luther King Jr. signaled a deep disillusionment in our system and ourselves. The Vietnam war split the allegiance of families and loved ones. We questioned everyone and everything. Young protesters raised their voices in outrage, challenging the system, rejecting tradition, and turning to sex, drugs, and rock 'n' roll. The boundaries between good and bad blurred as Hollywood aggrandized the antihero.

Neighborhoods mutated as those who could afford it migrated to the suburbs and bought a second car. With the introduction of fringe shopping centers and malls, many downtown merchants and family-owned neighborhood stores were forced to close their doors. The scourge of segregation and the brutal slayings of Civil Rights activists embroiled us in more dis-connectedness and complexity than we had bargained for.

The Sassy Seventies: The Rise of Consumerism

By now the women's movement had raised its voice and our consciousness, if we were paying attention. With Watergate and Nixon's resignation our faith in political leaders hit a new low. We turned to consumerism as a pick-me-up, and for the first time we became active agents in ad campaigns as company names and insignia began appearing on our clothes. Feeling a surge of middle class affluence, we excelled as consumers, affording the cost of cars and other big-ticket items by the size of the monthly payments instead of the purchase price.

Costs went up but that didn't stop us; credit cards distanced us from the sting of big spending. Two-family incomes made the idea of carrying a debt load less onerous than in the past. We enjoyed increased consumer opportunities, too, as stores stayed open seven days a week. The structure of the past gave way to "anything goes."

Movie content and even television shows became more shocking and violent. Toward the end of the decade, money for human services and government entitlement programs began to disappear while the price tags on houses, land, and cars went up.

We withdrew into our homes, locked our doors, discouraged drop-in company, and stayed off the streets at night. The exodus to the suburbs continued. Meanwhile, privacy fences and garage door openers limited our daily contact with neighbors, driving yet another wedge into our already tenuous connections.

The cost of living continued to rise and so did the divorce rate and the number of single-parent families. The boomers were maturing. So were our parents, and as much as it hurt, we had to find someone to take care of them because we'd become too busy to do it ourselves. As we found ourselves coming of age, our lives had become more complex, more costly, and definitely more conflicted.

The Egotistical Eighties: Access, Overload, and Excess

If we thought consumerism reigned in the seventies, that was just a warm-up. Despite the high prices, our consumerism reached new levels. Mall strolling and shopping became a national competitive pastime for people of all ages. Chain stores and supermarkets were open for business twenty-four hours a day, and ATMs assured us of instant, accessible cash.

Losing our common enemy with the end of the Cold War ruptured our already precarious connection to one another. In our communities we witnessed a disturbing increase of homeless people on our streets and we had to kiss some of our compassion good-bye so we could cope. In the midst of a wellness-inspired craze for health clubs and personal trainers loomed the grim reality of AIDS. While all of us were in some way touched by its horror, this controversial illness gave us further reasons to disconnect rather than unite.

Meanwhile, personal computers offered endless capacity for communication in a world that was already pumping out more information than we could handle. Phil Donahue broke new ground with his revolutionary talk show format, and cable TV opened the door for new programming, new standards, new audiences, and stronger positioning for the corporate news media. VCRs changed our movie-viewing habits. The gap between print and TV journalism narrowed with the introduction of *USA Today*, whose dispensers suspiciously resembled TV monitors.

Plagued with too many choices of what to watch or read, besieged with junk mail and more periodicals than we could keep up with, overwhelmed with work-related communications and information, we found ourselves on permanent fast forward, overloaded in a complex, consumptive world that refused to stop changing. Meanwhile, we clung to our careers with fervor, bringing home our overstuffed briefcases each night, lest we fall behind.

The Nasty Nineties: Talk Is Cheap

In the nineties, TV talk shows popped up like daffodils in the spring. The fierce pressure for ratings quickly drove the standards downward. Elsewhere in the media, narrow casting became the norm: special interest TV channels and periodicals proliferated, splintering people and their passions into smaller, select groups, giving them less in common to talk about. Sensationalism ran rampant with sex, violence, and intimacy from the talk show set to the big screen. Movies became a vehicle for mass marketing products instead of a medium for ideas or entertainment.

The Internet, on-line news groups, LISTSERVs, and chat lines exposed us to just about any topic of interest, plus endless shopping and spending opportunities. Continually accelerating technological change created a lust for pagers, personal cell phones, system upgrades, personal web pages, and constant E-mail contact, regardless of need. People who complained about being pressed for time somehow managed to spend hours on-line each day, connected to their computers instead of their loved ones.

Driven by increased competition from a global market and the desire for higher stock values and larger profits, corporate downsizing created major upheavals for thousands of workers and their families, many of whom were middle-aged and looking forward to the happy conclusion of a successful career. Merging conglomerates dominated the business scene, limiting our options while fortifying their market share.

Between rampant ad streams, the media presented news laced with undertones of melodrama, creating the perception of a hostile, dangerous world despite a slight drop in crime rates. Customer expectations continued to rise but the quality of contact suffered on both sides of the counter. While the subject of service was on everyone's lips, most organizations failed to deliver. Meanwhile, service personnel suffered from the strain of being abused by hordes of cranky customers.

While we lost our mortal enemy when the Cold War ended, we found new ones, thanks to talk shows fostering hate and divisiveness. We displayed our disdain for the poor by disenfranchising them financially as we secured ourselves within the stronghold of gated subdivisions. We didn't show much compassion for our kids, either, as public school monies dried up and we voted down local millage increases. Special programs, sports, and enrichment classes were cut back or outright eliminated as we invested in Wall Street instead of our children.

As population continued to increase we reached new levels of competition for space, time, and attention. Race relations once again surfaced as cultural diversity became an issue in our workplaces and communities, and as minority voices cried out for their rights the rest of us queued up, greedily vying to vent our special issues, personal agendas, and biased opinions.

Increased speed limits added to the turmoil of our already revved up lifestyles and the pressures of compressed time, computers, competition, and customer contact complicated our lives to the breaking point. Emotional eruptions in our homes and workplaces, our streets, and even on commercial airliners reflected our time-compressed lives, inner conflicts, and inability to cope.

THE FUSION OF PAST AND FUTURE

Thus ends our short course on cultural crankiness. If you're middle-aged you probably remember most of these events, but perhaps like me, you didn't think much about them at the time. But now you can get a sense of how they helped frame and shape our culture. You'll recall additional events, too, and connect them with one or more of the Ten

Trends. Even if you were born in the sixties or seventies you can probably identify how these events have contributed to some of your current conflicts.

For the Skeptics among Us

Some may argue that they are virtually untouched by historical incidents. Guess again. We *are* affected by our past. We can be profoundly affected by what we see, hear, and experience, particularly in our formative years, carrying images, words, feelings, and whole experiences in our memories, even in our cellular structure. We bring with us into adulthood a composite of what we heard repeatedly while growing up, some of which was encouraging, some not. Positive or negative, these messages leave their mark. Lots of us seek counseling to rid ourselves of the dysfunctional ones.

It's not just messages from our past that influence our behavior. Every day we're exposed to hundreds of commercial messages. Are we influenced by them? We'd like to say no, but advertisers disagree! Think about the hundreds of thousands of ads you've heard in your lifetime; how many can you still sing or recite, word for word, although they haven't been aired for years?

We're not only influenced by the commercial messages surrounding us but also by the messages behind the messages. Ads exist to sell products, but watch them closely for embedded messages of fear, power, sex, status, and wealth. Our desire to belong, achieve, prosper, and be loved, plus the appeal of strong visual images, are what prompt us to buy. Corporations invest billions of dollars to figure out which messages have the most impact. Political spin masters spend untold hours crafting the right speeches, slogans, and pictures to gain our vote.

The question is not "Have you been influenced?" The question is "To what extent have you been influenced?" The effects are subtle, gradual, subconscious. Not easy to detect. But if you're conflicted by a negative body image, a sense of inadequacy about your face or personality, discontent because you don't have enough, or driven by a compelling desire to be rich because you think it will make you feel better, you've been affected. *Infected* might be a more appropriate word. Examine your attitude, values, expectations, and sense of entitlement to determine the extent to which you've been molded as a consumer. We'll revisit part of this issue in chapter 3.

A Slow, Killing Simmer

When I discuss crankiness and the anger that fuels it, I'm describing a fuming, unrelenting sense of anger, hostility, and alienation that simmers for months, even years without relief. Eventually, all it takes is a triggering incident, usually minor, for the hostile person to go ballistic: a clerk makes a mistake, a line moves too slowly, or a driver does something stupid. These people often make the headlines when they unleash their pent-up anger and hostility. We even have a phrase for it: *going postal*.

In their book, *Anger Kills*, authors Redford Williams, M.D., and Virginia Williams, Ph.D., lay out the facts about hostility: how it can harm our well-being, undermine our relationships, and even shorten our lives. They explain how to transform hostility into healthy expression. When properly channeled and controlled, anger can serve us. It can mobilize us to initiate massive change, as Candy Lightner did when her daughter was killed by a drunk driver. If you ever think one person can't make a difference, I'd offer Ms. Lightner and Mothers Against Drunk Driving (MADD), as testimony to the power of raising your voice against irresponsible behavior. But a long-term unfocused anger would not have served Candy Lightner nor her daughter's memory. When mishandled, anger can make us sick or provoke desperate acts. Maybe in your more cranky, hostile moments you've wondered about the precariously thin line that separates you from the berserk people who make the nightly news. I certainly have.

Hostility short circuits our compassion and replaces it with contempt, encouraging us to blame and strike out. But in our attempts to hurt others, we hurt ourselves. It pays to trade hostility for hope, anger for optimism, and greed for generosity. Becoming more compassionate, kind, and civil doesn't mean you'll be taken advantage of (some of the kindest people I know have a keen eye for deceit). It also doesn't mean you'll never have a bad day, or that you'll never get mad. But it does mean you can express your anger in positive ways and keep crankiness from hurting you. Or someone else.

What Did You Expect?

At the bedrock of our anger epidemic lies a compelling, complicating presence in our lives: the workings of "the Expectation Machine." Imagine a conglomerate of illusions, impossible-to-deliver promises, and erroneous beliefs that feed into a highly fantasized version of "the perfect life," and you have the Expectation Machine. Its fallout affects us both at an individual and societal level.

For example, each of the last five decades brought with it a set of promises and expectations. While most of these promises were never realized, advertisements, media images, and the intriguing illusions of futurists persistently fed our hope for a future far out of our grasp. Our cynicism rose, but so did our expectations. If you're thinking this makes no sense, you're right.

Enter the commercial fuel that powers the Expectation Machine. Ads deluge us with idyllic images and promises of a perfect world. If you could watch a film festival of the commercials from each decade you'd catch the continual escalation of imagery, persuasion, and seduction. Reality suffers in comparison, but we keep irrationally hoping for the right product (or the right combination of them), so we can have as good a life as those perfect people on the screen.

Review the eighties and nineties and you can track how our expectation curve morphed into new proportions. Boomers exhibited their unrestrained capacity for spending as no preceding generation had, buying into the alluring promises of ads and nonstop shop-till-you-drop encouragement. And it isn't over. Take a close look: We're surrounded with compelling billboards, print ads, captivating TV images, and enticing catalogs bludgeoning us with the notion that we need—and deserve—everything that's out there. The Expectation Machine lives on, gaining strength as we go.

I'll admit I'm sensitive to this issue, having raised three small kids while living at poverty level for five years: half of that time I was working forty hours a week and the other half I was on public assistance, working on my community college degree. But our world was less materialistic then. I can't begin to imagine what it would be like today, living at subsistence level, being constantly inundated with such compelling messages. I'd feel outraged and cheated over having so little in a world that taunted me and my kids with the promise of so much.

THE CONFUSION OVER EXPECTATION
AND ENTITLEMENT

One of our inalienable rights is the pursuit of happiness. We're not *guaranteed* happiness, but some of us think we deserve happiness without having to do the pursuing! That's one of the reasons so many of us buy lottery tickets; we think wealth means happiness.

Most people assure me they could handle the pressure of newfound wealth. They say they *deserve* to win the lottery more than other people because they'd know how to handle it. Yet, many lottery winners squander their fortunes until they're back to square one. They don't just lose their fortunes, either. Many instant millionaires end up alienated from their families and rejected by long-time friends who greedily *expected* to share the profits, feeling *entitled* to a windfall by virtue of their kinship or friendship.

The confusion over expectation and entitlement has shaped us into insatiable consumers, obsessed with *wanting* and *needing* instead of appreciating what we already have. With a tremendous leap of fuzzy logic many of us have come to perceive *expectation* and *entitlement* as one and the same: "If I want something, this must mean that I *deserve* it. If I deserve it, then I'm free to do whatever it takes so I can get what is *rightfully mine* in the first place. I'm *entitled* to get what I want and I want it now!"

Great Expectations

In case you're wondering, expectations don't exist at the forefront of our consciousness, yet they influence virtually every decision we make. Once you become more aware of how your expectations influence your actions you'll be able to exert more control over your moods and choices, resulting in fewer embarrassing, knee-jerk reactions and far less frustration.

You see, regardless of how realistic or far-out your expectations may be, when they don't materialize, you experience disappointment. It's that simple. Think about some of the major letdowns you've encountered in your personal life or job. Could they have been prevented if you had been more definite or realistic about what you expected beforehand? Sometimes people disappoint us because they simply don't know what we want or expect from them.

If you do some investigating, you might just be surprised at what you actually *expect* from yourself, your loved ones, life, work, or your favorite hobby. This book will help you identify, clarify, and get a better sense of how your expectations drive your decision making. You might also gain some insight into other people's expectations.

Grating Expectations: The Code of the Cranks

While we're on the subject, just in case you live with, work for, or must spend significant amounts of time with people who fit the cranky profile, the following may help you better understand why they behave as they do. Here are some of the underlying expectations harbored by our cranky citizens who think they have a constitutional right to unleash their insolence on the rest of us:

—The Cranky Code—

- I am entitled to what I want when I want it.
- My time is important and I should not have to be inconvenienced by others.
- I have a right to be impatient or rude when other people are behaving stupidly.
- I am entitled to special privileges because I am who I am.
- My family should know I care about them without my having to prove it or say it every day.
- I'm a taxpayer; I own part of this road and I have the right to drive as fast as I want.
- I not only have the right to pursue happiness, I *deserve* to be happy and I'll do whatever it takes to achieve it.
- I'm entitled to cheat a little bit in order to get ahead. If I don't take advantage someone else will, and then they'll be a step ahead of me.
- I work extra hard but don't get paid for it so I'm justified in helping myself to a few "souvenirs" from my office to offset what I am rightfully owed.
- I'm too busy to mince around with false politeness and should be able to tell people exactly what I think without having to worry about their feelings.
- I must be more *in the know* than everyone else so I can stay "one up" on them; otherwise they may take advantage of me.

- I deserve the newest, the biggest, the best, and the most. It's my right.
- I'm going to die one day so I may as well get as much as I can right now.
- So what if I'm being rude—I never have to see this person again so what difference does it make?
- My opinions and views are more valid than anyone else's.
- My emergencies take precedence over anyone else's emergency.
- The world is unfair and opportunities are limited, so I may as well get all I can while I can, regardless of who or what stands in my way.

DIVIDED OR UNITED, WE'RE ALL IN THIS TOGETHER

In reading the Cranky Code you probably sensed the dis-connected-ness, the superiority and separateness, and the attitude of entitlement embedded in each statement. Maybe it reminds you of people you know: those who are quick to take advantage, who talk but don't listen; those who try to bully or badger you. Our cranky population is vast, we've all been infected to some extent, and those with raging conditions are causing all kinds of trouble for the rest of us. But now let's turn to you for a moment: When you get exposed to cranky behaviors, what's your typical reaction? Do you stay focused on how good it feels *not* to be combative or do you get cranky, too?

Crankiness Is Communicable

Crankiness is contagious: One person's brooding behavior can trigger an infectious aftermath of gigantic proportions. Here's what I mean: You get up in a good mood, but by the time your family is done with you, or a few crabby coworkers and customers have roughed you up, you've caught their crankiness as if it were the flu. Yes, even a mellow, mature, naturally courteous individual like you can be infected if you're not careful.

For example, has some surly stranger recently annoyed you to the point that you ended up taking it out on someone else? Think about how unfair this is to you, or those around you, when the anger or irrita-tion you unleash is sparked by someone you may never see again.

Just like when you catch a cold, the onset of a foul mood is subtle. It sneaks up on you and in the blink of an eye, things are out of control. Start paying attention to the frequency and intensity of your moods. For the next few days, monitor how *often* you get cranky while noting the *extent* of your contrariness, too.

An Unconscious Infusion

Moodiness is often an unconscious habit and people who live by the Cranky Code don't realize what they look or sound like, or the shoddy way they treat others. They simply behave without thinking. *They don't understand that any mood or behavior repeated over time becomes second nature.* They haven't a clue; they are simply doing what comes "naturally." Pay attention to the habitual ways you think and act; observe the patterns you've built through the years, and you might learn some things about yourself that other people already know!

We all know that to some extent, other people affect us, and we affect them, so pay close attention to how you react to rudeness. You can't control how other people behave but you *can* control how you do. You don't have to "catch" crankiness! You even have a built-in defense system that can help you resist being contaminated.

YOUR BUILT-IN IMPUNITY: EMOTIONAL IMMUNITY

The internal protective mechanism that can safeguard you from cranky outbreaks is your "emotional immune system (EIS)." Similar to your physical immune system, your EIS is located in your mind and its maintenance is up to you. You may take a multivitamin every day to benefit your physical immune system, but how about your emotional immune system? Your mind needs to stay in peak condition, too, and while there's no magic pill on the market, you can treat yourself with your own personal brand of "mental vitamins"!

Your EIS Protection Plan

Anytime, anywhere, you can fortify your emotional immune system to resist being infected by people's contrary behaviors. There are just a few simple steps to follow. When exposed to a negative person or difficult circumstance, stop and immediately quantify the size of the problem:

- Is this a small, medium, or large annoyance?
- Is it simply unsettling or downright dangerous?
- Is this a minor conflict or mortal combat?

If you're willing to take a moment and truthfully answer those three questions you've taken the first step in boosting your EIS. Next, you want to match the level of your reaction to the severity of the problem. Ask yourself:

- Do I plan to get mildly irritated or wildly upset?
- Can I blow this off or will I blow up instead?
- How long do I plan to stay upset and why?

If you've been contaminated by the Cranky Bug you may never have asked yourself questions like this before; you just got mad instead. Well, guess what? Your willingness to stop and ask these questions can change your life. People are initially skeptical when I explain this process, but later they tell me how well the EIS strategies work. There's absolutely no need for you to fly off the handle impulsively every time something goes wrong. That's what cranky people do. They don't realize they can *consciously choose* how to respond to what happens to them—but you do!

Here's an example: A professor friend of mine told me that one of her students came to class visibly upset. On the verge of tears, the student explained he couldn't take the final exam because his fiancée had just called off their engagement. He was distraught and couldn't eat or sleep. He was too depressed to study, let alone be tested. My friend asked him, "And how long do you *plan* on being depressed?"

The student was stunned by the question. Then he said, "I dunno. Two weeks, I guess." My friend said fine, come back in two weeks, and he did. Three months later the student confided that until this incident, he didn't understand he had so much control over his moods. His professor had helped him discover the power of his EIS.

It's high time you discovered the power of your EIS: When misfortune strikes, categorize the event (inconvenience, irritation, crisis, tragedy) and treat the situation accordingly (big upset or little upset, long lived or brief). Make your reaction appropriate to the seriousness of the circumstance. Once the incident has passed, do what you can to prevent it from happening again and then move on to better things.

Immunize Yourself

Long-term emotional wear and tear can make us vulnerable to physical illness. Why sacrifice your health over people you can't change or circumstances you can't control? Cranky people undermine their health by being perpetually provoked. And no, you can't eradicate crankiness from the world but your EIS can help you resist infection. It's like an antibiotic and you're in charge of the dosage.

You keep your EIS in peak condition by taking a nice deep breath when you're exposed to stressful situations and keeping your body as relaxed as possible. You enhance your immunity by finding the humor in a tense situation, even if you only laugh silently. You keep yourself in good shape when you remind yourself that irritating events occur all the time and you can handle them. You benefit every time you reaffirm that you cannot control everything that happens to you but you can control your reaction. And now you know that whenever you treat a small incident like it's a big one or replay a stressful event over and over in your mind you compromise your EIS.

There will be times when bizarre thoughts spontaneously pop into your mind, but you can interrupt them before they take hold. The minute you realize you're on a negative track, think or literally say the word *stop*! or envision a Stop sign. Don't allow the negative thought to continue. Consciously switch your mental channel and put a positive image in your head instead. This may initially require a bit of concentration but the more you practice, the easier it will get.

When you allow fear, insecurity, or toxic people to pollute your perceptions you weaken your EIS. When you take responsibility for what you see, feel, or do, you fortify it. By keeping your EIS in peak condition you increase your capacity for resisting people's bad moods, regardless of the number of exposures. You stay emotionally healthy by choice.

A KIND THOUGHT

The point is that those of us who are still capable of composure need to retard the cranky contagion before it goes any further. You want to look for the ways you've been contaminated and obliterate them. Consciously boost your EIS and help others fortify theirs, too. That's your gift to yourself and humankind. Consider for a moment the words *mankind* and *humankind*. What are the last four letters in each of these two words? What if you decided to diligently practice the "kind" part? Think of the results if we all slowed down and took an extra moment to engage in more simple acts of human kindness.

There are many, many people out there who are in desperate need of a friendly smile, a gentle touch, a listening ear, or encouragement and support. What if you exposed others to courteous, kind behaviors instead of cranky ones? You could infuse untold numbers of people with human kindness, and what a gift that would be. Your consideration could fortify the frazzled nerves of someone who is on the verge of coming down with a bad case of crankiness. You could prevent a local outbreak.

THERE IS A PROBLEM AND THERE IS HOPE

No one person can immediately change the tenor of our society but scores of us can. As we change at an individual level, so will our society. We *can* reverse the cranky trend and replace it with common civility the same way it began; one event at a time. I try to do one good deed a day. It may be a quick note or phone call to an old friend, assisting someone who needs help, giving up a convenient parking spot to someone less mobile than me, or contributing to a good cause.

My daily good deed began one summer when I impulsively stopped at a little girl's roadside stand after she and her friend waved me down. I bought a few pieces of "jewelry" the two girls had fashioned from a crude concoction of wood, thread, and a lot of of tape. I still remember the grateful mother's face as, standing behind her excited daughter and friend, she emphatically mouthed the words, "Thank you!" Always remember that it takes very little to help another person feel good. What better time than right now to slow up, adjust your attitude, and live your life with just a little more human kindness!

Each of us can do our part in creating a safer, saner society. If this seems like a major undertaking, it is. But you can do it; we can do it, one incident at a time, one person at a time. Envision the power behind a series of positive individual acts by a *legion* of people across our nation who care. One by one, with small but steady force, we can make a difference—first in our homes, then our workplaces, schools, and communities.

We know that lasting change begins on the inside and works its way to the outside. We also know that small changes are nearly invisible at first, but persistence and gradualism win out. Our culture is at a crossroads right now and we can either intensify the anger epidemic or eradicate it.

Knowledge is power. Understanding is empowering. Once we clearly grasp the influence of the Ten Trends and the Expectation Machine that fuels our crankiness, the better our capacity for warding off their influence.

Compressed Time

FEED THE RUSH

While my friend Mary Bradshaw was on vacation she accidentally sliced her finger. A medical assistant by profession, she hated the thought of going to the emergency room on Christmas Day so she decided to treat the wound herself. After rushing to a drugstore and quickly grabbing medical supplies off the shelves she then endured a tediously long line. With throbbing finger, Mary watched as a league of time-compressed shoppers bought box after box of Christmas decorations at half price. These people had hurried away from their homes (and probably their families) in the middle of the holiday to stock up for next year! Christmas wasn't even over, but these shoppers had already kissed it good-bye in their rush for the next one.

We've all watched the compression of time through our holidaze: one gala spending opportunity flowing into the other. As one celebration ends, retailers put up signs advertising the next one, like an ever-shrinking commercial time capsule. But it's not just consumer pressures that feed the rush.

Ads and articles tease us with convincing images of a seamless life where home, work, and health are perfectly balanced. That's the fantasy. The reality is that many of us are frazzled from our hectic daily marathons, plagued with guilt when we can't do it all, or filled with resentment when we do. There's a price to pay for having it all. Or simply trying. The thought of quality time or even a few stolen moments of relaxation seems like a daydream to many of the worn-out, worn-down people I meet in my work, especially single parents whose days are doubly demanding and discouragingly long.

People say it feels as if they're living on a fast moving treadmill that gains momentum with each new day. This is not an illusion.

Between increasing pressures at work and multiple demands at home it's no wonder we're cranky. Some people mistakenly think constant rushing and hurrying will relieve the pressure. Others give up their hobbies or personal time. Some try to gain an extra hour or two by going to bed later and getting up earlier. We could probably solve some of the cranky problem if more of us would just get a good night's sleep once in a while!

SMALL ADJUSTMENTS, BIG RETURNS

This chapter will help you evaluate how compressed time is affecting you. You'll get a sense of how your management of time influences the other issues in this book and the intricate ways the Ten Trends play off one another. Everything is connected. A lack of balance or mismanagement in one area spills into other areas, and before long, you feel hopelessly out of control. Of course you'll feel cranky if you're moving as fast as you can and are still falling behind! That's the problem with most of us today.

It's as if someone were turning up the speed dial on our social treadmill every night while we're sleeping and the next day our world is spinning just a little bit faster than it was the day before. Maybe you feel close to the breaking point from trying to keep up the pace, but you're not sure what you can do to change it. The pressure of time urgency fuels the compulsion to be even busier and this contributes to our overall crankiness: Who has time to wait, be courteous, or help others? Time is a rare and scarce commodity and nobody wants to squander it. *Carpe diem* (seize the day) has given way to *grab the moment and run*.

The bad news is that if you're a victim of compressed time you'll have to put in some effort before you can regain a sense of order in your life. The good news is that the rewards are there. You'll feel more relaxed, in control, and at peace with yourself. There are many small adjustments you can make to help regain a sense of control over your time. You'll find numerous ideas and suggestions in this chapter and I encourage you to try them. As you already know, living under the ongoing pressure of time compression takes an enormous amount of effort, with few real rewards. If you're willing to go through the work of making some small changes in your attitude and behavior, you'll feel the benefits immediately.

Remember the reality: *You will not live forever*. Life may be a timed event, but a prolonged fast pace is a short-term fix that merely creates the *illusion* of accomplishment while you simultaneously lose ground. Gandhi said there had to be more to life than seeing how fast we could get through it. I agree. Speed is not the only criterion for measuring a productive life!

Think about how the Expectation Machine's external messages, myths, and illusions shape your perceptions about time. Do you have realistic expectations about what you can actually accomplish each day? Have you fallen prey to the promise of *bigger, better, faster, more, now?* If you can identify the beliefs that feed your compulsion to "do it all" you'll isolate the core of your distress, giving you something concrete to work with instead of a vague, chronic sense of frustration.

You already have a sense of what's out of balance in your life. You even know some of the steps you can take to relieve the pressure you feel. You just haven't made the decision to do anything about it yet, and that's where I come in. My job is to help you confirm, clarify, and then confront these issues. From there, I hope to encourage and inspire you to take some positive steps in your personal anti-cranky campaign. There are many small improvements you can make that will help you feel more enriched and well rounded. As in making any personal changes, sometimes the hardest part is owning up to the problem. Once you get past the denial and excuses, it all gets easier.

FAST FORWARD

Find the Stop Button!

My younger brother Steve came over for dinner one night. We put on some music, talked for a while, and then sat down to eat. Halfway through dinner we looked at each other in bewilderment, realizing we were both gulping our food, trying to finish the meal in record time. We had no clue about what was happening until we caught the music. It was the Rolling Stones album, *Between the Buttons*. The cut that was playing kept gaining in speed from start to finish. We had begun our meal in normal mode but were finishing it in fast forward. If Steve and I hadn't figured it out we might have ended up with strands of spaghetti on the ceiling or ourselves. We laughed, relaxed, changed the music, and settled back into our normal pace.

Cranky Quiz

COMPRESSED TIME

Scoring the Cranky Quiz

Score 1 point for every *yes* and 0 for every *no*. Count a *sometimes* as a *yes*. Add your total: 3 points or less (Cool) means you're in good shape, 4 to 7 (Warm) indicates a need to slow down, and 8 to 10 (Hot!) indicates a raging cranky infection. You'll find anti-cranky solutions for each quiz item in this chapter.

1. ___ Do you feel hurried and rushed every day, always busy yet always behind, with no real relief in sight?

2. ___ Do you get annoyed at long lines, time-consuming transactions, traffic bottlenecks, flight snafus, and so forth?

3. ___ Are you so busy that you skip or hurry through meals and have trouble finding time to exercise or have fun?

4. ___ Do you expect the people around you to speed up to your pace rather than you slowing down to theirs?

5. ___ Do you wake up tired and go to bed wired or have difficulty sleeping?

6. ___ When driving, do you get mad and flash your lights at other drivers, grumble, gesture, try to pass, or slow down in front of them?

7. ___ Do you exceed the speed limit whenever you think you can get away with it?

8. ___ Does your mind constantly race ahead, always keeping you a few steps ahead of yourself?

9. ___ Are you a multitasker; that is, are you prone to work on two or three things at once rather than one at a time?

10. ___ Do you feel "time impoverished," as if there's never enough of it, regardless of your efforts to catch up?

Cranky Quotient _____

My compressed time condition is (circle one)   Cool   Warm   Hot!

Ingrained and Entrained

The same thing happens to you every day and you may be as unaware of what's going on as Steve and I were during our spaghetti dinner sprint. You wake up feeling pretty relaxed, but by the time you've spent a few hours in our high-speed world you've cranked up your gait (walking, breathing, speaking, eating—you name it). In fact, your regular pace of doing just about everything is faster than it was five years ago unless you've consciously slowed down. It's called "entrainment."

You have gradually, unknowingly synchronized your patterns and rhythms with a hurried-up external world. It's pretty subtle. However, the dilemma is much larger than that. Our commercialized, materialistic, winner-take-all, go-for-the-gusto, do-it-now lifestyles relentlessly feed into our already quick pace. You experience the effects of entrainment every time you return to work after a long weekend or vacation and have trouble kicking back into high gear. You had begun to settle into your slower, natural pace. This gives you a sense of how you're affected by the world around you.

Try This on for Sighs

There are symptoms that tell you when you're being squeezed by time compression and sighing is one of them. Pay attention to how often you sigh and what kinds of feelings or thoughts accompany it. Yes, sometimes we sigh with contentment but more often it's an indicator of fatigue, stress, or impatience. Listen to the sighs of irritation as people stand in a long line (maybe you'll even hear yourself!). Sighing often results when you breathe from your chest instead of your diaphragm or when you hold your breath; both are signs of stress. Pay attention. If you catch yourself sighing, figure out if you're tired, frustrated, or aggravated. Check your pace, the speed of your thoughts, your breathing patterns, and make whatever adjustments are in order. You can't change the world's pace, but you are definitely in charge of your own.

CRANKY QUIZ ITEM # 1:
CHRONIC TIME PRESSURE AND URGENCY

> 1. ___ Do you feel hurried and rushed every day, always busy yet always behind, with no real relief in sight?

Have You Got the Time?

Now that you understand entrainment, you can look at your life with different eyes. Maybe you've been so sped up and buried in busyness you haven't even stopped to question what you're doing or why. Like a patient with an undiagnosed condition, you knew something was wrong, but you couldn't put your finger on it. It's hard to realize that busyness is *addictive*. It feels good. It feels productive. It conveniently shields us from having to think about interpersonal conflicts, troubled relationships, and areas of our lives we'd rather not think about. We sometimes bury ourselves in busyness so we don't have to grapple with the reality that one day we are going to die. Well, we *are* going to die so let's be mindful of how we spend our time before we go!

Anti-Cranky Alternatives for Quiz Item # 1: Chronic Time Pressure and Urgency
Create Your Own Wake-up Call

One reason so many of us are cranky is because we're out of touch with what we value. We think we know what's important to us. We can quickly rattle off the litany of all we hold dear, just like reciting multiplication tables in third grade. But in our frantic attempts to achieve success, happiness, and fulfillment, it's distressingly easy to abandon what really counts and sometimes it takes a *"wake-up call"* to get our attention. Because of that, I've chosen to lead with the one issue most meaningful to me. You could call it a crash course on core values and priorities, because every problem, conflict, or inconsistency you face will always cycle back to this core. Your values and priorities are the "home position" and the first place you want to visit whenever things aren't working as you'd like.

In 1984 I was forced to take a long, hard look at what I truly valued when my twenty-one-year-old son, Robbie, was killed in a work accident. He was dead by the time I was notified so there was no way to say good-bye. There was some distance between us at the time of his death and we never had a chance to resolve our differences. Up to the moment he was killed, if you had asked, I would have professed, maybe even boasted, that I was living in sync with my values. But I wasn't, really, and I had to learn my lesson the hard way.

It's impossible for me to express how much it hurts even to write these words. But like so many of the people I work with every day, I was blithely zooming along, buried in busyness, pretending I had all the time in the world. Meanwhile, I was neglecting some core values and I didn't even get it. When I got word that my son was dead, my world came to a standstill. I got knocked off the treadmill and never crawled back on.

There are wake-up calls and there are Wake-up Calls. They come in a variety of shapes and sizes. The loss of a dream. Regret. Guilt. Broken promises. Missed opportunities. Loss of a job. Death of a loved one. Heart attack. A life-altering accident. A parent with Alzheimer's disease. A child on drugs. Chronic illness. Terminal diagnosis. Sadly, in our attempts to have it all, some of us lose it all. In that wake-up moment, life becomes precious, clear, and heartbreakingly brief. The list of what's most important becomes very short.

Yes, experiencing the worst helps put life's minor inconveniences or annoyances in perspective. I've spoken with other parents who have lost a child and though their words differ, the sentiment is the same. Our worst-case scenario has already happened. We've survived the worst life has to offer and we recognize that we wasted a lot of time worrying and whining over things that didn't really matter. We emerge from our tragedy different; deeper. It changes us forever.

What really matters in your life and what would knock you off the treadmill? You can create your own Wake-up Call by sitting down and visualizing your own worst-case scenario. Pick any of the above extreme circumstances, or one of your own invention. As vividly as you can, imagine what you would think and feel. Then project the outcome that might result by asking these three simple questions:

- What would change in your life?
- How would this affect the way you live from day to day?
- What lasting lessons would emerge?

You can probably imagine I wish I'd spent some time on these three questions; living by my values would have spared me a load of guilt and additional heartache. This is a heavy exercise, and an important one, so don't just think about it. Write your answers down on a piece of paper and review them periodically, especially when you're irked or frustrated.

I encourage you to engage in this exercise at a visceral level so you can work through your gut, not your intellect. This will help you sort out what really matters. Once you get the core issues clarified, handling the rest of the items in this chapter (or this book) will be a breeze. Maybe, unlike me, you can reap the benefits of a profound lesson without having to go through all of the pain. And now, having graduated from your crash course, we'll lighten up the tone and look at the side issues that spin around the core of compressed time.

Visit Your Bureau of Personal Standards

Your life will always include some trivial tasks, chores, and projects. You can't make all of them go away but you can lighten your load. Here's what I mean. There are some things you do, not out of desire, but out of obligation, guilt, or sheer fussiness. Maybe you hold on to the high standards instilled by your mom or dad, but secretly you don't give a damn. It's time to recreate your *own* personal standards. Not everything requires 100 percent effort all of the time (sweeping the garage or making the bed, for example). It doesn't have to be perfect. It just needs to be *done*. Or maybe it doesn't—that's up to you.

If you're a parent you may have to adjust your neatness standards to accommodate your kids, like tolerating a few fingerprints on the wall or crumbs on the floor. Many parents who hold lofty standards clean up after their kids. The kids are smart enough to know that if they wait long enough, Mom or Dad will do it for them, but Mom and Dad haven't figured this out. There's a simple solution: If the kid's room is messy, don't clean it; shut the door!

It's not always kids we feel compelled to clean up after. Sometimes it's our spouse. Quit being so quick to pick up after those you love. It's their job; you have your hands full just taking care of yourself, right? Whenever your lifestyle changes (having a baby, changing jobs, starting an exercise program, taking a class), assess and then adjust your standards to accommodate new time demands. Think twice before caving in to someone else's standards. Remember the times you've lapsed into a cleaning frenzy when a parent, friend, or relative was coming by. By the time you made everything immaculate, you felt almost resentful about their visit; where's the joy in that?

Visit the Quick Stop!

Convenience stores are everywhere and they usually live up to their name. A quick stop, get what you need, and you're back on the street in no time. Well, here's a free convenience item you can use to increase your self-awareness and adjust your pace whenever you need. Just visit the Quick Stop! This means, stop everything you're doing for just a few seconds, literally. You may think you're too busy to Quick Stop! but try it. Just as it sounds, it's fast, it's simple, it's convenient.

Just momentarily stop and quickly review what's going on. Ask yourself: *What am I thinking? How am I feeling right now?* The stopping is essential. It's hard making corrections (or sometimes even thinking straight) when your body is whipping along at warp speed. Only when you Quick Stop!, only when you halt your body, do you put your mind in a receptive place so you can think objectively and analyze your situation more clearly.

You may resist this. You may think you don't have time or it won't make any difference, but it will. Stopping is always the *first step* in identifying a problem or searching for a solution. That's the importance of the Quick Stop!

Visit it several times a day; briefly review what's happening with you, mentally and physically. *Consciously* decide what you need to do next. By adding the Quick Stop! into your routine, your thinking will become more clear, you'll be more mindful of what you're doing, and entrainment will be less a problem. You'll feel more in control. If you need a memory jogger, put a brightly colored sticker on your watch or planner. And now, here's a chance to practice: put this book down for a just a moment and take a Quick Stop! Please remember the questions: What am I thinking? How am I feeling right now?

CRANKY QUIZ ITEM # 2:
INSTINCTIVE IMPATIENCE

> 2. ___ Do you get annoyed at long lines, time-consuming transactions, traffic bottlenecks, flight snafus, and so forth?

I Want Patience and I Want it Now!

We live in an era of instant gratification. We can pick up the phone, order an item from across the country, and have it delivered overnight. Thanks to jet travel, we can have ourselves delivered somewhere overnight, too! When we're short on cash we can walk up to an ATM and get money instantly. While instant capabilities and conveniences are great, they foster impatience. We have zero tolerance for inconvenience anymore. We hate having to wait. The attitude is, "My emergency is more urgent than your emergency." We can't bear the thought of someone else's problem taking precedence over ours. And when someone or something gets between us and what we want, we get very cranky.

Up in the Air

There was a time when air travel seemed just short of a miracle; in just a few hours we were transported from one side of the continent to the other, or from one continent to another. We dressed up for the occasion, munched macadamia nuts, adjusted our cloth napkins, and felt like royalty, even in coach class. Well, it's a new dawn. The European produced *Airbus* says it all. As airlines systematically trim down their services (including the size of the seats we sit in), our crankiness increases in direct proportion to their cutbacks. Enter "air rage."

I seldom take a flight without hearing passengers griping about something. Of course, much of it is justified. Services have indeed been stripped, and the trend continues. With so many people flying these days we're lucky to have a package of pretzels tossed in our laps. Of course, we passengers play a part in this, too. Some of us come aboard looking as if the airline staged a mass come-as-you-are party. But truthfully, our dignity suffers. When we're herded onto the shuttle that drives us to our commuter plane, or hurried to our seats so the "on time" quota is met (despite our late boarding), sometimes I want to yell, "Baaaaaa!" like the sheep in the movie *Babe* just for fun.

Actually, I'm impressed that the intricate lattice work of the hub-and-spoke system works as well as it does. There's only one small factor that can muck up the system faster than you can say supersonic—weather. With all the disclaimers printed on our ticket, maybe airlines should include a consumer warning that reads in big block print: OUR TICKET AGENTS ARE NOT RESPONSIBLE FOR THE WEATHER.

Maybe that would help the screaming masses settle down and smell the Jet A fuel, instead of bombarding ticket agents with frantic appeals to *do something because I've got to get there!* Of course, we don't want to miss our meeting; yes, it's hell to lose our first vacation day because of a blizzard; and naturally, we want to get home after a long business trip, but hey. None of these instances are truly the end of the world; they just feel like it. Planes can't fly in ice storms, sleet, thunderstorms, blizzards, or tornadoes, and even if they could, would you really want to be on board?

Everybody loses when somebody totally loses it over uncontrollables. Those angry, aggressive passengers who scream at ticket agents make the rest of us pay (witness the growing contempt the airlines are directing toward passengers).

The problem is that crankiness compels us to find someone to blame for our intolerance toward inconvenience. We can't even begin to comprehend that we need to look no further than the mirror.

Anti-Cranky Alternatives for Quiz Item # 2: Instinctive Impatience

Try the Patience Project

In 1997 I decided to dedicate the entire year to a self-improvement project, and the behavior I chose to work on was patience. They say be careful what you ask for: 1997 gave me a bumper crop of opportunities to stand in long lines, wait in traffic, and endure sluggish consumer transactions and delayed or canceled flights. Every time I felt my impatience begin to raise its nervous little head I reminded myself about my year-long "patience project." I smiled. I relaxed. I learned something: We all want to improve but most of us just aren't persistent enough. We try a new behavior for a couple of weeks, fail at it most of the time, and then give up.

But giving yourself a full year to focus on *one single behavior* tips the scale in your favor. Try it. Some days you'll be extremely successful, other days maybe you'll forget, but for once, time will be on your side! Spend 365 days practicing patience (or any other much-needed behavior), and you'll be a different person when the year ends.

Toward the end of my patience project I spent six hours on the tarmac at Dallas–Fort Worth airport in a crowded airplane, as the pilots waited for a massive storm system to pass. Our aircraft had to be refueled before we could leave and we hadn't even gone anywhere! I was able to laugh at the irony instead of getting angry over circumstances that were beyond my control.

A similar situation happened at Detroit Metro recently when communications broke down between our shuttle driver and the gate agent. Our little bus drove to six different parked commuter planes before it finally found the one headed for Lansing. Luckily, the plane couldn't take off without the passengers! Once again, I snickered over a situation that would once have boosted my blood pressure. Patience can be yours. Give yourself the gift of 365 days to work on it. The airlines alone will provide you with many opportunities to practice.

Take Some Reality Bites

So maybe you're considering a year-long patience project, but you still need an interim strategy to keep your feet on the ground every time you have to wait. Here's a more extreme, but fast-acting antidote: Take a bite of reality. Wishing, complaining, and hoping things were different will only contribute to your crankiness. "Reality Bites" will lessen it. Take waiting, for example. You simply are going to have to stand in lines or sometimes wait for what you want. *Take it*. Flights will be delayed, even canceled. *Endure it*. You will be inconvenienced. *Count on it*.

People are going to do things that irritate you. *Expect it*. You will have to do things you don't want to do from time to time, like exercise or drive the speed limit. *Put up with it*. You'll occasionally have to let someone else's emergency take precedence over yours. *Live with it*. Inconvenience, waiting, and delays are a part of life and you know better than to expect anything else. *Acknowledge it*. Uncontrollables are a part of life. *Accept it*. These hassles won't change, but *you* can! Smile, spend a moment feeling grateful that these nuisances don't happen every day, and get on with your life. Quick, extreme, effective. And I know it will work for you.

CRANKY QUIZ ITEM # 3:
IMBALANCE AND SELF-NEGLECT

> 3. ___ Are you so busy that you skip or hurry through meals and
> have trouble finding time to exercise or have fun?

Time for a Personal Battery Recharge

We can only put out so much energy and then we need some kind of recharge. Without it, our spirits arrest. We get tired and feel unrewarded. I suggest putting your name at the top of your "To Do" list every now and then. My friend Chris Clarke-Epstein, who travels the world, is faithful about getting a massage wherever she goes. Chris works very hard and figures she deserves a bit of pampering when she's on the road. Even in passenger briefings, flight attendants tell us to put on *our own* oxygen masks before assisting anyone else. Sounds like a principle we could apply elsewhere.

If you're wondering how I get renewed, it's riding my horse. When I go to the barn I enter a different world and lose myself in an activity that was once a childhood dream. Maybe you think I'm lucky that I have the time and money to ride. It's not luck. Like you, I have many demands in my life. I make the time to ride. It's an integral part of my life.

For years now, I've made riding an affordable priority, in terms of both time and money. It's a *choice*. What renews you doesn't have to be a hobby and it doesn't have to cost money, but it does have to happen. If it takes you longer than ten seconds to answer the question, "How do you renew yourself?" go back and review the section on wake-up calls for a quick dose of inspiration.

Anti-Cranky Alternatives for Quiz Item # 3:
Imbalance and Self-neglect
Take Care of Yourself so You Have Something Left for Others

Have you ever had a "self" day? If you can afford it, make a day trip to a spa and get the works. If you're on a low budget, hole up in your home for a day of solitude. Turn off the phone ringer. Read, nap, soak in the tub, look out the window and watch the light change. If that seems too quiet for your taste, go do something you haven't done in a while: see a movie, go out to dinner, get a manicure, go to a ball game, take a nature walk, visit the new gallery in town, attend a lecture, take a golf or tennis lesson, get a hair cut, spend a few minutes relaxing in a darkened room with a scented candle.

Maybe that night you could cuddle up with your sweetie for some quality time. Order dinner, have it delivered, and eat by candlelight. Just indulge yourself in something you consider special and delightful. Poorly nourished spirits feed crankiness. Keep your spirit full.

Make Your Health a Priority

If good health appears on your list of values, then make a healthy food choice rather than skipping a meal or eating fast food because you feel pressed for time. Avoid food emergencies by carrying bagels or fruit with you. I've found you can't kill a bagel, regardless of what you do to it. Carry one in your purse or briefcase. Apples travel better than bananas and they're easier to eat than oranges. Even granola or power bars are a good alternative to candy or snack food but check the fat grams first.

The same goes for exercise. If health is a priority, you have to do it. You don't achieve much by *thinking* about exercising; you have to actually do it! People say they're too tired to exercise, but mild exercise actually increases energy. There's no excuse for neglecting your health. If you want to live to a ripe age, remember the words of musician Eubie Blake: *If I had known I was going to live this long I would've taken better care of myself when I was younger.*

Soak It All Up

I had a wonderful insight the first time I spent the night at my son's home shortly after he bought it. Ron doesn't have a shower, and while taking my first bath in years, I realized how our cultural transition from baths to showers had stepped up the pace of our day. If you're inclined to shower rather than soak, once a week start or end your day with a bath instead.

Make it a ritual: pay close attention to the temperature of the water and how it feels on your body. Note which parts of you are not submerged and how that feels, too. Listen to the sounds the water makes as you wash, splash around, and rinse yourself. Smell the air; the fragrance of the soap. Feel the moisture in your nose and on your face.

Feel the sensation of the washcloth and towel against your skin. Closely observe all aspects of the experience from start to finish. If you find yourself feeling especially hyper one morning, stop yourself. Take a bath. You'll find it makes a difference when you start your day on your fanny instead of on your feet.

CRANKY QUIZ ITEM # 4:
PRESSURING OTHERS TO SPEED UP

> 4. ___ Do you expect the people around you to speed up to your pace rather than you slowing down to theirs?

I Got Rhythm

If the world were perfect you could take a holiday, travel to some secluded spot, read this book in peace, evaluate your existence, and return home a few weeks later a new person—relaxed, renewed, revitalized. I doubt you can afford that, so let's take a quick "economy tour" instead. Take a moment and envision the ocean. Close your eyes and remember how it changes from one day to the next, in color, flow, energy, and sound, yet there is always an underlying rhythm. Just as the ocean has its own rhythms that rise and fall with the wind and tides, you have your own rhythms, too. Because entrainment alters your natural pace, you need to put your rhythms back in sync.

Anti-Cranky Alternatives for Quiz Item # 4:
Pressuring Others to Speed Up
Adjust Your Rhythm

Now that you know about your tendency to synchronize unconsciously with your surroundings, stay tuned into your physical rhythms. Observe your heart rate, both active and resting. By knowing exactly how your body feels when you're comfortable, you can duplicate this state when stressed and steer yourself back toward composure. Some incidents (or people) will trigger a change in your heart rate. Pay attention when this occurs. Breathing through your nose, not your mouth, take a few deep, extended relaxing breaths from your diaphragm (not your chest). This will bring your heart rate back down, and just like an athlete or performer, you'll feel more in control, regardless of the circumstance.

Monitor your mental rhythms, too. Note when your mind feels keen and alert and when it feels dull. Recognize when your thoughts are racing and chaotic, and when your brain is more still. If you feel mentally sluggish maybe you've been sitting too long. If you feel irritated or crabby, maybe you're tired or hungry. If your thoughts are racing maybe you've just drunk some caffeine, or you've exercised and activated your creativity. Maybe you're feeling nervous about something that's about to happen or ruminating over an unresolved problem. Maybe you dislike the person you're with.

Just as relaxation and deep breathing can physically calm you, they can also help still your mind. Note which habits and rituals enhance or interfere with your brain's natural rhythms, like drinking too much caffeine. Some of us have been in high gear for so long we don't know what's natural for us anymore.

Use a "Faux Pause" to Get in Sync

If you have a strong personality you may be surprised at how often you interfere with other people's rhythms. Start paying attention. Do you expect people to match your tempo or do you make an effort to get in sync with them? Note how your presence affects people. Do they talk faster or louder? Do they shut down and let you call the shots? When you're in the company of others, especially family members, observe their rhythms. If they're slower paced than you, dial down. If you want people to enjoy your company, entrain to their pace. At work or home, give your full attention to others when they need it. It's just common courtesy, but it's amazing how many of us only partially listen.

Managers often don't really hear what their employees are saying. People feel blown off, resentful. Children are perceptive; they know when they're being heard—or ignored. We all know we need to listen better, so I'll simply remind you to think about entrainment. Instead of trying to set the rhythm for everyone else, you can make a "Faux Pause" and try to get into their "personal time zone." You may actually end up saving a few minutes because you won't have to retrace your steps or ask for later clarification.

CRANKY QUIZ ITEM # 5:
SLEEP DEPRIVATION

> 5. ___ Do you wake up tired and go to bed wired or have difficulty sleeping?

All I Need Is a Nap

If you're feeling chronically cranky, maybe it's because you're short on sleep. In the United States, at least one in six adults suffers from some kind of sleep disorder. Some of the reasons behind our sleeplessness include shift work, sleep apnea, depression, narcolepsy, restless leg syndrome, bruxism (tooth grinding), caffeine or alcohol use, and stress. Lack of sleep undermines work performance, interpersonal relationships, and peace of mind. It's also dangerous; an estimated 24,000 sleep-deprived individuals die in accidents each year, many of them on the road. In attempts to treat their condition, a lot of people experiment with over-the-counter medicines or herbal remedies. Some work; some don't. Many weary people also opt for alcohol, but contrary to popular belief, it's more likely to interrupt sleep than induce it.

A Different Kind of Wake-up Call

Whether you sleep well or not, there's also the issue of how you wake yourself up. If you're like most people, you use an alarm. Just think about that word—*alarm!* When I was a single parent I constantly woke up cranky and on edge. I now realize that the sound of my alarm set me off with a shot of adrenaline and a racing heart. Our whole family would have been better off if I hadn't been so rudely jarred into wakefulness each morning.

The conditions under which you wake up are only one small element in your life, but crankiness isn't caused by one big incident, it comes from a multitude of small, nagging sources. If you habitually get yourself up so late you feel rushed or frantic the minute your feet hit the floor, you're setting yourself up for a cranky day. This was a pattern of mine for years and it really affected my outlook. So did my inability to think ahead.

A few months into my first job, my car died and I didn't have money to fix it. Work was nine miles away—too far to ride my bike, and frankly, I wasn't that motivated. Until my parents loaned me a car two weeks later, I was going to bed at night without having made any arrangements for getting to work the next day. Each morning I was faced with the stress of having to find transportation, thanks to my inability to plan! Imagine waking up and having to beg friends, neighbors, family, or coworkers for a ride to work shortly after waking up. Once I even hitchhiked to work in the rain. As you can imagine, my "good" days during that out-of-control period were few and far between. How could they have been otherwise?

Anti-Cranky Alternatives for Quiz Item # 5: Sleep Deprivation

Just Say No to Caffeine

Research on the potential benefits or adverse effects of coffee consumption is inconclusive, but consider the physical facts: caffeine stimulates the central nervous system; elevates blood pressure, metabolism, and respiration; reduces blood flow to the brain; increases norepinephrine and fatty acid levels. This results in irritability, shortness of breath, anxiety, impatience, and combativeness. If you are a caffeine drinker, pay attention to how much you consume in a day because its effects last for up to six hours. If you drink cola, the combined caffeine and sugar may affect you more than you think. Try substituting plain water or herbal teas for some of your soft drinks, tea, or coffee.

Put Your Stress to Rest

Stress can affect your sleep cycle. Traumas can trigger sleep disturbances but they're usually temporary so we'll focus on chronic sleep problems instead. If you feel tired, try a short sit-up relaxation break after work. Aerobic exercise can both reduce your stress and help you sleep better, but don't do it too close to bedtime. If stress is your problem, remember the words of Dr. Hans Selye: *"It is not the event, but your perception of the event that makes it stressful or stimulating."* Does this sound vaguely familiar? Can you spell *expectation*? Practices such as the Quick Stop!, Faux Pause, and Reality Bites, will help lower your stress and put you in a more sleep-receptive state.

If racing thoughts and an overactive mind are keeping you awake, create a transition period. Don't flip off the TV or abruptly stop working and expect to nod off. Soak in a warm bath first. Instead of fretting about work, world unrest, famine, pestilence, or other unnerving concerns, let them go.

It's bedtime. You can't do anything about these pressing issues for the next few hours—maybe not at all. Make sure your room is dark. If outside light bothers you, buy a sleep mask or lined window shades. Try sitting up in bed, in the dark, for a few minutes to ease yourself into a sleep-ready state. Breathe deeply and relax. Visualize a place where you feel contented and safe. Go there for a few minutes and then slide down under the covers when you feel ready. As the owner of an often hyperactive mind, I find this method particularly helpful. Do whatever works for you.

Graduate from "Good God, It's Morning!" to "Good Morning, God!"

Make your mornings as pleasant as possible, because your first thoughts or experiences can set the tone for the day. Even if you hate to get up, give yourself at least fifteen minutes of grace so you don't have to rush around (trust me—the precious sleep you lose will be well compensated by the gift of extra time). Wake yourself up in as pleasant a manner as possible. I use alarms with soft sounds that don't make my heart race, but you could opt for music, nature noises, or maybe even a sunrise lamp. If you'd like to begin your day in a kinder, gentler manner, take a moment and listen to the morning sounds before getting up. Slowly stretch your body before you bound out of bed so that when your feet hit the floor, you don't have to worry about pulling a muscle or getting a cramp. Put a softer, lower-watt lightbulb in your bedroom lamp so your eyes aren't traumatized by brightness when you turn it on.

If, for some reason you wake up cranky, treat yourself especially well that day. The Law of Opposites suggests that when you most need to take good care of yourself you will be least likely to do so. It may take some discipline, but be nice to yourself. Don't listen to the news right off; play an inspirational tape or music that relaxes you. Soak in the tub if you have time. Find something to smile or laugh about. Keep a book of short inspirational pieces nearby and treat yourself to a couple of quick doses.

Acknowledge and accept that you're a little bit "off" without getting upset about it. Recognize that when you're in a down mood you'll tend to look for everything that's wrong so don't let it throw you when you notice the negatives. Force yourself to be nicer than usual to others and maybe they'll be extra nice back. Try to trace where you think your mood may have come from but don't get fixated on it. Smile more than usual. Limit your caffeine and don't use your down disposition as an excuse to overeat.

You may find it easy to get cranky or offended when you're off your game, so resist letting people or things get the best of you. Every now and then, review everything you feel gratified for. Of course, the list will be shorter on these kinds of days but at least you made the effort. Give yourself one small treat at some point and do one good deed. You may never find out exactly what caused your crankiness. Even if you figure it out give yourself credit for not letting your blue mood completely ruin your day. Chances are, tomorrow you'll be back to normal and feeling good again.

CRANKY QUIZ ITEM # 6:
RAGE ON THE ROAD AND OFF

> 6. ___ When driving, do you get mad and flash your lights at other drivers, grumble, gesture, try to pass, or slow down in front of them?

A Telling Tail

A woman told me about being tailed by a state trooper for nearly fifteen miles. A writer, she was doing what she usually does in the car; talking into her dictation machine, gesturing as she spoke. With one eye on the rearview mirror, she never exceeded the speed limit, but the officer finally pulled her over. When she asked him why, he responded, "Road rage." She looked at him, completely confused, and then he said, "I've been following you since you hit the county line. Your mouth and hands haven't been still one minute. It appeared as if you were about to go ballistic." In no other decade would this have happened.

Maim Street, U.S.A.

Many of us let off steam once we get behind the wheel and this hair trigger mentality is putting us all at risk. According to the National

Transportation Safety Board and the American Automobile Association, incidents of aggressive driving and attacks on the roads increased steeply in the mid-nineties, including high-speed duels that claimed the lives of innocent victims. Of course, we don't all shoot at or beat one another up; some of us just swear or gesture, slow down, or block someone from passing. But even minor displays of crankiness can trigger a retaliatory response in the other driver that could ruin your day. It could even ruin your life. A man is currently on trial for his part in a mad merging scene near Detroit in which the other driver was killed. These kinds of incidents are happening all over the United States.

You've witnessed these dangerous displays on the road and you know it didn't used to be this way: the phrase "road rage" didn't even exist until just a few years ago! You may have asked yourself what's changed. For one thing, today's highways are our modern melting pot: People from all walks of life, with all kinds of vehicles, and all kinds of lifestyles, converge and interact in the same space for a limited amount of time. There are more people on the roads. A lot more. Highway space hasn't increased much in recent years but the number of drivers has. We're jammed in closer than we used to be, with people we don't know or care about. We're driving longer distances every day and the repetition of this daily pattern is getting on our nerves.

Drivers Behaving Badly

Let's face it; most of us are preoccupied, overworked, overscheduled, and in a big hurry to get where we're going, even if it's somewhere we really don't want to go. Maybe you've wondered how it is we feel so entitled once we slide in behind that wheel. Some people theorize that our car is one of the few places where it seems we have a semblance of control. Of course, this is mostly an illusion, but being locked inside a car creates a sense of privacy and anonymity. Unless a cop is around we figure we can do whatever we want and not get caught.

Few of us realize that all of our personal pressures get in the car with us: money worries, time constraints, relationship problems, and self-esteem issues. The slightest incident or inconvenience can trip the delicate framework of our emotional "house of cards," and when that happens, all hell breaks loose. How could it be any different when we're fueled by an attitude of, "It's *my* car, *my* space, *my* schedule, and *my* time. *My* situation is more important than yours, so get the hell out of *my* way!" Below are the fine points we'd all love to cover with the cranky drivers of today:

—Remedial Tips for Road Rage Candidates—

1. Green means Go, red means Stop, and yellow *doesn't* mean wildly accelerate.
2. The operational word on a speed limit sign is *limit*, not speed.
3. A Stop sign is not a request; it's an *order*.
4. The right lane is for right turns and the left lane is for left turns, *not* the other way around.
5. In case the people around you aren't psychic, there's a special device to let other drivers know what's on your mind. It's called a turning signal. Use it *before*, not after you turn or switch lanes.
6. *Do not* read while driving. You might miss the plot.

Anti-Cranky Alternatives for Quiz Item # 6:
Rage on the Road and Off
Get a Grip

Let's figure out where you might fit in the "car wars" lineup. Please honestly answer the following questions:

- Is it common for you to express irritation or anger at other drivers?
- Are you a chronic speeder?
- Do you comment on the driving habits of others, even if you're alone?
- Do you spend most of your driving time in the passing lane?
- Do you get cranky when you're behind a driver who isn't in a hurry?
- Do you think seat belts are unnecessary or only for wimps?

If you answered "yes" to more than two of these questions, start practicing your stress management skills when you drive or take a course on anger management. When you're behind the wheel, breathe, relax, smile, and loosen your grip every few minutes. Just as you'd do with a Quick Stop!, let go of any negative thoughts. Chew on some Reality Bites. Hard and disappointing as it is to accept, you cannot control how other people drive.

You can, however, control how you feel. Slow down and don't take bad drivers so seriously. Excuse the pun, but chances are you'll never run into them again. If you're curious about whether or not you're infected with road rage, ask someone who regularly rides with you what kind of driver you are. Listen carefully to his or her answer. Better yet, if you can ever manage to eavesdrop on a conversation about your driving, you'll discover the honest truth about your highway habits.

Control Your RPMs

Here's a three-step approach to help you control road rage, but these concepts transfer to virtually any circumstance that drives your Cranky Quotient into the Hot zone. RPM stands for Restrain, Pull Away, and Monitor.

- Restrain yourself. Do not get behind the wheel if you are angry, frustrated, or exhausted. Restraint is your best preventive defense and if you're "in a mood," stay off the road! Walk; call a cab. Or a friend. If you've got the money, call a limo service so you can reward yourself for good behavior.
- Pull away. Avoid getting hooked by some stranger's antagonism. If someone ever tries to provoke you, keep driving. Do not engage in any eye contact, gestures, or acknowledgment. Get into a different lane, slow down, disappear into traffic, abruptly turn down another street. Drive to the nearest police or fire station if you can. Do not stop and get out of your car.
- Monitor yourself. Take a deep breath. Relax your hands and stay in control. Clear your mind of any thoughts of revenge. Every time you exhale, release your tension. Absolutely refuse to let a brief incident such as this, now passed, infect your present moment. RPMs can help you maintain a healthy distance from crankiness.

Separate the Symptoms from the Cause

Road rage is a deadly serious topic, and it's a perfect illustration of how crankiness can morph into mortal combat with the flick of a switch. What is happening on our roads today is a *symptom* of pent-up anger, not the cause. If you admit to having a problem when you're behind the wheel, please know it's not what happens on the road that triggers your anger; it's that bundle of unresolved issues you're carrying around. If you find yourself getting extremely agitated toward drivers who behave stupidly, understand that your anger is pointing you toward your personal issues. It's not the other party, it's *you*.

Instead of unleashing your anger at others, take a Quick Stop! and evaluate your behavior. Take some quiet time to go inside and figure out what's eating you. I agree that people do dumb things when they drive, and it's irritating to be inconvenienced by someone's bad judgment. *But on the road and off, how you react to others relates to your issues, not theirs.* A little blip of crankiness is one thing, but intense anger or spikes of outrage directed toward strangers is a signal that there's something in your life that needs attention. Figure that one out and we'll never have to hear about you on the nightly news.

CRANKY QUIZ ITEM # 7:
SPEEDING

> 7. ___ Do you exceed the speed limit whenever you think you can get away with it?

Life in the Fast Lane

Our highway death statistics are the price we pay for mobility and personal freedom. If we manage to make it to our destination in one piece maybe we should pause just for a moment and call ourselves lucky. I feel grateful for the miles I've managed to log without sacrificing life and limb.

Every day you and I observe drivers speeding along ten, fifteen, or twenty miles in excess of the speed limit, casually overtaking one car after another, their radar detectors on, just in case. No big deal. Or is it? Accidents happen, and it isn't always the reckless who die. Half of accident victims are just in the wrong place at the wrong time.

On any given day it could be you, me, or a loved one who leaves the house and never comes back. In the United States, over 120 unsuspecting human beings die on our roads each day. They head off to work, school, or to run a quick errand and never return. A small percentage of them leave in haste or anger, and they or their loved ones never have a chance to make up. That certainly encourages us to engage in meaningful good-byes every single time we leave the house, doesn't it?

Dying to Get There
Here's a topic I shouldn't even have to write about because we all know better, but each year approximately 500 people lose their lives in vehicle-train accidents. While no one can determine the exact circumstances of each incident, you know that some of these drivers were in such a hurry they tried to beat the approaching train. When people die under such preventable circumstances the grief is profound. *That they are often accompanied by a fatally injured family member or friend compounds the loss.*

When I visited our local state police post to research traffic statistics I read a fatal car-train accident report. Holding this document in my hands was a chilling experience. A once vital human being had been reduced to codes and numbers neatly arranged into data fields: a piece of paper representing one human life. A life lost because someone tried to save a few minutes. Sometimes our crankiness kills us.

Anti-Cranky Alternatives for Quiz Item # 7:
Speeding
Slow Down and Smell the Rubber
We have speed limits for a reason: safety. When we disobey speed limits we break the law. What could be more basic? Think of the stress involved in speeding along the highway, scanning for patrol cars, intimidating slower drivers to pull out of the passing lane. If you're a chronic speeder, calculate exactly how many actual minutes you save in one trip. Think of the times that a car you just passed ends up catching you at a light. Is the risk really worth the few minutes you gain? Considering the number of accidents and deaths that occur daily on our roadways, why push the odds? So here's my appeal: Please slow down. Drive the speed limit. Wear your seat belt. Be a positive role model for others. We could certainly use a few.

Making Tracks
None of us like to waste time. I live in the country near a railroad track and sometimes I'm irritated at having to wait for a slowly approaching train when I'm so close to home. There's always the temptation to

sneak around the bars. But since beginning this book I've been timing the trains. So far my longest wait is just over six minutes. Is that worth dying for? The next time you're tempted to beat a train, stop and time it instead. Or revisit the days of your childhood when you enjoyed counting the cars and reading where they came from. Take a Quick Stop! and then consider that somewhere today, a driver made a different decision from yours, but didn't live to tell about it.

CRANKY QUIZ ITEM # 8:
RACING MINDS AND LOST MOMENTS

> 8. ___ Does your mind constantly race ahead, always keeping you a few steps ahead of yourself?

Momentary Pause

A business owner hired me to assess his company. He was brilliant, charismatic, and amazingly energetic. He even had a *stand-up* desk, if that gives you a clue. He was constantly on the move, always a jump ahead. When talking with his employees, he quickly caught the point of the discussion (or thought he did), came to a fast conclusion, and briskly forged on. His fast-paced style forced everyone to communicate at his speed, not the individual's.

I could tell his employees had unanswered questions and frustration over these aborted discussions. I cut out a pair of "footprints" from a large piece of paper, instructing him to stand on this "management aid" whenever he spoke with his staff. He was to stand still and listen, stay mentally present, and not physically leave until the discussion was over (this to be determined by his employees, not by him). The footprints were his reminder to stop, listen, and stay *in the moment* instead of chauffeuring others through a high-speed discussion. Can you relate?

Anti-Cranky Alternatives for Quiz Item # 8:
Racing Minds and Lost Moments
Welcome the Moment

At work or home, make a conscious effort to bring yourself into the here and now. Quit thinking about everything you've got to do. Stop.

Look around. Listen. Feel what's happening inside you. Be quiet for a moment. Relax. Feel your breathing; feel your heart. When you're in the moment and self-aware you can more fully see, hear, feel, and experience what's happening around you and inside you. You can tune in to others. You can better identify the almost invisible forces that crank up the momentum in your life. The more you live in the moment, the easier it is to enjoy life's little pleasures. You rediscover the sources of self-renewal your spirit so desperately needs.

Push Your Reset Button

We have little influence over many factors in our lives but if we periodically center ourselves we can stay in the moment and maintain inner calm in the midst of chaos. The secret is in having a "Reset Button." When you start rushing, feeling out of control, or getting cranky, pretend you have a Reset Button that can instantaneously transport you back to *now*. First, let yourself refocus. Disregard what's happening "out there" and turn within. Take a nice deep breath and let it relax you. Thoroughly review your state of mind and body. Pushing your Reset Button means breathing, relaxing, refocusing. It brings you back to the present. You may need to do this a hundred times a day at first. Push your Reset Button anytime you need to so you can bring your full awareness back to now.

Share the Moment with Others

When someone is speaking, give your full attention. Don't jump ahead or interrupt unless you have a clarifying question. Refrain from finishing people's sentences, even if you think you know what they're going to say. Monitor the pace of conversations between you and your loved ones or friends and make sure you give people adequate space in which to talk. Let your kids or spouse speak for themselves. Give the moment to the other party so you can both enjoy the here and now. You can reverse this process, too: The next time you interact with someone who's operating at warp speed, keep your body language quiet and your tone of voice steady. Pause before you speak, stay calm and centered, and notice whether the person entrains to you.

CRANKY QUIZ ITEM # 9:
MULTITASKING

> 9. ___ Are you a multitasker; that is, are you prone to work on two or three things at once rather than one at a time?

If One Is Good, Then Two Are Better

During a stress management seminar I was explaining how multitasking adds to our stress level. A woman asked, "This morning, while I was eating a bagel, blow-drying my hair, and putting on my makeup, I reached over and flushed the toilet with my foot. Is that multitasking?" Indeed, multitasking is our attempt to attack two or more tasks at once, instead of working on one item at a time. Because most of us do it, people always ask what's wrong with multitasking. Well, it splits our focus, distracts us, forces us to stay two jumps ahead of ourselves, and undermines our ability to be in the moment. We're more likely to make mistakes when our attention is divided and in extreme instances, accidents can result.

Many of us multitask while driving. Look around and you'll catch people eating, smoking, talking on their cell phones, cleaning their car, combing their hair, shaving, putting on makeup or nail polish, and even *reading!* Who the hell is driving the car while all of this is going on?

I fight the temptation to multitask because it's often less of a time saver and more of a stressor; my technique suffers and I often end up making a mess. Granted, some multitasking works, but first we rationalize it, then we get compulsive about it. We then lose our ability to do one thing at a time, like eating. We do so many things when we eat (read, watch TV, talk on the phone), we get fidgety when food is our only focus.

Before I became a patient person I avoided one of the cashiers at a local grocery store because she's the complete opposite of multitasking. This woman carefully picks up one item at a time and gently places it in the bag. There was a time I wanted to bang my head against her cash register because I found her pace so tedious. Now I just relax and appreciate her work. This woman taught me the beauty of doing one thing at a time. And she *never* bruises my tomatoes!

Anti-Cranky Alternatives for Quiz Item # 9:
Multitasking
Embrace the Process

For simple stress reduction and relief from compressed time (and even increased safety), give up the practice of multitasking. It may at first feel awkward because you're used to juggling tasks. But once you adjust you'll feel more centered, more relaxed, and less scattered. Sometime soon, pick an appropriate period to practice the following:

Take a moment and center yourself. Ignore everything going on around you. Consciously zero in on whatever task you're doing as you do it, step by step. Slow down and embrace the process. Consciously notice every movement, every stroke, every step. Notice the subtleties of even the simplest movement. Multitasking triggers a sense of urgency by forcing you into the next moment rather than *this* one. Instead of increasing your stress by multitasking, embrace the process, so you can spend more time in the moment.

Give Yourself Some Sole Food

Eating is a big part of our lives, but mountains of food pass through our mouths without our ever tasting it. Every now and then, make a meal your sole occupation. Don't watch TV, read, or work. Before you grab your fork, look at the food on your plate. Smell it before you start eating. Savor the aroma. Pause, then take a small bite. Chew slowly. Taste your food; feel its textures. Empty your mouth before you take another bite. Lay your fork down. Reflect on how it feels to make a meal your sole focus.

Even in just reading this, you might feel resistant and want to bang your head ever so gently against the table, but please know that this reaction is simply a sign of how desperately you need an exercise like this. It's good for your mind and body to eat in peace. It lowers your stress, improves your digestion, and helps you eat less (it's easy to overeat if you're distracted). What you learn from eating sole food can be applied elsewhere in your life: the value of doing one thing at a time.

CRANKY QUIZ ITEM # 10:
TIME BANDITS

> 10. ___ Do you feel "time impoverished," as if there's never enough
> of it, regardless of your efforts to catch up?

The New Currency That Makes Paupers of Us All

It's hard to decide whether we actually place a high value on time or not. Yes, we all want more of it, and yet we squander what little we have on things that don't really matter. We seem unconscious of, or incapable of, reconciling our conflicts between getting what we think we want and doing what we think we must. We're all conflicted about time issues, and the inconsistencies make us cranky.

Our homes are filled with convenience items and we're more squeezed for time than ever before. Everything has sped up except our ability to keep up. We interrupt polite telephone greetings and hang up on answering machines because we don't want to wait fifteen seconds. Computers and printers are sluggish; microwaves are too slow, and fast food isn't fast enough. *Time is the precious currency of the new millennium and we all feel impoverished.* What happens when an entire culture becomes "time deprived" and feels as if bandits are stealing its precious, nonrenewable resource? How much faster can we go, and how time impoverished can we get before someone cries halt?

When Robert Reich resigned from his Secretary of Labor position he admitted he was giving up the most wonderful job he'd ever had, but it was also the most demanding. Reich said he wanted to spend more time with his family. I perked up when I heard him say, "Time management is a joke." He was right. In our chaotic, compressed world, time management can only go so far. *You're not just managing time anymore; you're managing choices, today and every day of your life.*

Anti-Cranky Alternative for Quiz Item # 10:
Time Bandits
Make the Transition from Time Management
to Life Management

"Time management" is something you're familiar with, and you're probably better at it than you think. Time management involves *practices*. It centers around efficiency and effectiveness techniques that help you handle your tasks, chores, and workload. It's invaluable for dealing with your external environment.

"Choice management" involves *principles*. It means sorting through what's important to you and what isn't. It's consciously and consistently living in accordance with your values and priorities. Just as it sounds, choice management is far more difficult than time management; it involves dealing with your internal environment. I'd venture to say that few of us are operating at this level. *Until we clarify what drives our behavior, we're merely going through the motions, and often the wrong ones at that.*

Then there's "life management," an idea whose time has yet to come. Life management involves *purpose*. The reason so many of us are time impoverished is because we haven't done the internal work, the spiritual work, to define who we are, what we believe in, and our purpose for being on this earth. Life management involves the day-to-day discipline of living by our principles. As you can see, we've moved up the ladder of abstraction, from the physical to the spiritual or metaphysical; from our "comfort zone" to "uncharted territory." This may not be the answer you were looking for. We human beings are infatuated with method, quick fixes, and hard answers—things we can *do*. Purpose doesn't come from strategy or technique. It requires a lot of *being* and thinking.

If you truly want to curb your time-compressed, frenetic life, you need to ascend to the top of that ladder and define what you and your life are all about. Chapter 13 will help. So will an elegantly simple book by Barbara Braham entitled *Finding Your Purpose*. Until you do this work, your day-to-day activities will lack connection, and the energy you expend will feel wasted. Forget time management for now; you're probably already doing it. Start making conscious choices about how you spend your time and make sure it's connected to your purpose. Once you get your purpose nailed, life opens up to you in ways you haven't dreamed possible. If all of us actually took these steps, it would cause a massive cultural shift.

A Dose of Reality about Compressed Time

Regardless of how busy you are, you still only have twenty-four hours per day, 168 hours a week. This is a reality that can't be changed here on Planet Earth. No matter how busy or how important you are, how well your mutual funds are doing, or what some far-out TV shows suggest, you cannot transcend the time-space continuum. This means you can do only so much in a day, or a week. It means that if you're late, hurrying up won't make you on time, and the last place you want to hurry is on the road. It means that more activity or a faster pace isn't always the answer, nor is blaming others for your stress. You can't make more time, but you can make better choices. You can *consciously* readjust your pace and dedicate your time to the activities and tasks that truly and legitimately matter to you. You can choose to drop the insignificant stuff that's making you crazy. While some cranky people will continue squandering their lives, suffering from their self-imposed "scarcity mentality," you can choose a different path; a more bountiful one.

Life is short and priceless. You don't know how much time you have. But you do know how to marshal your personal resources and enrich your existence. You can make each day count through *conscious, purposeful choices* about what you do, when, with whom, and why. If not, you'll continue treating the symptoms of compressed time and not the cause. As you know, things only get better when *you* do.

Communication
Overload

TOO MUCH, TOO OFTEN

any people consider all-you-can-eat buffets a great bargain. Maybe you've found yourself with a plate piled so high with food it challenged the laws of physics. You start out modestly, only taking small portions, but by the time you get to the desserts, the situation is hopeless. You utter a quick prayer trying to reach the table without an embarrassing spill, but the pressure isn't over. You end up eating more than you want so no one will accuse you of wasting food. Later, bloated and remorseful, you swear you'll do better next time.

Now, imagine this dilemma repeating itself day after day. We continuously face an abundant "media buffet," and many of us don't know when or how to quit, or even that we should. We have twenty-four-hour access to news and entertainment as well as instant electronic contact with one another. In the United States alone, thousands of newspapers are published each day. A Sunday edition of the *New York Times* contains more information than our forebears from a century ago could amass in their lifetime. Our brains are so stuffed with news reports, articles, ads, entertainment images, and endless opinions, it has spoiled our appetite for learning about ourselves.

Despite futurists' promises about the paperless office, we're still bombarded with, and buried under, perpetual piles. How many mounds of paper sit on your desk, jam your files, flood your living room or otherwise intrude into your personal space? These conditions won't change until you do. If you've been diligently trying, but failing, to keep up, here's some good news. Much of what you're exposed to is *not* information. It's simply data. Brain clutter. It's not essential and you don't have to let it litter your mind. Cliff Stolle, author of *Silicon*

Snake Oil, states, "Data is not information any more than fifty tons of cement is a skyscraper."

Wherever you go and whatever you do, you're not just observing the "information glut," you're *embedded* in the thick of it, like banana slices in Jell-O. We're all on overload, and it's making us cranky. With apologies to Mae West, too much of a good thing isn't always wonderful: Our minds, like our stomachs, can handle only so much in one sitting. And just like the process of overeating, it sometimes takes us a while to realize we've exceeded the limits of what our brains can comfortably handle.

Spend a moment reflecting on the structure of your typical day and whether you're surrounded by nonstop mental commotion. If your chores, concerns and queues of incoming data are stacked like incoming flights landing at O'Hare International over the Thanksgiving holiday, you're precariously poised for a bad case of crankiness! An occasional busy, demanding day filled with mental distraction is one thing, but an unrelenting succession of them takes its toll.

Crankiness is a sign that you're suffering from too much pressure, too often. Your judgment can suffer as you bound from one activity to the other without relief, and so can your mood. Somewhere, somehow, there has to be a limit. You can't always completely control your schedule or magically trim down your workload, but you always have some options in your personal life. How do you spend your personal time? The media would have you think that you can't survive without the latest headline, newest scandal update, or tonight's lineup of sitcoms and dramas, but sometimes turning your back on these things is exactly what you need.

Your brain needs relief from external noise and data dumps; give yourself frequent chances to relax, reflect, and renew. Remember the priority issue? Constantly keep in mind what's really important to you and where your energy is best directed. The more you overindulge in the *extraneous*, the less you can focus on the *essentials*. Log on to the Internet and you have virtual access to anything, anywhere in the world. But if you don't know how to get to the right place and find the right information while ignoring the unnecessary, you have access to nothing. It's the same way in your life: The energy you expend trying to keep up with what's going on in other people's lives could be better used on your own.

A MATTER OF QUESTION

Chapter 1 explained how your expectations are influenced by what you see, hear, and experience. They, in turn, influence what you choose to see, hear, and experience. Unless you're acutely aware of this process you'll tend to compulsively overload yourself with data, news, and media agendas without considering the process or the effects.

As you read this chapter please keep in mind the context of entrainment and time urgency as outlined in chapter 2. The media can instill a sense of immediacy on both TV and radio. Between news segments and even entertainment programs you'll be advised to stay tuned, watch the next installment, stick around, and tune in tomorrow, and if you don't, you'll miss something good. These subtle pressures suggest that you need more, not less, information, and this can push you into overload without your realizing it.

Examine everything you watch or read, and *why*. That we simply accept and don't question our media exposure is a significant statement about our culture. For example, regardless of how rich or poor we may be, TV now holds an unquestioned presence in our lives. Those few individuals who don't own one are looked upon as odd—social misfits.

TV's presence in our culture is now so established that instead of asking *if* we should watch TV, we ask *what* we should watch. We talk a lot about what we watch, but that *we don't question the watching itself* reflects its prominence in our lives. As an image-driven entertainment medium, TV profoundly affects our perceptions and expectations. By virtue of TV's unique nature, context and delivery *are* the primary message, the content is secondary. We're not asked to *think* when we tune in; we're simply expected to watch, with images, music, and laugh tracks guiding us along the way. If this strikes you as curious or unsettling, then you'll find Neil Postman's *Amusing Ourselves to Death* a thoroughly illuminating and thought-provoking book. Rather than simply accepting the presence of electronic influences in your life, explore their effect on you. Tally how many hours a day you're exposed to news, data bytes, headlines, and talk shows and the impressions they leave on you. Think about the more than two million commercials you'll digest in your lifetime and how those ads may affect your attitude, buying habits, and lifestyle.

Your mind can handle only so many concerns at once. If or when you find yourself feeling cranky, take a few moments to determine whether your mood is in any way related to "input fatigue" and the quality or quantity of what your brain is being fed. *From now on, expose yourself to more silence, more solitary time, and less sensationalism in any form*. Make some decisions about how you can minimize the ill effects of "communication overload" and lead a less mentally cluttered, more emotionally spacious life.

WHEN UNLIMITED DATA HITS A LIMITED ATTENTION SPAN

Out of Order

There was a time in my life when my television got switched on as soon as I woke up in the morning and stayed on until I went to bed. As a full-time homemaker with three small children, a dormant imagination, and a husband who worked two jobs, TV was my companion, news and entertainment source, and baby-sitter for my kids. Some years later, while I was attending community college, raising my teenagers, clinging to the dream of completing my education and making something of myself, one day the TV broke. It took me eight years to replace it. By then, TV had lost its hold on me.

News or Noose?

People complain about media overload, but when I suggest they watch less news or read fewer magazines they gasp, "But I *have* to know what's going on!" Do they? Do you? Is our urge to keep up motivated by personal curiosity, cultural expectation, or both? During the sensationalized O. J. Simpson trial, scores of busy, overloaded people somehow managed to carve *hours* out of their busy lives to watch the trial each day.

Does up-to-the-minute knowledge of the most recent plane crash, murder, terrorist activity, or political scandal enrich our existence or impair it? What do we actually *learn* from most reports? Several studies have shown that heavy TV viewers perceive the world as less safe than others. This "scary world syndrome" illustrates how we draw personal conclusions from what we see. Books, movies, and TV programs offer a composite of our most grisly depths: stalking, rape, murder, and terrorism under the guise of entertainment. Try to avoid that kind of content and you get it anyway, thanks to frequent flash previews.

Cranky Quiz

COMMUNICATION OVERLOAD

Scoring the Cranky Quiz

Score 1 point for every *yes* and 0 for every *no*. Count a *sometimes* as a *yes*. Add your total: 3 points or less (Cool) means you're in good shape, 4 to 7 (Warm) indicates a need to slow down, and 8 to 10 (Hot!) indicates a raging cranky infection. You'll find anti-cranky solutions for each quiz item in this chapter.

1. ___ Do you watch more than two hours of TV per day, including reruns?

2. ___ Do you begin and/or end your day with TV, radio, or a newspaper?

3. ___ Do you leave the TV or radio on for the purpose of background noise?

4. ___ Do you tune in to talk shows and celebrity specials or buy tabloids?

5. ___ Do you discuss movies, events, TV programs, or commercials with friends, family, and colleagues?

6. ___ Do you consider yourself "immune" to commercials and ads?

7. ___ Do you listen to politically oriented talk shows?

8. ___ Are you drawn to mysteries or suspense novels, real-life crime, or violent movies and TV thrillers?

9. ___ Are you surrounded with piles of paper (memos, magazines, articles) that you somehow never get to?

10. ___ Are you so information soaked that you can't assimilate the old data, let alone the new?

Cranky Quotient _____

My communication overload condition is *(circle one)*

Cool   Warm   Hot!

It's Both What You Say and How You Say It

It's midsummer in the Midwest as I write this piece and it's hot. It's also muggy. While projecting the five-day forecast last night, our meteorologist introduced not only the heat index, but the *misery* index. We viewers were not only told *what* the temperatures would be, but how we ought to feel about it. With the blink of an eye, the weather report switched from objective data to subjective interpretation. This may at first blush sound like a trivial matter, but bear with me.

News holds an important place in our lives, and it offers far more subjective data than we realize. The next time you catch a report, observe anchors and commentators slipping from fact to speculation and back again, with no distinction made. Note how often interviewees are asked for their opinions, "What do you think . . . " or "Why do you suppose . . . " instead of fact. "What took place?" "What else did you see? . . . " Observe how often objective reports get served up with a side dish of commentary or personal innuendo. The point? When boundaries are blurred, when objective analysis blends with opinion, we can miss the shift and automatically buy it as fact.

CRANKY QUIZ ITEM # 1:
TUBE TIME

1. ___ Do you watch more than two hours of TV per day, including reruns?

Sixty Channels and Nothing's On

With the introduction of remote control our TV watching became even more passive, but you wouldn't know it by the language. Channel surfing sounds so *active*. We hit the remote dozens of times and then announce in a brooding tone, "There's nothing on." Of course, that doesn't stop us from watching. Now that you know I was once a TV addict, I can report that these days, viewing lags well below average in our home. I watch three, maybe four hours per week.

Mind you, I'm not suggesting TV watching is inherently bad; it's just that for many of us it holds a constant, unquestioned presence in our lives. I'm simply urging you to *think* about what you watch and why, especially if the tube is on several hours a day in your home. Latest statistics show that the average viewer watches about twenty-eight hours per week. Many are unaware of how much time they spend staring at that colorful, animated screen. Are you one of them?

Anti-Cranky Alternatives for Quiz Item # 1:
Tube Time
Tune In to Why You Tune In
Statistics report that more homes in the United States have TV sets than indoor plumbing. Some of us are so accustomed to its presence we don't even realize it's on. If we're so tuned out when we're tuned in, why do we turn it on at all? The following questions will help raise your viewing consciousness:

- Are you aware of how many hours you spend watching TV per day (week)?
- Is there something else you could be doing that would bring you more satisfaction or pleasure?
- If your time on earth were limited (and it is), is there something else you'd go off and do instead of turning on the tube?
- Could you and your loved ones benefit from more "together" time?
- Do you habitually watch TV more as a diversion than actual entertainment because you're too tired or uninspired to think of anything else to do?

Watch What You Watch
Many of us watch TV out of habit. Before turning the set on, ask yourself, "Do I really need this?" Critically observe both substance and style, especially with news or interview programs. Pinpoint the good interviewers, and shows offering quality information so your time won't be wasted. I have little tolerance for the terse, rapid-fire hosts who stage more of an interrogation than an interview, badgering guests, looking for the hook. Their need to control the dialogue hampers an authentic exchange. But those who know how to draw out their guests have something to offer. Brush up on your observation skills and you'll separate the mediocre news programs from the few outstanding ones. When you watch TV for sheer entertainment, note the structure of the program and what makes it work. In short, actively question what you watch and be part of the process.

How Good Was It?

I'm not saying you shouldn't watch TV. I am suggesting that if you're parking in front of the set and passively taking it all in while complaining about how bad it is, you're wasting your time and energy. It's like a couple I overheard in a restaurant one time. The first one mentioned that the food wasn't very good and the second said, "Yes. And the portions are so small."

If you and your TV have a codependence thing, set up a system for measuring your level of interest in watching it. This will save you from using it as escapism or mindless diversion. You could use a 1 to 10 scale: the 1 represents extremely low importance/low interest and a 10 reflects extremely high importance/high interest. Set your standards high. If you find yourself staring at a value 5 or 6 program, do something radical; turn off the tube and walk out of the room. This way, you can watch less TV while enjoying it more and have some extra time to whittle away at your communication overload.

CRANKY QUIZ ITEM # 2:
THE NEWS AND OUR NEED TO KNOW

2. ___ Do you begin and/or end your day with TV, radio, or a
   newspaper?

And Now, the News

Wherever we are, in today's plug-and-play world, we have continuous access to news, data, and information. The Expectation Machine, that invisible force field that shapes our perceptions about our culture and ourselves, influences us not only to think we can keep up with split-second electronic media, but that we're *obligated* to do so. For in-depth coverage we can consult the *New York Times, Washington Post, Wall Street Journal*, and other high-profile newspapers, yet even they don't guarantee accuracy or objectivity. With CNN and *USA Today* we can catch headlines and news briefs and feel partially informed, feeding on snippets as we go about our day. As if this isn't enough, some of us take it to extremes.

I know a woman who keeps a TV on in her bedroom, bathroom, and kitchen so she doesn't miss one sound bite while getting ready for work. On her drive into the city she tunes in CNN on her car radio. She scans several papers and magazines daily so she can be up on the latest headlines, just in case (in case of what, I don't know). Compare her with another woman, who, with equal conviction, *avoids* the news and doesn't watch TV because she considers it an unnecessary intrusion in her life. You might appreciate knowing that both of these people are in the same profession. Would you hazard a guess about the overall pace each maintains?

Where do you fit in the "need-to-know" continuum and is this a healthy balance for you? In case you're curious, until beginning this book, I occasionally listened to Public Radio, seldom watched the news, and infrequently scanned a newspaper. I read mostly nonfiction and subscribe to two magazines on equestrian sports (my hobby). Call me lightly exposed if you like, yet headlines, current news features, and popular commercials still find their way into my consciousness. The distance I maintain from popular media helped prompt the writing of this book because I see things differently. In my work as a business consultant I've trained myself to catch the things many people pass by without noticing. One time, while exercising in a hotel workout room, CNN was on. I was amused to note that the longest feature presented during the hour's news loop was the "Business Minute."

No End in Sight

A disturbing aspect of news watching that doesn't get addressed is the lack of closure. Even with my low exposure, I find myself reflecting on stories that left me hanging. Did the innocent child injured in that drive-by shooting survive? Was that unfairly accused inmate released from prison? Did the residents of that community fully recover from that natural disaster? Maybe I'm just too sensitive, but I can't shake these images and I dislike worrying about such things. On the other hand, I would find it more worrisome if I were indifferent to these events. Maybe you feel the same way. This is a good time to reflect on the unanswered question: Where do unfinished news items go when they're not the news anymore?

Anti-Cranky Alternatives for Quiz Item # 2:
The News and Our Need to Know
Establish Your Own MDR

There's no FCC approved "Minimum Daily Requirement" for news, but it's worth considering. Even if you pride yourself on being a highly informed member of our society, you don't have to relinquish your "well-informed citizen" badge if you cut back a bit. You might even benefit. For example, why listen to a news loop for a second time if you heard it an hour ago? Why absorb a chain of superficial news bites that leave you with gnawing questions instead of knowledge? Why passively watch TV when there's someone in the room who passionately loves you and wants attention? Why put a vivid picture (a plane crash or image of war) to a headline you've already heard about?

Too many negative images can haunt your subconscious, prompting a combined sense of crankiness and woe. Prevent overload. Preserve your mental energy and time. Set limits. Establish a personal news MDR and stick to it. If you have a heavy day of news, find a positive antidote (a quick inspirational read, for example, or a few moments of journal writing) to prevent an onset of "data overdose."

From the First to the Last

Many of us begin and end our day with a heavy portion of news but did you know that during your first and last waking moments, your mind is in a state of high receptivity. If you have sleep problems, maybe your unrest comes from that late "bad news" report. Read something positive instead. Reflect on the pleasant parts of your day or aspects of your life you appreciate. Run through a perfect rehearsal of your favorite hobby. Recite positive affirmations until you fall asleep.

Plan a pleasant wake-up routine, too. Ease into your day by delaying your first portion of news. Play soft music. Read a positive passage to set the tone for your day. Try this for a week, morning and night, and see what effect it has. If you have small children, help make the first and last minutes of their day more agreeable, too. You won't be banished from society if you miss the first or last news report of the day but you could benefit mightily. Restraint is a powerful agent in lowering your Cranky Quotient.

CRANKY QUIZ ITEM # 3:
OUR NEED FOR NOISE

> 3. ___ Do you leave the TV or radio on for the purpose of background noise?

Surround Sound

A new friend invited me over for coffee after a movie. As we entered her home and headed for the kitchen she flipped on the TV. I asked if we were going to watch something. She said we wouldn't actually be *watching* it, that she merely kept the TV on for background noise. Silence has become such a rare experience in our culture many of us don't know what to do with it. Some psychologists suggest we've become afraid of silence, just as a child fears the dark. The unnerving part is that we don't realize how noise prevents us from actively using our brains and thinking about substantive things. Or, even worse, maybe we *do* realize it!

Every day, all day, we're surrounded by noise. Outside and inside, we hear constant noise from traffic, appliances, kids, pets, sirens, phones, computers, printers, TVs, stereos, radios, CD players. Some of us wear mini players as we walk, drive, or bike ride, lest we be forced to endure a silent moment. We're so attached to our electronic gadgets some of us can't go to sleep or wake up without one.

The Sounds of Silence

Where does silence fit into your life? When you're alone do you enjoy quiet surroundings? Some people get uncomfortable at just the thought; I can see it in their face and body language when I raise the topic. Background noise is *normal* for them. What's wrong with that, you may ask.

Silence offers your mind and body a chance to relax and regroup. It provides relief from external distractions. Most critically, it lets you explore what's going on in your head. For cranky people this is a problem. They avoid self-examination and use noise as a diversion. Otherwise, they might have to think about their behavior or admit that others aren't to blame for their bad mood. Maybe you're already comfortable with quiet time, but just for fun, read on.

Anti-Cranky Alternatives for Quiz Item # 3:
Our Need for Noise
Think about It

Noise obstructs inner reflection. When was the last time you sat in silence and simply *thought?* If you're unaccustomed to this practice, I encourage you to try it. Take three minutes initially and build up to five or ten. In the evening, take time to review what you were thinking or feeling as events unfolded and why you responded as you did. Consider what you might do next time if the situation were to repeat itself. My friend, Marilynn Semonick, calls it "simmering" and she does it faithfully. You really get to know yourself in quiet moments such as this. Maybe you could simmer on what it might take to help you feel more relaxed or less overloaded.

Let Your Mind Soak in the Silent Sp-ah!

Say the word *spa*. It rhymes with "ah!" Here's an exercise that offers relief from any kind of overload, and the more you practice it, the better you'll get. Just as someone who is out of shape can't immediately go out and run or swim a long distance, it may take a while to perfect your technique. But patiently persist; silence is truly a tonic in a clamoring world. Read the following and then try your first mental soak in the "Silent Sp-ah!"

Sit in a quiet room with no TV or radio; no music. Get into a relaxed position, seated upright. Close your eyes and take a nice deep breath, then let all of your breath leave your body in a long, slow exhale. Imagine stress and tension leaving with it. Now take another nice slow, deep inhale through your nose, drawing relaxation into your body. Gently feel the rise and fall of your chest. As you quietly inhale and exhale through your nose, shift your breath lower, feeling your belly expand as you inhale and contract as you exhale, using your diaphragm to push the air in and out. For the first few minutes, gently exaggerate your belly's expansion and contraction.

Continue your relaxed, deep breathing and let your focus softly wander to the thoughts passing through your mind. Let each one float by with no hurry, no analysis, no judgment. Now and then, let your mind smoothly shift from your thoughts to your breathing, and then back out to the assorted noises around you, letting everything drift lightly by. Slowly shift from one to the other, like the flow of a lava lamp.

When you come back to your breath, don't force it. Focus on how naturally and effortlessly you breathe in and out. You might become aware of or feel sensations you wouldn't otherwise notice. Let your thoughts and feelings drift by with a gentle, floating awareness, as if everything were held in suspension. Release any tension you feel. Soak up these delicious feelings, right to the end. After a few minutes, open your eyes and sit for a moment before you get up. Imagine the luxury of slipping into the Silent Sp-ah! every day, perhaps as a pick-me-up after work. Five minutes is nice; ten is good, fifteen is better. You'll emerge feeling refreshed and renewed.

Let Whatever Happens Happen

Some people will get hyper just reading about the Silent Sp-ah!, let alone trying it. Of course, that's the whole point! If you feel uncomfortable or fidgety when you try to relax, be assured this is normal. You may itch and twitch, wiggle and jiggle. Your mind may be filled with stampeding thoughts, like a herd of runaway horses. Bizarre things will careen through your head. Don't let them worry you. Just let them go by. Allow your mind to settle lightly on your breathing or whatever is going on around you. You may realize that birds are singing or children are playing in the distance. You may feel or hear something you've never noticed before.

At some point, you'll begin thinking about the hordes of important things you should be doing. Stop! Here's our news flash. We're called human beings, but we live like human *doings*. We place a value on productivity, but disapprove of inactivity. As a result, you may initially feel uncomfortable sitting still. Here's why:

1. You're not used to it. We have a tendency to reject anything new or unfamiliar unless it tastes exceptionally good or feels great on the first try. The Silent Sp-ah! may not feel wonderful at first but that's exactly why you need it. Consider this your first clue.

2. At the outset it will seem as if nothing is happening, but that's exactly what's supposed to happen—nothing! You don't even have to *do* anything with this idea; just let it be. Can you stand it?

3. You may feel almost an instant panic at being so still. Your body and brain aren't used to stillness and as a result, everything inside you may rebel. If you find yourself feeling cranky or complaining that this isn't working, this is your second clue. Stay put: Your discomfort is a sign that you desperately need more quiet time in your life. The more you protest, the more you need it. How's that for a conundrum?

4. A lot of us are hung up about making mistakes. Our performance anxiety inhibits our ability to just let go. When it comes to the Silent Sp-ah!, don't worry about whether you do a "good" job of relaxing. Just do it. Regardless of what happens, you still benefit.

5. Relaxation is a skill anyone can learn. Just like golfing, swimming, or riding a horse, it takes practice and discipline. We're often willing to invest all kinds of time, effort, and money to learn a sport or craft, yet we're arrogant enough to think that relaxation should be there any time we want it, no questions asked. Not so! Just like the flow of a flawless golf swing, the more familiar you become with sitting quietly, the smoother it will feel. It takes time, but it's worth it.

6. You may be thinking you don't have the time to relax, or you don't need it. This is your last clue. *Your level of resistance is in direct proportion to the extent of your need.* Your ability to relax and let go is the secret to combating crankiness and the Ten Trends that cause it. Cultivate this capability and you take the first steps toward decontaminating your life. Who would have thought the statement, "Go take a soak," would have such a positive context?

Now Hear This

If you suffer from tinitis (constant ringing in your ears) you may at first find it difficult and distracting to sit in silence, but let your focus go outside of yourself and away from the noise in your ears. It's good for your mind and body to get away from everyday noises (traffic, TV, radio, machines) regularly, even if the silence isn't perfect, and even if it's only for a few moments. Let your attention softly and casually go where it wants, from the rise and fall of your breathing to soft outside noises and back again. You may find yourself momentarily forgetting about the noise in your head without your having to rely on outside sounds to keep you distracted from it. I have tinitis and sometimes it feels as if I carry a field of crickets and cicadas in my head. I've found that my ability to shift focus takes me away from the noise. It's always a refreshing, welcome break.

CRANKY QUIZ ITEM # 4:
TABLOIDS AND TV TALK

> 4. ___ Do you tune in to talk shows and celebrity specials or buy tabloids?

I Can Quit Any Time I Want: Addiction, Adoration, and Arrant Curiosity

"Princess Di Is Alive and Living with Elvis in Secret Las Vegas Hideaway." Okay, I haven't actually seen this headline but it's no less bizarre than most. Yes, you want to be informed, but this isn't *news*. Make the distinction between news and "media motes." Do you really need gossip?

If a sensational news item doesn't relate directly to your life, where's the benefit? What's behind the compulsion to watch every TV program, see every movie, read every magazine, follow every scandal, or know who's being stalked? Is it simply more distraction to keep you from monitoring your own personal issues, or to console yourself that life isn't so bad after all? Life is too short to spend it absorbing half-truths about strangers. In *Breathing Space*, author Jeff Davidson suggests you give up trying to follow someone else's fifteen minutes of fame. I agree.

Sometimes this means overcoming your morbid curiosity (relax, we all have it). Like you, I scan those teaser headlines while standing in the checkout line. Yes, I'm intrigued and even tempted, but I refuse to waste my irreplaceable time reading unfactual reports about people I'll never know. In no way is your life, or mine, enriched by the factual or fictional escapades of strangers.

Of course, celebrities and TV personalities don't *seem* like strangers to us because their faces are in our living rooms every day. We're comfortable calling them by their first names. Oprah. Rosie. Geraldo. Sally. And so on. With this familiarity comes a sense of endowment, as if it's *our right* to know about these people's private lives, whether they like it or not, whether it's accurate or not. I sometimes wonder if Princess Diana would be alive today if we all hadn't felt so entitled to a piece of her.

Anti-Cranky Alternatives for Quiz Item # 4:
Tabloids and TV Talk
Curb Your Media Addictions: Just Say No

Do talk shows or tabloids provide you with substantial insights about yourself? Is the quality of your life enhanced by keeping close tabs on someone else?

Some of us are addicted to scandal and shocking stories. If you find yourself faithfully tracking tabloids or secretly tuning in to sensational talk shows, get a grip! As with any Twelve-Step Program, admission is the first step. You can kick your habit right now, in the privacy of your own home. No public confession; no personal embarrassment. Simply admit you have a problem and resolve to recover, now. From today on, don't buy that tabloid; don't tune in. Be strong. You can do it!

Think Before You Spend

If you're a compulsive collector who spends your hard-earned money on books, magazines, or mementos about someone you will never know, ask yourself *why*. It was spooky watching the "Diana" merchandise appear so quickly after her disastrous death. *Why* were these products produced and *who* benefited from their sale? Explore why you feel compelled to own such things. From now on, instead of compulsively heading for the mall so you can purchase the latest piece of celebrity memorabilia or the newest installment of an infinite series of collectibles, stop and think about what you're doing: The manufacturers are betting you won't!

If you find yourself unable to resist anything soft and cuddly with a cute face, find out what the word *neoteny* means. It might help immunize you. Now, your argument might be that if you don't buy the newest addition your collection will be incomplete. That's exactly what I'm suggesting. You're being held hostage by a cleverly designed marketing ploy of a company that wants your money. They can do it only with your cooperation. Hey, go collect a few insights or sunsets instead. They're free!

CRANKY QUIZ ITEM # 5:
PERSONAL COMMENTARY ON THE MEDIA

> 5. ___ Do you discuss movies, events, TV programs, or commercials with friends, family, and colleagues?

Sometimes We Don't Know What We Don't Know

Some of us don't let a little thing like lack of knowledge get in the way of free expression. A week after O. J. Simpson had been taken into custody some colleagues and I were discussing the case. A woman who lived in the Brentwood area said in a tone filled with conviction, "Look, I don't know him, but he's my neighbor. He couldn't have done it. This was a professional job!" Professional job? And just how many professional killers has *she* hung out with? Then it hit me like a bolt. Here we were, arguing with one another about people we didn't know and an incident about which we couldn't possibly learn the truth, yet each of us acted as if we had the inside scoop!

This was a defining moment for me. As one easily given to commentary about virtually anything, I vowed to quit being so free with my opinions unless I had first-hand experience or had seriously researched the topic. As you can imagine, this has severely limited my public discourse. I've been both amazed and amused at how little this leaves me to say at parties and social events. I'm becoming a better listener.

When a woman asked my opinion about the Clinton impeachment proceedings, I summoned my newfound self-restraint and rather smugly replied, "I make it a policy not to comment on issues when it's impossible to have all the facts." I expected (and hoped) this would pretty much kill the conversation but she, apparently unburdened by any such self-imposed boundaries, launched into her version of the issue. Oh well. I listened.

Anti-Cranky Alternative for Quiz Item # 5:
Personal Commentary on the Media
Is It Truly Newsworthy?

What's happening in the news often gets discussed more than what's happening in our own lives, and here's why: The news is conjecture. It's safe. It's remote. Because most of us watch the same TV shows and news reports, this creates the illusion of a bond: We can "tsk" together over the awful things that go on and feel comforted these incidents didn't happen to us. We can agree it's a cranky, whining world out there.

I once went to a dinner party where the host was the only person I knew. There were six of us and while the people were friendly and nice, after two hours I found myself eagerly anticipating dessert so I could finish it and bolt. It wasn't until the next day I realized the source of my restlessness. In the entire evening, no one ever talked about himself or herself. It was all news, school, work, local politics, or sports. I didn't know these people any better by the end of the night than I did when we were introduced. When I meet someone, I like to get acquainted, to find out who he or she is. I love hearing people's stories. The dinner party's dearth of personality left me hungry for substance.

Now that I've danced around it, let me get to the point: An occasional discussion about news and media events has value, but there are distinct disadvantages when current events become our major focus:

1. It prevents us from being known, from being "somebody." We don't get a chance to cover personal information such as who we are, what's happening in our lives, our philosophy, ideas, personal interests, and even real-life problems, challenges, or achievements.

2. It invites judgment. Given sketchy, limited, usually unverified data, we decide upon the goodness or badness of an incident without attempting to gain a complete understanding of the situation or the circumstances surrounding it.

3. It encourages us, like the woman from Brentwood, to make things up, express erroneous opinions, even live vicariously. We can go overboard in our interpretation without experts to counter our theories with pesky facts or bothersome data. We're free to draw our own (incorrect) assumptions. Without a reality check to intervene, we're free to treat these assumptions as fact, and we do.

4. It interferes with our discussing real-life, real-time events that matter to us. This is especially critical for couples; intimacy suffers when we only discuss superficial, remote topics with our partners (more on this in chapter 4).

5. We lose self-reflection time. We can't concentrate on our own behavior if we're hung up about what others are doing. Because we have no control over other people's behavior, our Cranky Quotient sky-

rockets. In other words, if you focus on people's negative attitudes or behaviors, you'll end up just as cranky as they are!

In short, it never hurts to know what you're talking about. You might wish to remember this the next time you get drawn into a flurry of personal commentary.

CRANKY QUIZ ITEM # 6:
COMMERCIAL EXPOSURE

> 6. ___ Do you consider yourself "immune" to commercials and ads?

It's a Mad, Mad, Mad, Ad World

You can tell the time of year by the products featured in TV ads, particularly over-the-counter medicines. Flu season. Cold relief. Allergy season. Itch relief. Antacids for holiday season relief. Sometimes I think an interplanetary visitor, a Martian maybe, might perceive television as the Command Central of our society. After all, it tells us what we should wear, eat, drive, how we should look and live, and what it takes to make us happy and successful. Quite an image, isn't it? Maybe I'm overstating my point, but small children can be as naïve as that Martian, and kids from age two on up are considered a *major* targeted market by corporate advertisers. Imagine a focus group composed of eighteen-month-old babies evaluating a TV show intended for that age market. I'm not kidding. Did you catch the word? That's exactly how corporations label us, as *markets*, from crib to coffin, and most of us don't even realize it.

We're so inundated with compelling inducements to earn, spend, and accumulate that even when we don't buy the product itself, we can buy products that *promote* it—caps, T-shirts, jackets, even a "Pepsi Stuff" duffel bag. I was surprised to discover that Nike is first and foremost a *clothing* manufacturer, not a shoe company; the Whoosh stripe can be displayed on virtually every part of the body. Just for fun, the next time you go to the mall, count how many logos you see on people's bodies. We wear labels and brands as status symbols; rather brilliant marketing, if you ask me. Is it mere coincidence that the sale of specific dog breeds skyrocket when one is featured in a series of commercials or a movie? And we think we're immune.

Billboards, print ads, and commercials are a huge part of our culture. Key words and phrases quickly slip into our language. In the eighties, the phrase, "Where's the beef?" from a Wendy's commercial was used in Mondale's presidential campaign. In a social setting if you want a good laugh, simply repeat the punch line from a clever commercial. Everyone knows the context. They laugh and you feel brilliant.

We're all more affected by advertising than we like to think. Consider how your self-esteem and self-perception have been influenced by commercials, ads, and media images. Have you ever felt self-conscious about your body because you're too large (or too small), too hairy (or not hairy enough)? Have you ever felt inadequate because you only remotely resemble the models or celebrities who promote the products you buy? Are you bothered by signs of aging? Did you take up smoking so you could feel more grown up or sophisticated like the people who looked so cool when they lit up? Did you ever secretly purchase a special product or article of clothing, hoping it would work its magic on you? I have. You may think you're immune to ads, but they get to you, in more ways than one.

Anti-Cranky Alternatives for Quiz Item # 6:
Commercial Exposure
Drop Consumer U: You've Earned Your Credits in the Work-and-Want Life Course

According to the Statistical Abstract of the United States the average person is exposed to 16,000 commercials a day. Would corporations spend billions of dollars per year on ad campaigns if they didn't work? Think about how often you see a particular ad. Do you think a company buys that air time just for fun? Do you really think the repetition has no effect?

Remember learning your multiplication tables and repeating the drill innumerable times until you got it? When developing a new mental or physical skill we learn to repeat the movement until it's right. If repetition is the secret to our success in building a skill, how could recurring commercial exposure not enjoy similar results? Think of what seeps into our subconscious when we're besieged with countless messages to buy, spend, wear, eat, collect, and own.

Look for the Message Behind the Message

Something triggers us to buy a particular item at a particular time but few of us stop to figure out what it is. For example, when people buy a sweatshirt that advertises their favorite TV program or sports team, maybe it's because they needed to stay warm, but could there also be an underlying need for inclusion or belonging? Others will read that shirt and immediately identify; instant bonding, just like Super Glue. Again, this appears as no big deal but why this sweatshirt at this time?

Now, what inspires you to make a purchase? If you're thinking *need*, think again. There's more. Figure out which ads hook you and why, and you'll increase your resistance to their message. It will also help you distinguish want from need.

Just watch teens to get a sense of their tenacious need for inclusion and how it hinges on wearing the right brand of clothes, shoes, or accessories. Ask them if what they hunger for is a want or need, and then try to figure out where they might possibly get the idea that their self-esteem hangs by a designer thread.

Turn Down the Volume; Don't Just Tune Out Your Mind

People say commercials don't bother them because they mentally tune them out. Yes, you're desensitized from so much exposure. But for full immunity from the compulsion for *bigger, better, faster, more, now,* you need to abstain. When a commercial comes on, literally turn down the volume or hit the mute button. This way it won't reach your subconscious. You might think you're not listening, but the messages are still getting through. When you mentally tune out during a commercial, you're merely dulling your senses to what's around you. Everything just becomes noise and you slip into a semitrance state. Too much of this and you chip away at your self-awareness. There are benefits from even a few seconds of silence. Turn it down.

CRANKY QUIZ ITEM # 7:
PROSELYTIZING PROGRAMS

> 7. ___ Do you listen to politically oriented talk shows?

Look Who's Talking

When I'm on the road, I periodically tune in talk shows such as Limbaugh, Liddy, and the likes to find out what they're up to. If I can't find the Big Guys there are a lot of small ones out there; local AM stations feature their own personal pundits, including Christian radio. Though I should be used to it by now I'm still surprised at the unself-conscious partisanship. Maybe I've been teaching team-building seminars too long, but I start breaking out in a rash when I hear people huffing and puffing from a testy, squared off, us-versus-them posture, regardless of what side or issue they represent.

Political matters are complex and knotty; there are always two sides to every issue and both come with their biases and misleading banners. I'm all for critique and analysis. But malice or name-calling oppose intelligent inquiry. Some people say these shows are just entertainment. I contend that conscious engagement in condemnation incites animosity and this inhibits our ability to evaluate. We can't make clear, rational decisions when anger or hate fills our hearts and minds.

The sad news is that everybody ends up a loser when debasement replaces debate. This "draw the line in the sand" mentality aborts any hope of discourse. As we scurry from the perilous middle ground to firm up our position of righteousness we forget the real purpose of this exchange: There's a problem and we need a solution. *Intelligent dialogue is impossible in the presence of a face-off.* Only when we abandon the right-wrong, black-white mentality and sift through the infinite maybes and nebulous grays with tough, searching questions and intelligent dialogue, can we truly examine any controversial issue.

The Perils of Pundits and Political Agendas

As Deborah Tannen states in *The Argument Culture*, we don't know how to cover two sides of an issue anymore without rolling up our sleeves or going for the throat. Regretfully, we sacrifice wisdom when we substitute dogma for discussion. Where's the learning when there's only one opinion? Like a touchy ulcer, my emotional indigestion kicks up when I hear Limbaugh's lines, word for word, on people's lips, because when someone else distills our ideas for us, we end up with an assortment of jumbled half-truths threaded together on a perilously thin strand. Let me clarify that it's not Limbaugh. It's that we eagerly swallow reconstituted opinions rather than research and formulate our own.

My objection centers around the *process* we follow, not the person. It could be anyone, from any side.

Whether covering political issues or popular culture, call-in shows allow viewers and listeners to air their opinions, but when undercurrents of rancor prevail I question the merit of this format. Thanks to my degree in human communication, I hear not only what is said, but appreciate how it's said. In listening to voice tone, skillfully constructed phrases, pauses, repetition, and intentional inference, I wonder if the popularity of these shows results from the cunning tactics of the hosts, the innate crankiness of the audience, or both.

Anti-Cranky Alternatives for Quiz Item # 7: Proselytizing Programs

Check Out Your Purpose

Call-in shows, opinion polls, and interactive formats reflect our desire to speak out and interact with those who share our views. We have to realize this is different from open exchange. If you're an avid fan of a proselytizing program, ask yourself exactly *why* you tune in. When have you learned something that enriched your life or benefited you personally? If it's validation you're seeking, ask yourself why you need it. Do you relish the thought of being right? Wars have been fought with both sides thinking God was their co-pilot. We all have opinions, but if you find yourself getting indignant or disgusted with dissenters rather than initiating a dialogue with them, figure out whether listening to opinionated programs generally raises your Crankiness Quotient or lowers it.

Take a Field Trip

When I was in the third grade we got to take a field trip. We visited the Post Cereal Company in Battle Creek, Michigan, and it was a thrill to see how cereal was made (you can even smell it cooking as you drive into town). I got to eat one of my favorite breakfast cereals, Grape-Nuts, embedded in ice cream. Obviously, I never forgot it. Maybe it's time for *you* to take a field trip to somewhere you've never visited so you can broaden your horizons. Watch or listen to a program that offers a counterpoint to your strongly held beliefs.

Get your hands on some media watchdog materials and check the veracity of sources you may have taken as gospel. When you listen to someone who holds a different view, instead of immediately refuting or condemning their message, look for the kernel of truth in it. Our society is incredibly complex and it's self-defeating to pretend political issues can be one-dimensional. A field trip can broaden your perspective and reduce your tendency to judge or dismiss so quickly. You might find yourself less cranky and more comfortable with dissenting views, or at least capable of listening with more understanding.

CRANKY QUIZ ITEM # 8:
GRAPHIC PORTRAYALS

> 8. ___ Are you drawn to mysteries or suspense novels, real-life crime, or violent movies and TV thrillers?

Imagine This

When Alfred Hitchcock's classic thriller *Psycho* hit the screens in 1960, movie goers were electrified. Images of the famous shower scene were etched in people's minds so indelibly that, decades later, hordes of us still lock the doors before stepping into the shower. Hitchcock's mastery lay in his restraint. We really didn't *see* anything: Our imagination did it all. Today, imagination is unnecessary. We get graphic action, breath-stopping chase scenes, violence, sex, cruelty, and a *lot* of killing. How many people have you or I watched get blown away in our lifetime? I'd hate to know. Novels, too, have picked up the pace, with striking descriptions of horrific acts, mirroring and exceeding that of real-life crime.

Whatever we watch, read, or experience registers: Through repeated exposure we become systematically desensitized to the most unspeakable of acts. As adults we think we're not affected, but don't be too sure. And what about our kids? Look at the headlines. While the actual percentage of teen crime has dropped, the starkness of violent acts and the subsequent lack of remorse are chilling. Kids think it's cool to not be terrorized by on-screen action and suspense, but what vital ingredient is lost as they repeatedly stifle their natural instincts?

Anti-Cranky Alternatives for Quiz Item # 8:
Graphic Portrayals
Get Selective: Abstain and Gain

Memory is selective. You've had moments in your life you wanted to capture forever: feelings, images, sounds, thoughts, even smells. But in attempting to recall, you only get a series of disjointed shots, like a bunch of outtakes from a badly edited film. Yet that same leaky mind of yours has stored traumatic experiences from your childhood, in detailed sequence, and they surface at the oddest times. How frustrating that our retrieval system can be so unreliable and unpredictable; we're not always in charge of what sticks.

My friend Holly Steil was asking her mom if she had felt concerned when all through kindergarten Holly drew pictures using only black crayons. Her mother replied, "That wasn't you, dear. That was your sister." To Holly it had all seemed so *real*.

The plot thickens. Psychologists tell us that our subconscious meticulously files and stores our experiences, both *real* and imagined. *Our brains are unable to correctly discern between fantasy and reality.* Imagine, if our minds are unable to differentiate between what we *actually* experience, versus what we only think, read, or witness on the screen, what happens when we're frequently exposed to graphic, brutal portrayals? Could this contribute to your crankiness? Here's one way to find out: Give up this grim fare for six months and then assess your mood, attitude, and general outlook. After doing so, I decided to abstain permanently. Maybe you will, too.

Repeat after Me

We're told that practice makes perfect. You probably know that an Olympic athlete's daily training regimen involves several hours of repetitive practice, drills, and visualization. Sports psychologists teach athletes to refine their *mental pictures*—to visualize perfect practice and flawless execution every time. Successful performance requires frequent repetition of these mental pictures, blending conscious desire with subconscious programming. The brain accepts these images as actual; real. This is how athletes improve their physical prowess.

Now think about kids who watch violent movies over and over again, or spend hours playing aggressive computer, video, or virtual reality games. What kinds of mental pictures result from such intense activity? *These kids are spending hours practicing, drilling, and visualizing violence.* Where do the mental pictures go when they're done? I won't venture so far as to say this is a factor in teen violence, but I certainly do wonder.

The learning nugget for you is this: Instead of filling your mind with repeated images of death and destruction, use the skills of world-class athletes to *improve* your life. *Repeatedly put pictures in your head designed to help you learn, grow, and enrich your life.* Practice, drill, and visualize until you make it happen.

CRANKY QUIZ ITEM # 9:
BURIED WITH BACKLOG

> 9. ___ Are you surrounded with piles of paper (memos, magazines, articles) that you somehow never get to?

Catching On to the Myth of Catching Up

The promise of a paperless society is still just that: a promise. Do you have an ever-growing stack of books, newspapers, magazines, and to-read items you've been wanting to attack? Sorry. This is the age of communication overload. Welcome to Never-Never Land. Just as Peter Pan proclaimed he'd never grow up, today we sing the New Millennium medley, "I'll never catch up!" Face it. You can do a lot, but you can't read it all, see it all, hear it all, or do it all.

You'll never catch up on *everything*, no matter how hard you try, so relax. Sit a spell. There will always be more options, obligations, and opportunities than you can possibly handle. You have to make some choices. *You'll never catch up. You can't do it all. So quit trying!* For tips on paper management, read Jeff Davidson's *Breathing Space* or Barbara Hemphill's *Taming the Paper Tiger*. If your disarray has hit crisis level and you're tempted to call 911, contact a member of the National Association of Professional Organizers instead.

Anti-Cranky Alternatives for Quiz Item # 9:
Buried with Backlog
Lighten Up Instead of Catching Up

To lighten your communication overload, sift through your mail before opening it. Toss the junk without opening it, including that catalog; you don't *need* anything. Ditch that flyer, too. Now, let's go back to that stack of articles, magazines, and papers that have been collecting dust the past year. So you hoped to read it all one of these days—an admirable intent. But by now most of it's out of date. Throw it out. It'll only hurt for a minute. Occasionally, extreme measures such as this are necessary to sustain your mental and physical well-being. Don't you wish everything was this easy!

Get Set to Set Limits

It's hard to accept that time is limited and one day we'll be gone. That's partly why we overload ourselves. If you want to combat your over-load, you need to analyze where you put your attention, time, and energy.

- Evaluate the time you spend reading, what you read, and how it serves you.
- Review your magazine subscriptions and decide which are *absolutely* necessary.
- Do the same with newspapers.
- Audit your TV time (and car radio news time) and determine whether you need to cut back.
- Assess the amount of reading time you spend on work-related material and if this commitment is short-term (organizational changes or a training course) or permanent and how you might be able to cut back (a speed-reading course, maybe?).
- Examine your habits and personal patterns to figure out whether you have a tendency to take on more than you can handle. After one of my programs a couple went home and added up their mag-azine subscriptions, which totaled twenty-three; six of them on golf. They cut back to nine magazines (three on golf) and said in a year they'll reevaluate.

CRANKY QUIZ ITEM # 10:
TOO MANY, TOO MUCH

10. ___ Are you so information soaked that you can't assimilate the old data, let alone the new?

More of More

It took years for cable TV to reach our area and by then we figured we could live without it. But when I travel I sometimes sit in a motel room with a remote in my hand, clicking through the procession of channels and I'm staggered at the endless offerings. When I stand in front of a magazine rack my mind sometimes stalls out because there are simply too many choices. The same thing happens on the Internet. Scan the self-help section in the bookstore. So much good information; how can we absorb it all? In this book alone, you'll have more ideas than you can immediately apply. Some you'll grasp instantly and others you'll just ignore. After a second reading they may jump out at you, not because they've changed, but because you have. There's so much out there. The question isn't Can you find good ideas, it's, Which ones will you use first?

Anti-Cranky Alternatives for Quiz Item # 10:
Too Much, Too Often
Create an Idea Incubator

Many good ideas fall by the wayside because we don't have time to process them immediately. It takes time to think things through, and we just never get around to it. Losing an idea or forgetting it can make us cranky. Grab hold of a good thought and let it incubate. That's how I conceived and wrote this entire book, stumbling onto one idea at a time and later developing it. A concept or phrase would pop into my head at inconvenient moments but I'd make a quick note in my Idea Book with enough detail to remember the context, and set it aside. Writing it down is the secret. As my friend Kim Kauffman says, the mind is like a self-cleaning oven. You already know your retrieval system is fickle—don't trust your memory!

In total, I filled six notebooks and worked out of fourteen file folders stuffed with articles or tiny strips of paper with hurried notes. But it wasn't the writing alone that was important. It was the self-reflection—

ruminating over the ideas and letting them germinate until they took on a life of their own. Self-reflection and idea incubation are the keys to interpersonal growth. This process takes time, but you can plant the seeds almost anywhere, any time, and let them grow by writing your thoughts down and letting them develop. This is why I suggested you buy a notebook to accompany your reading of this book. By capturing your insights on paper you stand a better chance of applying them every day.

Trim Down the Option Glut

You can't lighten your life until you figure out how you unknowingly overload yourself. Think twice before turning on the news. If you're compulsive about TV watching, give up cable for a while, or pare down your cable package. Skip the reruns and make sure that anything you watch is a quality experience. If you're bone tired, instead of plunking yourself down in front of the tube, go take a Silent Sp-ah!

Don't buy a magazine (or subscribe to one) unless you know you'll read it. Request to be taken off mailing lists of catalogs or newsletters in which you have no interest. Know your compulsions and discipline yourself in these areas. If you're already overscheduled, don't offer to help someone do something just because it seems like a good idea. Throw away that trial subscription card and you won't have to make a later decision. Turn off that talk show. Decide to live without that latest miniseries: Can you really afford six or ten hours of TV watching? Remind yourself that there's always more to see, do, and buy than you'll have time for. Take a big helping of Reality Bites on this topic so you can help your days get leaner and cleaner!

Monitor Your Choice Management

Get disciplined about looking at the kinds of entertainment choices you make. Consciously and carefully choose what you read, watch, or hear. Make room for quiet time so you can regularly reflect on your life and renew yourself. Resist being swayed by media messages about what kind of person you should be, how you should look and live, the model of car you should drive, or the size of home you should live in. Monitor the kinds of images you carry in your head based on what you read, hear, or see, and whether graphic material enjoys an extended shelf life in your brain. Regularly choose quiet over clamor and engage in entertaining activities that support your ongoing personal growth: watch a video on Yoga or Tai Chi rather than a horror film, enjoy a half hour of inspirational reading or writing in your journal rather than reading a graphic mystery or true crime. You'll benefit, and so will everyone around you.

A DOSE OF REALITY ABOUT
COMMUNICATION OVERLOAD

You can't stop the endless waves of data and information that surround you, but you can make decisions about your exposure level. You're the one who ultimately chooses the messages that go into your head. Get more conscientious about this process or communication overload will get the best of you.

You already know how the urgency of compressed time complicates your life. It makes you vulnerable to communication overload, which brings with it the prospect of your getting even more frazzled. If you begin feeling overly burdened and unrewarded you might try to replace the missing pieces in your life with material possessions (clothes, expensive car, home, costly trips, designer dogs) or escapist activities (computer games, mood shopping, compulsive exercising, habitual TV watching), all of which have the potential of disconnecting you from what (and who) is really important in your life.

Maybe this gives you a sense of how the ten trends overlap and play off one another. Poor time and choice management contribute to overload, which erodes our relationships at home and at work and corrupts our attitude, possibly our health. Before long our entire existence is infected. That's why we need to act now, to take small but definitive steps toward combating these trends. We need to understand that at the root of the anger epidemic is not one big, easily identified affliction, but a series of small, almost undetectable, seemingly unrelated, easily dismissed symptoms that throw our life out of balance. Add them up and you get C-R-A-N-K-Y.

As you've probably suspected all along, there's no one miracle makeover. But you can rebalance your life with a succession of small adjustments. Consciously chip away at your overload by making disciplined decisions such as less TV time, not buying that tabloid, or opting for a few moments of silence instead of a talk show or string of commercials. You can also fight input fatigue by giving your precious mind a few moments' rest now and then. You need it.

In chapter 2, I stated that there's an innate source of wisdom deep inside you, just waiting to be tapped. Here's what I mean: You already have at least a vague notion about why we've transformed into a cranky culture. You've noticed many of the symptoms; you've even talked about them with friends or loved ones. You've observed the decline of people's attitudes as I have. Chances are you've also witnessed the buildup of pressure in your own life, too.

You intuitively know the areas of your life that are most out of balance and where you're most vulnerable to crankiness. Pay attention to your instincts. Let the combination of your inner wisdom and the ideas in this book steer you toward constructive solutions.

Yes, you can regain some control over your life. But first you need to quiet yourself long enough to discover what you know, and clarify what you need to do. It's hard to focus your energies in the midst of so many distractions and alluring options. When the servings are unlimited, it's easy to get carried away and heap more helpings onto a plate already piled high. Don't be wasteful of your personal resources. Think long term. This is your life, and unless Shirley MacLaine is right, it's the only one you have.

Dis-Connectedness

WE'RE LINKED TO EACH OTHER
BUT ARE WE CONNECTED?

As Rob Hall, professional mountain climber and guide, lay slowly freezing to death on the slopes of Mount Everest in the disastrous 1996 expedition, he was able to speak via satellite phone with his wife, Jan Arnold, at their home in far away New Zealand. It must have been excruciating for her, also an experienced climber, when she first heard his feeble voice. She knew her husband would never make it off the mountain. He would never see their unborn child. How anguished she must have felt, knowing this would be their last and final connection.

After seeing the footage of this eerie, heartbreaking scene on a PBS special, I'm still haunted by it. The Halls' story is a poignant reminder of life's uncertainty. Perhaps it prompts in you a desire to take better care of your important relationships and make each day count.

PHYSICALLY CLOSE AND
EMOTIONALLY DISTANT

When I talk about relationships in my speeches many people confide in me afterward. What I hear helps explain our epidemic crankiness. Couples tell me it's hard to sustain a loving relationship when both of them leave the house early every day and return late, frequently feeling tired, cranky, or preoccupied. What energy they do have often gets directed toward their kids rather than each other. They don't want to disconnect, but they feel it happening as they try to keep up the pace of their hectic lives.

Some people talk about still living with their partner after many years, sharing the same space, unable to express their love, or that they've reached a point where they no longer even try. They complain that money pressures, child rearing, and long work hours are slowly eroding the closeness they once enjoyed. When relationships begin to fray so do our nerves, and the way is cleared for a classic case of low-level, long-term crankiness.

I recently heard a conversation between three young women about how even before marriage, two of them were already frustrated because their fiancés were so uncommunicative and they feared it would get even worse with time. The eldest in this discussion, a woman of thirty, said that eight months before their wedding date, she had given her future husband an ultimatum: go to counseling or go their separate ways. He opted for counseling and she said he opened up in ways she hadn't imagined.

The other two women looked at her in astonishment, convinced that their men would never do such a thing. They hadn't even taken their vows, and already they feared disconnection. Are they an exception? Probably not. We are imperfect people living in an imperfect world that does little to prepare us for lifelong commitments.

RELATIONSHIPS ON THE LINE

Many of us are spread too thin, working hard, trying to control our busy schedules, and striving to achieve "the good life," while worrying that the dream is slipping through our fingers. All that plus working on a relationship, too? Yes, it's a lot to ask.

Between the stepped up pace of our culture and extended work hours, who has time to maintain close, thriving relationships? Even our larger homes contribute to the dilemma. Last year I attended a party in a large, sprawling home. The woman made a comment about how much she enjoyed having company. Small wonder. Her home has such a hackneyed design that she and her husband can both be present, but lose complete touch with each other in both sight and sound. Few of us realize how expanded physical space can interfere with intimacy, yet most of us want a big, beautiful home.

The commercial pressures that exist at every turn entice us into thinking that we not only have the right, but we're almost *obligated* to go for more than what we have. After all, it's the American Dream to better our lot in life! In our efforts to accumulate the proper possessions and create the ideal lifestyle, it's deceptively easy to end up disconnecting from what really counts: our loved ones, even ourselves. As our close connections begin to crack and strain, we feel the repercussions, but that doesn't immediately stop us. We'd rather think that things aren't so bad, and that maybe next week or next month, or next year when the loan on the car or the furniture or the stereo is paid off we'll have time to reconnect. At last, everything will be in order. Maybe. Maybe not.

ALL IN THE FAMILY

Granted, healthy, nurturing families and enduring friendships do exist, and that's something to celebrate. We all deserve people in our lives with whom we can laugh, listen, and feel safe—places where we can be ourselves, speak our minds, and even engage in friendly argument without reprisal. If that describes your family, count your blessings. If not, you'll find some ideas in this chapter that can help you reconnect with those you love or redefine the roles of people in your life who deserve to be thought of as family.

What comprises a family unit includes a range of situations these days: from low-income couples who exhaust themselves every day, barely surviving, to dual-income middle-class families whose children enjoy (and expect) all the advantages. Add overworked single parents who struggle to make ends meet; blended families who grapple with issues of identity, rivalry, and inclusion, and cohabiting couples or same-sex families at all economic levels, with and without children. Some of these families are connected, intact units, while others are emotionally distanced and disconnected.

It bears saying that someone else's family can look much better than your own because you're looking at its dynamics from the outside in rather than the inside out. Your lack of historical perspective can cast things in a light that doesn't actually exist. Comparing your apples to someone else's oranges can cause you to feel discontented and cranky about your kin. Nobody's perfect, so why pretend otherwise?

In her own inimitable style, Dr. Joy Browne states in *The Nine Fantasies That Will Ruin Your Life* that the phrase *dysfunctional family* has lost its meaning and you're better off thinking in terms of "family function" instead of dysfunction. As with many other areas in life, you'll be further ahead if you focus on what's *right* about your loved ones rather than what's wrong. If you simply accept your relatives for who they are rather than wasting your time wishing they were different

Cranky Quiz

DIS-CONNECTEDNESS

Scoring the Cranky Quiz

Score 1 point for every *yes* and 0 for every *no*. Count a *sometimes* as a *yes*. Add your total: 3 points or less (Cool) means you're in good shape, 4 to 7 (Warm) indicates a need to slow down, and 8 to 10 (Hot!) indicates a raging cranky infection. You'll find anti-cranky solutions for each quiz item in this chapter.

1. ___ Do you secretly consider intimate relationships both desirable and disappointing?

2. ___ Are you and your lifemate too busy or tired for intimacy or lovemaking?

3. ___ Are you ever resentful toward the people in your life who make too many demands on your time and energy?

4. ___ Are you more likely to stay silent rather than speak out in a conflict because you hate to argue?

5. ___ Do you generally find it hard to get excited or enthusiastic about things anymore?

6. ___ Are you concerned about the way kids are being raised these days?

7. ___ If you're a parent and had it to do all over again, would you have kids?

8. ___ Have you had first-hand experience with divorce, either as a child or adult?

9. ___ Do you find family get-togethers or holiday gatherings potentially stressful?

10. ___ Do you and your significant other have trouble communicating?

Cranky Quotient _____

My dis-connectedness condition is *(circle one)*   Cool   Warm   Hot!

(after all, wishing hasn't worked so far), you won't plant those sour little seeds of discontent or disapproval. Just think, if you're a little less cranky around your family, it might encourage them to lighten up a little bit, too!

I consider this the most important chapter in this book because your closest relationships influence every aspect of your life, personally and professionally. Emotional connections are directly linked to your purpose. They are the central ingredient for combating chronic crankiness. If you were to ask me where you should begin making significant improvements in your life, I would say right here. Right now.

ROMANCING ROMANCE

Real Life, Real Love, Unreal Images

In the United States, more marriages fail than succeed, but we don't let a little thing like statistics stop us from making romance, love, and the dream of living happily ever after a cultural obsession. True, at least we've fixated on a happy dream, but we're far more *fixated* than happy. What's wrong?

That same relentless Expectation Machine that prods us toward *bigger, better, faster, more, now,* in terms of possessions, prestige, and prosperity, also ignites our fervor for the perfect partner. We're indoctrinated (far more than we know) by romanticized images about "love" everywhere we turn. Who among us doesn't carry memorable scenes in our heads from such classics as *Casablanca*, or its more recent representations, *Pretty Woman* or *You've Got Mail!* Given our images and expectations, how can real life measure up?

Reconnecting in a Dis-Connected World

We fall in love, we fall out of love, and sometimes back again. Who we love and how we love says more about us than it does our partner. In this chapter we're going to explore the many aspects of relationships and their implications, highlighting some of the defective romantic notions we harbor about intimate and family relationships while offering a series of workable strategies and rational insights. We'll also explore methods for handling interpersonal conflict and rough ground. It's a demanding hike, but the view at the top is infinitely rewarding. I hope you'll stay on the path as we examine the hazards that create dis-connections plus the helpful steps that can bring you back.

CRANKY QUIZ ITEM # 1:
IS THIS ALL THERE IS?

> 1. ___ Do you secretly consider intimate relationships both desirable and disappointing?

Real Versus Ideal

A friend sent me a greeting card. On the front panel was a young, cute, well-built guy, bare from the waist up. The caption read, "What we're looking for." On the inside was an unshaven, stogie-smoking, paunchy middle-aged guy in an undershirt, scratching his backside. The caption read, "What's looking for us." While I found this hysterically funny, it's not that far from reality. Many of us keep looking for the "big dream" and when we're faced with a reality that doesn't measure up to our expectations, we wonder if this is all there is.

A Compulsion to Connect

We all want to be connected. It's emotional, biological, sociological. It's wired into our circuitry. At some point, under some circumstance, most of us meet someone, something clicks, and we fall prey to commercialized romanticism. As fantasy and illusion stage their dramatic entrance, our common sense and rationalism bolt for the back door. Just review your own romantic expectations as you've carefully (or clumsily) traversed the tricky turf of our cultural obsession for dating, falling in love, and getting married.

A Compulsion to Expect

One of the reasons our divorce rate is so high is because we have the expectation that relationships should be easy, but they aren't. We expect them to be self-sustaining, but they aren't that, either. We're told that love is the answer, but with apologies to the Beatles, it takes far more than love to make it work. We're infatuated with the idea of "happily every after" but nobody told us that in real life, the cameras keep rolling and the action doesn't stop until you (or the relationship) die. Funny how our minds work: After a big wedding, parents often say, "Well, it's over now." But it's only just begun! Few expectant parents can look at a belligerent fifteen-year-old and say, "Look, dear; we're having one of those!" *We would rather cling to the dream of what we want than deal with the reality of what is.*

It's that simple. This principle applies to every subject in this book. It's so easy. It's so hard. You could spend a lot of time visiting your own Expectation Machine and sorting through your personal line of demarcation between fantasy and reality. Once again, it's the difference between romanticism and rationalism.

Anti-Cranky Alternatives for Cranky Quiz Item # 1: Is This All There Is?

It's Your Life: Paint Your Own Reality

Before I get labeled as a crass anti-romantic let me set the record straight. I'm an emotional person. I enjoy romance in my relationship with my life partner, Rob, but it's my own personal brand of romance instead of the commercially packaged variety. If you have any doubts about this issue, consider the depression so many people experience during the holidays, particularly those who live alone. Some of the songs are enough to make *me* cry! This reflects the folly of buying into a cultural image and expectation. I encourage you to construct your own. Take your brush and paint your own picture; create your own ideal of romance and reality. Don't settle for someone else's paint-by-numbers set. When you hold your own brush you can paint what you want. You can even paint outside of the lines if you're so inclined. If you want better relationships, if you want a deeper, more fulfilling life, quit buying into the commercial stereotypes of what you should look like, how you should feel, and the kind of life you should be leading.

The only person you really need to please is yourself, and if you have a compassionate partner, he or she will support you in your cultural rebellion. Paint your life. Trust that you have the talent. Choose your colors. Only settle for the lines you draw yourself. You have that right. You have that responsibility. Your life, your relationships with others, and your spirit will absolutely thrive. Crankiness will fade from the picture.

Oh yes, you'll have to wash your brushes, and maybe buy new ones. And you'll have to change canvases from time to time. Maybe you'll have to substitute colors, or mix your own, but you can do this. You have the equipment; you have the resources. It's that "purpose" thing again, and purpose is your frame. I have only one request: Please, for your sake, make sure that the images you're trying to live up to are ones of your own making, without the influence of pumped-up expectation or cultural innuendo. Do that, and you'll create a masterpiece.

Be a Rational Romantic

Once you cut away the cultural trappings of what romance *should* be and, instead, define it by your own standards, you'll enjoy more fulfillment in your relationship and fewer disappointments. I know a woman who figured this out in the first year of her marriage, after her husband forgot both her birthday and their anniversary. She was devastated that this loving, sensitive man she married could be so thoughtless. However, it soon dawned on her that this was more *her* problem than his; she had come into the relationship with an expectation that he would share her emphasis on special dates. Now, after their first year together, she knew this wasn't so.

She recognized that her notion of romance was different from his and that his forgetfulness had nothing to do with how much he loved her. Her approach of "psychic relationship management" ("if you really loved me you'd remember these important dates") wasn't working. She decided to try a rational approach. She now tells him when a special date is coming up. He never forgets because she helps him remember! She's happy; he's happy; they're happy.

Some people argue that it's not the same if you have to announce such things to your partner, that he or she should *know*. Why? Show me where this is written on a stone tablet! Why all the guesswork? Why *expect* romance and end up cranky or disappointed because someone failed to match your undeclared performance standards? Why expect someone to be responsible for your emotional well-being? If, in reading this, you're protesting that your partner *should* care enough about you to remember special dates, I'd argue that *you* should care enough about him or her to help!

If your concept of romance revolves around the way things *should* be instead of how they *are,* I encourage you to read *A New Guide to Rational Living* by Dr. Albert Ellis and Robert Harper. Ellis is the creator of RET, Rational Emotive Therapy, and while he has written dozens of books, this one influenced me more than any book I've ever read. In fact, I never even finished it. Once I understood RET, I just started practicing it, and it helped me change my life!

Please know that when you combine romance and rationalism, your relationships will take on a new depth and closeness. You'll be able to prevent yourself from sliding down the slippery slope of unfulfilled expectation. You'll get more of what you want when you want it because you help put it there; isn't that what a good relationship is all about?

Shorten the Wedding Plans, Stretch Out the Romance

A wedding lasts only a day, but a marriage needs to hold up for the long haul. Knowing that newlyweds have a fifty-fifty chance of their relationship surviving, maybe it's time we focused less on a perfect wedding and more on the imperfect relationship that follows. Romance takes its toll, financially and emotionally; family feuds erupt from the pressures of planning a perfect wedding. Even the betrothed battle over details. Brides often border on hysteria during their "big day," with many spending half the time in tears. Soon afterward, the romantic expectations of the "hormonal haze" give way to the disillusionment of everyday realities, with unsuspecting couples pathetically unprepared for the transition.

Perhaps if we approached the process of getting married more rationally than romantically, the marriage itself wouldn't feel so anticlimactic. What if a couple were to set aside some of what a wedding would cost and use it for early counseling so they'd have a better chance of staying together? If you're getting married, or one of your children is, consider this alternative as an investment in the future, not a one-shot cost. Here's my proposal:

Imagine a couple who for eight or ten months prior to the big day, carefully plans every step of their *marriage* instead of the wedding. Rather than working with a wedding counselor about engraving and entrees, they and their marriage counselor cover every detail of how they will handle problems as they arise. Imagine this couple discussing and planning in depth the areas that most invite disagreement or conflict (money, sex, children, leisure time). Envision this couple learning the communication techniques that will enable them to resolve clashes or conflict, in effect, creating their own instructional manual for their life together.

One of my friends said she and her husband would never have married if they'd engaged in this kind of prenuptial education. Another said she was so swept away in lust and longing it wouldn't have made any difference. Not romantic enough, you say? Too rational? That's proof of our unrelenting indoctrination by the Expectation Machine. Here are the typical reactions I get:

Yes, it's a good idea.
Yes, it could prevent some bad marriages and save a few mediocre ones.
Yes, this approach makes a lot of sense.
No, I'd never do it because it's not romantic.

Please, dear reader, excuse me for a moment while I go scream into my pillow.

CRANKY QUIZ ITEM # 2:
LACK OF QUALITY TIME

> 2. ___ Are you and your lifemate too busy or tired for intimacy or lovemaking?

I Love You but I Don't Have Time to Say It Again

If you're trying to live life by a schedule, you already know that relationships operate independently of the clock. Your kids live in the moment. They don't care what you're doing when they need attention, nor will they quietly wait till you're free. Ignored spouses have their own way of getting your attention, too.

Work can be a handy escape when home is an emotional drain, but it only postpones the inevitable. If you consistently leave home early and come back late, stop and figure out why. *Regardless of how you justify your long hours away from home or your preoccupation when you do show up, your family knows what you consider important and what you don't.* Shape up before life hands you a wake-up call: you might not get a second chance to tell a loved one he or she ranked *first* in your life.

Hey Kids: It's Quality Duty Time

Quality time is often more myth than reality, and few of us have defined it in our own terms. What exactly does "quality time" mean to you? How about your loved ones? If you haven't discussed it, you need to. *Quality exists in the eye of the recipient, not the donor.* It doesn't work to cram in ten minutes of what *you* consider quality time at *your* convenience.

- Does your family feel neglected? Let them answer this question, not you.
- Do your kids look at you with dropped jaw when you shower them with attention? Consider this a big hint.
- Do you repeatedly disappoint them with broken promises? Rent the video *Liar, Liar* and watch it with your kids. If you squirm, consider this another hint.
- When you do show up, are you so preoccupied you're really not there? You may think your physical presence is quite enough; not so!

It's a busy, fast-paced world out there. It's easy to lose perspective. I give you credit if you're lavishing your loved ones with attention because it's something more of us need to do. If you want another perspective on this topic you'll enjoy Mary LoVerde's book, *Stop Screaming at the Microwave!* which offers numerous tips on how to stay connected to those you love, including how to create a family "memory jar."

Anti-Cranky Alternatives for Cranky Quiz Item # 2: Lack of Quality Time

For Parents: Put a Value on Your Time

Evaluate your interactions in terms of *high* or *low* quality, keeping in mind that the value of your time and attention depends on your children's assessment, not yours. Kids are perceptive. If you're dutifully metering out fragments of obligatory attention to appease your conscience, be assured, they know. This isn't a connection, it's self-deception. If you're wondering how to assess time value, read your child's facial expression, voice tone, or level of enthusiasm. If you have any doubts, ask.

Court Your Partner, Revive Your Relationship

The illusion of love and romance is seductive yet it's hard sustaining passion over time. Romance can pale against the backdrop of work, kids, bills, chores, and other distractions. Even childless couples and empty nesters may find they share less and less in common, thanks to disparate demands. However, relationships can remain vibrant and spicy. *If you want a zesty, long-sustaining relationship, continue the courtship.*

Take walks. Talk. Shower together. Groom each other. Instead of working late at night or watching TV, sit or lie in bed together. Snuggle more. Make both sexual and nonsexual time for each other. Make dates for lovemaking and just make dates. Buy little gifts for each other. Listen as intently as you did in the early days while still under the influence of the hormonal haze. Reminisce over special early experiences; how you met, your first date. Laugh together. Listen to each other's stories of growing up, even if you've heard them before. Read to each other. I suggest *1001 Ways to Be Romantic* by Greg Godek, or any of his other books, if you want to add a spark to your relationship.

CRANKY QUIZ ITEM # 3:
CONFLICTING AGENDAS

> 3. ____ Are you ever resentful toward the people in your life who make too many demands on your time and energy?

Love Me, Love My Agenda

She wants to spend Saturday at the antique fair. He wants to do yard work. Both would like company. Neither wants to take the kids to their game. Sound familiar? You and your partner each bring a distinct personality and set of individual interests and priorities to your relationship. Each of you has expectations of the other, and it's inevitable your agendas will conflict. This is seldom planned; it's more a slow, gradual takeover, until someone starts feeling taken advantage of.

The old joke men sometimes make about their "Honey Do" list is rooted in the agenda issue, as is the wife who's expected to take up golf because that's her husband's favorite sport. But it isn't always a spouse or lover who drives your agenda; it can be a parent, sibling, or friend.

Examples include the person who always insists on driving or choosing the movie, restaurant, or entertainment venue. As you read the following, if appropriate, substitute the word *friend, parent, roommate*, and so on for *partner*.

- Does your partner hint, wheedle, or demand your active involvement in his or her interests, so you "go along to get along" instead of doing what you want?
- Do you rarely get to choose how the two of you spend your time?
- Have you given up any of your interests because they aren't worth fighting over?
- Do you ever lie or make excuses to get out of something you don't want to do?
- Are you pressured to accompany your partner to places you'd rather not go?
- Does your partner refuse to reciprocate, despite your requests?
- Are you beginning to feel resentful about your time not being your own?
- Are you doing any of the above to your spouse or partner?

These questions will help you determine if someone else is directing your life or if you're doing the dominating. Of course there's give and take in every relationship, but that's the point. A problem exists if it's all give on your part, or all take.

Anti-Cranky Alternatives for Cranky Quiz Item # 3: Conflicting Agendas

Analyze the Agenda: Yours, Mine, or Ours?

If your agenda isn't your own, don't get mad and don't get even. After all, you've been an active participant up to now and we already have too many cranky people in the world. Maybe you didn't realize the severity of the situation until this moment. Maybe you've hinted or joked about it, hoping the real message would get through, but it won't. Conversely, if, in reading this, you've discovered you're driving the agenda, you need to back off. Consider the following questions before you say anything.

- How long has this been going on?
- What kinds of positive changes would be appropriate?

- How can you broach this issue without blaming (or intimidating) your partner?
- What might be a close-to-ideal option for both of you?
- Might you need a counselor or mediator to sort through this issue?

The visions of what each partner wants out of a relationship are usually very different: The two of you need to talk about what you want and why, without sacrificing either's basic agenda. You'll increase mutual trust, improve your communication, and achieve more intimacy. You'll stay connected. If you ignore the problem, you'll move farther apart. Unresolved issues grow into anger; anger grows into resentment. Resentment gives way to contempt. Contempt fuels retaliation, which results in a blowup of hard feelings and unchecked emotion. You can do better than this.

Don't Just Take It; Talk It Out

When a relationship is new and exciting who wants to think there will ever be conflict? We think a fight means something's wrong. We try to tolerate our differences, but everyone has a breaking point.

The Expectation Machine deludes us into thinking we can somehow pull it off; that our relationship will be different from everyone else's and we'll live happily ever after with no hard times. I, too, was once so self-delusional. How any lifelong partnerships last without extensive training escapes me. Maybe the following will encourage you to talk things out with your partner instead of merely tolerating them:

1. Every relationship has its areas of disagreement or disharmony; it's a natural and normal outgrowth of human interaction. Handling issues as they come up will strengthen your relationship, not destroy it. But refusing to raise difficult issues fosters emotional dishonesty, bringing with it the potential for disconnection.

2. Expressing anger to a loved one is both a right and a responsibility. How else will you and your partner get to know each other's likes and dislikes unless you put it into words? You owe it to each other (and yourself) to speak your minds openly.

3. When expressed responsibly and without malice, anger can strengthen a relationship. Partners who learn how to handle conflict in a

rational, nondefensive climate find themselves moving closer to each other, becoming more intimate.

4. Unexpressed or poorly expressed anger can damage a relationship beyond repair. When unaddressed, anger festers into active resentment. This erodes trust and respect, paving the way for more anger and ultimately dis-Connectedness.

5. Anyone can be taught how to handle conflict fairly and effectively. It's a matter of learning what works, what doesn't work, and why. From there, it's a case of application. Just for fun, sit down with your partner and make a master list of the tactics people use that do not work when there's a disagreement. Have fun with this. Laugh over the obvious futility of some of these gambits, like ordering someone to calm down and be logical when he or she is upset (the two of you might admit to using some of them, too). But you've just done a good thing. Keep the list. Use it as a reminder of what to avoid.

CRANKY QUIZ ITEM # 4:
FEAR OF FIGHTING

> 4. ___ Are you more likely to stay silent rather than speak out in a conflict because you hate to argue?

If You Could Read My Mind You Wouldn't Like Me Anymore

Considering the negative modeling seen on soaps, on TV shows, and in movies, we almost never get exposed to effective conflict management, so how could we expect to be good at it? Of course, it's uncomfortable fighting with someone you love. You'd rather avoid the whole thing. Instinctive reactions such as withdrawal, aggression, accusation, blame, or intimidation don't work very well. What's a person to do? Well, I'm suggesting you *fight* for your relationship, but in a way that lets you and your partner stay close and connected. You need some rules. People say it seems odd to have rules for fighting, but we have rules for every other endeavor in life, even war!

Anti-Cranky Alternatives for Cranky Quiz Item # 4: Fear of Fighting

—Ten Guidelines for Resolving Conflict—

1. *As a couple, agree to keep your relationship "tuned up."* Engage in relationship preventive maintenance. Talk with each other. Read John Gray's *Men are from Mars and Women are from Venus* together so you can laugh over your different styles and expectations. Take a class so you can learn to argue *without malice or power plays*. Handle conflicts as they happen because the longer you wait the bigger the issue gets. The only exception to the immediacy rule is when either (or both) of you are too (truthfully) tired or not feeling well. Reschedule the discussion for another day and time. Postponements often provide a welcome cooling-off period, helping to prevent a heat-of-the-moment blowup.

2. *Use language that keeps you in the here and now*. Let go of past anger and resentment and stay *in the moment*. Handling issues in real time keeps the argument smaller and more manageable. Here-and-now language prevents retorts such as, "If I hear you say that one more time . . . " or "Why can't you just listen for once!"

3. *Stay together until you resolve the issue or call a truce*. Sit down, facing each other. The less distance between the two of you, the better. No jumping up and leaving the room. No door slamming. No screaming. By staying close to each other, eye to eye, knee to knee (even holding hands), you can both talk quietly. If you're afraid you might forget to say something important, write it down. Yes, I'm suggesting the two of you show up for conflict discussions with clipboards and notes. This helps you focus on specific issues and incidents without getting sidetracked.

4. *When your partner speaks, listen*. Don't interrupt. Don't defend yourself. If necessary, visit the Quick Stop! to stifle your defensiveness. You are being given a chance to find out how your partner interpreted your behavior. Chances are you didn't *mean* to do or say what you did, *but whatever you may have intended didn't come across*. Maybe you didn't even *do* what your partner thinks you did, but listen anyway. You can explain your side later. If you truly listen to your partner, you increase the chances of being heard when you speak.

5. *Maintain a positive intent.* When your partner opens up, you're being given an inside look at him or her. Try to understand what you're being told. See the situation from your partner's viewpoint. Don't try to outshout or ensnare. If you attempt to back your partner into a wall he or she will either counterattack or shut down. This isn't about winning. Hold on to the vision of maintaining a connected relationship that reflects effective choice management and life management.

6. *Let go of having to be "right."* Most of us learned how to fight dirty as kids. Well, it's time to learn how to fight clean. When you speak to your partner, give up your need to be right. Conflict is often more a question of *perception* than a clear right or wrong. Focus on creating positive results for the two of you instead of getting hung up over who is right. The harder you try to be right, the more wrong you'll be.

7. *When it's your turn to talk, express yourself in a nonblaming way.* Explain what you thought and felt, and why. Take responsibility for your behavior. When your goal is preserving the relationship, not scoring points, you'll naturally choose language that encourages your partner to listen and still feel connected, in spite of the emotion.

8. *Mutually "outlaw" escalation tactics.* Counteraccusals such as "Well, *you* do that, too!" or "I wouldn't have done that if *you* hadn't said . . . " blur the issue and create side skirmishes. (I was once very adept at this mind game. I ended up trading it for good listening skills.) Generalities such as "Why can't you (men) (women) (Virgos) (computer programmers) understand . . . " or "There you go again!" derail the discussion and lead to more anger.

All inclusive statements are also self-defeating: "You're *always* late . . . " or "You're *never* on time . . . " Your partner will always find the one exception: "No I'm not. Back in 1997 when we went to Pat's wedding I wasn't late; I was *early*!" If you and your spouse created the master list of tactics that don't work, this was probably on your list.

9. *When you ask a question, give your partner time to respond.* People contemplate at different speeds. Some speak and then think (like me); others think before they speak (like Rob). I have waited up to three actual minutes for my partner to talk (yes, I've timed it). I used to want to shake him when he did this. I'd sit and wonder how it could take him so long to formulate what he wanted to say, knowing I could

instantly say it *for* him if he'd only let me! But my restraint helped build our connection, which has lasted over two decades and weathered many storms.

10. *End your conflict with an eye on the future*. As your discussion comes to a close it helps to outline preferences for the future. "If this situation were to repeat itself, I'd like to see (you) (us) . . . " or "The next time, please ask rather than assume that I . . . " This way, you might be able to prevent some relationship issues from incessantly popping up like ducks in a shooting gallery.

As you read these ten strategies, it's probably obvious these methods are intended to keep you focused on the *subject* of the conflict rather than inciting side skirmishes or escalation. With practice they'll become second nature. *Don't let something as important as an intimate argument become a free-for-all!* If you'd like to do further study on ways to communicate with your partner under pressure, read the infinitely practical *Tongue Fu* by Sam Horn. Her lists of "words to use" and "words to lose" alone are worth the price of admission.

Do Not Try This at Home

Actually, *do* try this at home but if you need help getting over your discomfort with fighting, do something about it. In my own relationship, it took Rob and me two couples communication classes (including facilitated videotaped fights with instant replay) and several counseling sessions before we developed our fair fighting skills. We even had a friend mediate a couple of our arguments and her feedback was very helpful. Go ahead and try these ground rules. If you have difficulty sticking to them find a counselor or mediator so you can practice in front of a qualified, neutral third party.

Managing conflict is a learnable skill, just like cooking or car repair. Granted, it's far more emotional, but the point is that it can be taught. The biggest prerequisite is desire. Divorce may be the best option for some couples, but many relationships could be salvaged if more of us knew how to *argue without malice*. What a pity this important skill isn't a part of the wedding package!

CRANKY QUIZ ITEM # 5:
EMOTIONAL DISTANCE

> 5. ___ Do you generally find it hard to get excited or enthusiastic
> about things anymore?

Backing Off, Shutting Down

Sustained demands on your mental and physical resources can result in
chronic stress and mental fatigue: Your mind and body can handle only
so much. These are the conditions under which crankiness thrives.
Emotional withdrawal, or dis-connectedness, is one way of trying to
cope with the overload, but it has drastic side effects. In the short term,
you can put your feelings on hold but in the long term, you become
emotionally disabled, incapable of experiencing a full range of emotions. The more emotionally distant you become, the more disconnected you get, from others and from yourself. The result, of course, is
ruptured relationships.

Numb and Numb-er

We have a lot on our minds these days. Between time constraints,
money worries, child rearing, relationship conflicts, health issues, job
concerns, and constant change, our emotions are putting in overtime.
Then there's our daily blitz of news: natural disasters, accidents, terror-
ists, shootings, drugs, and scandal. As if that's not enough, add the violence, homicide, and horror we watch for entertainment! With our
feelings strained to the max, some of us end up herding our personal
conflicts into an "emotional holding pen," fearing that one more issue
will throw us over the edge.

We pass by homeless people on the street and pretend they don't
exist. We know people in our community go to bed battered, hungry, or
suffering each night, but we can't resolve our own conflicts and concerns, let alone other people's, so we tamp our compassion down
tighter. This mental distance provides temporary relief, but it comes
with a price. Our priorities blur. We lose compassion. Meaning and significance leak out of events that once stirred us. We become observers,
not participants. All the while it gets harder to care, harder to connect,
and much easier to be cranky.

Moving Inward Means Moving Onward

We can approach life with fortitude or fear. Instead of shutting our-selves off or running away from something that disturbs or threatens us, we need to move *toward* it and work through it. We need to stay recep-tive to whatever comes our way. In his illuminating book, *Timeshifting*, Stephan Rechtschaffen discusses the rewards of experiencing all of our emotions instead of escaping them. He suggests that sifting through our insecurities, fears, anger, *and* bliss is how we find the inner peace and happiness we all desire.

If you're thinking this relates to the discussion in chapter 2 about practices, principles, and purpose, you're right. *To sit at the top of the mountain you must first traverse its rocky slopes; the magnificent view is reserved only for those who are willing to do the work.* Somewhere along the journey we discover that joy and heartache exist on the same path. The Expectation Machine seduces us into thinking we're sup-posed to be happy all the time without having to do a lot of work. This couldn't be more wrong!

Anti-Cranky Alternatives for Cranky Quiz Item # 5: Emotional Distance

Begin Your Own Emotional Rehabilitation Program

Maybe you've forgotten which came first—caring too much or caring too little—but the result, not caring, is the same. Ironically, the problem is the solution: to live fully, you have to care. *You don't have to care about everything but you need to care about something.* Resuscitate your sense of humor. Rent some videos; watch stupid comedies. Read cartoons. Look for moments of levity and reasons to smile.

Rescue your dreams; chances are, they've been sitting there, waiting for you to find the claim check. Last year I received a card from a woman who had attended one of my speeches. She was fulfill-ing a life dream (getting her master's degree) and announcing the big news to everyone who had helped, supported, or encouraged her. She said my comments about positive persistence inspired her to keep working on her dream. I sent her one of my books as a celebration gift.

If you've lost touch with your dreams, I'd suggest you go back to your childhood and think about your early passions, because that's where many of our dreams took root. My childhood dream was to own a horse but it didn't happen until I was in my early thirties. My first horse was given to me; he was a sickly guy and I nursed him back to health, mostly through love and affection because I didn't have a lot of money to spend.

In fact, I learned to ride bareback because I couldn't afford to buy a saddle when I got my horse. I barely had enough money for board, but the father of a high school chum offered to keep my horse for only twenty dollars a month. I gave up cigarettes and alcohol so I could afford my long-time dream, and I've had a horse in my life ever since. I've fulfilled other parts of that dream, too, including competing in shows with some measure of success. For twelve years I dreamed of taking my horse to Florida for the winter (as my trainer and some of my friends did) to escape the snowy Midwest, and I finally accomplished that, too. Don't let your dreams fall by the wayside and gather dust. Keep envisioning, hoping, planning, and taking small steps toward making your dream unfold.

Emotional rehabilitation also involves revisiting your priorities so you can further your personal renewal. Take small, consistent steps that enhance your well-being (smile more, eat better, exercise, show appreciation, add quality to your life). Revive your sense of appreciation of friends and loved ones you cherish, your health and physical capabilities, sunsets, soft rains, evocative music, or art (whatever feeds your spirit). Use that list as a tonic on days you're feeling down. When in doubt, connect with others; it always solidifies your connection with yourself.

Give Your Relationship some R & R: Review and Revitalize

Many relationships lose their vital connection. If this has happened to you, then you need R & R. Maybe it's been a while since the two of you had some fun. While you could do the following exercise in your head, writing it down will be more meaningful. By the way, "loved one" can mean an adult or child.

- What are all the pursuits you and your loved one enjoy doing together?
- What are the circumstances when the two of your feel most connected?

- When do the two of you get so immersed that you lose track of time?
- When was the last time the two of you engaged in one of these pastimes?

Maybe it's been a while and you're thinking you'll do this as soon as you have more time. In what millennium will that occur? What good is tomorrow's money, success, or goals if you lose your vital connections today? You'll only have the time if you take the time: Revitalize your relationship while you still can. In fact, put this book down for a moment and go make a quick connection!

CRANKY QUIZ ITEM # 6:
CULTURAL QUANDARIES

6. ___ Are you concerned about the way kids are being raised these days?

Kids Ain't What They Used to Be

While every generation has provoked concern from its elders, today's teen crime, rudeness, violence in schools, smoking, and drug abuse are serious problems. In her book, *The Way We Really Are*, Stephanie Coontz suggests that today's teens suffer from a sense of "rolelessness." Generations ago, it was common for kids to miss a day of school to bale hay or help bring in a crop. No longer do they shoulder that kind of responsibility in our society and with this freedom has come a role vacuum.

Where can kids actively contribute anymore? Middle-class parents pay to have the household chores done and the lawn maintained, and kids are left out of the maintenance loop. Many don't work because of extracurricular activities and those who do have jobs find themselves in unrewarding positions that teach little about life or the work ethic. Only a few schools offer active community service programs where students can volunteer. *The most clearly defined social role for our offspring is that of consumer*. No wonder "mall mania" is such a common affliction among our youth!

In our sanitized society there's a shortage of safe places, public or secluded, where children and teens can play or just hang out. Not so long ago, when the world seemed safer, kids played in less than safe areas: dumps, gravel pits, woods, streams, railroad yards, vacant land, and construction sites. All this without signing a waiver! In today's litigious society, we wouldn't think of turning our kids loose in such areas. But other than school yards or municipal parks, where *can* they go? No wonder kids watch so much TV or experiment with drugs— we're boring them to death!

Anti-Cranky Alternatives for Cranky Quiz Item # 6: Cultural Quandaries

Campaign for Significant Space

Look around and note if your community caters to adult spaces while ignoring its kids: count the number of cafés, coffee houses, restaurants, bars, gyms, speciality shops, and biking or hiking trails designed for the over twenty-one crowd. Then check out the neighborhood (or even your home) for spaces intended just for kids. Maybe you're old enough to remember playing softball in vacant lots, climbing trees in old orchards, or sitting in rickety tree houses large enough to accommodate you and your friends. Where is the equivalent for today's youth?

Raise your voice on this issue. Write letters to the editor. Bring this topic to the attention of local leaders. Campaign for more ball fields, play areas, safe spaces, and community centers where kids can go. Before I started this book it hadn't occurred to me how few of these places and spaces exist anymore. No wonder so many of our kids feel cranky and disconnected!

Temporarily Adopt a Child—or Several

How long has it been since you visited a school? If your kids are grown, maybe it's been a long time. If you don't have kids, maybe you've never visited one. In either case, I urge you to make a trip. You might be touched, as I was, to discover the limited resources some schools have. With two-income households so common, volunteers are limited, too. Many people complain they're too busy to spend time with their own kids, let alone someone else's.

When I watched my grandson's soccer practice this fall I was impressed with the volunteer coaches and grateful these people are willing to commit several hours a week to these kids. Could you volunteer at a local school or a community outreach program? A couple of hours a week might not make much of a difference to you but it could make a lasting difference for a youngster who needs an adult's positive influence.

Share Your Expertise with Tomorrow's Citizens

Schools at all grade levels are always looking for guest speakers. Are you a computer whiz, manager, dog trainer, race car driver, artist, poet, involved in an unusual occupation, or just plain crazy about your job? If so, consider Career Day at a local school. Or simply offer to visit a high school class and talk about what you do. In case it's not obvious, there are distinct advantages to this type of volunteerism. You get to contribute, which is always a good feeling, and this approach is a clean, one-shot deal; no long-term commitment, no series of meetings, no major sacrifice on your part. I've spoken to all four of my grandchildren's classes and I loved doing it. You, too, have something to offer. By sharing your expertise, you'll contribute to the advancement of future citizens and leaders of our country.

CRANKY QUIZ ITEM # 7:
PARENTAL PERPLEXITIES

> 7. ___ If you're a parent and had it to do all over again, would you have kids?

Parents Ain't What They Used to Be

When comedian Brett Butler was asked if she planned to have children one day, she replied, "I've never wanted to be the recipient of that much ingratitude." For many of us this comment brings both a smile—and a nod.

Parenthood, the most important job we could ever have, requires no entrance exam, no mandatory training, no minimum qualifications, no license. Some of us become parents for all the right reasons and some of us don't. If you're a parent, was yours a well-thought-out decision? I was sixteen when my first child was born. I chose to have three kids because my parents did; a jury could never find me guilty of putting too much thought into that life decision! Is this hard for me to admit? Of course. But I'm not alone in my lack of logic or planning. I hear a lot of young women stating they want a big family because they like babies. Maybe we'd have fewer cranky parents (and kids) if we put more thought into the parenthood issue before the fact. It's impressive that so many couples want to do the right thing by learning Lamaze and birthing training. What an intelligent way to get their new family off to a good start!

However, this is life and the cameras keep rolling. The birth of a child signals a beginning, not an end. Where are the classes that cover the first eighteen years after the baby's birth? If we emphasized the importance of caring for our children *after* their birth, we'd all be better off, including our kids! Being so young when my first child was born I could have desperately used some coaching about baby and child rearing. Though everyone treated me like a grown-up, I was still a kid myself. I was terrified those first few months, feeling very alone and isolated. My parents were living in California at the time, I was cut off from my peers, and my husband wasn't much help when it came to caring for babies. His mother tried to help but she wasn't all that knowledgeable, either. I wish there had been a better way.

Anti-Cranky Alternatives for Cranky Quiz Item # 7: Parental Perplexities
Revisit the Parental Role
If you're thinking about having children or are just beginning your family maybe you're currently exploring the awesome responsibilities of parenthood. Here are some questions I wish I had asked:

- Why do I want to be a parent?
- Am I emotionally prepared for the relentless demands?
- Are my images of parenthood a projection of personal fairy tales or objective, rational thought?
- Have I asked people about both the positives and negatives of parenthood?
- Can I afford the time, money, and resource consumption?
- Am I in a stable relationship that shows promise of lasting?
- Is my partner as committed to parenthood as I am?
- Will we share the responsibilities equally?

- Are we willing to seek guidance and training to prepare us for this role?
- Do we recognize that "having a baby" translates into "*creating a human being*" to whom we will *always* be responsible?
- Are we willing to have only one child, or to space our children in such a way that we avoid overloading ourselves mentally, physically, and financially?
- What other issues do we need to address before we move forward?

Perhaps you're thinking that life would be different for many of us if we had considered these and similar questions before embarking on life-changing decisions. If you're wondering why we're not better at this type of far-flung thinking you'll find an explanation in chapter 11.

There are also questions for anyone facing the prospect of a second marriage where children may be part of the picture:

- Are we both committed to providing child support for noncustodial kids?
- Are we, as a couple, in sync with how we will treat each other's kids?
- Are we prepared to help our children adjust to one another?
- Do we have adequate time and space to do so?
- Are we committed to offer the best stepparenting possible so the kids will be cared for, physically and emotionally?
- Are we prepared to seek family counseling if we need it?
- If we want a child of our own, are we prepared to wait till the proper time?

The Expectation Machine leads us to believe that just because we have the ability to produce a baby physically, it's our right to do so and somehow we'll figure out how to take care of it. Of course, this isn't so.

Recreate Roles, Responsibilities, and Rituals

In today's marriages, women still log more hours on home responsibilities than men: arranging child care, shopping, cleaning, disciplining kids, and cooking. If roles and responsibilities in your home are strongly one-sided, or if your kids suffer from the rolelessness we covered earlier, here's a suggestion that will benefit everyone. Establish a "family council."

Discuss roles and responsibilities and let everyone have input.

You'll be impressed with some of the ideas your kids come up with, and how perceptive they are (even in helping devise their own "punishments"). Let everyone share responsibility for keeping the home in good condition; the kids can choose where their skills or interests best fit with cleaning, dumping garbage, cooking, pet care, lawn, or home maintenance.

Hold your family council meetings weekly, even if only for a few minutes. Keep in mind that what kids observe in their parents helps shape their concept of that role for the future. Discuss not only chores and physical maintenance but relationships, too. The family council approach offers an opportunity for exchanging ideas and addressing problems before they get out of hand. Try it, even if your kids are too young to participate fully. Let them witness a family ritual they'll soon be a part of. You might just find things taking a sharp turn for the better when everyone in the family has a clearer sense of where he or she fits and how each contributes.

CRANKY QUIZ ITEM # 8:
DIVORCE DOLDRUMS

> 8. ___ Have you had first-hand experience with divorce, either as a child or adult?

Split Happens

While the U.S. national divorce rate hovers just over 50 percent, some of us are wearing out the carpet from repeat jaunts down that fateful aisle. Is it hope, denial, or optimism that keeps us pairing up, regardless of the statistics? A safe guess would be "all of the above." Most of the people I know are in second marriages, and a few are in their third. It's the rare couple who stays together anymore, yet we like to think there's someone out there for us, someone with whom we can be happy and, in turn, make happy. But that's not the whole picture. There's this person from our past; someone we dreamed or hoped was *the one* for us, but as it turned out, he or she wasn't. Yet, this is often the person with whom we have children in common, and therefore he or she represents a piece of our history we can't eradicate. Enter the "ex."

Anti-Cranky Alternatives for Cranky Quiz Item # 8: Divorce Doldrums

Make a Clean Break and Keep It Clean

If you have a former spouse I hope the two of you have a workable relationship because it makes no sense to keep fighting the same battle over and over again like those Civil War reenactment buffs. You don't have to be best friends, but if you have children in common you must be on civil terms. If you still actively resent, dislike, or hate this person, free yourself of that baggage because you and your kids will suffer from it. Once you're divorced, leave it all behind and get on with your life. Deep down, you know your credibility suffers when your kids see you acting their age.

You also know it's self-defeating to feel jealous of the relationship your kids have with your ex or his/her companions. If your former spouse doesn't play by the rules it will be hard to resist such contemptuous tactics, but don't take the bait. Your kids are probably smart enough to figure out what's really going on.

If you're the custodial parent you face the inequality of being the disciplinarian. Your kids get to go away, have fun, and then come back to their responsibilities and rules. Yes, this may be unfair, but resentment only complicates the picture. Some divorced couples engage in devious acts "for the sake of the children," but that's just for cranky people, not you. There are extreme cases: some exes are conniving, abusive, and dangerous. In that case, you may need to involve the law or take drastic measures. In general, though, you will be well served by steering clear of cranky codependence.

Be There to Pick Up the Pieces

Divorce recovery takes time. You can heal faster by consciously making healthy choices. Visit the Quick Stop! when you get swept away with anger or resentment. Chew on a few Reality Bites about life after divorce. Make a brief visit to the "altar of self-pity," absolve yourself, and then move on. Focus on the relief you feel instead of replaying negatives. What do you now know about yourself? What lasting lessons might help you in the future?

If divorce happens to a friend, just be there to listen and offer your support. Your presence gives the newly separated person some stability in the midst of interpersonal upheaval, and you will be providing a welcome haven. Resist playing rescuer or judge. If a couple you're close with or your parents divorce, avoid taking sides unless one of the parties is obviously, blatantly culpable. After all, they may reconcile. When long time, live-in partners break up, acquaintances and family seldom treat the split as seriously as a divorce, yet the attending emotional pain and physical divestiture is equally acute. If this happens to someone you know, keep in mind that he or she could use a friend.

Step Up to the Stepchild Issue

With our high divorce and remarriage rates, the blended family is well represented in our culture. Each child brings his or her own history, much of which is unknown to the new parent. It takes time for everyone to find a rightful place in the new family. Being on good terms with your ex or your spouse's ex will help the kids adjust to their new circumstances. You can solidify your blended family by making a concerted effort to know and understand your stepchildren, regardless of their ages, and treating them as fairly and individually as you do your own. Be patient and allow your new family structure to establish itself over time. Barbara Glanz's book *Care Packages for the Home* offers dozens of activities to help keep families of all kinds connected.

Keep It All in Balance

Women are usually expected to take on more of the parenting, but it often works if the custodial parent assumes the disciplinarian role and the new partner lends support. Clarify your role and establish a bond before you take on too much parental responsibility. If you play the role of disciplinarian, balance it with nurturing. Sibling rivalry is confounded by the "step" issue, and kids will look for incidents of preferential treatment. Working with a family counselor can help your family clarify roles, responsibilities, and rules during the forming stage. Don't feel it's too late if you and your spouse have been together for a while and are still struggling with these issues. If the kids are going to be around for some time yet and you plan to stay married, find someone to help you work through your difficult issues.

CRANKY QUIZ ITEM # 9:
FAMILY TIES

> 9. ___ Do you find family get-togethers or holiday gatherings poten-
> tially stressful?

From Holiday Cheer to Cranky Celebrations

If the world were perfect we'd all enthusiastically await the annual holiday ritual where everyone would join hands and sing "Home for the Holidays" in front of a glowing fireplace in flawless harmony. Okay, maybe this is a stretch. As the holidays draw near, I hear two distinct songs. The first is a cheerful refrain about reconnecting with loved ones. The second involves a chorus of grumbling about spending time with relatives whom, as we change, feel a little more like acquaintances than kin. Suffice it to say that some of us go home because it's expected while others of us wouldn't miss it for the world.

Family gatherings provide an abbreviated opportunity to touch base with those who share the most significant portion of our historical taproot. We have a chance to reminisce and review, update one another, lend support during a trauma, or celebrate the triumphs. While these visits are inherently rewarding, there exists the potential for friction. An accepting, commonsense outlook can prevent crankiness from seeping into an otherwise special event.

But there is another side. For some people, family gatherings are stressful. Not knowing what your situation is, we'll try to cover both bases briefly. Whether you eagerly anticipate family gatherings, or would rather endure a root canal, I'd like to offer a few suggestions that can help keep your holidays more cheerful and less cranky.

Anti-Cranky Alternatives for Cranky Quiz Item # 9:
Family Ties
Don't Sweat the Small Stuff

Family gatherings, like many other good things, have a limited shelf life. That is, you're all together for a little while each year, so enjoy everyone with that spirit. There may be occasional irritants that can incite crankiness but with a little bit of effort you can keep them in perspective. Yes, Aunt Martha will probably drink just a wee bit too much wine and get weepy as she's done in the past, and Uncle John will most likely talk too loudly as he's always done, but so what? Your older sibs might still try to treat you like a kid, but you can handle that. You know they care about you and if they give unsolicited advice they're just trying to help.

If you host the holiday and your mom and dad stay a couple of days longer than ideal, go with the flow. Enjoy them now because they won't always be around. Take advantage of their presence and know they have the best of intentions, even if you're a full-grown adult and they still wait up for you when you stay out late. This is your *family* and these people care about you. Look at them with a soft lens on your heart. Relax. If any little currents of crankiness stir up, send them packing. The very comment that momentarily struck a nerve today might be something you'll long remember because it's so characteristic of the person saying it. Don't sweat it. Just sit back and enjoy the show. You'll gain a few insights into what makes your parents or siblings tick and you might even learn some important things about yourself.

Avoid Cranky Celebrations: Try the K.I.S.S. Method

If your family falls into the category of "cranky kin," perhaps the K.I.S.S. method will work for you: "Keep It Short and Seldom." Limit your number of visits per year. Arrive late and leave early. Limit your exposure to those who may not always have your best interests in mind. As a preventive measure, don the cape of your emotional immune system and let its powers help protect you from behaviors that may otherwise prompt in you a regression to emotional adolescence. Remind yourself that you're an adult and no longer need parental approval, nor do you have to compete with siblings who try to edge you into a subservient role.

Show up if you must, but don't be an active participant. If someone tries to hook you, don't take the bait; let the person be disappointed, not you. Casually (not angrily) leave the room. Visit the Quick Stop! and then gnaw on a few Reality Bites. Push your Reset Button. Remind yourself that how other people behave makes a statement about them (and their hang-ups), not about you.

If your situation is extreme—that is, you bear an unhappy past and go home only to be assailed with criticism, put-downs, or guilt—this goes beyond crankiness. Ask yourself *why* you're going out of your way to appease people you'll never be able to please. Maybe it's time to withdraw permanently, but before you take this difficult step, read *If You Had Controlling Parents* by Dan Neuharth, who outlines numerous constructive ways of preventing your past from contaminating your present.

Add a New Branch to Your Family Tree

Friendship is sometimes defined by who you can call at four in the morning and get a listening ear. If there are people in your life with whom you can safely disclose, share trust, and be unconditionally accepted, they may not be blood relatives, but they are part of your inner circle and deserve to be thought of as "family." The support and acceptance you get from these friends (and give them) is the ultimate of connectedness. Every now and then, let these individuals know how special they are.

CRANKY QUIZ ITEM # 10:
RUMPLED RELATIONSHIPS

> 10. ___ Do you and your significant other have trouble
>   communicating?

Cranky Couplings

We've all been around cranky couples—two ordinarily nice people who have let their relationship slide onto thin ice, people whose tone of voice and look of resignation tell far more about them than you want to know. This doesn't have to happen. Couples who keep their relationship vital and satisfying seem to maintain an ongoing appreciation for each other. They let the small irritants fall by the wayside instead of making big issues out of them.

But couples who lapse into crankiness tend to look at their partners in a critical manner. There's always an issue, a flaw, someone at fault for something. They seem overwrought, even on occasions when they should be enjoying themselves, as on vacation, or when going out together.

My heart goes out to these dour duos who live with such a lack of enthusiasm. I want to go up and cajole them—tell a joke, tickle them, make them smile, and help them relax! I feel sensitive about this because when I look at cranky couples I see myself from many years ago, when life was hard and I felt old, despite my tender years. I know from experience that dis-Connectedness is an unsettling, unsatisfying way to live and little bouts of crankiness can escalate into bigger confrontations if we're not careful.

Anti-Cranky Alternatives for Cranky Quiz Item # 10: Rumpled Relationships

Assess Your Situation

If your partner has become increasingly withdrawn, negative, or critical of you; if it feels as if he or she is drifting away for some unknown reason, do something about it now. Let me gently remind you to come from a position of compassion, because if you accuse, threaten, or criticize, this will only serve to increase the distance between the two of you.

You need to be clear on how you'd like the situation to change. What do you want out of this relationship? What did it used to be like? What factors have changed for the two of you? What are you willing to do so you can regain what you once shared? The more clearly you can envision the outcome you desire, the easier it will be to discuss these issues with your partner.

Maybe in reading this section you realize *you're* the one who's backed off. If so, you need to answer these same questions and decide what you'll do next. This is hard, serious work, but after all you've read in this chapter, you recognize the cost involved in disconnecting from those we love.

Your relationship with your partner truly deserves to be all it can be. Go back to why you chose this person with whom to share your life, what wonderful traits and qualities initially attracted you, and try to rejuvenate them. Revitalize yourself, too. Bring laughter back into your relationship. Revisit what you want from each other. If you need to, work as a couple (or singly first, if that's appropriate) with a counselor. In the meantime, go back and reread the section about R & R and courting your spouse, and do it.

Correct Cranky Communications

If you and your partner have digressed into a pattern of cranky communication it might take a little while to (1) recognize it, and (2) change it, because how you communicate is habitual. But if you're persistent you can do it. The first order of business is to become more aware of how you express yourself (your words, your tone, your attitude).

Listen to your tone of voice. If it sounds harsh, critical, or cranky, stop! Say your statement over again. If it feels awkward doing so, just say, "Wait a minute. That didn't sound right. Let me try again." And then speak in a more positive tone. Pay attention to the words you use. If you realize you've said something that might cause your partner to feel cranky or uncomfortable, restate it. "That's not what I meant. Here's what I wanted to say." Use new, better words this time.

Once you increase your self-awareness, you can work on the hidden element of your communication: intent. Actually, intent *precedes* what you say or how you say it, but most of us aren't immediately aware of how intent influences communication. Once you have the presence of mind to monitor your tone and words, you'll be able to focus on your intent.

Having a positive intent means you're trying to inform your partner, not criticize. You're being constructive, not cranky. You want to express, not demand; explain, not defend; connect, not disconnect. Even if you're angry, you can communicate in a tone that conveys seriousness without hostility, or as stated earlier in this chapter, you can express anger without malice. This is sometimes called "hate the sin, love the sinner," or "separate the person from the behavior."

There are always two messages that get transmitted whenever we communicate: the one that's said literally and the one that's implied. It's like parents who look at the clock while saying to their child, "Do you know what time it is?" The parent isn't really asking what time it is; he or she is implying that it's *bedtime* and the child needs to get ready for bed. Depending on the parent's attitude (intent) this could be a constructive interaction or a cranky one. Voice tone or facial expression provide the clue.

Think about how you can explain what's on your mind without disconnecting from your partner. One of the most effective ways to do this is to explain your perceptions by using "I" messages.

Using an "I" message means you will focus on how your partner's behavior affected you instead of emphasising what he or she did ("you" message). "You" messages describe the other party's behavior and imply blame. "I" messages describe your honest reaction and imply connection.

"I" message: "I felt concerned when you didn't call to tell me your meeting was running late." Implied: *I was afraid something had happened to you.* "You" message: "You never called to tell me you'd be late tonight." Implied: *You don't think I'm important.*

You may have figured out that if you focus on positive intent, the implied message will complement your words. But if you have an ulterior or hidden intent that, too, will be implied, and ultimately it's the hidden message that will be communicated. Cranky couples engage in a lot of implied communication; listen to how voice tone makes a word like *dear* or *honey* sound cold or resentful.

"I" messages and positive intent will help you stay connected with your partner and reduce incidents of cranky miscommunications. If the way you've been communicating hasn't worked very well, I hope you'll give this a try. The world already has enough cranky couples: we need more connected ones!

A DOSE OF REALITY ABOUT DIS-CONNECTEDNESS

The stakes are always high where our emotions are involved. That's why some of us find it so hard to talk about relationships. We're very vulnerable when it comes to romance, intimacy, marriage, family, conflict, divorce. It's a complex portrait, and our job is to sort through what works for us and what doesn't. For every relationship problem, there's a potential positive outcome if we're willing to look for it. Staying connected, not just with our loved ones but even within our communities, is one of the keys to quelling the anger epidemic.

Deep down, each of us recognizes that as human beings we're all linked in some cosmic way, and connectedness begins in our homes. A few extra moments of tenderness, empathy, careful explanation, or understanding can make all the difference. The more closely connected we are with our loved ones, the better our ability to reach out to others so we can unite in our efforts to combat cultural crankiness.

Our connectedness transcends all educational and socioeconomic levels, race, age, ethnicity, or physical capability. When we observe a tragedy we experience a sense of sadness. When we see a child or animal mistreated we feel a stab of pain. When we witness an act of love or compassion we feel hope. And when we look into a baby's eyes we embrace joy. These are examples of our connectedness.

The stronger your connections, the deeper your compassion. But when you lose your compassion, you also lose your passion. When passion fades, your emotional connections begin to fray. By staying fully alive, vibrant, and keeping yourself closely connected to those who matter in your life, you'll fully experience your passion—and compassion. Best of all, you'll pass it on. You're the critical link!

Cost

POOR, BROKE, AND PAYING THE PRICE

It was two weeks after my husband walked out, and despite my panic, I struggled to make the transition appear smooth for the kids' sakes. I was interviewing for jobs and had no money. As marriage was the only way of life I had known, I was still emotionally and financially dependent on my husband, feeling wholly unprepared for being on my own. I came home from a job interview and found our dog, Skippy, lying next to the road. He was awake, though not particularly alert. As I picked him up, one of his hind legs swung back and forth. With a sinking heart I realized he had been hit by a car and his leg was broken.

I hurried him to the vet, hoping against hope that I was wrong. They told me it would cost $35 to mend my dog's leg. They may as well have said $350. Or $3500! I tried to call my husband to see if he would cover the cost but I couldn't locate him. There was no way I could commit this much money to a dog when I had three kids to feed. Sobbing and shaking, I signed the form authorizing the veterinarian to put our family pet to sleep. I still remember how powerless I felt, making this decision, my first as a single woman. Little did I know that many of the costs I was about to pay over the next few years would have far less to do with money than with my impoverished way of looking at the world.

THE PRICE OF HIGHER COSTS
AND LOWER SAVINGS

We all have our own reasons for how we handle money and it's a loaded issue for most of us. Government reports tell us we're better at spending than saving but we already know that. Just a few decades ago (before the Expectation Machine revved up its engine) our collective Cranky Quotient was lower, and so was our sense of entitlement. We hadn't yet been massively infected by the "work-and-want" mentality. Of course, there were things we all wanted, but as a society we hadn't yet reached the apex of unbridled consumerism. We were not yet "buyers with attitude." We still considered expectation and entitlement as separate concepts, and most of us didn't make purchases with an undercurrent of contempt. Not so today.

Whether we realize it or not, many of us attempt to emulate what we see on TV and in movies: a storefront life with the perfect backdrop that suggests we deserve only the best, that what we have is never enough, that life is a constant upgrade parade, and we are *almost obligated* to maintain an upscale lifestyle.

Here's the high-cost version of the house that Jack built: We buy a house ("starter castle") in the country with twice the square footage of our old home in town; that means a lot of floor space we need to cover with either carpeting or wood. The house is so big that everything we own could go in one room, so that means having to buy more furniture. The new place features walk-in closets in the master bedroom and that means we have to buy more clothes, or there won't be anything to put in those world-class closets.

Then there's the three-car garage, designed to accommodate not only our two cars but to provide ample room for all of the power equipment we need to buy. The five-acre plot our new home sits on means we have to buy a small tractor so we can keep the grass mowed, and we'll need a rototiller so we can put in a garden. Now that we live in the country we need to trade in the old Corolla for some kind of four-wheel drive vehicle for when it snows. We also need a leaf blower and a snowblower, too, for the front sidewalk and back deck. Our new starter castle is so big we can't possibly maintain it ourselves so now we need to find someone to come in once a week and straighten it up. You probably caught it, but notice there's not one "want" in the above series of statements. It's all "have to" and "need." This is how we talk these days. The house is costly enough, but just imagine the rest of the expenses involved in living this upscale life we just "have" to have!

Many of today's oversized homes have *showcase* rooms the owners furnish and arrange as a showoff factor to impress company. All that's missing from this perfect picture are the velvet ropes to isolate this "off limits" area so guests won't actually try to walk on the carpet or sit on the sofa (family members already know better).

The madness of trying to create and keep up appearances is too much for some of us. Financially and interpersonally, we crack under the strain. According to Juliet B. Schor in her brilliant book, *The Overspent American*, at least 30 percent of us are living beyond our means. Personal bankruptcies are at an all-time high.

Crankiness is a natural by-product of our social compulsion to drive the right car, live in the right home in the right area with all the right furnishings, have the right job, send our kids to the right day care or schools, wear the right clothes and accessories, belong to the right clubs, and go to the right vacation spots. Perhaps we think that having the best will somehow mean we are the best. Self-esteem issues aside, this madness might be acceptable if we could afford it, but many of us are so busy trying to create the right life that we've turned our existence into a nightmare of debt. This social condition, called "affluenza," is characterized by an internal emptiness we think we can treat with physical possessions. We don't realize that the relief we're seeking can't be bought.

I, too, have fallen into the credit trap. When I was married and our kids were small, even with living costs far lower than they are today, my husband and I were miserable money managers who bought everything on credit. Like many families, we lived from paycheck to paycheck, with no savings tucked away for emergencies. We existed under a constant shroud of denial, hope, and absurdly short-term thinking.

Our combined lack of restraint and poor money management resulted in a humiliating climax: Our family physician refused to examine the kids when they had chicken pox because of our long-outstanding bill. With monthly payments that outstripped our income, we had to go through the embarrassing, expensive process of loan consolidation for a second time. For many families today, the story is the same, only the numbers are bigger. Poor money management is a costly prospect that involves far more than dollars.

"NECESSARY" LUXURIES

The cost issue is a major source of crankiness. We have to buy the necessities but we want to buy the luxuries. The easiest way to do this is to redefine luxury items as necessities (answering machines, microwaves, stereos and CD players, additional TVs, dishwashers, cable service, cell phones) so we can feel justified spending our money on them.

It's easy to confuse want and need when we visit the "world of wealth" every day: After seeing so many spacious, beautifully furnished homes on TV or in movies we begin thinking this upscale way of life is how everyone should live. If you remember *Dynasty* or *Dallas*, ask yourself if these shows influenced our perception about how large a house should be, or how lavish a lifestyle?

Movies, too, can skew our perceptions. I still remember my granddaughters gasping at the fancy bedroom and oversize closet of the girl in *Clueless*. Like a Dick and Jane primer, we learn the drill early on: "What I see, I want. What I want, I buy. When I buy, I borrow. When I borrow, I pay." The problem is that there's always more to see and want than we can buy. We pay later, up to 18 percent. Given this pattern, who has money left over to save?

Our constant exposure to the obscenely high earnings lavished on sports figures, entertainers, and corporate executives seeds our disquietude about money. Why should we have to live on such a pittance if these people are worth so much; aren't we worth something? We're simultaneously resentful of, and awed by, celebrity, fame, and prestige. Money talks. It tells us what we consider significant. Compare the incomes of gifted athletes to that of gifted teachers and ask yourself what this says about our society. I recently had a conversation with a former police officer, who after twelve years on the force, quit and went to work for UPS. He immediately doubled his income by switching careers. What we pay certain people and who we consider celebrities is a telling reflection of the world in which we live. The value system of a culture is mirrored in its citizens.

MY MONEY, MYSELF

Our conflicting perceptions about money also cost us dearly in self-esteem. The money we make, or lack of it, defines our lifestyle, and we in turn allow our lifestyle to define who we are. Equating income with self-worth sets us up for a big fall. Those of us who aren't rich and famous feel cheated. Some of those who "make it big" struggle with their newfound wealth through serial relationships, drug and alcohol abuse, even suicide. We cluck at their tragedy while still longing for "the good life," thinking that money is the answer to all our problems.

Coming to terms with our attitude toward money and how we handle it will go a long way in reducing crankiness. Most of us want more money than we have, and a lot of us spend more than we should. Those of us who like to save money don't actually enjoy the act of spending it. Go figure! We all know that money is often a highly charged issue of contention between couples. In short, most of us place too much emphasis on this nagging necessity, using money as a measure of social (and personal) worth. These attitudes come with an interpersonal price.

Between the ever-increasing cost of living and the relentless drive to earn, spend, and accumulate, many of us are stretched beyond our means. We seldom consider the costs of placing too much value on money and too little on a meaningful way of living. This chapter will help you get a grip on cost. You'll gain a better sense of what money means to you, discover some options for modifying your inconsistent money management practices, while enriching the part of you that pays really big dividends: your spirit.

THE COST OF LIVING

Poorer Than We Want to Be, Richer Than We Realize

A friend of mine who visited a remote town in Russia last summer talked about the rows of empty shelves where they shopped. In one store she found two boxes of cereal. Two *boxes*; not two brands. That was it. Her experience reminds me that even when my kids and I lived on welfare we were still wealthy in comparison to other people in the world.

I'm astonished at the choices beckoning us every time we walk into a store. On your next trip to your local megamarket, take a moment and view the spectacle. Calculate the square footage of food items and merchandise. Note the almost infinite variety of products and brands. Contemplate the number of *nonfood* items you can buy, including prescriptions, clothing, photo processing, toys, or fresh-cut flowers.

Some markets offer one-stop shopping that could sustain a life cycle from birth to death, excluding the casket, and who knows, maybe there's a special order department! As you scan the acres of goods, reflect on your expectations about product presentation. Do you reject a rumpled package or dented can, a piece of produce with a bruise or

Cranky Quiz

COST

Scoring the Cranky Quiz

Score 1 point for every *yes* and 0 for every *no*. Count a *sometimes* as a *yes*. Add your total: 3 points or less (Cool) means you're in good shape, 4 to 7 (Warm) indicates a need to slow down, and 8 to 10 (Hot!) indicates a raging cranky infection. You'll find anti-cranky solutions for each quiz item in this chapter.

1. ___ Are you living from paycheck to paycheck, depending on money you haven't yet made to pay the bills at the end of the month?

2. ___ Are you the kind of bargain hunter who drives across town to save a buck or refuses to pay full price for anything?

3. ___ Do you spend money on impulse purchases or luxury items you seldom use?

4. ___ If you're married, do you and your partner ever fight over money?

5. ___ Do you feel trapped in a job you hate but can't afford to quit?

6. ___ Do you go overboard and spend too much on parties, ceremonies, or holidays?

7. ___ Do you tend to get carried away and spend more money than you should on gifts?

8. ___ Do you worry about money, often wish you had more, and dream about winning the Lotto?

9. ___ If you have investments, do you follow Wall Street numbers religiously?

10. ___ Does it ever feel as if the price you pay for your lifestyle is too high for what you get in return?

Cranky Quotient _____

My cost condition is (*circle one*)   Cool   Warm   Hot!

brown spot? When I catch myself doing that I imagine standing next to someone who would consider that sagging head of lettuce or that slightly soft green pepper as a *treasure*. But our bounty doesn't come free: as you scan the rows of products remind yourself of the hidden costs in the foods you buy including transportation, processing, packaging, presentation, promotion (and even pesticides). We consumers also end up absorbing the cost of products that don't get purchased; produce and other perishables, or anything with an expiration date.

More Places to Spend Than Save

In our ad-driven, consumer-based culture, somebody somewhere wants your money. Billboards, print ads, commercials, and shopping channels clamor for your complicity and your cash twenty-four hours a day. How can you resist? It isn't a car, it's *performance*. It's not just clothing, it's an *image*. It's more than a beer, it's a *party*. It's not simply a product, it's an *experience*.

As consumers, we carefully choose our product brands, hoping to run faster, jump higher, look better, feel better, have more charisma, be more attractive, be more fulfilled. Life becomes a perpetual motion machine that exchanges our time and energy for hard-earned money, and trades those dollars for the promise of *bigger, better, faster, more, now*. We spend our lives exchanging and upgrading because whatever we have is never enough. We're always a step behind the American Dream.

At What Cost?

Money doesn't fund just dreams, though; it's nearly as essential to our survival as oxygen. We need a certain amount to survive, but how much is enough? No one has as much as they they think they need. But there's a cost for this insatiable mentality. Just for starters, how many times have you heard a couple reminiscing about their early years when they were poor and struggling to establish themselves. In the midst of today's comfortable life and a house filled with possessions, they sigh, "Those were the best years of our lives!" How could they look on such hard times with so much fondness?

Money is a hot issue for most of us. Just bring up the subject of income at a party and watch everyone's gaze drop to their feet: We all want money but nobody wants to talk about it. We don't want to admit how much we have or that it isn't enough.

We don't want to seem cheap nor do we want to be thought of as extravagant. If the topic of cost does come up, based on someone's look, voice, tone, or body language, we may quickly modify how much we paid for an item, either shaving off a few dollars or adding a few, so we won't be thought either a braggart or fool.

The fact is that most of us have unreconciled issues and conflicts about money; our spending and saving habits say a lot about our personality and philosophy. People raised by parents who experienced the Depression often internalize their parents' values. They tend to be more frugal, often going without or postponing a purchase until they can pay cash rather than buying on time. Boomers are more inclined to think in terms of monthly payments rather than whole cost. They're willing to stretch their financial limits so they can get what they want now, protesting that this is their inalienable right.

What is money to you? Do you love it? Hate it? Do you consider it a necessary evil? Do you count pennies and squirrel money away whenever possible or do you spend it recklessly? Do you manage money or does it manage you? And how much of your time do you waste being cranky about not having as much money as you'd like?

CRANKY QUIZ ITEM # 1:
SPIRALING COSTS, STRAINED INCOME

> 1. ___ Are you living from paycheck to paycheck, depending on money you haven't yet made to pay the bills at the end of the month?

Show Me the Money

For the sake of simplicity, let's look at two extreme ways of handling money. Income level has little do with either; these are ingrained attitudes. First there are the frugal thinkers who save a dime whenever possible so it can be tucked away for the future. Don't expect these types to buy your lunch. Even though these people may want something, they won't buy it unless it's on sale. They live for retirement, denying little luxuries and big ones, as they wait for their future to unfold.

The frivolous thinkers live for today, sometimes squandering large sums of money on impulse purchases or expensive possessions.

They seek status, think upscale, and consider spending money their birthright. They accrue substantial debt load, live from paycheck to paycheck, and struggle to make ends meet.

Maybe you're somewhere in the middle. I hope so. It doesn't always pay to put everything off for tomorrow (you don't know how long you'll live), nor do you want to squander everything. We've all been advised to spend a little, save a little, enjoy today, and keep an eye on the future, but who among us practices such self-restraint?

Don't Give Yourself More Credit Than You Deserve

Then there are credit cards: easy to attain, convenient to use, hard to pay for. Credit cards allow us to spend money at an extra cost, both at the counter and through the ATM. There's an insidious component behind credit card use that financial institutions and stores are banking on: Credit cards spare us from enduring the pain of pulling cash out of our wallets and watching it disappear, or writing a check and watching our balance dwindle. Just a quick, tidy transaction and technology takes care of the rest.

Until we receive our statement, that is. Just so you know, I went through my own brief phase of ATM codependence and I certainly paid for it. And even though I know better, when I use my credit card the transaction still doesn't feel as "real" as when I use cash.

Splitting the Cost

We all have to deal with the high cost of living and we each have our own method of coping, from clipping coupons to going without. The point, of course, is to develop a workable system of money management that fits with who you are. It's less a question of right and wrong and more one of balance. But there is one issue that many must face, and that's child support. Too many noncustodial parents follow the "out of sight out of mind" principle. The ex-husband of one of my best friends always claimed it was *against his nature* to pay child support.

Divorce wreaks havoc in a family budget, on both sides of the split, and cost complicates the lives of both the custodial parent and the one who pays. Like many other low-income single parents, my husband's nonpayment of child support made my already difficult life even more so in the early years after our divorce.

Conversely, the ongoing commitment of outgoing support payments complicates the lives of those who remarry. It's a difficult prospect either way. The costs of child support, and the issue of having more children in a new marriage requires extensive consideration to assure that the financial and emotional costs aren't too dear.

Anti-Cranky Alternatives for Cranky Quiz Item # 1: Spiraling Costs, Strained Income

Clarify Your Perceptions about Money

You'll do yourself a favor by sitting down and sifting through your perceptions about money. The following questions will help you clarify some of these issues.

- What do you consider the basic necessities in your life?
- What do you define as luxuries?
- Do you ever (intentionally or unintentionally) confuse the two?
- Do you use the words *want* and *need* interchangeably?
- How often do you buy something as an act of defiance; that is, you want it, you deserve it, and therefore you refuse to worry about how you'll pay for it?
- Would you consider your debt load well within reasonable limits?
- Do you have a "wish list" of material possessions you want to own?
- Are you impressed or envious of people who make more money than you?
- Do you have less money saved than what you consider desirable?

Explore what money means to you—how you perceive it, how you spend it, and whether you save it. Pay attention to the moments when your sense of entitlement kicks in, when you start telling yourself you *deserve* something rather than admitting you simply want it. Be brutally open about how you spend money. Don't let denial or rationalization get you into trouble.

Curb Cost Crankiness

If you're living from paycheck to paycheck, strapped with monthly payments, credit card interest, or borrowing to make ends meet you've been infected with the cranky ailment of work-and-want. Put a moratorium on your spending. Stash your credit card away so you can't use it. Don't buy that third TV. Don't get another pet so the one you already own will have company. Don't replace the carpet just because it has a stain. Buy a throw rug. Rearrange the furniture.

Carefully monitor your spending habits. If this is a long-term pattern, face the fact that you're using money to treat something it can't cure—anger, loneliness, frustration, fear. If you don't detox, your Cranky Quotient will sail higher than the Dow during a bull market. Draw up a budget and follow it until you've paid off some of your balances. Again, quit using your credit card. If you can't discipline yourself to take these steps on your own, find a therapist or financial counselor to help you curb your compulsive spending.

Follow the Paper Trail

Your spending patterns are a telling reflection of your values: Pay more attention to where your money goes and especially when you "spend with an attitude." Follow the paper trail. Force yourself to review your check log in detail every time you balance your account. Put all of your credit card slips in a special spot and review them weekly. Some credit card companies now provide their "members" with an annual report, logging every transaction over the previous twelve months. It's quite an experience to read this telling record. If your credit card company provides you with one of these reports, keep it. Read it every month for reality therapy.

Face Up to Your Interpersonal Payments

If you're responsible for child support payments and spend a lot of time whining about it, get real. The money is for the kids. Hard as it is, having children and helping sustain them as they grow is a reality of divorce or parenthood. Little did we think when those precious babies were conceived and born that there would one day be a divorce. After the split it can be tough facing up to all that responsibility. It may feel unfair to shell out money week after week, but hey, you had an active hand in helping create these human beings and they depend on, and deserve, your support. Do the right thing.

If you and your current spouse feel overloaded, if you feel the hot breath of compressed time and cost on the back of your necks, if you're having relationship problems or getting impatient with the kids you already have, *think long and hard about having another*. Some couples decide to have a baby because they think it will mend a troubled relationship or lessen lifestyle pressures. This only worsens the trend.

If you feel that the work-and-want syndrome has its grip on you, take a quick inventory. Stroll through your home and note which possessions you consider truly important and essential. Then review the nonmaterial aspects of your life that you most value. *Chances are, your list will be short and will have more to do with relationships than ownership.*

CRANKY QUIZ ITEM # 2:
COST COMPULSIVENESS

> 2. ___ Are you the kind of bargain hunter who drives across town to save a buck or refuses to pay full price for anything?

At Whose Cost?

Two men friends were in the market for a new videocam. Both were partial to Sony products, so together they headed for the local Sony electronics store to research available models. They spent nearly two hours in the shop, asking questions, assessing equipment, and deliberating over which features would best fit their needs. As it ended up, they both wanted the same model, and the shop had several in stock. The first man bought his videocam on the spot but the other held off.

Having benefited from the efforts of a willing, capable salesclerk who took time to answer all of his questions, the second man drove across town later that day and bought his videocam at a discount chain store, saving himself forty dollars. The first man said he placed too much value on the salesperson's expertise and goodwill to save a few dollars. But the second man, whose income far exceeds the first, prided himself on his ability to save a few bucks, at the expense of the salesclerk who educated him.

You've probably heard the saying, "Some people know the price of everything and the value of nothing." The price of an item is an issue, yes, but when you buy something, don't just consider the sticker price. Considerations such as time, service, convenience, quality, guarantee, and even local commerce are all factors in this thing called cost.

Anti Cranky Alternatives for Cranky Quiz Item # 2: Cost Compulsiveness

Resist Insisting on a Bargain at all Costs

For some of us, a few extra dollars saved can mean food on the table. I know what that feels like. But there are people so fixated on *price* they sacrifice convenience, time, and even personal gratification to get a deal. They make an hour-long trip across town to save five dollars; they comparison shop from store to store when the price only varies a few bucks; they'll even settle for a lesser product because the item they want isn't on sale. It helps to ask what other kind of cost is involved in a transaction. Is what you're giving up equal to what you gain? Could this transaction end up costing you more than you bargained for in terms of time or inconvenience? Your consumer decisions gain more scope when you employ more than the one measurement of cost.

If You Buy It, Be Happy with It

A woman I know had always bought used cars. Finally, one spring she ordered a brand-new vehicle, getting the exact color, style, and interior she wanted. Her excitement lasted until fall, when one day she saw a commercial for the same make and model she had purchased six months earlier, only now it was $2,500 less than she had paid. The financing was unbelievably low. She got depressed and swore she'd never buy a new car again. Her thrill over achieving her dream—a new car—lasted only six months. From then on it was regret and crankiness over losing so much money. It didn't count that she got exactly what she had dreamed about. What mattered more was the money she could have saved if she had waited till fall and bought something off the lot. Instead of feeling *good* over getting the car she wanted, she chose to feel *bad* about what she didn't get: a deep discount.

CRANKY QUIZ ITEM # 3: HASTE, WASTE, AND POOR TASTE

3. ___ Do you spend money on impulse purchases or luxury items you seldom use?

License to Spend

How we view money inevitably connects to how we view ourselves. For example, if I perceive myself as someone who likes to stay healthy I might join a health club, but that doesn't mean I'll actually make use of it. Because I *want* to be in shape and *intend* to start working out, I continue paying for my membership and justifying the cost because that's the person I want to be. Canceling my membership would mean having to admit that I'm a couch potato who would rather veg out than work out. This thin slice of reality might make me cranky so I continue the costly charade.

There's also our public self and our private self, and they don't always match either: The person who buys drinks for everyone may have a self-concept of generosity, but he or she may actually be looking for recognition or respect. Our compulsion to be well-dressed may be prompted by insecurity or a need for acceptance. Sometimes our inner needs are the motivating factor for those impulse purchases we make, where a few hours or days later, in retrospect, we find ourselves wondering, "What was I thinking?" Whatever it was, at the moment it seemed fully justifiable. It was the right product at the right time for all the wrong reasons.

Anti-Cranky Alternatives for Cranky Quiz Item # 3: Haste, Waste, and Poor Taste

Stop before You Shop

If you're long on excuses and short on money you need to evaluate your self-image and spending profile. A friend of mine laughs over her ten-year-long health club membership that she only started using two months ago. She regrets the money she wasted but says at least she's paying the original low fee so when she's sixty she'll break even.

From misplaced motivation to thinly disguised "retail therapy," we all blow money from time to time. I've been known to buy an outfit that didn't quite fit when I tried it on, but I was planning on losing weight and it was such a bargain, how could I resist? Two years later it still didn't fit (I'm amazed how some fabrics can shrink just hanging in a closet) and I carted it off to the consignment shop with the tag still on.

Poor consumer choices may be a big or small problem for you: It depends on the frequency—and the amount. If impulse purchases or "mood shopping" are an issue for you, don't go to the mall when you're cranky or depressed. If you have to go, don't take your credit card. Always give yourself a three-day cooling off period before removing the tags from whatever you bought. By then you'll probably be over your "consumer moment" and you can return it.

Watch for Wasteful Ways

Look for ways you waste money. Maybe you buy food that gets thrown away, clothes that simply hang in your closet, or appliances that idly sit on the kitchen counter collecting dust. Make a rule that you absolutely won't buy it unless you *know* you will use it. Intent isn't enough. Liking the idea of owning something isn't enough. You have to *know* you'll use it!

Shopping on price alone can also be wasteful. The lowest cost isn't always a bargain. There were times I thought I was getting a good deal but I ended up having to trash what I bought and start over because of cheap, shoddy construction. My most recent mistake involved a low cost, poorly constructed cutting board that will soon be deep-sixed. I'd have been better off spending twice as much money, and that's what I'll do next time.

Remember the 1-to-10 value scale of watching TV? You can also set up a similar want-and-need scale for consumer purchases. This will help you think before you buy. For example, if you're getting ready to go on vacation, don't buy perishables. You may be too busy planning and packing to eat them. If you need clothes for the trip you may be better off buying them locally than in a pricey tourist shop. For casual, everyday clothes (jeans, T-shirts, sweatshirts) think *gently used*. I buy almost all of my "play" clothes at consignment stores, some of which are brand names and perfectly broken in.

And last, don't buy from a position of compulsion or scarcity. I once knew a woman who always had to have her cupboard filled with canned goods and staples because she feared running out. This wasn't a rational concern; she lived a block from the store. This related to her having grown up poor where food was always an issue. If you have some old hang-ups like this, work on them. You probably have enough current money issues to worry about without having to recycle old ones!

CRANKY QUIZ ITEM # 4:
MONEY GAMES

> 1. ___ If you're married, do you and your partner ever fight over money?

Slaving, Spending, Scheming, Steaming

Money is a source of conflict for many couples. He, an avid target shooter, sneaks into the house and down the stairs with his new rifle, hoping she doesn't catch him. He's prepared to lie about how much it cost, justifying this untruth because he wants to avoid a scene. He figures she can't estimate the true worth of a firearm, so what's the problem? She may be equally deceitful about that new holiday dress hanging in the closet. He would never understand the value of something she can only wear once or twice a year, so why get into it?

What's the problem here? Each party figures the other doesn't need to know. Each is willing to lie instead of telling the truth. Both are employed; each makes good money; it's not as if they can't afford these purchases. Both parties say they want to avoid unnecessary conflict, but with all this secrecy and subterfuge they may be opening the door for more than they bargained for.

The problem isn't money. It's trust. Neither party has faith in the other, though they wouldn't admit it. They probably don't even know it. Rather than enjoying mutual support, each person slides into secrecy instead. The relationship is compromised because these little deceptions often bleed into other areas. If you find yourself engaged in such trickery, you need to reconnect with your spouse or partner before the gap between you widens. Each of you has a right to spend a *certain* amount of money on whatever you want without being accountable. Let money be a working part of your relationship instead of becoming a wedge between you.

Anti-Cranky Alternatives for Cranky Quiz Item # 4:
Money Games
Blow the Whistle on the Money Games

There would exist fewer lies and deceptive games between couples if both parties had money that each could spend with no accountability to their partner. Call it a "financial freedom agreement." Yes, we all need to be responsible about how we handle money, but no, we shouldn't be held accountable for every single cent; this invites "money games."

I remember how hard it was, as a full-time homemaker, to have no source of personal income. Later on in my marriage, I earned money cleaning people's homes and doing ironing by the basket, but in the early years if I wanted money, I had to ask. Sometimes I grudgingly got it and sometimes I didn't. More than once I lied about how much the groceries cost so I could pocket some spending money. The financial freedom agreement is easier to achieve in a dual-income family but even when there's only one wage earner, each party deserves access to "me" money. After all, it's a *partnership*.

Share the Wealth: Yours, Mine, and Ours

Nothing strains a relationship like one party wielding pressure over the other about whose money it really is and exactly where it should go. For the sake of this discussion I am excluding compulsive spending, gambling, debt accumulation, or a series of failed investments. I'm talking about average couples with some discretionary income who want to minimize pressure and pettiness over money. If you've ever misled your partner about any expenditure, stop! Sit down and talk. Consider the advantages of earmarking income as *yours, mine, and ours*. In addition to your savings or checking accounts (separate or combined), each of you can open separate *spending* accounts in which you keep money you are completely free to do with as you wish. How you spend that money is your choice. No guilt, no recriminations; no lies, no explanations required; only celebrations and fun show-and-tell sessions so you can show off what you bought.

CRANKY QUIZ ITEM # 5:
GOLDEN HANDCUFFS

> 5. ___ Do you feel trapped in a job you hate but can't afford to quit?

Help! I'm Employed and I Can't Get Out

After conducting a day-long stress management seminar for a new client I came home feeling as if I had been bludgeoned. My shoulders, back, and legs ached. Never had a day of work hurt like this! What made this program different from any other? I had spent seven hours with fifty angry support employees—secretaries and office clerks—who hated their employer and their jobs. Yet, most of them had no intention of leaving because this company paid them more than anyone else would.

Talk about *cost*! They were trading health, peace of mind, and quality of life for money and they were damn mad about it. This was incomprehensible to me. I've been in jobs I hated and I chose to leave because I wasn't willing to sacrifice my well-being for the sake of a wage. I'm not suggesting my way of thinking is the only way. What I am saying, though, is that decisions based on money alone are inherently flawed because the consequences will come back to haunt us every time.

Anti-Cranky Alternatives for Cranky Quiz Item # 5: Golden Handcuffs

Do a Bubble Wrap

If you hate your job and feel stuck because of money, it's time for creative rebellion. If there is truly an excellent reason (not an excuse) keeping you in a job you dislike, then you need to create some emotional free space so you can remain effective in such a nonnurturing environment. Ruminate on some Reality Bites. Dust off your emotional immune system and use it liberally while at work. Read Viktor Frankl's *Man's Search for Meaning* to keep your attitude on track. Do your job.

Stay away from office politics or bellyaching (I once had weekly lunches with a friend who hated her job as much as I hated mine, and we had to call off our lunches because we both got so depressed afterward). Visit The Emergency Department and write your own encouraging statements to help you get through each day. Let your positive affirmations wrap you in a special protective bubble that shields you from the surrounding toxins. Do a good job and give yourself credit—a lot of it. Firmly refuse to complain and avoid negative discussions with coworkers.

Prepare for the Break

In the meantime, update your résumé. Embellish it with truthful exaggeration. Read it often to remind yourself of how valuable you are. Examine your budget and figure out the minimum income you can live on while envisioning your ideal job. Work on the vision fervently, including duties, income, conditions. There's a better job already out there; you just need to find it. Network. Conduct some "information interviews" so you can discover what's out there and where you might fit in.

If you need guidance, work with a creative career counselor. If you can't afford that, look for free resources. If you're staying in your job out of habit, fear, or because the money is good, you pay an exorbitant cost. Forfeiting your spirit for the sake of a few extra dollars is a way of subdividing your soul and selling it off, plot by plot. There's something better out there waiting for you; your job is to figure out what it is and where it is.

If, after reading all of the above, you still won't budge because you feel hopelessly, absolutely trapped, here's a last-ditch proposal. If you must stay in a job that gives you nothing but a paycheck, then create an outlet for keeping your soul intact. Reach out beyond your job for fulfillment, reward, or satisfaction. Take a class, find a hobby, do some volunteer work, or choose a pastime that feeds your spirit. It's the least you can do for yourself.

CRANKY QUIZ ITEM # 6:
THE COST OF SOCIAL EXPECTATIONS

> 6. ___ Do you go overboard and spend too much on parties, ceremonies, or holidays?

Whose Celebration Is It, Anyway?

In chapter 4 we explored our deep, instinctive need for connecting with others in a meaningful way. Social gatherings offer an opportunity to celebrate with others, and we commemorate nearly every life cycle event, from birth to death. Hosting some of these affairs can be a costly proposition. Some of us are able to throw a huge gathering or gala event without a trip to the mortgage lender, but when it comes to the big once-in-a-lifetime festivities such as weddings or Bar Mitzvahs (even graduations), some of us go overboard. This extravagance may be caused by sheer excitement, but some of it may have to do with social expectations. It's worth investigating.

Costly Celebrations

If a wedding looms in your future, think of the advertisers, printers, caterers, clothing and department stores, musicians, entertainers, and resorts who rely on this institution. The cost of a formal wedding in the United States now hovers around $18,000; that's a healthy down payment on a starter home in many small communities! With the high cost of this one-day event, the *marriage itself* takes a backseat to engraving and invitations; picking the right day, time, and site; silver or china patterns; gift registration; the guest list; photo shoot; ceremony; reception; food; and entertainment.

The first runner-up in the "spend as much as you can in one day" cavalcade of social events would appear to be Bar Mitzvahs, still lagging behind costly weddings, but showing great promise as a contender. We seem to have an unlimited capacity for pricey parties whether or not we can afford them: anniversaries, graduations, birthdays, and of course, let us not forget the annual holidaze. Is it time for us to revisit that word *enough* once again? Do we need to stop and ask what we're *really* celebrating on these special occasions: the honoree or our ability to outdo our friends by turning our wallets inside out?

Anti-Cranky Alternatives for Cranky Quiz Item # 6: The Cost of Social Expectations

Know the Purpose Behind the Party

Once again you're faced with an opportunity to clarify your intent and practice restraint: I can feel your excitement. This is a simple one, though. Just ask yourself two questions:

1. What's the occasion?
2. What's your purpose?

Honestly answer these two questions and the details will fall into place. If your purpose is to impress (be honest here!), then refinance the house and go for it, but don't get cranky later and complain about how much it cost you. If your intent is to simply celebrate a special occasion, invite the people who matter to you and let the party begin.

Life gets complicated when we get hung up in *shoulds, musts*, and *have-tos*. (It *must* be perfect. We *should* rent this hall because it's fancier. We *have* to hold as big a party as the one we just attended or it will be too embarrassing.) Life stays simple and more affordable when we stay on purpose. Whatever the event, by celebrating your special occasion in a simple, sincere style, it's the honored person who stays the center of attention, not the stuff that surrounds him or her.

Look for the Costs of Other Social Expectations

Do your friends make more money than you? If you're the low wage earner of the lot, this could affect the kinds of cost choices you make. In *The Overspent American*, Juliet B. Schor cites peers, or one's reference group, as the most potent influence on our lifestyle and spending habits. If all your friends regularly convene at a pricey bistro or belong to the best spa in town, maybe you've followed suit despite the stretch marks on your pocketbook. Is the car you drive a reflection of your desire to appear successful? If your best friends host a huge wedding for their kids you may feel pressured to do the same for yours.

You may choose vacation spots, leisure activities, a new home, or a high-status college for your kids because of your friends, only maybe they can afford it more than you. It's possible you're spending considerable sums of money because of the lifestyle you're trying to maintain. Is it ego? Insecurity? An attempt to keep up with those around you?

Think about the cranky consequences of trying to maintain a lifestyle that outpaces your income. It pays to make sure that how you dress, what you eat, where you go, and what you do for pleasure are *your* personal choices and not those dictated by your impression of what someone else expects.

CRANKY QUIZ ITEM # 7:
THE COST OF FRIENDSHIP, KINSHIP

> 7. ___ Do you tend to get carried away and spend more money than you should on gifts?

The Cost of Gifts and Giving

There's hosting an affair and then there's being invited to one. In addition to weddings and Bar Mitzvahs the pleasure of your company will be requested at birthdays, holidays, births, graduations, anniversaries, new jobs or promotions, illness and recovery, and retirement. When celebration is upheld in a noncommercial context, it connects people. But when we try to keep pace with an ever-growing list of socially prescribed "gift buying days," we disconnect.

For some people, gift buying is quid pro quo, and while we like to say it's the thought that counts, there's a price to pay for buying a gift that's too big or too small, or not buying one at all. If you spend too much you're extravagant, and the recipient feels pressured to up the ante next time. If you spend too little, you're cheap and the other party feels insulted. If you don't buy at all, you're a Scrooge and you lose face.

Commercial pressures and relentless romanticism spur us on, especially during the holidaze, as we stretch our creativity and credit limits, going in debt and spending more than we can afford. Once again, the Expectation Machine has corrupted a once enjoyable practice by sucking the meaning out of it.

Anti-Cranky Alternatives for Quiz Item # 7:
The Cost of Friendship, Kinship
Redefine What Giving Means to You

Ideally, a gift is a token of appreciation, commemoration, or a celebration. It brings pleasure to both parties without obligation or indebtedness. It's a low-pressure, high-pleasure experience when done with an open heart.

As an author, I had to learn this, because initially, when I gave away a book, I wanted (okay, I expected) some display of recognition or gratitude from the recipient. I once got a letter from a woman who said her employer had one of my books and she wished she could afford to buy her own. I was touched by her note so I sent her a free copy. I never heard from her. I still give books away but I do it for the sheer joy of giving because I now believe that true gifts come in packages with ribbons maybe, but no strings.

You'll enjoy your gift giving more if you keep it simple and affordable. Should you get criticized by a greedy receiver, next time give the person one of those charity certificates that reads, "A gift to the (Cancer Society) (Domestic Abuse Shelter) (Red Cross) has been given in your name." Maybe that will make the point.

One last thought: If you buy expensive gifts because you're looking for recognition, spend that money on a counselor instead so you can reconcile your self-esteem issues. You'll feel better and so will those around you. Can you see yourself giving with no expectation other than experiencing the joy of pure generosity and not caring if others keep score? This approach will save you hours of cranky calculating over who owes whom for what.

Reinvent the Practice

Knowing *why* you give influences *what* you give. Once you get away from obligatory purchases you can focus on appropriate presents for the people you care about. If you can afford it, think about giving meaningful experiences rather than physical possessions: a trip to the planetarium or a play for a special youngster, a horseback riding lesson, or modeling classes. Pay for a discovery flight (an introductory flying lesson) for someone who's always dreamed about flying a plane, a massage certificate for the overachiever who doesn't know how to stop and smell the aromatherapy, or a lesson with a local pro for the serious sports enthusiast.

If you get carried away with extravagant gift buying and can't trust yourself, allot a specified amount of money (cash) and don't let yourself have any more. Leave your credit card at home. Ask a friend if you need help sticking to your program.

If your budget is limited, keep in mind that some of the best gifts cost very little. My friend Mary window shops and bargain hunts. When she sees something a friend might like she buys it. This item goes into a special drawer for the "proper giving time." This eliminates panic shopping and poor decisions.

Then there are free gifts, such as the gift of *you*: an hour of undivided attention, a sunset walk, a home-cooked candlelight dinner, a series of back rubs, head rubs, foot rubs, or whatever the recipient treasures. One Christmas while my kids and I were on welfare I made each of them a handmade coupon book of low-cost to no cost treats: a favorite meal, special favor, getting to stay up an extra hour, a trip to the museum—experiences I knew they valued. In our commercialized, time-compressed world, such personal gifts can be far more meaningful than material things.

Resist ritual gift exchanges simply because the calendar says you must. Give what you want when you want because it adds meaning to the relationship. Of course, you have to explain your newfound attitude or someone's feelings may be hurt. But freeing yourself of social expectations leaves you and your loved ones more room for true enjoyment of each other's generous spirits.

CRANKY QUIZ # 8:
COLD CASH, HOT ISSUE

> 8. ___ Do you worry about money, often wish you had more, and dream about winning the Lotto?

So Much, So Many, So Little, So Few

My first house, bought in the sixties, cost less than the car I drive today. That boggles my mind. The home Rob and I have lived in for fifteen years, a small, inexpensive ranch style, has nearly tripled in value since we bought it. House prices are so high I marvel that young couples can afford even a tiny one. Then there's furniture and car payments, food, clothes, insurance costs, kids, pets, children's education, recreational expenses, and any emergency that may come along. For the mobile middle class, add the frequency of second homes, third cars, time shares, health and golf club memberships, and other indulgences, and we have an impressive monthly outflow of money in our society.

Yet I constantly hear young people say, "I just wanna be rich." People in my audiences tell me they fantasize daily about winning the Lotto. Most of us seem convinced that life would be much better if we just had more money. Yet a windfall can seriously mess up our lives if we're not ready for the complications it brings. I suggest to my audience members that they "get their act together now" just in case they do win the Lottery, so they can enjoy it to the utmost with the least amount of hassle.

Anti-Cranky Alternative for Cranky Quiz Item # 8:
Cold Cash, Hot Issue
Money: Come to Terms with It at All Costs

Take some time to clarify the role money plays in your life. If you discover that you place too much emphasis on money, you need to demystify it. For example, if you're fixated on winning the Lotto, figuring all your problems would disappear if only you had more dough, explore why this escapism appeals to you. There's more than money at stake with this fantasy.

Some money concerns are legitimate. If you have a limited income you may be plagued with feelings of powerlessness and vulnerability (I remember how it felt when I could barely scrape enough together to buy groceries).

On the other hand, if you're driven by a scarcity mentality that makes you afraid to blow even small sums (despite your considerable savings or comfortable lifestyle), think about a few counseling sessions to help you let go. There's an interpersonal cost in placing too much emphasis on money. You want your relationship with it to be harmonious and healthy, like all the other relationships in your life.

CRANKY QUIZ ITEM # 9:
TAKING STOCK

> 9. ___ If you have investments, do you follow Wall Street numbers religiously?

Don't Ask, Don't Tell

We may have been told that money doesn't buy happiness, but there's a long line of us who can't wait to disprove the theory. When the stock market burps we all reach for the antacid, reflecting the incomprehensible linkage between our financial well-being and the whimsy of Wall Street speculating. I know people who can recite their investment numbers but they don't know their blood type. In a health emergency, which would be more important?

Many of us let our stock profiles define who we are and when it comes to the cost of investing, personal values can take a backseat to earning potential. You can watch the numbers soar when a big company announces a personnel cutback, but there's a price we pay for following the profit line. When I question the practice of investing in make-a-profit-at-all-cost cranky corporations, people typically say they don't even *know* for sure who they're invested in, and then admit they don't really care. They're attracted to profitable companies and in many cases this refers to corporations without a conscience.

Let's face it, when companies cave to the ultimatum of greedy stockholders fixed on short-term gains, the long-term consequences are devastating. Unsuspecting workers are terminated, communities are dismantled as production moves to another country where labor is cheap, and the earth is compromised through hazardous, environmentally damaging practices. You owe it to yourself, and your community, to find out who they are. It's called ethical investing.

Anti-Cranky Alternatives for Cranky Quiz Item # 9: Taking Stock

You Are More Than Your Portfolio

It's nice to have a nest egg growing and working for you, but if you catch yourself trying to scan the stock quotes on the TV screen when your spouse is getting affectionate, it's time to regroup. The same applies if you do a daily calculation of how much your pension will be worth the day you retire. And last, if the only time you feel perky is on the days when your stock's about to split (or you get cranky when it doesn't), hit redial and give yourself a wake-up call! Balance can be yours, at far less a cost than the price of skewed priorities.

Support Supportive Companies

Whether investing in a company or buying its products, find out about its philosophy and way of doing business to see if it matches your value system.

- Have you had first-hand contact with this company and was it a positive experience?
- Does it manufacture a product you approve of and fully support?
- Does this company treat its workers with respect and support their well-being?
- Are goods locally produced or does it outsource its operations so it can pay cheap wages while charging a premium to customers?
- Has it recently engaged in radical downsizing despite its profitability?
- Does this company engage in what you consider responsible advertising?

As a consumer, and especially as an investor, your support is an endorsement of a company's practices (including its advertisements and how it treats employees or customers). If you disapprove of its policies or practices you may not want to do business with it. But boycotting a corporation out of principle can be wildly inconvenient and almost impossible because choices may be limited, or it's just not worth the hassle. This is one of the reasons customers stay with a bank with whom they've had a bad experience; the paperwork involved in divesting and moving on is more onerous than the nuisance of continuing to do business with it. But always consider your options and exercise them when you can.

If you hold your personal ethics in high regard and you're enjoying a high return from a particular corporation, investigate *why* it's so profitable. We know money talks, but so can our principles. In my value system I'd rather support a compassionate company with marginal returns than an uncompassionate one that makes me rich.

CRANKY QUIZ ITEM # 10:
HIDDEN COSTS

> 10. ___ Does it ever feel as if the price you pay for your lifestyle is
> too high for what you get in return?

Costs That Have Nothing To Do With Money

I once knew a scruffy, poorly dressed doctoral student who was living off the interest from an inheritance. He's the only person I've ever met who was that rich. To his credit, he didn't flaunt it, but to his detriment, he couldn't fully enjoy his wealth either. Maybe that's why he dressed as he did. This guy suffered severe health problems and I've often wondered if his internist ever played psychologist long enough to say, "Hey, just accept it. You're rich. Have a nice life!" Maybe you're thinking about how quickly you could accept the burden of great wealth if you just had the chance. I have, too. But let's talk about some hidden costs in life, some conflicts that may be eating at you in much the same way that rich, scruffy doctoral student was affected.

We know our priorities aren't expressed in what we say, but in what we do. And priorities seldom come in a perfectly matched set. Here's what I mean: When people find out I have my own business they sometimes mention how wonderful it must be to be self-employed. I remember a woman telling me she would love to have my job because of the travel and excitement of meeting new people. I explained to her that it usually meant traveling alone, staying in marginally comfortable hotel rooms, paying my own insurance and health-care costs, and having a lot of uncertainty over income. After hearing this she said, "Oh, I wouldn't like your job after all!"

Living Your Values and Loving It

Any couple who shares core values about lifestyle, money, or politics has a built-in advantage, and it's something Rob and I truly appreciate about our relationship. We both value independence over security. Early on, we joked about how it would have helped if one of us cared more about financial stability, but it's worked out just fine in the long run. We cherish our freedom and happily pay the price when there isn't much work on the books and money is short. We haven't been able to do everything we want, but maintaining a semblance of freedom has been worth the sacrifices.

Though we need a certain amount of income to sustain our lifestyle, money takes a backseat to independence, companionship, adventure, and peacefulness. Let me put it this way: Rob and I have created our own "spiritual stock market" through interpersonal risk venture. We view our relationship as a valued commodity. We've put years of work into exploring ourselves, knowing each other, and enhancing our life together.

We work to keep each other up and have profited from our efforts. Our "spiritual stock market" has flourished from hours of substantive conversations, shared experiences (both happy and sad), empathic listening, and mutual encouragement that have resulted in spiritual and intellectual growth. The counselor we worked with some twenty years ago would be proud to know our relationship has appreciated through the years!

Anti-Cranky Alternatives for Cranky Quiz Item # 10: Hidden Costs

Venture toward Your Values

Do you desire a different lifestyle and dream about it, yet you've taken no significant steps toward making it happen? Maybe you don't want to pay the price, whatever that may be. In other words, maybe your values are actually telling you something by keeping you where you are. Maybe you've let your dream appreciate to a high-inflation level, while your reality has seriously depreciated. If so, you need to rebalance these issues. Before you can either move forward or accept what you have, you need to answer the question: What do you value?

If you value freedom over security, then owning your own business could be a dream come true, as long as you were willing to pay the price. If this is the case, a perfect starter book for you is Elaine Biech's *The Business of Consulting*, which outlines the step-by-step process of starting a business of any kind. On the other hand, if you value security, then keeping your "real job" is probably the best option.

Only you know what will work best. To clarify these issues, think about the values behind your behaviors. How do you feel about independence, security, risk, status, money, creativity, structure, innovation, stability, and frugality? Investigate the areas where you feel most discontent and determine whether your restlessness is an idle distraction or a compelling dream you intend to realize, regardless of the cost (or consequences). I encourage you to clarify whether what you're dreaming about (or complaining about not having) is actually what you want. You might already be in the perfect situation, or close to it, without even realizing it.

Invest in Your Own Interpersonal Stock Market

Create your own interpersonal stock portfolio: Put the same energy you might expend in learning about stock values and investments into your personal profile. You'll profit by getting to know yourself inside and out. Pay attention to the ups and downs of your internal numbers and what might be happening in your world to make your moods fluctuate. Study yourself the same exacting way you examine the profiles of companies in which you put your money. Simply invest in the best: yourself!

Don't take your life for granted; place a high value on your time and energy. Make this a joint venture with your spouse and watch your "mutual appreciation fund" appreciate even more. In case you're thinking this is just too cute or way out there get past the wordplay. There's a substantive message here and I hope you'll be imaginative enough to try it. Take an "interpersonal risk venture" with the most precious commodity of all: your life. Include the most precious person: your lifemate. See what happens when the two of you invest in your intellectual and interpersonal capital together. You have everything to gain and nothing to lose.

A DOSE OF REALITY ABOUT COST

Money is an essential element in your life and how you feel about it goes far beyond the cost of living or the price you pay for any material item. How you handle money affects your relationships with others and even your relationship with yourself. If you're saddled with more debt than you can comfortably handle, do an in-depth assessment of your money-handling patterns, both the good and the bad. Be brutally honest about what you find. Beyond the essentials, be more conscious of when you spend money, why you spend it, and how you feel at the time. You need to understand what motivates you to spend before you can modify the behaviors that get you into trouble. Is it expectation? Entitlement? Anger? Be particularly cautious about using other people's money (credit cards, debt consolidations, or loan programs such as home equity). What looks like a good deal is indeed often a good deal, but more for the other party, not for you.

Ideally, you want to maintain a happy balance between your ability to save, your ability to spend, and your capacity for enjoying both activities. Yes, it can be hard to do this when money is limited, yet you condemn yourself to long-term crankiness by refusing to accept the reality of your income and lifestyle. There are costs in thinking that the world owes you and it's self-defeating to be resentful that some people make more money than you do. Similarly, caving to social expectations you can't afford (extravagant parties and gifts) will also get you into trouble. The solution? Quit connecting income to self-worth, or being convinced that money is the answer to what ails you.

Look for the price you pay by buying into the chronic sense of discontent instigated by the Expectation Machine. Figure out if you use income or material possessions to measure your self-worth, or if you run yourself into debt to keep up appearances or gain recognition. Here's the point: If you're hung up on *looking* successful, you're not really successful.

If you find yourself frequently depressed, worried, or cranky because you can't afford your current lifestyle, it's time to revisit your core values and priorities. *Just as we might eat for reasons other than hunger, we also spend money for motives other than need. If* you've ever pigged out on bad food as a form of self-contempt please know you can spend money out of self-contempt. This idea is worth serious consideration, especially if you engage in occasional (or frequent) reckless spending bursts that blow your budget all to hell and leave you feeling empty and angry afterward.

Examine the attitudes you've internalized about money, status, saving, spending, and gift giving. Whether you feel affluent or impoverished, rich or enriched, has as much to do with your state of mind as the actual measurement of your income or wealth. You'll profit by spending some serious time thinking about how money fits into your life and the interpersonal costs you might be paying that have nothing to do with numbers.

Competition

A MULTITUDE OF DEMANDS
AMONG DWINDLING RESOURCES

In our yard there are several bird feeders we keep stocked all year long. We love watching the birds swoop in for food; each species has its own way of dealing with the competition. Chickadees, for example, fly to the feeder and take only one sunflower seed at a time, retreating to a branch where they crack and consume their tasty booty. Goldfinches flock to the thistle feeder, all eating at the same time, with occasional flurries of friction. Then there are the boisterous blue jays who travel in groups, assaulting the feeders, driving off all the other birds. They wildly rake through the seed with their bills, throwing it every which way. After several minutes of greedily filling their gullets, they noisily fly away. The smaller birds slowly return to pick through the spoils.

In many ways, the feeder activity in our yard mimics the competitive activities found in a free-enterprise society, with examples ranging from elegant thrift to abject greed. Competition rules. It abounds from the roadways to the workplace, home to hobby, and back again. Our personal lives are tremendously affected by relentless business competition; the constant battles for growth, better positioning, and higher profits. Competition is what has made the United States a great nation and it's also our undoing.

We are all affected by the unceasing drive for profit and market dominance, as witnessed by career instability, higher costs, fewer consumer choices, a volatile Wall Street, mergers, hostile takeovers, downsizing, and a widening gap between the haves and the have-nots. The expectation behind these behaviors implies a scarcity mentality; that there's never enough. More is better. More is necessary. Is it?

If bigger is better, why are companies downsizing and cutting back on services in the midst of unprecedented profits? Who benefits from merger mania when it reduces our choices as consumers? And who are the losers when the corporate drive for *bigger, better, faster, more, now* encourages greed instead of good business practices? Do we have too many "corporate" blue jays and too few chickadees?

COMPETITION AND THE CHANGED CORPORATE CONTRACT

Market competition has indeed changed how we live and do business. Not so many years ago, workers could spend their entire career in one job with one employer. "The Corporate Contract" was an unspoken agreement of longevity and mutual benefit between employer and employee. That's unheard of today in our mobile society, where people change jobs with the same ease as they change cars, and employers change terms of employment—and retirement—with little warning and less apology. Call it the "new loyalty," or lack of it; this attitude has certainly had an impact on the way we do business today.

COMPETITION AND PERSONAL COMPULSIONS

Of course, competition doesn't exist only in business, we feel its effects in all other aspects of our lives. Sociologists write about competitive consumerism and our ceaseless attempts to keep up with, or outmatch those around us. Our compulsion to collect, accumulate, and buy was reflected in the bumper stickers we saw a few years ago: "He who dies with the most toys wins." Just for perspective here, let's acknowledge that he who dies with the most toys is *dead!* Deep down, we know that wealth, spending, and ownership aren't the secrets to happiness, but that doesn't stop us from trying to do at least as well as everyone around us.

It's easy to detect the symptoms of our cultural value for competition; just watch the extremes we go to, even in pleasurable pursuits! It's not enough to be a jogger, we want to be *runners*. For the runners among us, there are marathons, and as if that's not enough, triathalons will prove we're *really* in shape. If we want to be in the elite category, we run the Ironman. Even in staying healthy, we feel the hot breath of the *bigger, better, faster, more, now* closing in on us. Walking is for slackers; if you really want to be a serious exerciser, you need equipment, a personal trainer, a health club membership, classes in aerobics, kick boxing, spinning, or whatever tends to be the latest craze. If you think competition doesn't exist in virtually every area of your life, just look around. The houses we live in; the cars we drive; the clothes we wear; the size, location, and furnishings in our offices at work; even our pets reflect our drive to measure up.

At work you can catch other aspects of personal competition. The most obvious is the constant one-upping that occurs even between friends. But people actually vie over their areas of dysfunction, too. I've seen friends argue over who has the fullest, most impossible-to-meet schedule, boasting about how busy they are and how hard it is to fit it all in. Listen to two friends trying to make a casual dinner date and it quickly starts sounding like a comical, complicated skit, reminiscent of "Who's on First?" Small wonder we suffer from bouts of crankiness when even what we do for fun has to be tightly slotted into a schedule or evaluated in terms of what other people might think. It's as if the word *enough* has lost all meaning.

Competition can be a subtle driver and it starts early. By kindergarten, kids can discern who's good-looking or popular and who's not. A few years later and the seeds of peer pressure have firmly taken root. As if that's not enough, new parents feel the pressure, too. Before their baby has cut its first tooth, ambitious parents are already mapping out this child's future, knowing they're already wait-listed for the best day care facility. From there, they and other harried parents frantically lay the groundwork so they can find the most suitable college this lucky baby will attend some eighteen years from now.

This chapter will help you sort through both the obscure and obvious undercurrents of competition in your workplace and personal life. You'll find many suggestions that will help reduce the competitive pressures you're experiencing, personally and professionally, as you strive to find your rightful place in our touchy, turbulent world.

Cranky Quiz

COMPETITION

Scoring the Cranky Quiz

Score 1 point for every *yes* and 0 for every *no*. Count a *sometimes* as a *yes*. Add your total: 3 points or less (Cool) means you're in good shape, 4 to 7 (Warm) indicates a need to slow down, and 8 to 10 (Hot!) indicates a raging cranky infection. You'll find anti-cranky solutions for each quiz item in this chapter.

1. ___ Does your employer expect you to work longer hours with no extra benefits of any kind?

2. ___ Has your employer downsized, reorganized, outsourced, merged, or changed its pension plan in the last few years?

3. ___ Is there more competition in your field of work than there used to be?

4. ___ Do you observe commonplace rudeness and a general lack of courtesy at work?

5. ___ If you take time off are you concerned that someone else might edge in on your job in your absence?

6. ___ Do you frequently bring work home?

7. ___ Do undercurrents of competition sneak into your work or personal relationships?

8. ___ When attending a concert or game do you tune out at the halfway point, trying to figure out the best way to beat the crowd when it's time to leave?

9. ___ Does it seem that wherever you go, you're always competing with somebody else for time, space, service, products, or attention?

10. ___ Do you have mixed feelings about competition, sometimes avoiding it, other times getting carried away?

Cranky Quotient _____

My competition condition is (*circle one*) Cool Warm Hot!

EVERYBODY'S AFTER SOMETHING

Revisiting the World of Bigger, Better, Faster, More, Now

We all feel the effects of corporate competition. If the marketplace isn't shifting, the culture is. If management isn't instituting some new practice, product, or marketing approach, it's thinking about it, or recovering from the last attempt. If a company isn't acquiring some other enterprise, it's a target for one of its competitors. That's the nature of competition and everyone is affected, private and public sector alike. We've metamorphosed into a global economy where a scarcity of resources or a significant monetary setback on one side of the planet has an impact on the other side. The results of such intense competition have been just short of earth shaking for many of us: downsizing, reorganizing, outsourcing, merging, overtaking, privatizing, capsizing.

In a world of higher costs and intensified competition, public sector agencies and educational institutions have adapted a new survival strategy: trying to mimic corporate structure. In the eighties my state government clients made a major shift in their language: citizens and clients became "customers." Since that time state agencies and schools have been busy drafting mission statements and strategic plans while redefining lines of accountability. This was a necessary move, for they, too, had begun facing competitors that didn't exist just a few years ago: each other! Not only did they watch their funding pie shrink, they also, out of necessity, began targeting some of the same limited client populations. This unhappy predicament resulted in competition among agencies that had previously worked together in an atmosphere of cooperation.

Just Holding Your Own

We're trying to carve out our space, too. The disheartening news is that continual competition is a necessity in today's work world, *just to maintain* our positions. It's not enough to do a good job. There's that extra mile to run; that enduring effort we must expend so we can simply hold our own. Once in a while we get to stand in the winner's circle, but all of a sudden, someone else has edged us out and we're back on the track, running like hell, looking for a strategic spot to occupy. This means you'll sometimes come to work when you're sick. You'll show up when you're tired. And sometimes you'll be sick and tired! This is why you feel cranky or frustrated from time to time. This is life today in the fast lane and your first order of business is to find the pace that will work for you.

By all indicators we can plan on this pattern to continue. Every day, with unrelenting regularity, we vie with others for recognition, secure employment, personal space on the road and elsewhere, food, goods, services, time, attention, and maybe even potential lovers in the personal ads. How could we *not* be cranky with all this constant positioning and elbowing going on? It's like the infinite redundancy of the cartoon where a guy is watching TV and on the screen is a guy watching TV and on his screen is the same picture, and so on. Competition exists at virtually every level of our lives.

Overworked and Worked Over

Personally and professionally, it takes a lot of effort just to hold our own. Despite the optimistic predictions of futurists who have consistently (and erroneously) predicted shorter work weeks over the last forty years, author Juliet Schor says we're working more and enjoying it less, and that salaried employees are hit the hardest. In her book, *The Overworked American*, Schor states that today's working adults average only $2^1/_2$ hours of free time per day. No wonder we feel overloaded, time compressed, and disconnected! And although more men are helping out on the home front these days, employed mothers are still hit the hardest, with their second full-time job beginning the moment they walk through their own front door.

CRANKY QUIZ ITEM # 1:
MORE WORK, LESS SATISFACTION

1. ___ Does your employer expect you to work longer hours with no extra benefits of any kind?

Open for Business

We used to joke about "banker's hours" but even financial institutions are now expanding their business day so customers can do their banking before and after work. Doctors, dentists, and health clinics have done the same. Some insurance companies have increased their hours of operation with claim departments providing nonstop access for policyholders and service centers open twenty-four hours a day, seven days a week. I consider the intent commendable, but as a business consultant I find it worrisome because expanded hours infringe on employee needs. In fact, they also infringe on a customer's time, too. Customers have no "days off" anymore.

Imagine receiving a phone call on Sunday afternoon only to be asked if you're happy with the service you've been receiving. I can just hear you saying, "I was *very* happy with your service until now—I can't believe you're interrupting my personal time to ask this question!" Telemarketers, another subject entirely, prove every day how little value they place on our time, but those with whom we already do business tread a fine line between exceptional service and outright annoyance. I don't pretend to have an easy answer for this dilemma. It's hard to make everybody happy. Even service is a game of give and take, and for both customers and employees, when is enough *enough?*

Anti-Cranky Alternatives for Cranky Quiz Item # 1:
More Work, Less Satisfaction
Balance Employee Needs and Customer Needs

As a consultant, I'm convinced that satisfied employees give good service and dissatisfied employees don't. As for extra work hours for the sake of increased service, I know that workers get frustrated when it's all give on their part, and all take on the side of the company. If you're a manager and your organization is demanding more and more from its employees, there needs to be fair exchange somewhere or morale will plunge.

Everyone has a breaking point and people will hold back (some will leave) if they feel taken advantage of. Think of the direct effect on customers. Look for indicators of discontent before the situation hits a crisis point. Give something back to those on whom the organization depends: employees. *They will tell you how to treat them if you're willing to listen.* The sad news is that the cranky managers don't care. Some have told me so. I like to think they're the exception, and among my clients, they are. Meanwhile, make it easy for your employees to help you gain and maintain a competitive edge.

Turn the Problem over to Those Affected by It

One of my clients, an executive, instituted a series of focus group meetings during a period of intense organizational restructuring. He facilitated meetings with employees who had been moved to a new building, encouraging them to raise issues of concern so they could prioritize and address them. Tough questions were asked and answered, first about the changes the company was initiating, and then about logistics. One of the first issues, van pooling, was immediately addressed. Actions were promptly taken on other priority items (vending machines, access to medical services, and picnic tables for outdoors). Based on comments and feedback, the company even modified a work hours policy it had initiated only two months before.

One department created its own work life issues committee and the benefits were immediate. With extensive input from peers, the committee devised a complex work schedule to accommodate new extended business hours. There were three shifts that had to be covered by five teams (five members on a team), but two of the teams were incomplete. There was a required minimum number of employees who had to be accessible by phone during each shift and it would be necessary to keep at least one or two support staff on board at all times. No one would have the same set hours every day, and at least one day per week each employee would "swing" to another shift.

This meant that on appointed days, employees would come in earlier than usual, and other days they'd work later to accommodate extended evening hours. They could now expect to work some weekends and holidays too. Many of these employees were parents and had family obligations or day care arrangements to consider. Some of them were in the van pool. Others were now traveling a longer distance since moving to the new facility.

Creating a schedule to meet so many legitimate needs had seemed an impossible task to me (and the managers), but by working cooperatively (interviewing each individual and discussing the schedule demands ahead of time) and minimizing the competitive aspects (asking everyone to be as flexible as possible), the committee came up with a schedule that everyone was willing to follow. Imagine the "buy-in" that results when people get to generate their own solutions! You could probably benefit from a similar approach in your workplace; it takes the heat off managers, places power in the hands of employees, increases trust at all levels, and results in a more solid, satisfied team.

Don't Sink: Establish "You, Inc."

Maybe you're not a manager and have no say. Maybe you're in a "golden handcuffs" situation as described in chapter 5 and you can't immediately bail out of a bad system. Don't let your spirit get beaten: establish *You, Inc.* From now on, pretend you're in business for yourself. Don't tell anyone about it, but let *You, Inc.* be your personal inspiration for good performance: Run your job the way you'd run your own business. You'll build your work skills, preserve your reputation, and better position yourself for a transfer or new job when things change. While you're at it, read *How to Be the Person Successful Companies Fight to Keep* by Connie Podesta and Jean Gatz. The authors make an important distinction between what it means to be employed and *employable.*

Determine how employable you are. I recently spoke with a woman who had no idea about what *You, Inc.* meant, but she had lived it. She had just left a job she hated, but none of her coworkers (or customers) had a clue. She had disciplined herself to come in with a smile and leave in a good mood. She left that position under the best of terms. Face it. People talk. It's unnerving how word gets around; it doesn't pay to be a complainer. In this competitive work world, crankiness could be your undoing. You owe it to yourself to do a good job, even if you're in a bad system.

CRANKY QUIZ ITEM # 2:
UP WITH PROFITS, DOWN WITH PEOPLE

> 2. ___ Has your employer downsized, reorganized, outsourced, merged, or changed its pension plan in the last few years?

The Price of Profitability

Do more with less. This phrase sets people's teeth on edge, especially those who have experienced downsizing. Most of the workers terminated this last decade were everyday people like you and me who gave honest effort in exchange for their wages. Many were valuable, experienced employees, but as retirement loomed in their future, these workers were viewed as more of a liability than an asset. Why pay a pension year after year when you can rid yourself of the burden? Buy them out. Force them out.

Review the list of corporations who waged the largest personnel cutbacks in our country and feel the chill when you realize that thousands of people were let go *in the middle of record profits*, and it's still happening. Michael Moore's *Downsize This!* offers an illuminating account of this social and economic calamity. For years, Moore has cataloged the decline of his hometown, Flint, Michigan, as it suffered systematic cutbacks by General Motors. Maybe you saw where it all began with his unusual documentary, *Roger and Me*. Living within forty miles of Flint my entire life and growing up in a GM family, I can identify.

When a major employer chooses to outsource or close a plant the consequences are immense. Entire communities decline with little hope of recovery. Families suffer; marriages break up; people become ill. Crime and domestic violence increase. Countless lives are ruined so a few stockholders can enjoy higher profits and already overpaid executives can increase their salaries.

Those who do survive this slash-and-burn policy take on double duty. Not only do they absorb more work, they're expected to adjust immediately. *Ironically, in most organizations, when emotional needs are the greatest, support and reinforcement are at their lowest*. How absurd that people are expected to remain productive as they simultaneously heave a sigh of relief, mourn for those who are gone, and stifle the guilt they feel for being spared. Business as usual? I don't think so.

How much is enough when it comes to profit, power, or market share? As thousands of people are let go, CEOs simultaneously increase their salaries. In some corporations, workers endure pay cuts to safeguard their jobs, being promised further compensation when the company again becomes profitable. Many companies then renege on this commitment. Wasn't that one of the issues behind the 1998 Northwest strike?

More Corporate Crankiness

Where will it end? The ever-besieged airlines are beginning to draw their own crosshairs in the middle of their logos, shooting themselves in the nose wheel, as it were. In the midst of peak profits one of the majors has just announced they're cutting back on food service once again. If they get away with it, the rest will follow suit.

Air rage may be a problem, but it also exists in reverse and nobody's talking about it. Do you feel the undercurrents of contempt from airlines and their employees? Delta's offer of a $2.00 discount to customers who sidestep travel agents and book their own flights via the Internet mimics the bullying blue jay behavior that I witness in our yard every day. Are the airlines attempting to push travel agents out of the marketplace?

My travel agent, Bev, has always been my ally. When push comes to shove with the airlines or car rental outfits, I never have to wonder whose interest Bev is looking out for. Will this profession one day be a thing of the past because insatiable stockholders would stop at nothing short of *bigger, better, faster, more, now?* There are probably other examples around us where services are endangered or disappearing right before our eyes, but we haven't noticed yet, and those responsible aren't talking about it.

Anti-Cranky Alternatives for Quiz Item # 2:
Up with Profits, Down with People
Learn the Difference between Acceptance and Approval

If you're a victim of downsizing, it's a long, hard road to recovery. Note I didn't say *back*. Things may never be the same, especially if you enjoyed a high income. Knowing that things will be different makes adjusting very difficult, but eventually you have to come to a level of acceptance so you can move on. Keep in mind, this doesn't mean you have to *approve* of it.

In his unusual, in-your-face book, *The Unfair Advantage*, Dr. Tom Miller makes an intelligent distinction between acceptance and approval. Miller helped me realize it's possible to accept a less than perfect situation *without* having to approve of it, helping me adjust to circumstances I might have otherwise resisted or rebelled against in a self-defeating way. For me, the existence of domestic violence represents a constant gnawing at my soul. That some women and children live in an environment of constant fear and cruelty brings me to tears. There's no way I can approve of this deplorable behavior but I must accept that it exists. I volunteer my time at the local domestic shelter and donate my speaking honoraria to this cause.

Thanks to Miller's insightful distinction between acceptance and approval I was able to move beyond my disapproval and into action. Maybe it will help you, too, in any area in which you feel conflicted. You can say to yourself, "I don't like this. It shouldn't have happened. It's unfair. I disapprove." Yet, you can still accept the reality and move on. It may sound paradoxical, but you can both disapprove of, *and* accept the same situation.

After discussing this issue, one of my seminar participants said his nineteen-year-old-daughter has two large tattoos on her back and she sports a nose ring. He accepted her right to do this, but as her father, he definitely didn't approve! *A major life upheaval is a far more serious issue, but it's still the same process. Separating acceptance and approval shortens your recovery process.* Whether you're struggling with a job loss or some other tough circumstance, this simple distinction will help you make peace and move on. I also recommend *How to Survive the Loss of a Love* by Harold Bloomfield, Melba Colgrove, and Peter McWilliams. This book isn't just about death, it's about losing anything you seriously care about.

Take One Step at a Time down the Road to Recovery

Other than serious illness, injury, or death of a loved one, job loss looms as one of the grimmest predicaments we can face, because it involves all aspects of our well-being: money, personal identity, security, self-esteem, relationships, even health. If and when it does happen, it's self-defeating to project too far into the future: your best strategy is to take one day at a time. The first step is to release your anger and indignation so you can begin the healing process. This doesn't mean taking out your frustration on others. It simply means allowing yourself to admit how you feel. Yes, it's unfair. It's hard. And it will take time. No, it shouldn't have happened, but it *did*.

When you're ready (or maybe just before you feel ready), start looking for income possibilities, even temporary employment. The

"Law of Opposites" tells us that when you most need to be confident you will feel your most insecure, so you may have to force yourself to take the first steps. And when you most need to appear positive you may feel your most negative, but smile anyway. This is a good time to sink your teeth into some Reality Bites. Keep a tight lid on your stress and let your emotional immune system keep you from losing perspective. These constructive, one-step-at-a-time activities will help you heal your aching spirit.

Rebuild Your Résumé as You Rebuild Your Life

Losing a job may feel like the end of the world, but hang on to your hope. Although it feels like the worst possible time, you need to create (or update) your résumé. With an eye on possible positions that might work for you (stretch the limits a bit), list all of your work-relevant experience, and then write a skill summary that reflects the specific *work skills* you've developed through the years. You'll feel better about yourself when you see this list on paper. Truthfully embellish your strengths.

Next come your *transferable traits*. These are personality characteristics you possess that set you apart from others: innate skills and abilities that transfer from job to job such as creativity, patience, the ability to organize ideas, a good sense of humor, or the ability to handle pressure. Ask your spouse what he or she sees in you. If you think it would help, find an outplacement counselor. It's hard engaging in this kind of exercise when you feel down, but it can help rebuild your bruised ego.

Help Yourself

Sit down and list the priorities in your life—that is, what you hold dear—and read this list whenever you need a moment of encouragement. Read your skill summary frequently to bolster your confidence. Avoid negative people. Talk with survivors of downsizing who "right sized" into a good or even better situation. I can't list how many people who, years after being terminated, have told me, "It was the best thing that ever happened to me." Though they initially viewed their job loss as a crisis, many of them in fact ended up with better jobs. Some became consultants. Others who found less lucrative employment discovered how much they'd hated the job they'd lost, and they wouldn't go back for anything.

One thing all of these people had in common was that in the midst of their crisis it was hard to envision anything ever being right in their lives again. If you reach a point where you feel like giving up, give it just one more try instead. Reflect on the "rich" part of your life: health and relationships. Review the parts of this book you've found most insightful, and above all, commit to putting these ideas into practice. They work!

CRANKY QUIZ ITEM # 3: NEW CONTENDERS

> 3. ___ Is there more competition in your field of work than there used to be?

Educating Ourselves About the Competition

One of my favorite clients, a public school superintendent, recently called to ask if I'd help institute a district-wide program emphasizing customer service for teachers and staff in order to compete better with their latest market threat: schools of choice and charter schools. My first thought was that overworked and underpaid teachers would have to take time away from their lesson plans and enrichment projects to learn about marketing and service strategies.

These teachers (like people in other professions) are being asked to take on something they've never had to do before. Competition complicates our lives by adding new responsibilities with few to no added resources, and definitely no extra compensation. This at least takes the mystery out of where some of our workplace crankiness comes from, doesn't it?

Anti-Cranky Alternatives for Quiz Item # 3: New Contenders

Know and Nurture the Nature of Your Business

Let's cover the bad news first. You have to understand the nature of the business you're in. Remember the classic example of railroads thinking they were in the railroad business, not the *transportation* business? If market competition changes the nature of your job (as with these teachers) you have to adapt. If you refuse, you could end up on the street. It's not necessarily that you'd be fired, but your employer could be taken out by the competition. Understanding the nature of your work makes it easier for you to accept its new complexity. Absolutely refuse to get cranky over this issue; channel your energy into resilient action instead.

Now here's the good news. At least a few of the new skills you'll build as the nature of your business changes are probably things you should have been doing all along (such as the teachers practicing good customer service).

Do you know the nature of the business you're in? You find it by focusing on the *results* of what you do rather than the process. For example, teachers may think they're in the education business but they're actually in the business of endowing knowledge, cognition, and independence in children and young adults, preparing them for their roles as future citizens of our country. The better you understand the nature of your work the easier it will be to nurture it: Take the emphasis away from the job description and focus on the *results*.

Add and Subtract

Here's another note of comfort. As you add new dimensions to your work you'll probably find a few activities that no longer apply, so as your responsibilities broaden, look for tasks that have become unnecessary and leave them behind.

Organizational change can cause people to feel isolated and alienated, but that doesn't have to happen. Transition teams help all the staff go through the process together. They can gain experience and learn from one another. Using our example of teachers one last time, they could organize service teams, perhaps including selected parents or community members with an interest in school improvement and service enhancement.

They could launch special public meetings and create publications, making the efforts visible to district residents. The point? There's always some kind of positive action that can be taken instead of wasting our energy resisting the inevitable. Look at it this way; if the street has been cordoned off, join the parade. This makes you look like a real team player, and hey, it never hurts to earn a gold star for good performance!

CRANKY QUIZ ITEM # 4:
AN UNCIVIL ACTION

> 4. ___ Do you observe commonplace rudeness and a general lack of courtesy at work?

Hot Collars and Cold Climates
I grew up in a self-conscious world that refused to admit that TV or movie characters had bladders, but today, on the screen and off, we now hear public pronouncements that someone is going to take a pee. The lines between private talk and public talk have blurred so completely there are almost no limits on what one might hear anytime, anywhere. Even at work, we let it all hang out. From corporate execs to unhappy customers, we could just as easily be sitting on the bleachers at a ball field as in a business office.

It's not unusual to hear managers grumble, customers yell, or work colleagues snipe at one another. A cheerful "Good morning" may be met with a cranky "What's good about it?" I always look for competitive posturing when I work with sales reps and I'm seldom disappointed. Depending on the culture, their teasing ranges from good-natured ("Hey, don't you owe me a lunch for that lead I gave you last week?") to mean-spirited ("I knew I could count on your numbers to make me look good!").

Crankiness doesn't crop up just within work teams though: A friend of mine, while booking a flight, was appalled at the price. Looking for sympathy, he said to the ticket agent, "Wow, this fare is really expensive!" and she replied, "If you don't like it, take the bus!" There used to be a bumper sticker that read, "We don't care, we don't have to." Originally it was aimed at the telephone company but today the airlines may have picked up the honor.

Back to Basics
If you're sitting in a staff meeting and feel as if you're dodging slings and arrows, look at your watch. If it's morning, remind your-

self that some of your cranky coworkers might still be reeling from their recent brushes with road rage. Just as we need to push our Reset Button several times a day, we also need constant reminders to revisit the now almost uninhabited land of "common courtesy." Of course, you can't *force* others to behave in a more civil manner, but maybe you can be the catalyst behind reintroducing respect into your workplace.

The best way to begin is with your own example. Later on, perhaps you can suggest that your work team draft its own Code of Conduct for how you want to treat one another. Developing such a code is a powerful exercise. I've facilitated the process with township officials, committees of all types (including the work life committee that developed the challenging work schedule), volunteer boards, and customer service teams. This exercise has never failed! It leaves people with a concrete sense of purpose and positive actions to employ.

Anti-Cranky Alternatives for Cranky Quiz Item # 4: An Uncivil Action

Begin within to Create a Kinder, Gentler Workplace
The logical beginning for turning the tide from crankiness to courtesy is within yourself. You may be crankier than you think, or at least perceived that way by the people around you. For the next two days, closely monitor yourself.

- Do you treat others in a friendly manner when you arrive at work or leave for home?
- Do you appear friendly (face, vocal tone) when speaking to customers or coworkers?
- Do you tend to use positive words (*challenge, opportunity, yes, I'll give it a try*) rather than negative ones (*problem, obstacle, no, I can't do that*)?
- Are you more likely to compliment than criticize people?
- When a mix-up occurs do you look for solutions rather than someone to blame?
- Is it more like you to take responsibility than pass the buck?
- When coworkers need a sounding board do they tend to seek you out?

- When you leave work are you focused on the good things you did rather than the bad things that happened to you?

You can imagine that monitoring these behaviors requires self-awareness. Some people worry they'll turn into a robot if they pay such close attention, but in truth, the opposite happens. The higher your self-awareness, the more natural it will feel to respond appropriately, to ward off those embarrassing knee-jerk responses you'll regret later.

Self-monitoring makes you more adept at reading people, too. As you note subtle shifts in vocal tone, facial expressions, or mood, you can immediately respond to these cues, asking "Did I explain myself clearly enough?" when someone looks confused or "Was it something I said?" when a person looks upset. *The person who controls the language controls the situation.* Self-awareness helps you say the right thing at the right time and prevents you from saying something that might prompt crankiness in others.

Purge the Surge: Take Anger 101

Under certain circumstances our crankiness can leap over the line. Since the mid-nineties, anger management programs have been springing up around the United States in response to people's outbursts at work (and on the road). If you often find yourself gritting your teeth, making fists, or feeling your heart wildly thumping from adrenaline surges when something goes wrong, you're a prime candidate for such a class.

Whenever you feel a rush of anger coming on, if you happen to be on your feet, immediately sit down. Head off the surge by taking a deep, relaxing breath all the way down to your belly button. Release the tension in your jaw, neck, and shoulders. Are your hands drawn into fists? Open them. Quickly review the thoughts that inspired your outrage. Summon all of your self-control and process this experience. Remind yourself about uncontrollables: the world is neither perfect nor fair and things won't always happen as you wish. Review the emotional immune system approach of figuring out how upset you should be and how long you should stay upset. Run through some of the Reality Bites that pertain to this specific situation. Help make your workplace as habitable as possible: Save the extreme reactions for extreme circumstances. When you get a chance, reread the EIS section in chapter 1.

Create a Code of Conduct

This is a consensus building exercise in which your work team will develop, as a group, a set of realistic behavioral guidelines you are all willing to follow. These must be actual, doable behaviors. For example, rather than writing down "Have a good attitude," you might suggest, "Smile when you say hello." You want *behaviors*, not concepts. You all must agree on every item. If you have a mission statement, make sure the code complements your mission. You can even make the Code of Conduct a self-governing document by including a strategy for how you'll handle it when someone violates the code. There are only two categories.

WE WILL   WE WILL NOT

Everyone makes his or her own list first on a separate piece of paper, and then one member "scribes" everyone's lists onto flip chart sheets for all to see. All ideas are recorded, then discussed one by one and everyone must agree before an item makes the final list. Next, each one is tweaked to make sure it's a doable, observable behavior (not just a nice concept) that everyone is willing to live with. Some items may be combined for the sake of clarity.

After the code has been finalized and agreed upon, the list is transcribed and given to every member. Encourage people to bring their codes to meetings. Mention it as you begin. One board I worked with had their code typed up and placed in a see-through plastic stand-up frame that sits on the table every time they meet.

Just the act of discussing these behaviors results in a substantive exchange. Teams walk away from this experience with a better sense of who their colleagues are and how they all fit together. People feel motivated because everyone gets actively involved in the process. They are, in effect, creating their own ground rules and establishing an environment of their choosing. Work groups can create a Code of Conduct for staff meetings, team building, customer service, or other special functions. One per team is usually enough, although a separate code for customer service standards could be valuable. I encourage work groups to consider their Code of Conduct a living document and to revisit it from time to time for possible additions, deletions, or modifications. It's a wonderful exercise and a perfect antidote for transforming a potentially cranky workplace into a more courteous, civil one.

CRANKY QUIZ ITEM # 5:
WHAT, ME WORRY?

> 5. ___ If you take time off are you concerned that someone else might edge in on your job in your absence?

The Firings Will Continue until Morale Improves

The posters and cartoons on people's office walls reveal a lot about their attitudes and the culture in which they work. I first saw the quotation about firings while working with a company in the middle of a major downsizing. I smiled when I saw it but took the message to heart because disapproval or contempt often lurks beneath witticisms. This might inspire you to scan your own work-space collection if you have one, and consider what you're telling customers, coworkers, your boss, or top management about you.

What I call the "nasty nineties" left a mark on our workplaces in the form of longer hours and new responsibilities without benefit of added compensation. Most of us have felt we must just accept this as the way it is. Perhaps you feel the hot breath of ambitious colleagues hovering over you, eager to work longer and harder to get ahead. Sadly, women who take extended maternity leave (or even those who request it and are refused) often sacrifice future promotions because they get labeled as "not serious" about their careers. The same can happen to men who opt for family leave. Some workers have given up taking long vacations because they worry about being replaced while they're away. Those who do take time off frequently travel with pagers, laptops, and cell phones so they can stay in touch. With pressures like this, how could productivity, service, and morale *not* suffer?

Culture Shock

In reading this book you've become aware of the subtle ways the Expectation Machine influences how we see the world. Maybe this knowledge has already prompted you to assess the assumptions you hold about your job. Most workplaces are so unstable these days you can't expect a long, smooth ride, and just as it pays to know the nature of the business you're in, it helps to understand the corporate culture and politics of your organization. You don't necessarily have to be a player, but you need to at least know the rules of the game, or know someone who does.

Here's what I mean. When I was a sales rep for Xerox, I spent time with my friend Carol, who understood the culture and inner workings of our company. She never disclosed her sources, but she always knew what was happening. When our branch was getting ready to introduce a new copy machine to the sales force (always a secret process), Carol knew beforehand.

Although the unveiling ceremony was a month away, she knew all the copier's specs. Speed, cost, and features. But on the day of the sales meeting, as the drape was removed from the new copier, Carol dropped her jaw as if she were the most surprised person in the room. Management never suspected. Without my savvy friend, I wouldn't have had the foggiest notion of what was going on.

Anti-Cranky Alternatives for Cranky Quiz Item # 5: What, Me Worry?

Develop Your System Savvy

You can measure how close you are to the information loop by how often you're surprised. If you know about trends, changes, and new products or strategies before they're formally introduced you're well networked. If you're often surprised, you need to buddy up with an information source like my friend Carol (note I said *friend*; this process isn't merely sucking someone dry). You also need a support colleague, a trusted coworker with whom you can discuss work issues without having to worry about confidentiality. Sometimes information and support can be embodied in the same person. If you want a historical viewpoint, talk with someone about to retire or even newly retired. They're divested of internal politics and can give you a big-picture perspective.

Take people to lunch. There's always a time limit so you don't have to feel prevailed upon, and it's fascinating what people will tell you when you spring for the tab. If you're short on networking skills, read *How to Work a Room* and *What Do I Say Next?* by Susan RoAne. You'll develop a genuine skill for connecting with others.

Level the Playing Field
You can thrive in an environment you understand, or barely survive in one that baffles you. Just as you wouldn't wear a pair of dress shoes for a hike in the Grand Canyon, or hiking boots to an important business meeting, you need to understand your work climate. As an outside consultant, I always conduct a quick assessment of a client's culture as a first step in working together.

Some years ago I was asked to present a seminar for physicians and administrators of a large, nationally known hospital. In our hour-long planning meeting, my contact person spent forty-five minutes telling me about the hospital's culture and fifteen minutes on proposed content. That told me everything I needed to know about the institution's highly political culture and I designed my program accordingly. It was a big hit. Here are eight questions to help you better comprehend your corporate culture:

- Who are the people driving the decision making—the formal and informal leaders?
- Which behaviors and practices are encouraged and which are discouraged?
- Do people feel free to chat, discuss work problems, laugh, and enjoy light moments?
- Do people generally put more energy into politics than producing results?
- Are employees generally well informed or are they kept in the dark?
- Is two-way negative feedback and constructive criticism accepted or discouraged?
- Do customer complaints result in positive changes and improved systems?
- Are employees treated with consideration or disrespect?

Understand your work culture. Although in some instances, one person can make a difference, it's self-defeating to fight a hostile culture alone. It's even more futile to spend all your time wishing it were different. The next time you switch jobs, carefully interpret whatever you're told. I like to think that interviewing for a job is a lot like buying a horse; it isn't always what the seller says, it's what the seller *doesn't* say that's significant. Listen to words, tones, and undertones. Spend a few minutes in the cafeteria alone and eavesdrop. Pay attention to what people hang on the walls so you have an inkling of the culture and whether it's the right fit for you.

CRANKY QUIZ ITEM # 6:
HOME WORK

6. ___ Do you frequently bring work home?

Taking Your Work Home with You

Maybe you remember the thrill of buying your first official briefcase and how proud you felt while marveling at the smoothness of the leather and its delicate smell. You felt like a real adult. That same treasure, now weather-beaten and fatigued, overstuffed with papers, file folders, and documents, represents an albatross that migrates with you from work to home and back again. If you're simply carting this dead weight back and forth without actually touching it, quit going through the motions. On the other hand, if "home work" has become a way of life, you need to stop and smell the Wite-Out.

Anti-Cranky Alternatives for Cranky Quiz Item # 6:
Home Work
Do That "Priority Thing" Again

Competition can get the best of you. If you get too sucked up in its wake you lose your perspective, and this can certainly happen with work. Remember priorities and the perils of dis-Connectedness? Set a time limit on how long you'll work (or when) and stick to it. There's a difference between occasional flurries of extra work and daily occurrences. If your loved ones have a startled look in their eyes when you walk in the door, it's time to get reacquainted. Is any career truly worth the price of personal relationships?

It isn't always the literal work we take home with us, by the way;

sometimes we carry the residue of other people's crankiness. Whatever form it may take, physical or emotional, be extremely selective about what you bring from your workplace to the inside of your home. Your family deserves the best of you.

Turn Your Work Time Around

Many people avoid the "home work" bind by making small changes in their schedules. Some people go to work an hour early because there's no one around to disturb them. Others take their lunch hour at one o'clock instead of noon. They get a lot done between noon and one because there are fewer people around to interrupt them and they receive few calls during that time because it's presumed they're out. When they come back from lunch at two o'clock, the post-lunch phone call flurry is over, and they can return the calls at their convenience, without being interrupted.

CRANKY QUIZ ITEM # 7:
COLLEGIAL COMPETITION

> 7. ___ Do undercurrents of competition sneak into your work or personal relationships?

Teamwork by the Seat of the Pants

One morning, while getting dressed for work, I grabbed a new pair of panties I had bought on impulse at an outlet mall because of the wide, lacy waistband. I stepped into them and noticed a thread, which I immediately and irresistibly pulled. A split second later, I stood clad in only a wide, lacy waistband! One swift motion made the difference between my being covered or exposed.

Later that day in a team building session, it occurred to me that it's a very delicate thread that unites a team. The connections between one person and another can be influenced by the most unconscious action. If the thread that runs through the team gets compromised by one person, the team's entire backside may become exposed.

Trying to Keep Up

But teamwork can be a hard value to instill. In theory, people are supposed to happily join up and direct their efforts against the competition, but in reality employees compete with one another over parking spots, equipment time, conference rooms, office space, furniture, and even job titles. Departments compete for status and budgets. Workers vie for the boss's attention or approval, try to outdo one another, or withhold privileged information to maintain a slight edge. Some say this kind of positioning keeps people sharp, but it can also spark sabotage, turf wars, and politics.

Competition sneaks into our personal lives, too. In chapter 4 we discussed family dynamics and as much as we'd like to think we outgrow our need for acceptance or recognition, long-term rivalries still exist among grown siblings.

Watch for undercurrents of competition in your friendships, too, from good-natured joking to mean-spirited one-upping. If you mention buying a new set of golf clubs and one of your pals either suggests you paid too much or bought the wrong brand, that's competition raising its prickly little head. A little bit of teasing is fine, but constant testing, subtle put-downs, or a refusal to validate you are indicators of a one-sided friendship. You're not the one with the problem; your friend is.

Anti-Cranky Alternatives for Cranky Quiz Item # 7: Collegial Competition

Keep an Eye on the Future

Long, enduring friendships (and occasionally love and marriage) result from work affiliations. Calculate the number of hours we spend with our work team, and it makes sense we'd want to get along. Interpersonal competitions foster crankiness, distract us from our job, and have the potential of escalating into ugly episodes. One of the best pieces of corporate advice I've ever heard is "Make no enemies: in this turbulent world, one day you could end up reporting to the person you least like." Yet people will bait and challenge you. It's hard to keep your cool when your collar's heating up. The three steps of RPM from chapter 2 can apply to cranky coworkers, too:

- Restrain yourself from immediately responding when someone makes a caustic comment.

- Pull away mentally so you don't let your ego get dragged into an argument.
- Monitor what your face and body are doing so you look calm and in control.

The hard truth is that you will have to work with a few people who have an emotional allergy to cooperation and civility. Be nice anyway. Work on your emotional immune system and Reality Bites skills when surrounded by troublesome teammates. They aren't affected by your reactions, but you are. If you need people's help or cooperation to get your job done, why would you want to do something that could alienate them?

Make Your Friendships Mutually Rewarding

If you have friends who criticize you, put you down, or try to pressure you to be someone you're not, ask yourself if it's worth the price. Avoid friendships that take a toll on your self-esteem or peace of mind.

CRANKY QUIZ ITEM # 8:
A JUMP ON THE CROWD

> 8. ___ When attending a concert or game do you tune out at the halfway point, trying to figure out the best way to beat the crowd when it's time to leave?

Ready, Set, Go!

A woman who attended one of my programs comes from a family of sports fans—parents and kids alike. One day, a neighbor who was taking his kids to a football game offered to take her youngest son. When the woman later asked her son how the game was, he started crying. It took a few minutes for her to figure out why. It seems the neighbor was more interested in avoiding the traffic out of the stadium than in knowing who won the game. Her son was crushed at not getting to see the end of an exciting surprise win. The neighbor's inability to be *in the moment* precluded the full enjoyment of the game not only for him, but for the kids who were with him.

Anti-Cranky Alternative for Cranky Quiz Item # 8:
A Jump on the Crowd
A Peace of the Whole

Our competitive spirit shows itself in odd ways. For example, think about the times when, at the end of a movie, you've watched people spring out of their seats and sprint for the exit before the credits start rolling. You know these people weren't fully present as they watched the end of the film; they were already somewhere else. Their brains had already left the theater while their bodies were momentarily left behind.

In chapter 2 we discussed the practice of being *in the moment* as an antidote to compressed time. Let's revisit this idea. If you decide to attend a movie, sports event, or any large gathering, accept *all* that comes with the package: the atmosphere, the energy of the crowd, the excitement of witnessing the event in person, plus your arrival and departure. I'm suggesting this attitude because the minute you lapse into worrying about your exit, you have disengaged. You're no longer a participant (even though your body is still there). My point is to go and make the best of an *entire* experience or stay at home.

Use Reality Bites to help you stay *in the moment*: I came here to enjoy this experience and I'm going to stay focused on it. I *can* do this. I knew there would be a crowd. I *accept* that. After the event is over, people will be in a hurry to leave and it will be crowded. I *acknowledge* that. People may get cranky in their rush to get out of here. I can *avoid* that by taking my time when it's over.

In effect, when you stay focused on the present, your sense of competitiveness subsides. Think about how much effort some people waste trying to get two seconds ahead of everyone else. Despite their rush, they only get so far and then they have to wait. In attending any special event that involves a huge crowd, probably half of the attendees start thinking about leaving when the event is only halfway through. If they're so fixed on leaving, why did they show up in the first place?

Think of the peace of mind you give yourself by getting fully immersed in what you're doing in *this moment*, not the next one, even if it means threading your way through a traffic queue as you leave. Walk, don't run to your car. Go to the bathroom. Finish your soda or read your program. Take your time. Watch people leave. The longer you wait, the better off you are because most of the cranky people are now already in their cars, jammed in next to one another, grumbling, trying to beat everyone else out. Congratulate yourself. You have the intelligence to choose the lane less traveled.

Focus on the gift you're giving to others, especially children, by your example: a whole, unhurried experience, with time to talk about the game and do your own instant replays as you depart *with* the crowd instead of against it.

CRANKY QUIZ ITEM # 9:
LOST IN THE SHUFFLE

> 9. ___ Does it seem that wherever you go, you're always competing with somebody else for time, space, service, products, or attention?

No Room for Cooperation Anymore

You've been circling the block in pelting rain for several minutes, searching for a parking place close to the store. You have no coat, no umbrella. You desperately need to buy a birthday cake. It will be frozen, but if it sits in the car all afternoon it will thaw. The problem is that if you don't find a parking spot in the next thirty seconds you'll have to buy the cake after work, but that means it will still be frozen when you get home.

Then, you see it. Taillights flick on, a car begins pulling out, right in front of you. As you look heavenward, muttering, "There *is* a God!" a red sports car comes from nowhere and zooms into the space, beating you out. You can't believe it. Couldn't that driver see you? Wasn't it obvious you were waiting? Don't you wish you weren't such a nice person right now?

Compare that "mean streets" mentality with a scene we happened upon in rural North Dakota last spring. There was a two-lane bridge under construction with only one open lane. On each side of the bridge sat a handmade placard with the words, "Please Take Turns." If everyone had this kind of attitude we'd feel less compelled to compete for space in line at the store, bank, pharmacy, on the road, or at work.

Anti-Cranky Alternative for Cranky Quiz Item # 9:
Lost in the Shuffle
Plan for the Worst, Give Praise When You Get the Best

An engaging radio play, *Moon over Morocco*, offered this sage advice: *Trust in Allah, but tie your camel first*. It may sound negative to suggest that you prepare for adversity, but have a Reality Bite on me. Frustrating, nagging incidents happen every day; why continue acting surprised or disappointed? People will do things that may annoy you. This is a cranky world, remember? Expect a few minor setbacks and take them in your stride. Of course you want convenience, but so does everyone else.

In reality, you *are* competing with hundreds, even thousands of people for time and space on this planet. Invariably you'll bump up against someone with similar or identical needs. You'll have to wait your turn. As our population increases, our resources become more limited. *We all can't be in the same place at the same time all getting the same thing. It's impossible.*

You'll have to wait now and then. You will occasionally be inconvenienced by other people who are getting their turns before you get yours. Take it with resolve instead of resentment. Maybe you noticed, we've cycled back to Dr. Miller's distinction between acceptance and approval.

But you'll get yours, be patient. On that fateful day when the universe says, "Next!" and it's you, when that light changes to green as you approach the intersection, or when your suitcase shows up first on the carousel after a long, tiring flight, whisper a word of thanks. You finally got your turn. There is some justice, after all!

CRANKY QUIZ ITEM # 10:
COMPETITIVE BY NATURE

> 10. ___Do you have mixed feelings about competition, sometimes avoiding it, other times getting carried away?

Competition-R-Us

As individuals we tend to value what our culture values. If our society valued cooperation rather than competition, people would behave differently in airports. They wouldn't rush to be first in line to board a plane that has assigned seating.

People would stand several feet away from luggage carousels, patiently waiting for their bags; they wouldn't crowd and hover, elbowing for space long before the plane is unloaded. They wouldn't drag their entire family up there with them, leaving vertically challenged (short) people like me at a disadvantage. Watching people express their competitive nature can be amusing when you have enough sense to not be part of the spectacle!

Competition Can Crop up Where You Least Expect It

My mother, Julie, is a quiet, friendly woman. One of her most commonly invoked phrases is "Just as long as there are no hard feelings." She's the type who seeks smooth waters and there's only one exception to this rule: If you play her in a game. I can't say it any other way; my mother is a ruthless competitor. Even my kids got sick of playing Candy Land with Grandma Julie because she couldn't stand to lose! Although Mom no longer plays Ping-Pong or badminton, she still plays a mean game of golf, pool, and backgammon. My sweet mom is a cutthroat competitor who will innocently suck you in and then stomp you, but she's so nice about it, you don't mind (unless you're under twelve).

Most of us have a competitive streak. Just watch parents on the sidelines at a soccer or basketball game. Hear them roar when they think the referee has made a bad call. Whether it's at the Little League game or the office staff meeting we all have ways of unleashing our sense of competition. That's how seemingly meek, modest folks turn into Godzilla at a moment's notice.

People show a healthy competitive spirit when they organize by work teams to meet a new quota or see which department can create the most decorative Valentine's Day or Halloween display. Some offices stage contests at work to see who can lose the most weight in an allotted time, complete with weigh-ins and prizes. Friendly competition can sprout out of the most innocent conversations, and all of a sudden people are flashing photos of their kids, grandkids, boats (and yes, maybe even horses)! It's just part of our nature.

Performance Zone or Pressure Zone?

Some of us are afraid to acknowledge our competitive side, giving up before the game even begins. Others of us can't quit playing after it's over. The healthy expression of competitive spirit puts us in the "performance zone," where we rally our mental and physical resources so we can surpass ourselves. But competition ceases to bring out our best when it undercuts our appreciation of the activity or corrupts our sense of fair play: This throws us into the "pressure zone," where we clutch and lose our focus.

At work (even more than on the playing field), it is very much to your advantage to stay in the performance zone. You'll be able to control what you say and how you say it. You won't clutch. Back on the playing field, while it's fun to beat your opponent and win the game, keep in mind that true competition always demands finesse. When you try too hard you tense up; when you don't try hard enough, you flounder. Intense focus and concentration can put you in the performance zone but, paradoxically, you can get there only by relaxing and getting into the flow. It always helps to remember that the person you're really competing against is yourself.

If, hours after a racquetball or golf game, you're still gnashing your teeth and replaying every stroke, get a grip. Hey, the game is over! Don't you do this for fun? Whatever happened to your *in the moment* skills? Sure, you want to improve, but focusing on what you did *wrong* only reinforces the negative. If you must do an instant replay, at least focus on *correct* technique, not mistakes.

Working on It

It may not help to replay how you might have blown a game, but reviewing a work discussion that didn't go well can be very productive (provided you maintain a proper outlook). Review the situation and isolate the moment where the discussion got into trouble. Trust yourself; your instincts are probably accurate. Using the conflict and communication guidelines from chapter 4, figure out what you can do to repair the situation. Keep yourself in the performance zone by focusing on positive intent: resolve to learn a lesson rather than try to teach someone else a thing or two.

As soon as possible, do whatever damage control you can. Maybe you can revisit the issue tomorrow and keep the discussion on track this time. When work colleagues are involved, don't even think about winning or losing. Think about *results*. When it comes to work relationships it's always helpful to communicate with the future in mind, and the best way to exercise your competitive spirit at work is by constantly looking for ways to be a more positive influence to others. In other words, make it easy for people to give you what you want or need from them. Seek to connect rather than compete, ask instead of tell, and compliment instead of criticize. You'll end up getting more of what you want, and so will everyone else.

Anti-Cranky Alternatives for Cranky Quiz Item # 10: Competitive by Nature

Acknowledge Your Competitive Instincts

Like my mom, you may not think of yourself as competitive, but it's a natural instinct. There's nothing wrong with it. Maybe you don't see yourself as competitive because you don't actively participate in a favorite sport or craft, consequently you have few ways to express this drive. But you might try to win an argument, outwit someone you're not crazy about, or even tell someone what you really think of him or her! Those are social expressions of the competition you don't release on a playing field. I've met a lot of young women who appear civil, meek, and quiet, yet they say road rage is a big issue for them. If your competitive instincts are there, waiting to be tapped, you have to find the appropriate channels for them.

The Best Kind of Competition

At work or in a sport, the purest, most effective form of competition is *against yourself.* Continually look for ways to raise your "personal performance bar." Resist the "comparison trap," where you compare your weaknesses with other people's strengths. The more you focus on the quality of *your* effort, the less you'll concern yourself with what others are doing. That's *real* competitive spirit, setting your own standard and living up to it. Whenever you feel yourself getting sucked into nonproductive competition with work colleagues, have the intelligence to head for the bench because this can come back to haunt you.

A DOSE OF REALITY ABOUT COMPETITION

Competition exists in virtually every area of our personal and professional lives. Free enterprise competition is what allows people with brilliant ideas or superior products to flourish in our culture. I'm even aware that my twin granddaughters, Ashley and Samantha, competed with each other for space and nourishment in their mother's womb; that's how essential it is in our world.

As with so many other things in life, competition has both an upside and downside. Competition is healthy when it drives an individual toward self-improvement, or when it propels a company toward product enhancement. But the benefits of competition cease when organizations forsake their people in the name of expediency or profit, regardless of the human price. In business, sports, or everyday life, competition tarnishes the human spirit when the only motivation is to win at all costs. When hollow victories are the only spoils, there are no winners. We all lose.

Applied in the proper amount and under appropriate circumstances, competition acts as "brain spice." It brings out your unique characteristics, intensifies your personal capabilities, and adds a tinge of excitement to your favorite activities. Of course, too much competitive spirit can leave a bad taste in everyone's mouth. There are some cranky people out there who consider every conversation, every interaction, and every contact as a competitive event. Consequently, they're always on their guard. They've lost their ability to enjoy their connections with others because they're always keeping score. They long ago sacrificed their ability to stop and smell the roses, or to savor an activity for its own sake. These people always bring their tally sheet. There's a time and a place for competition, but sometimes a conversation is just a conversation, a game is just a game, and there's no need to figure out who's ahead.

My friend Barbara Foose was once a world-class competitor in the most exciting (and dangerous) equestrian sport of three-day eventing. Barbara is still an energetic, competitive athlete who can clear a fence so beautifully it takes my breath away. She loves to compete, but today she does it for fun only. As she continues adding to a collection of ribbons and trophies that fill a room, Barbara has transferred much of her competitive spirit into a full commitment for leading a life of quality.

She states that the "real victory" is not in winning ribbons but in living a life you love.

Today Barbara is a certified equine massage therapist, performing bodywork on sport horses to help them better handle the stress of their discipline. Helping equine athletes minimize discomfort while enhancing their physical potential has become her first love, and she pursues it with the same level of passion as she did her riding career. Barbara's truck bumper sports a sticker that reads, "Whinnying Is Everything." I hope her example will help you commit your energy and competitive spirit to create a life you love.

Customer Contact

MORE PEOPLE THAN WE CAN HANDLE, MORE PRESSURE THAN WE NEED

ook at the major concerns of any business or public sector organization in the United States and customer service will be on every list. Ask consumers their top gripes about anyone they do business with, and you'll find service on their list, too. We all play a role in this thing called service whether we're giving it or getting it, and it's not always a rosy picture.

Good or bad, customer contact is a reality in our lives, and its quality (on both sides of the transaction) is influenced by the Ten Trends outlined in this book. Our lives are far more complex and complicated than they used to be and the pressure takes its toll, at work and at home. As busy, overloaded customers, we want speedy, affordable, convenient service. If we don't get what we want, we'll go to the competition, unless our choices are limited or it's too much of a hassle to switch.

It's probably no surprise to you that discord in our personal relationships can affect how we connect with people at work, and turmoil in the workplace can cause us to take a load of service stress home with us. If you're leaving the house in a good mood and coming home cranky, in all likelihood the culprit isn't the workings of alien forces, it's the quality of the people contact you've had that day.

WE CAN'T ALWAYS GET WHAT WE WANT

As consumers, we're promised a lot but those seductive images created by the Expectation Machine don't always hold up to reality and some of us get riled as a result. I remember hearing a heated exchange after a rental car agent told a couple whose long-delayed flight had just arrived that their reservation had been canceled and there were no other cars available. They stood in shock as the agent snipped, "Well, there's a big difference between four o'clock and eight o'clock. You should have called!" Breaking under the strain of two uncontrollable events during the first hours of a short, expensive vacation, the couple went ballistic, hurling the F-word and every other insult they could manufacture. That the couple *could not have called* went right over the employee's head.

The problem with some of our cranky customer contact is that, as in the case of this unfortunate couple and the compassionless rental car agent, there are valid arguments on both sides. It's true they were late, even though they couldn't help it. The employee didn't know if they'd arrive. There was only one car left and better to rent it than have it sit in the lot. Customer conflicts are often complicated like this, with no easy answers to be found. It's disheartening when you don't get what you expected as a customer and it's even worse when you get poorly treated! Of course, employees shouldn't have to take a lot of abuse from customers, either.

And this brings us to the issue of dis-connectedness in service. Customers are busy, distracted, and bordering on overwhelm. The longer they have to wait for what they want the less satisfied they'll be. Customers no longer deal with neighborhood merchants; most transactions involve strangers talking to strangers. This lack of relationship inhibits emotional investment for either party; chances are, they'll never see each other again. This is the excuse lazy service people use, as do surly customers.

SOMETHING IN COMMON

We all have our own sob story about cranky customers or employees. Both you and I have tolerated more than one rude, indifferent, or incompetent service person who frankly should not have been in a job with public exposure. On the other hand, there are customers who use threat, manipulation, and social blackmail. This means that bad service is an equal opportunity experience.

I DON'T HAVE TO CARE ABOUT
SERVICE, DO I?

Many employees who work face to face with customers really haven't a clue. Somehow they missed Common Courtesy 101 in their upbringing and they certainly weren't given any on-the-job training. They don't even realize they should care about their customers. In a grocery store recently, while reaching for my money I realized my driver's license was missing. I shrieked in surprise and alarm, quickly reviewing everywhere I had been that afternoon and projecting what a hassle it would be if I couldn't find it.

The face of the twenty-something cashier never registered any visible change of facial expression. As far as I could discern she was completely, profoundly, absolutely unfazed by my dilemma. As she took my money I swear, the look on her face was somewhere between "Whatever!" and "Boring!" In spite of my emergency, I wanted to laugh. I hadn't seen that much indifference since the day I tried to teach two of my kids a self-esteem seminar during their early teen years! (I did find my license on the floor of my car.)

GO AHEAD, I DARE YOU!

Then we have customers who walk around with a chip on their shoulder, just daring someone to knock it off. To them, everything is an emergency. They're out to kick ass and take names. Their emotional immune system is on the endangered species list and threatened with extinction. The only thing they know how to do is unleash an outburst to get what they want and the rest of us suffer for their lack of civility.

So we have "customers with attitude" and service providers who could use *more* of an attitude (of service, anyway). Crankiness prevails when customers and service personnel get too preoccupied with their own problems and pressures. They either don't realize how impenetrable their self-absorption is, or they don't care. There seems to be little motivation for either side to go out of its way to express the humanity they share. This is regrettable, because in our busy, bustling, overloaded culture, meaningful connections, even brief ones, are a desperately needed tonic. For the recipient, yes, but even more so for the donor.

Many of us have not yet come to realize that whether working with customers or being a customer, we benefit by making the most out of every contact. That's what this chapter is all about—how you can profit by positively addressing, and finessing, every single contact with others, at work, at home, and in between.

MAKE YOURSELF A SERVICE STAR

When I was a child, I loved to draw. Whenever I drew a star I always added lines (to represent rays of light) that went off in all directions. We're going to use that image so you can graphically depict where you fit in the customer contact picture.

Because I'll refer to the concept throughout this chapter, I'm going to ask you to create your own "service star." Please draw a star in the middle of a standard size piece of paper. Write your name inside your service star.

Now, draw one of those "ray" lines for every customer (or customer group) you serve, externally and internally: the public, vendors, coworkers, people from other departments, suppliers, your supervisor, and top management. Include anyone you come in contact with. For the rest of this chapter, when you read the words *people* or *customers*, this means *everyone* who appears on your service star. Yes, everyone, even if you don't like the person.

SERVICE: MAKE IT EASY ON YOURSELF

Everyone benefits from good service. When I finish a customer service seminar, people often tell me they never realized service was so all encompassing; they thought it related only to their jobs. They had never connected the idea of service to other areas of their lives. People say I opened their eyes to how important service really is, both in serving our customers and when we're the customer, too. I hope to do the same for you.

Cranky Quiz

CUSTOMER CONTACT

Scoring the Cranky Quiz

Score 1 point for every *yes* and 0 for every *no*. Count a *sometimes* as a *yes*. Add your total: 3 points or less (Cool) means you're in good shape, 4 to 7 (Warm) indicates a need to slow down, and 8 to 10 (Hot!) indicates a raging cranky infection. You'll find anti-cranky solutions for each quiz item in this chapter.

1. ___ Do you think that people are more rude and discourteous than they used to be?

2. ___ Are you irked by the increasing number of self-serve, automated systems, and fewer face-to-face transactions than in the past?

3. ___ Do you get riled about having to wait in slow lines, fill out time-consuming forms, or endure inconvenient service systems?

4. ___ Do you realize that service personnel with the heaviest public contact (receptionists, secretaries, clerks, servers, etc.) are the lowest paid and least respected?

5. ___ Do you tend to complain when service is bad but say nothing when it's good?

6. ___ Are you always expected to satisfy your customers even though management doesn't necessarily support your efforts?

7. ___ Are you seeing an increase of unhappy, complaining, or rude customers?

8. ___ Is it almost as difficult to deal with your manager or work colleagues as it is cranky customers?

9. ___ Do you find being nice to your family difficult after a long, hard day at work?

10. ___ Are you so tired and overloaded it's impossible to think about getting involved in any kind of volunteer work or community service?

Cranky Quotient _____

My customer contact condition is *(circle one)*   Cool   Warm   Hot!

SERVICE: WE HAVE CONTACT

One Is the Onliest Number

One person can make a difference. This occurred to me recently when, in a small parking lot in a busy, downtown area, one poorly parked minivan took up two spaces and edged into a third by parking parallel in an angled lot. This display of inconsideration screwed up an entire parking row and held the potential of causing a cranky chain reaction. I'll bet some drivers got pretty miffed as they circled through the disheveled line of parked cars, inconvenienced because of one person's thoughtless actions.

When it comes to customer contact and dealing with the public, one person can definitely make or break the simplest transaction. A man described his family's experience on their return home from a two-week vacation out West. After arriving in Minneapolis, where they were scheduled for a brief layover, he and his wife and two kids were informed that their flight had been canceled. They faced the bleak prospect of being held hostage in the terminal for the better part of a day, waiting for the next flight home.

Seeing their look of dismay, a savvy Northwest ticket agent suggested a trip to the Mall of America, outlining the best transportation options there and back, plus a few choice activities and rides. What could have been a grueling six-hour wait became one last round of family fun, ending the vacation on a high note. Referring to the woman who salvaged their day the man said, "Luckily, we happened to get the *right* person." Is that what your customers would say about you?

Customer Contact: It Works Both Ways

There are leagues of service people who exude a "Don't get excited—it's just a customer" attitude. No doubt you've endured the surly server or cranky clerk who acts as if merely acknowledging your presence should be enough. It's especially grating when this place of business is the only one in town. But then, too, there are the customers who figure if they scream, demand the impossible, or threaten to take their business elsewhere, they'll get their way. Sometimes they do.

Companies can actually encourage customer misbehavior without realizing it. In their attempts to gain a competitive edge, boost business, and lock in customer loyalty, some stores are so fanatical about their liberal return policies that customers can misuse, break an item, or return a product that was purchased in a competitor's store and get a refund. There are commercials to this effect.

I've witnessed service employees (even managers) not showing a whole lot of concern until a customer threw a temper tantrum as the rest of us stood and watched. I recently watched a woman get an upgrade by pitching a fit because the hotel had messed up her reservation. While I commend the sentiment, I question the practice of rewarding customers when they go ballistic. This encourages nonresponsibility on the part of the consumer, which in turn leads to other forms of thoughtlessness and rudeness.

This Would Be a Great Job If It Weren't for the People

When a new client hires me I like to begin by interviewing selected individuals so I can learn about their jobs and work environment. I include two questions in my interviews and the answers are always the same:

> Question: *What do you like most about your job?*
> Answer: *"The people."*
> Question: *What do you like least about your job?*
> Answer: *"The people."*

Your people exposure is probably higher today than it was in the past. Merging companies and crossover markets have created an expanded customer base of all ages, personalities, and expectation levels. Your service star is visual proof that you serve many people. Just as their expectations differ, so do their styles. Like a chameleon who changes color to match its environment, you can adapt to these different styles. This is what I call "style flexing."

Between phone calls, faxes, E-mails, and face-to-face exchanges, you are *on call* each day to perhaps hundreds of people who want your time and attention. The better you can style-flex, the easier it will be, but it still translates into a lot of responsibility for one mere mortal.

One Person Equals One Organization

When I ask audiences how many people it takes to turn them off to an organization the answer is always the same: "One." Well, *you* are that one person. To your customers you represent your entire company. Think how many times you yourself have said, "I will never deal with them again!" after a bad exchange with just one company representative. You can be the one individual who makes your organization look great, or awful. This principle also applies to internal service: There are departments in every organization that are considered either a real pain to deal with or an absolute pleasure, and it's often because of one individual. That's how powerful service is: one person equals the entire operation. The next time you feel unimportant or forgotten, remind yourself that every contact with a customer is a critical one.

CRANKY QUIZ ITEM # 1: DOUBLE TROUBLE

> 1. ___ Do you think that people are more rude and discourteous than they used to be?

Two Sides to the Coin but Something's Missing

Rudeness. Indifference. Incompetence. Threats. Accusations. Tirades. And that might describe a good day! Customer contact isn't always the pretty picture commercials paint. There are employees in service positions who work because they have to, and every day when they show up for their jobs they check their imaginations and spirits at the door. Like Rhett Butler, they just don't give a damn.

On the other hand, service employees will tell you about customers who scream, hurl obscenities, or have temper tantrums that would make a three-year-old look composed. Some people lie, cheat, skip out without paying for meals or merchandise, write poison pen letters, or threaten bodily harm. On both sides of the counter, people are casting their crankiness on others as if it's their birthright. They've been infected with the "I'm the only person in the world" virus.

Anti-Cranky Alternatives for Cranky Quiz Item # 1:
Double Trouble

Revisit the Basics

On both sides of the transaction, customer contact revolves around one simple rule, *common courtesy*. But most of us have had experiences that qualify for the "Customer Service Little Shop of Horrors Handbook." So, for the truly service impaired here's *The Official Service at-a-Glance Cheat Sheet!*

When you greet someone, say *hello*.
If you want or need something, say *please*.
If you get it, say *thank you*.
If you must disappoint a person, say *I'm sorry*.
If you or an associate screw up, say *I apologize*.
If the other party screws up, say *that's okay*.
If someone offers a compliment or says thank you, say *you're welcome*.
If there's a problem, say *no problem*.
When the person leaves, say *good-bye* or *thank you*.

Say It Like You Mean It

Courtesy and good manners are simple and classic: smile when you connect with someone, whether you're the customer or serving one. Say all the right words in a friendly voice because tone can make all the difference. Think about how the meaning of the phrase, "I'm just doing my job," changes as one's tone of voice changes.

Don't Take Bad Service with You

You can't control how customers or service personnel treat you, but you're in charge of how you react to their treatment. "The Serenity Prayer" reminds us to distinguish between the things we can change and those we cannot. Think of bad service incidents as an *opportunity* to practice your patience or self-control. The RPM (restrain, pull away, monitor) method enhances your presence of mind so you can ward off confrontations. I hope you've already discovered how this simple self-awareness strategy can help you ward off crankiness.

Bad service does happen to good people, so if a customer or service employee breaks every rule in the book, find your sense of humor and file the event so you can entertain your friends with one of those "How bad was it?" stories. *You certainly don't deserve bad treatment, but when you get it, why take it with you?* In other words, once a frustrating exchange with a demanding customer (or rude employee) is over, let it die a natural death. Leave the incident behind you, where it rightfully belongs.

Create Your Own Customer Service Tag Team

When I went to renew my driver's license this year, little did I know it would be an unforgettable experience. That's because when I visited the Secretary of State office in East Lansing I was served, not by one state employee, but by a customer service tag team. I got to meet three imaginative, energetic women who keep each other "up" regardless of what happens. One of them has a sister who is gravely ill. She said that the support of her tag team means more to her than words can express. They joke together, pitch in when there's an emergency, and boost each other's moods. I urge you to establish your own tag team so you can get support when you most need it, and give it out to others who could use a bit of a lift.

CRANKY QUIZ ITEM # 2: THE MYTH OF SERVICE

2. ___ Are you irked by the increasing number of self-serve, automated systems, and fewer face-to-face transactions than in the past?

Looking for Service in All the Wrong Places

We used to call them *service stations* but now they're the place where we fuel our own cars and buy snacks or something to drink. It seems the age of self-serve skulked in while we weren't looking: We now have do-it-yourself beverage stations, ATMs, E-tickets, self-checkout grocery lanes, express car or hotel registrations, voice mail menus, Internet commerce. Someone's been sucking the life out of service without changing its name. But that's okay; sometimes self-serve is more desirable than service with a sneer, but should we still call it service? It's the *false expectation* we resent; the time wasted wandering through a football field–size discount house with a product in hand, desperately searching for someone in a red vest who might be able to help us. Note I said *might*. We often leave frustrated and empty-handed.

Savvy airline captains know the benefits of making one of their "Now folks . . . " announcements, because cramped passengers get restless and resentful when they're kept in the dark. Southwest Airlines is a good example of how we'll accept spartan service (open seating, luggage self-schlepping, and no food) when we know what we're getting ahead of time. They specialize in low cost, no frills, on-time flying and have capitalized on it.

Increased Expectations and Decreased Dividends

Downsizing has affected customer contact: We find ourselves standing in line longer, languishing on hold, or being attended by temporary employees who lack the know-how or authority to really help us. As demands increase, it seems there are fewer people ready and willing to serve this demand. I interviewed some pilots who admitted that the level of service on commercial air carriers (space, food, and personal attention) has decreased while the number of passengers has increased.

Anti-Cranky Alternatives for Cranky Quiz Item # 2:
The Myth of Service
Price, Value, Service: Pick Any One

When it comes to fast food, we need to recognize that quality and service take a backseat to convenience. With discount houses, we should expect there will be fewer employees to help us, fewer well-known brands to choose from, less impressive packages and presentations, and crowded spaces. As discussed in chapter 5, there's a cost to pay for shopping with only price in mind. This came back to me during a recent business trip when I forgot my dress clothes and had to buy an emergency outfit at a discount store. I was uncomfortable taking off my clothes in doorless dressing stalls that offered no privacy. It took me a while to remember that what I considered poor service was the normal way of doing business for this chain.

Raise Your Voice as a Customer

If you don't like the kind of service you receive, or you feel a company's systems are inconvenient, flawed, or inconsistent with their ads, let it be known. I'm not suggesting you get cranky and yell. I'm suggesting that most businesses assume customers are happy until they hear otherwise, and they won't be motivated to improve service unless they know how bad it is: *In the absence of feedback we make up our own version of reality.*

If you don't say anything, you may be sentencing yourself to future bad service. Try to get to the right party, though—someone who can do something about it. Chances are, the person who gave you the bad service probably won't be too interested in your opinion. Let the owner or manager of the business know what it's like to do business with it. If you're met with resistance or indifference, you still have leverage: You can go out and tell everyone you know. Word of mouth is still the most powerful form of advertising.

CRANKY QUIZ ITEM # 3:
YOU AS A CUSTOMER ON HOLD

> 3. ___ Do you get riled about having to wait in slow lines, fill out time-consuming forms, or endure inconvenient service systems?

Consumer, Heal Thyself

How many times a day do you find yourself having to wait for something or someone? As the practice of waiting becomes more common in our time-compressed business world, our patience has proportionately decreased. Like crankiness, impatience has become a chronic condition.

Yet, because we all share the same space and time continuum, we have to wait our turn to merge onto the freeway, park our car, enter the elevator, and be seated, served, or waited on. And then we get to wait some more while we reverse the process: get off the freeway, retrieve our car, get out of the elevator, pay for our meal. Face it: Waiting has practically become a national pastime, and it's a short trip to Cranky Land if you keep getting upset over it.

Anti-Cranky Alternatives for Cranky Quiz Item # 3:
You as a Customer on Hold
Wait a Minute

Whenever you're waiting in a long line, stuck in traffic, or sitting on hold, remind yourself that there are even bottlenecks near the summit of Mount Everest where climbers, while exhausting their precious oxygen supply, may have to wait an hour or more in extreme conditions before they can proceed to the top. Take comfort in knowing yours is not a life-threatening wait. You already know better than to make yourself miserable, right? The reality is that you can wait patiently or perturbed, but you're going to have to wait. You can *not* wait, but that may mean not getting your product or service, or skipping your appointment. Those are basically your choices. Single yourself out from the cranky people by taking a deep breath, smiling, and congratulating yourself on how well you handle life's little frustrations.

Be Proactive and Plan Ahead

The business world won't make special exceptions for you or me. Much as we don't like the idea, we'll have to sit and wait like everyone else. Plan how you'll handle waiting time. Carry reading material, a work project, or your planner with you at all times so you get something done. Read an article. Make a phone call. Watch people for amusement. By all means, stay in a good mood so your annoyance doesn't transfer to the person you're waiting for, especially if you're in sales. Your attitude is far more transparent than you'd like to think, and if by chance, anyone is watching you, make sure your face and body language look pleasant and alert.

Keep cassette tapes in your car in case of a delay on the road, or find a radio station that plays calming music. Soothe, don't *seethe*. If you have a cell phone and you're running late, call ahead and explain. Then relax, because here on earth, if you're already late, hurrying will not make you on time. Yes, it's inconvenient. And yes, it will happen. Remember Reality Bites from chapter 2? If you have to wait, accept it. As you know, you can't control the circumstance, only yourself.

CRANKY QUIZ ITEM # 4:
HIGH EXPOSURE, LOW REGARD

> 4. ___ Do you realize that service personnel with the heaviest public contact (receptionists, secretaries, clerks, servers, etc.) are the lowest paid and least respected?

Can't Get No Respect

When Xerox Corporation hired me for a sales position years ago, I was required to travel with an experienced sales rep. One of the superstars was a man with a strong ego who didn't like to waste his charm on secretaries and receptionists. His target was their boss, the decision maker, and he considered all others inconsequential. Then one day the manager of a large company informed him that the very people who would be using the copy machines—the support staff—would be making the decision about which brand to buy. They didn't even invite him in for a demo!

Many low-status positions involve high public contact (switchboard personnel, secretaries, receptionists, tellers, technicians, servers, bussers, custodians). These people have more exposure to customers than executives; they're the ambassadors of an organization but lack the respect or compensation they deserve.

Anti-Cranky Alternatives for Cranky Quiz Item # 4:
High Exposure, Low Regard
Give Respect, Build Rapport

Regardless of your position, help fight corporate crankiness by showing respect to people in low-status jobs. You'll gain loyalty, trust, and maybe even a favor. People at the support level see a lot, hear a lot, and know the inner workings of their organization. They may be short on status, but they have far more power than you might realize. Treat them right and they'll come through for you in a pinch.

While compiling five years of client documentation so I could earn my CSP (Certified Speaking Professional) designation through the National Speakers Association, I got caught in a political crossfire. In one company, the manager who hired me left the state shortly after I completed a series of six programs. The owner's son, now the CEO, refused to take my calls. So I called the department secretary with whom I'd had several cordial conversations four years before, explained my dilemma, and she helped me locate the manager who originally hired me. It's simple: Be nice to people. They'll remember you, and hey, you just never know when you might need a favor.

Serve the Ones Who Serve You

Executives can be absent from work for days, even weeks, attending training sessions, retreats, and conferences while their secretaries are lucky to accrue three days a year. Bosses confide that it's hard having their secretaries out of the office for more than a day at a time. Kind of makes you wonder who's running the place, doesn't it? I hope you take the time to say hello, learn support people's names, and treat them with kindness because they're probably part of your service star. It's unnerving to discover how many managers and executives walk by without acknowledging support staff.

If it's within your power, help make it possible for support people to receive the kind of training and pay they deserve. Every day I deal with support people who make their boss and their organization look good. I compliment them, but they deserve more. They deserve to be better compensated for their skills. If you have employees who understand what customer contact is all about, treat them as well as you do your customers.

Look for the Cranky Cam

In the movie *Defending Your Life*, people who had just died were put "on trial" before they could go on to the Next Stage. They had to explain and defend the best and worst moments in their lives. It would then be decided whether they would be returned to earth for another go at it, or get that Great Promotion in the sky. As a means of determining their fate they had to watch film clips of their lives: both significant and trivial incidents, from the heroic to the humiliating. If these people had known they would one day be subjected to such "reality therapy" at the end of their lives, do you suppose it would have affected their everyday behavior?

Imagine that there's a "cranky cam" recording your every move, and each night you have to review how you treated people that day. Would the presence of a cranky cam cause you to change your behavior? If so, use this idea to help you achieve new levels of courtesy with everyone in your service star, especially those who have little formal power or authority.

CRANKY QUIZ ITEM # 5:
COMPLAINTS VERSUS COMPLIMENTS

5. ___ Do you tend to complain when service is bad but say nothing when it's good?

Silence Isn't Golden

When I ask people their number one gripe about service, most will say, "Being ignored." Yet, ironically, many of us ignore those who wait on us. I've noticed that when people get into large groups the veneer of common courtesy tends to vanish. If you travel by air, note how few people say "Thank you" when a flight attendant serves a beverage or snack. If you attend a conference, notice how few attendees thank, or even acknowledge, the person serving their food or pouring their coffee. Most will continue their conversation with a colleague and silently receive their food or beverage, otherwise ignoring the person delivering it. Though this is a little thing, I perceive it as a reflection of the sense of entitlement we cart around.

Anti-Cranky Alternatives for Cranky Quiz Item # 5:
Complaints versus Compliments
Speak Out for Good Service

If we're quick to complain about bad service we also have a social responsibility to recognize and compliment excellent customer contact. So what if the person is simply doing his or her job? Human nature being what it is, we seem more prone to notice and reinforce the negative. Where does that get us? Well, for one, it gets us cranky.

What's the sense of making a big deal out of what we don't want, but not saying anything when we get what we *do* want? We're reinforcing the wrong behavior! I'm not saying overlook bad service; I'm suggesting you recognize and compliment *good* service so the provider will continue this behavior.

Speak Out about Bad Service

While it's nothing we sit around and hope for, bad service happens. Here are some strategies for when you're on the receiving end of second-rate service:

- Accept that service is a numbers game and sooner or later you were bound to run into someone who doesn't get the concept of customer contact. Tell yourself this is a momentary incident and no big deal. Don't get cranky. You'll soon be out of there.
- If the person seems distant or preoccupied you can try to break their trance by initiating a conversation. Give a compliment. Draw attention to something personal—a sticker, badge, or button the person may be wearing, or equipment he or she is using.
- If the employee seems indifferent, kindly ask if he is having a rough day; this brief display of empathy and support can turn things around.
- Complain to the offending person in a constructive, objective manner so she won't feel personally attacked. She may or may not take your words to heart, but if you stay calm and don't take things personally, you can walk out feeling good about how you handled the incident.
- Soothe your momentary stress by invoking your "attitude of gratitude." Be thankful *you* aren't burdened by such incompetence or a foul temperament.
- Try humor. If you can think of a funny remark you might catch the person off guard. This illuminating moment may be just the wake-up call the person needed.

CRANKY QUIZ ITEM # 6:
SERVICE TO A FAULT

> 6. ___ Are you always expected to satisfy your customers even though management doesn't necessarily support your efforts?

Do as I Say, Not as I Do

One day my hairdresser, Elyse, introduced me to another client as I was getting ready to leave. Elyse told her I had written a book on customer service and the woman immediately launched into a tirade about service. Her company had recently initiated a top down service program with little preparation on the employees' behalf and very little participation from management. She said the employees hated their training sessions and mocked the service slogans. They considered the whole thing a joke. She was so hot about this issue I knew it was useless to defend the merits of service training, so I empathized. Her company is no exception.

Service personnel have told me about managers threatening them with what would happen if they didn't excel in service. Some supervisors keep a running tally of dissatisfied customers and use it as leverage. I say, "Whoa!" What we have here is a perfect way to obliterate motivation, not generate it.

Customer contact is everybody's business, from entry level to executive. It can't be forced. Good service naturally springs forth when it's part of the culture, where positives are celebrated and mistakes corrected. When everyone buys in to customer contact it becomes the most natural thing in the world. There's no better example than the Disney Corporation. Tom Connellan's *Inside the Magic Kingdom* illustrates the simplicity and beauty of a good service program.

Anti-Cranky Alternatives for Cranky Quiz Item # 6: Service to a Fault
Check Out What Life Is Like for Your Customers

I asked a manager one time, "What is it like to work for you?" After a moment of silence he said, "I think I'd quit!" What is it like doing business with you? Are you friendly, helpful, polite? These behaviors are simply common courtesy and should be practiced by every person in the organization, at all levels. Phone your organization sometime. Listen for voice tone, diction, mood. Call a few different departments and decide for yourself if customers are receiving quality contact.

Evaluate every step your customers take, from the parking lot to their destination; look for friendliness, neatness, and quality. Is signage adequate? Is your workplace attractive to outsiders and comfortable for employees? Do the walls need a coat of paint? Are work areas organized? What conversations might customers hear as they pass by workstations, walk the halls, or ride the elevators?

People who work in hospitals tell me they really didn't have a grasp on customer contact until they (or a family member) became a patient. That was their wake-up call. Traveling as much as I do, when subjected to a motel's loud, inefficient climate control system that wakes me up every time it cycles, I think all hospitality managers should be forced to spend a night in one of their rooms.

Make It Easy for Customers to Do Business with You

Good customer contact lies in the little things. If you're a manager, ask employees how delivery systems complicate or interfere with service. Find out if employees suffer unnecessary interruptions because each new customer is forced to ask the same question. Flawed systems inconvenience everyone. If customers keep complaining about the same issue, change it. If customers gripe about having to jump through a series of hurdles to get what they want, simplify your systems. If you're not a manager and lack the authority to do any of the above, see if your work group can initiate a customer service task force.

Seek an Environment That Goes Beyond Lip Service

People skills are always in demand and if your organization has a double standard about service ("Get out there and treat our customers right, dammit!") maybe you need to find an employer that cares about its people. Don't do anything rash like quitting your job today but start looking for an environment that supports, reinforces, and rewards employees who want to do a good job. Considering that you spend close to one-third of your life at work, you deserve to be in a climate that fits your style and supports your efforts.

People often suffer health problems from staying in a job they hate. If you're experiencing distress over your job, take a long look at your personality, work style preferences, and where your best abilities lie. If yours is a case of poor management, or lack of support, consider looking for employment that is more compatible with your needs. Chances are, you'll be in the workforce for a long time. The work cultures that support customer service internally and externally are out there, and maybe they're looking for someone just like you.

CRANKY QUIZ ITEM # 7:
CRANKY CUSTOMERS

> 7. ___Are you seeing an increase of unhappy, complaining, or rude customers?

Customer Contact Takes Its Toll

Cranky customers take the old adage, "the customer is always right," and push it to the limit, especially when they're wrong. They'll do what it takes to get their way, from whines to screams, accusations, and threats. I read about a Detroit woman who is every service provider's worst nightmare, wreaking havoc wherever and whenever she can in the name of getting deep discounts and free merchandise. This customer from hell profits from her crankiness and is proud of it. Knowing it's the squeaky wheel that gets the grease, this woman must *slither* from one transaction to another! I hope she, and others like her, don't end up in front of you. No wonder the word *customer* sometimes inspires rolled eyes and a deep sigh.

Customers from Hell

Some pesky customers behave outrageously. One alarming manifestation of crankiness is "air rage," wherein airline passengers, perhaps fortified with a combination of alcohol, arrogance, and anxiety, flip out during a flight. Some have even gone so far as to assault airline personnel and other passengers. Crankiness and undercurrents of unchecked rage are all around us, even in grocery stores. My friend Susan, on more than one occasion, says that impatient shoppers have intentionally jammed her heels with their grocery cart when she didn't move in the line as fast as they thought she should. These bizarre incidents are becoming more and more common and they have to stop.

There's a fine line between crankiness and outright cruelty, and it appears that the conduct of customers from hell knows no bounds: Toll booth workers report being cursed at, spit on, handed hot coins, and having lit cigarettes butted into their palms. If you're wondering what's behind these unbelievable behaviors, I have a hunch: Many of us are mad at ourselves for our out-of-control lives and we're taking it out on others. We as a nation need to hit the brakes, locate our lost compassion, and rescue our self-restraint.

Anti-Cranky Alternatives for Cranky Quiz Item # 7:
Cranky Customers

Dealing with Ignorant or Upset Customers

In this context, ignorant means that some customers who ask the impossible or take offense simply don't understand your business, so don't confuse ignorance with antagonism. Educate these customers, explaining the process clearly and simply so they know exactly what you can or cannot do, and why.

When working with an upset customer, avoid negative phrases such as, "We can't do that." Say instead, "Here's what we *can* do . . ." or explain, "We established this policy because . . ." Once you've explained the policy, reasonable customers will understand why you are unable to meet their request. Even a statement of empathy, "I wish I could do more . . ." can help ease the customer's disappointment.

For many customers, getting their way is secondary to feeling good about the interaction. A simple apology can mean the difference between a satisfied customer or an aggravated one. People constantly tell me, "If only someone had said they were *sorry* I wouldn't have been so upset. But nobody seemed to care!" Customer contact improves when we remember the old saying that people don't care how much you know until they know how much you care.

Recover from Mistakes

There will be times you (or your organization or department) screw up and you have an unhappy customer in front of you. As bad as it may feel to own up, how you handle this situation from here on can make you look like a star or a schmuck. In fact, you may end up apologizing for someone else's mistake because it's the thing to do. This is called "service recovery." Getting defensive, making excuses, blaming someone else, or getting mad at the customer are losing strategies.

Admit the error (even if it's someone else's), offer to make it up, thank the customer for being understanding, provide an immediate answer, or offer a tangible benefit. Research has shown that unhappy customers who leave in a positive frame of mind demonstrate a stronger future loyalty than those who have never been upset. Look at your unhappy customer as an *opportunity* to make you and your organization look like heroes, where everyone goes away feeling good.

Handle Your Customers from Hell

You will face hostile, out of control, belligerent customers who operate beyond the bounds of crankiness; they're mad at the world and determined to make you pay. Unfortunately, it's your job to do your best with fervid folks as well as friendly ones. Your best bet is to listen. If you need, visit the Quick Stop! to steel yourself. Granted this isn't always easy, but sometimes people calm down after they've vented. Stay calm; getting defensive will only escalate matters. Sometimes it helps to set limits diplomatically: "I'll be happy to help if you'll be kind enough to explain what happened."

If you know you're going to be besieged by a stream of obscenities and personal slurs, talk to your manager ahead of time about the best way to handle it (most offices create an informal policy about how much ballistic behavior is too much). For the sake of your courteous customers, you need to resist getting infected by someone else's toxic tirade. Use the skills offered in earlier chapters to slough off your stress and renew your outlook. Be grateful these extreme situations don't happen every day. Remind yourself that regardless of what someone else says or does, you're in charge of your thoughts and feelings. You can leave those nasty words behind.

CRANKY QUIZ ITEM # 8:
CRANKY COLLEAGUES

> 8. ___Is it almost as difficult to deal with your manager or work colleagues as it is cranky customers?

Struggling to Soar Like an Eagle When You're Working with Turkeys

Sometimes it isn't our customers who get us down, it's the people we work with. One cranky employee can contaminate an entire work group, and a bad or negligent boss can create upset for the entire work team. If you have tried absolutely everything and you're convinced that the person making your work life miserable is mentally ill or toxic beyond rehabilitation, your best bet may be finding a new job. But make sure you exercise every available option first.

A woman attended a series of seminars I was conducting. After each program she talked about how miserable she was in her job—that she hated her boss and had suffered extreme stress from this troubled work relationship. She was under a doctor's care and seeing a therapist. This woman was a government employee and reluctant to give up her retirement benefits, which she would have to do if she quit. Her hope was to stick it out until she could get out. Two years later we ran into each other.

When I asked how everything was going, she exclaimed, "Wonderful!" I asked if she had changed jobs and she said no. I asked if her boss had died. She said no. I asked if she had transferred into another department and the answer was the same. "Nothing has changed," she said, "except me." After coming to grips with her desire to stay and the reality that her boss was unlikely to undergo a personality transplant, she decided to work on her attitude. Her manager's bad moods no longer got to her; she was happy, healthy, and having a good life.

Anti-Cranky Alternatives for Cranky Quiz Item # 8: Cranky Colleagues

Develop a Teflon Temperament

Some people constantly gripe and complain, others brush things off: They tolerate, laugh, or dismiss the same incidents that cranky people anguish over. There's one big difference between those who gnash their teeth over everything and those who refuse to bite: The latter possess a "Teflon temperament." They are emotionally more durable than others; they don't let the bad stuff stick. This isn't something they were born with. A Teflon temperament is often the result of a wake-up call, a significant event that helps the person understand that getting upset over unimportant matters is a personal choice. They learn to "not sweat the small stuff," to borrow a phrase from Richard Carlson. These people safeguard their own health and peace of mind by shrugging off life's irritations. You can, too.

The next time things start getting to you at work or at home, ask yourself:

- Just whose problem is this, anyway?
- Am I being too sensitive or is there something I may be missing?
- Just how important is this incident: Is it truly worth getting upset about?

- Will my getting upset change anything?
- Who or what will be served by my choosing to get cranky over this?
- Who or what will be served by my staying calm and composed?
- What if I let this incident go and focus on something pleasant or productive instead?

Some people say to me, "Right. Like I'm really going to stop and ask these questions!" My answer is yes, you are. If you're serious about becoming less cranky and more composed, self-awareness is exactly what it takes. You might recall our discussion in chapter 2 about choice management.

Some of our behaviors are conscious, some are unconscious. We have no control over unconscious behaviors but a *lot* of control over our conscious actions. Given that, why get infected with someone's bad mood when you can consciously ward it off? In my book *The Customer Service Companion*, I created a Customer Service Alphabet and "U" is my favorite. It states, *"U is for Understanding that while people can sometimes ruin a moment, only you can ruin your day."* A Teflon temperament is the perfect antidote for letting the antics of cranky customers or coworkers slide off your back.

Serve Others to Serve Yourself

Solid customer service skills reach into all aspects of life just like the lines that extend from your service star. You can practice good customer contact with your coworkers, manager, and other work colleagues, and then take these skills home to your family and friends. At work and home, when you consciously initiate positive behaviors you influence how others will respond to you. Would you like work colleagues to treat you better? Start treating *them* better.

If you want more compliments from your boss, give more compliments (be sure they're genuine). The same goes for coworkers. Look for a positive attribute in someone you're not crazy about and comment on it. It's amazing how people come around with the slightest encouragement! After reading an article about this strategy I decided to test it, and volunteered for a project with a woman I disliked. Just like the article recommended, I looked for favorable traits instead of faults (I already knew her flaws). I complimented her on on her strengths. In the process, she changed, and so did I. We didn't become best friends, but we got along better and I found that she no longer automatically irritated me. The lesson? *Serving others well serves you well.* By bringing out your best you help bring out the best in others, and vice versa.

Assess What You Bring to the Party

Before you complain too much about the cranky, demanding people in your life, ask yourself if your mood is 100 percent positive 100 percent of the time. The first step in assessing what you bring to the party is to take a Quick Stop! so you're in tune with what's going on in your head and how your body is feeling. The second step is admitting that, once in a while, you're the source of someone else's stress! Then you're ready to ask some questions to determine whether crankiness is edging out your customer contact skills.

- Do you want to scream when people interrupt you? Wait: Is what you're being asked to do part of your job? If so, it's not an interruption; it's your job.
- Do you want to grit your teeth when people ask you dumb, repetitive questions? If so, try to "beat them to the punch" and answer their question before they ask it. Sometimes people honestly don't know.
- Do you dislike someone at work and get a gut full of adrenaline every time he or she speaks? If so, you need to redefine this relationship. Push your Reset Button! If your head fills with negative thoughts, banish them with positive, repetitive encouragement. The other person isn't the one making you crazy. You are. Adjust your outlook so you can sidestep the misery.

On really tough days when it feels as if you've lost all tolerance for others, ask yourself what kind of job you could possibly get that entailed *no* people contact. If you could find such a job would you even like it after the first few days?

CRANKY QUIZ ITEM # 9:
TAKING SERVICE HOME

> 9. ___ Do you find being nice to your family difficult after a long,
> hard day at work?

Treat Your Family Like Customers and Your Customers Like Family

People often say it's easy to handle cranky customers, but family is another issue. They say after a rough day it's tempting to take work problems home, but this is a costly option. You're better off developing a system for isolating what happens at work and at home so you can leave your feelings in the appropriate place. After all, your customers want your best, but your family *deserves* your best. One woman told me she began loving her job once she mastered this process.

She said "My employer 'rents' me eight hours a day. While I'm rented I'm expected to be kind to customers and cooperative with coworkers. If I start getting stressed I look at my watch to remind myself I'm still 'on rent.' At five o'clock I leave my rented problems at work and head for home with a clean slate. In the morning I try not to mix my personal problems with my rented ones." She said this distinction helped her maintain separation between personal stress and work stress.

Anti-Cranky Alternatives for Cranky Quiz Item # 9:
Taking Service Home
Create Your Own Decompression Chamber

SCUBA divers know the danger of ascending to the water's surface too fast. In extreme circumstances, they need to be placed in a decompression chamber until their bodies adapt to the change in pressure. Well, customer contact causes pressure, too. If you've had a particularly bad day it's possible you'll take your stressful condition home with you unless you take preventive measures:

- If you drive to and from work, have a *long* and *short* route home. That is, on stressful days, take the long, scenic route home so you can decompress. Leave the most efficient route for the good days.

Think of your car as your decompression chamber: The additional drive time allows your body and mind to adapt to the change in pressure, just like a decompression chamber for a diver.

- If you have small kids, they may greet you at the door like little bodies of Velcro, ready to attach themselves to your legs permanently. It's hard getting a toddler (or even a teenager) to understand you've had a bad day. If a few moments of decompression are impossible once you walk through that door, take a deep relaxing breath and remind yourself how empty life would be without their presence. Welcome their need for your full attention. Many working mothers tell me that if they can give their little kids some immediate attention (even though it's hard) that the kids quickly tire of their presence or get distracted and then they can take a few minutes to relax.

- Create a "stress separation ritual" by systematically releasing your tension as you change from work clothes to home clothes. As you take off each article of clothing, one item at a time, envision that you are systematically removing the day's stress. By the time you're fully dressed with your new, fresh clothes, envision yourself fully renewed and ready to relax.

Each of these techniques requires discipline and time to incorporate, but by cultivating them, you'll feel better and so will those around you. Think of it this way: If you consistently bring anger, frustration, and resentment home with you, you're the big loser and so are those you love. Why waste time feeling bad when you can make the choice to feel good instead?

Fake It Till You Make It
Often called *as if* thinking, the fake-it-till-you-make-it strategy helps you practice new behaviors, like trying on a piece of clothing before you purchase it. Remember my year-long patience project from chapter 2? Well, I faked patience a lot in the beginning, but by working at a *behavioral* level, there was really nothing fake about it: Practice is practice! I soon found myself tolerating inconveniences that had once raised my Cranky Quotient into the red zone: a clerk's cash register running out of tape in the middle of my transaction; two slow walkers, ambling side by side, filling a narrow hallway so it was impossible to

pass; people with twenty items in their cart standing in an express lane. These were my ultimate tests. I passed!

Behaving *as if* I were a patient person (instead of my old impatient self), gave me a moment to regroup. I no longer sighed or got irritated. I didn't think mean thoughts about the person who was holding me up. I just went with the flow, took a nice deep breath, and relaxed, considering those moments *opportunities* to practice my new skill of patience.

People often tell me they couldn't do that. Of course they could. They just don't, that's all. Call it "adult pretending" if you must, it isn't about just winging it or being a phony. It's simply an imaginative way to try a behavior on for size and undertake gradual self-improvement.

Companies who have a strong service culture follow a similar process. Disney employees (Cast Members) are a good example. They exude friendliness whenever they're "On Stage." Just imagine if Mickey or Goofy were having a bad day the one time your family got to visit the Magic Kingdom; it just wouldn't be the same, now, would it?

These individuals didn't talk or act this way before they were hired. *These are learned behaviors.* When these behaviors get perfected they spill over into other areas of life. I'll bet that the Cast Members who play Mickey and the gang don't go home and kick the dog, either, and here's why. When you practice it enough, service *becomes* you. You become it. You take home the good things, not the bad.

Help Yourself by Serving Others

Customer contact skills can be applied virtually anywhere, at any time, with anyone who's part of your service star. These skills go beyond the workplace, too. The common courtesy of service and basic human kindness works with everyone else in our lives. Everyone benefits, including you.

- When you help someone else solve a problem you tend to put your own concerns aside.
- When you smile (even if you don't mean it) your body benefits: Smiling decreases tension, improves digestion, lowers blood pressure, increases endorphins and oxygen levels, and boosts your physical immune system.
- Any behavior you practice for several hours a day becomes a

habit. You can literally change the way you think and behave by internalizing and practicing good service.

- You become a kinder, gentler person.
- You go home feeling good about yourself instead of bad about others.

The result? Less stress, more satisfaction, at work and at home. Service is one case where it definitely pays to take your work home with you.

CRANKY QUIZ ITEM # 10:
THE OTHER KIND OF SERVICE

> 10. ___ Are you so tired and overloaded it's impossible to think about getting involved in any kind of volunteer work or community service?

There's Community Service, Too

Maybe you've noticed the word *community* popping up in conversation lately. This is because our cranky culture has inspired a deep need to reconnect and many of us are responding. Communities are actively initiating projects to create a resurgence of local spirit and interconnectedness among its citizens. Schools and local government agencies are joining forces with today's youth to redefine their position in our society. Reports indicate that volunteerism is on the upswing, and this is good news. As human service agency budgets have been systematically slashed through recent years, there's been a need for local citizens to reach out and help the less fortunate. The call is being answered.

People are becoming more active in their churches and metaphysical pursuits, bolstering the spiritual community of their choice. Even professional communities are establishing local "brain trusts," where executives from different fields come together to discuss business strategy and local issues. Professional and trade associations offer a "community of practice." It seems that everywhere we turn, there's a renewal of fraternity and community in the works. Maybe you'd like to do your part. If so, this could be a great time for you to get involved in the highest form of service: community service.

Anti-Cranky Alternative for Cranky Quiz Item # 10:
The Other Kind of Service

You're a busy person. You may be wondering how can you possibly take on another commitment, but please seriously consider getting more involved in your community. Volunteerism is beginning to enjoy a resurgence but that so many people got away from this practice is yet another symptom of our cranky, self-absorbed culture. Community service isn't just a make-work project; it's tied to purpose, and I guarantee that what you give will come back to you in ways you can't even imagine. Community service offers an opportunity for you to reconnect, not just with others, but with something deep within yourself.

Choose a cause you can fully embrace. With a little bit of digging, you'll find you have endless choices. Just for starters, consider the causes of child abuse or domestic violence prevention, AIDS awareness, sex and drug education for teens, environmental organizations, or adult literacy programs. Help those who have legitimate reasons to be cranky: Your community service efforts could make a difference in the life of someone who feels hopelessly disconnected or disenfranchised. It will make an even bigger difference in you.

A DOSE OF REALITY ABOUT
CUSTOMER CONTACT

Customer service holds a prominence in our daily lives and we can gain from its presence. Service involves politeness and common courtesy, and for those of us who learned these basics early on in our lives, it's easy to serve others with the right attitude. Be polite. Smile. Listen. Be friendly. Practice these skills when you're the customer and you'll get better service.

As for your customers, do your best to see that everyone in your service star ends up in a better frame of mind for having come in contact with you. It's also gratifying to think you can have so much of an impact on others. It's nice to realize that the people aspect of your job is the part that lets you exercise your uniqueness. Creatively handling a situation lets you break out of the routine and rise to the occasion. It's part of what makes you employable.

Service principles are simple, yet if we're angry, defensive, or engrossed in our own concerns, we aren't motivated to care about anyone else's problem. There are times when we simply forget, or other occasions when we just don't feel like being nice. But if service is your job you have a standard to uphold, regardless of how you might feel at the moment. As some people say, you can't afford to have a bad day if you work in service. It may help to remember that customer contact is one of those areas in life where you get back what you give out. You'll be further ahead by doing your job well and consistently connecting with people at a meaningful level.

Service for Us All

We will always have customers and we will always be customers. Both of these common activities can be taken to uncommonly high levels. Start preparing your kids for the day they'll occupy these two roles. Encourage them to treat others with respect at all times. Emphasize common courtesy. Make sure your youngsters know the basics of dealing with people: how to smile, say *please* and *thank you*, and generally engage in the practice of civil behavior. And because it isn't just what we say but what we do that counts, make sure your kids see you engaging in courteous behaviors when *you're* the customer. Let them see you connect with others, even strangers, under cordial conditions. If more of us had examples like this to emulate, people wouldn't be so cranky. The promise of service would equal the reality.

Computers

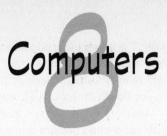

THE TECHNOLOGY TAKEOVER

omputers and electronics are everywhere, and they've revolutionized our lives in ways we don't even fully comprehend. When I bought my 1997 Ford Explorer, the service manager who explained the break-in procedure told me the engine's computer chip would "learn" how I drive. I asked him what would happen if my car's computer didn't like me.

In our country an estimated 45 percent of us own home computers and the number is growing every day. The online community is growing so fast no one can keep up. Within hours after some babies are born they have their own home pages so friends can take a look at the new offspring. You can get virtually anything you want via the Internet: It's vast, interactive, attractive, and potentially addictive.

TECHNO PHOBIC OR TECHNO CRAZED?

Techno phobic. Techno crazed. Think of the chasm between these two attitudes. You can watch the cultural disconnect take place at a party or social event. When the topic of computers comes up, the room quickly divides, as if someone had called a sophisticated line dance maneuver. The techno phobic immediately drop their gaze and turn silent while the techno crazed begin matching themselves up by compatible systems and software, like a digital New Age dating game. Their voices grow louder, drowning out the hushed tones of those who don't "do" computers. This social squaring off reflects one less, or one more, thing in common, with both sides feeling equally adamant.

Don't get me wrong: technology enriches our lives and gives us access to information and entertainment we might not otherwise afford.

Typical of many people, I'm more inclined to use the Internet for pleasure rather than work, which is always a great way to begin. Most often, I visit horse-oriented websites (dressage in particular), consult colorful weather maps or health news, and I sometimes look up words in the on-line Oxford English Dictionary. I appreciate being able to research a client's web page, and consider this an essential step in my getting to know them.

Generally, though, I'm a low-end Internet user, finding many sites tediously time consuming because all I really want is text—basic information, data, descriptions, or numbers. But I have to wait for elaborate, overdone visuals to load before I can get to what I want. Buy a faster modem you may think? I've done that. In my mind, it's still a major time sink. I recognize this is just a style preference. Funny, I can sit for hours with a book in my lap but I find staring at a computer screen far less fulfilling.

For people like me it would probably help to have a little warning sticker prominently displayed on the front of our computers that announces: Caution! Prolonged use of the Internet may cause bouts of crankiness! If you frequently use the Internet, you may have noticed that websites are becoming increasingly more TV-like, with music, color, and, yes, video, with as much "action" as the technology can offer. Products and services will be judged by their ability to put on a good show, whether or not they happen to be the most suitable or highest quality. While a website may shimmer with promise, the reality can be disappointing and some of us will get cranky over this.

Maybe you're one of the techno literati who casually cruises the Internet like it's your local interstate. Great. But if you find yourself burdened with compressed time or communication overload, the answer might be blinking right in front of you. On the other hand, if you're still hanging on to the edge of the technological pool, afraid to let go lest you be swept away, be warned ahead of time that watching a computer screen can be as big a waste of time as reruns or junk TV.

THE TECHNOLOGICAL ROLLER COASTER

Many business travelers tell me how exciting it was when the company issued their first laptops. At last, they could travel all over the country (or world) and stay linked to the company's mainframe. No more mid-dle-of-the-night faxes; no more early-morning phone calls. Just hook up that modem, dial the magic number, and voilà, instant communica-tions! So much for theory. One man told me he is by nature a very mel-low guy but he gets very cranky when his laptop freezes up on him, and it happens all the time. He hooks up his modem, dials in, starts down-loading his notes, files, and attachments, and then he waits. After sev-eral minutes of this, his computer freezes up and then he gets to start all over again. This isn't an isolated, infrequent occurrence and it really bugs him! As for alternatives, if he says, "Screw it" and waits till he gets back to the office, he's overloaded with missives immediately. At the moment, it seems there's no happy option for fixing this system except for gutting it out and somehow tolerating the crashes.

People tell me these frustrations often happen when too many people put too many demands on a system designed for fewer users. I can relate, because when America Online went through its massive growth spurt, I had my own bouts of crankiness waiting through hours of busy signals.

This chapter will take you through the various ups and downs of today's technology, how it affects you and how to approach it in a bal-anced manner. You might find yourself looking at some of your elec-tronic gadgets a little bit differently afterward. As always, the goal is to look for the best and discard the worst. Unfortunately with comput-ers, you're sometimes forced to buy the whole package. The point is that your attitude is critical when it comes to technology.

TAKING THE TREK THROUGH HIGH TECH

PC and Thee

Getting up to speed with computers can be daunting. Many of us worry that we're too old, too slow, too right brained, or too dumb to learn. I remember watching an experienced air traffic controller struggle as he reluctantly converted to computerized equipment: The way he jabbed at the keyboard was a telling motion. In just a few months, he retired.

The tutorial on my first computer, a Texas Instruments DOS-based model, described it as *Fast and Dumb*. That made me feel better, but I still had to get over my insecurities about tackling a whole new tech-nology, and it stretched me to the max. I still almost break out in a sweat when I remember learning WordStar, the first popular word

Cranky Quiz

COMPUTERS

Scoring the Cranky Quiz

Score 1 point for every *yes* and 0 for every *no*. Count a *sometimes* as a *yes*. Add your total: 3 points or less (Cool) means you're in good shape, 4 to 7 (Warm) indicates a need to slow down, and 8 to 10 (Hot!) indicates a raging cranky infection. You'll find anti-cranky solutions for each quiz item in this chapter.

1. ___ Do you feel as if you've been left stranded on the shoulder of the information highway?

2. ___ Do you carry a cell phone or pager so people can contact you, wherever you may be?

3. ___ Do you sometimes procrastinate because you know technology (fax, E-mail, overnight delivery) can bail you out?

4. ___ Do you ever feel outmatched by today's technologically sophisticated products?

5. ___ Are you more inclined to stay in touch with friends who have E-mail than those who don't?

6. ___ Do you spend an hour or more on-line each day?

7. ___ Given the choice, are you more likely to do a task in a high-tech manner (machine, power tool, or appliance) rather than low-tech (by hand)?

8. ___ Are you ever inconvenienced by constant product changes, improvements, or upgrades?

9. ___ Do unexpected electronic breakdowns make you impatient or cranky?

10. ___ When calling an organization do you get irked at having to interact with electronic voices instead of live human beings?

Cranky Quotient _____

My Computer condition is (*circle one*)   Cool   Warm   Hot!

processor. It was a complicated, anti-intuitive, software hellhole. No icons, no menus, no windows, only meaningless keystrokes with a logic that escaped me.

But because I had no other choices for software or hardware at the time, I persisted, determined to learn computer skills. I hated every minute of those early days, but I loved that I was conquering my emotional allergy to computers. My fear now replaced with loathing, I trundled on. I had faced my dragon and prevailed. The biggest lesson that emerged from this challenging period was my discovery that if I was able to stumble through the process and come out with no visible scars, just about anyone could. Like everything else, what it most requires is desire.

CRANKY QUIZ ITEM # 1:
LEAP ON OR GET LEFT BEHIND

> 1. ___Do you feel as if you've been left stranded on the shoulder of the information highway?

You Can Run but You Can't Hide

Computers have brought us to a new social intersection that reflects the combined forces of technological change, coming of age, and complexity. Instructions on new equipment once read, "So easy even a child can understand." Today they might rightly say, "So easy even many adults can understand." Kids don't worry that a computer will explode if you hit the wrong key; computers are just a normal part of life for them. When one of my clients and her husband bought their home computer, they unpacked it, grabbed the instructions, made some coffee, and sat down in the kitchen to review the installation procedure. Twenty minutes later, they walked into the living room and discovered their eight-year-old daughter had quietly (and correctly) hooked up the cables and turned it on.

I feel both impatience and empathy for people who stubbornly refuse to learn about computers, especially the ones who make themselves sick or choose retirement rather than learn a new skill. The number of older Americans who daily surf the Internet and chat with on-line friends demonstrates that computers are for any enterprising person who has a chair, desktop, wall plug, and at least a little bit of curiosity.

Anti-Cranky Alternatives for Cranky Quiz Item # 1:
Leap on or Get Left Behind

Get over Your Techno Phobia

If you've allowed yourself to get infected with techno phobia there's one word you'll want to keep in mind: *perspective*. A computer is only a machine and you're the human being. Ultimately, you call the shots. If you're worried about taking on the big challenge, relax. It's just a tool and you can learn how to operate it. Remind yourself it's merely a step-by-step procedure and you've been through this a gazillion times in your life. You know how to learn; you know how to take one step at a time. *Your attitude is the most critical component, not your ability*. The computer won't blow up; if you've heard about "crashes" that's just a figure of speech. A computer is merely a piece of equipment; it won't get cranky, or mad at you; it won't take things personally, so why should you?

Make the Learning Fun

If you're embarrassed about feeling dumb, just give yourself permission to learn. Approach learning computer skills as a child might: Play as you go, view the process with wonder, and laugh at your mistakes. I've disciplined myself to do this when learning something new and it relieves my performance pressure. I smile when I screw up, try to learn from it, and get absorbed in the process instead of worrying that someone else may be judging me. If I'm having fun, who cares? I smile during my riding lessons, especially when my instructor has to repeat herself. My smile is a reminder that I need to pay better attention and do what she says. As adult learners, we often forget that failure is a part of learning and taking on any new discipline is a "fail-as-you-go" process. Resist the trap of thinking you should already know how to do something you've never done. Just think about watching a baby learning how to walk, or witnessing a teen's first attempt at skateboarding.

As adults we have so many competencies, there are so many things we can already do, we don't keep ourselves on a constant learning curve. Consequently, our appraisal of the learning process gets corrupted—instead of focusing on learning we get hung up on how much we hate failing. This keeps us from stretching ourselves and that's why many of us only dream about things instead of actually doing them.

Don't let fear of failure immobilize you. Accept the immutable link between failure and learning: Watch yourself go through the process and acknowledge every step. Let Mary Kay Ash, who says she "failed her way to success," be your inspiration.

Take an Active Role in Your Learning

If your lifemate wants to teach you how to use the computer but the two of you almost divorced during your driving lessons, lovingly decline. If the two of you have distinctly different cognitive styles, trying to teach each other anything could be a bad move. Your spouse may not have the patience to work with you in the way you need. She or he may assume you know more than you know, or worse, end up treating you like a child. You may be better off learning from a neutral party. The last thing you want is to end up getting cranky at someone you love because of a lousy computer! But regardless of who teaches you, before you make your first move, think about the conditions under which you learn best.

- Do you prefer teaching yourself with a manual or do you like having an instructor?
- Do you prefer an orientation before engaging in hands-on practice, or vice versa?
- Do you need a lot of demonstration first or do you like to learn step by step?
- Do you want someone to push you or hold your hand?

Consider hiring someone to teach you the basics. That's what I did when I bought my desktop publishing software, and it was very helpful. In two hours I had the basics and the manual took me the rest of the way. It doesn't have to be an expensive proposition. My "teacher" was a friend of a friend and she charged forty dollars.

You can also expose yourself to technology in small doses. Sign up for a class. If you see a computer touch screen in a bookstore or anywhere else, put your finger on it. This is probably the most low-pressure situation you could find: You're alone, anonymous, and unobserved. The point, of course, is to do whatever works for you. Make it fun, even if you feel uncomfortable. Learning computer skills is a big step and it's worth getting excited over: It's a capability for both business and pleasure.

CRANKY QUIZ ITEM # 2:
TECHNOLOGICAL TETHERS

> 2. ___Do you carry a cell phone or pager so people can contact you, wherever you may be?

Technology as Time Saver, Technology as Time Waster

In a restaurant one night, I heard a man whining to his companions about never having a moment's peace. Both his beeper and cell phone went off during dinner. After quickly responding to his electronic umbilicals, he continued his complaints. I hoped someone might suggest he *turn off* his equipment but no one did. This man may have been technologically sophisticated, but interpersonally he was clueless! Whether he suffered from self-importance, or insecurity, who knows? But it was clear he had made himself a willing victim of technology.

Pagers and cell phones fragment our time and give us a false sense of connectedness, and some of us are downright compulsive about staying linked. I still find it odd when I see people using cell phones on sidewalks, or in stores, cars, educational sessions—even on hiking trails and beaches. People bristle when I suggest they turn these devices off. *Just because we possess the capability of staying in touch doesn't mean we're obligated to do so!* What's behind this compulsion anyway—are we all waiting for Publishers Clearinghouse to call?

Anti-Cranky Alternatives for Cranky Quiz Item # 2:
Technological Tethers
Pull the Plug

You may be required to carry a pager or cell phone for your work, but if you go beyond that, ask why. How many real emergencies might you experience in a day? Medical or mental health professions aside, if your answer is "several," then you either need to redefine the word, change jobs, or get a grip. Frequent interruptions intensify your sense of urgency and time compression; there was a time when you managed to survive just fine without this technology. What's different now?

People say they want to be available in case of an emergency. I can appreciate the intent, but think about how inherently negative this is! The telecommunications industry has done a fine job of selling the need to be constantly accessible via their technology, and I reject this pessimistic manipulation. If there's an emergency, I'll somehow be found. In the meantime I refuse to suffer hundreds, maybe thousands of interruptions while waiting for that fatal call.

If the bulk of your interruptions are really not life or death—that is, they could be handled by an answering machine or voice mail—it's time to pull the plug. Here's how:

1. Limit your cell phone use. Instant access creates the perception that everything *has* to be done now because it *can* be done now. This adds a layer of self-imposed pressure and feeds the itch for instant gratification. Put a value on your time by limiting other people's access to you. Maybe you've seen the poster that says, *"Poor planning on your part does not constitute an emergency on my part."*

2. Many couples mistake convenient contact as a form of intimacy. You may be *technologically tethered* but this doesn't compare to *being* together. Frequent, abbreviated calls are an enhancement, but not a replacement for one-on-one intimacy.

3. Restrict pager use to work hours unless you're on call. Yes, some parents use pagers to stay in touch with their kids, but this allows youngsters to interrupt and control Mom or Dad's time. How many calls involve trivial issues such as there's nothing to eat, how do I thaw a frozen butter crunch cake in the microwave, or where's my favorite sweatshirt? Ask yourself: Who's really calling the shots, and do any of these interruptions end up making you cranky? Pagers give the illusion of connectedness but the reality falls short.

4. Prevent interruptions. We let the phone interrupt face-to-face conversations all the time yet we are under no obligation to pick up that receiver just because the phone rings. When you need peace, turn off the ringer and let the answering machine do its work in silence. Aggressive telemarketers count on you to pick up the phone. Monitor or screen your calls so you know who it is before you pick up. If friends complain about this, remind them you found their call important enough to take.

With voice mail you may not be able to screen, but if you have the ringer off, you won't hear it, so it won't matter. A teenager may challenge all of this. He or she may find these strategies impolite or intolerable. Some kids can't stand the thought of disconnecting from their world. Given a young person's compulsion to stay linked, it's easy to understand why some families have separate lines for the adults and kids.

5. Honor your priorities. If you and a loved one are in the midst of quality time or a serious conversation don't allow yourselves to be interrupted by the phone. Let it ring or have your answering machine take the call. Stay *in the moment* with each other. If you don't have an answering machine, not to worry; the caller will try again. *But maybe the two of you won't.* Why risk losing the moment for the sake of an outside interruption? Think how bad you'd feel suspending important together time only to find a telemarketer on the other end of the line.

CRANKY QUIZ ITEM # 3:
THE LAST MINUTE

> 3. ___ Do you sometimes procrastinate because you know technology (fax, E-mail, overnight delivery) can bail you out?

Just in Time, Almost in Time

You know the feeling of racing against the clock, your heart pounding, your breath coming fast and short, your brain sucking every nanosecond out of those last fateful moments as the clock runs out. For those of us who actually enjoy this self-imposed torture, we now have more options for frantic down-to-the-wire flurries than ever before. We can now *literally* wait till the last minute! Just ship it overnight and pray the weather holds. If you choose other last minute methods of conveyance, hope the fax doesn't jam, the computer doesn't crash, or the ATM isn't down for repairs.

When I worked for Xerox they couldn't give away facsimile machines, let alone sell them. Today they're essential. Even people who don't own a fax can run to the nearest Kinko's or corner drugstore to send or receive a missive. Last-minute options abound: Even small libraries have computers their patrons can use. You can find faxes everywhere, go online in coffee houses and airports, get instant cash wherever you travel, and stay in touch with people all over the world. But despite these astounding capabilities, you can still end up behind the eight ball if you're inclined to procrastinate.

Anti-Cranky Alternatives for Cranky Quiz Item # 3: The Last Minute

Save the Last Minutes for Yourself

Technology comes bundled with its own Expectation Machine that tells us because computers and electronic contraptions can operate at warp speed, we should too, and technology can bail us out of almost any jam. Not so. A combination of old-fashioned, low-tech planning and self-discipline are what save you from last minute thinking, not technology.

You know the steps: Plan what you need to do, project how long you expect it to take, and put in a specific amount of time each day so you can chip away at the details. In this world of interconnectedness, postponing your part in the process can cause a crisis for someone else. Don't do the cranky thing of pretending you're the only person whose schedule matters. Your credibility could be on the line.

Make a promise. Set a deadline and stick to it. Early on, spend an hour assessing the material you need to act on. Don't skim it; absorb it. Make notes of what you need to do and take the first small step. Work the *first* minute, not the last one. How about weather, satellite glitches, power outages, equipment failures? Even if you're not exactly sure what to do, at some point you'll have to do something, so start now. You know this. Depend on your common sense, not the marvels of technology. Get your job done early and pass it on so you can spend that last minute indulging yourself.

Revisit the Mentality behind the Last Minute

In chapter 2 we distinguished between importance and urgency. If you have an item looming on your "to do" list that qualifies as *important*, get it done before it becomes *urgent*. Plan ahead because life is uncertain: unexpected crises can happen at that last critical moment you were so counting on. Remember what it felt like the last time your mild anxiety morphed into wild frenzy? Yes, it was exciting—until panic took over, and the crankiness you experienced wasn't fun at all. Just take the advice you'd give to others. Plan early; act early. Keep your deadline *ahead* of the last minute, just in case.

CRANKY QUIZ ITEM # 4:
PROGRAM ME, PLEASE

4. ___Do you ever feel outmatched by today's technologically
   sophisticated products?

Hello, My Name Is . . .

My computer bears my digital signature: secret passwords, color-coded
preferences, and altered defaults, with software configured and personalized for me. One of our TVs had to be personalized and programmed
for local stations before it was operational. From TVs to stereos to CD
players, home entertainment equipment has graduated to sophisticated
levels, and things aren't very simple anymore. Based on what I've read,
an astonishing number of us don't take full advantage of our VCRs
because the steps are just too complicated. It used to be if we had a
power outage when Rob was away, the digital clock would just keep
blinking until he got home. Now the clocks automatically reset using a
PBS carrier signal. Ain't technology grand!

Anti-Cranky Alternatives for Cranky Quiz Item # 4:
PROGRAM ME, PLEASE
Take a Minimalist Approach

As one who ventures only into the shallow end of the technology wad-
ing pool, I won't suggest you must know how to program everything in
your home. Instead, pick the areas for which you have some natural
skill, or have someone do it for you (even if you have to pay the person). Know what you need so you can get by, and keep the instructions
handy, just in case.

Granted, what I'm suggesting isn't the elegant way; it's the prag-
matist's way. If you're technologically gifted, skip over this part and
keep on hitting those keys. I'm just trying to save the techno deprived
from getting cranky.

Think before You Buy

When I bought my horse, Ladiebug, I wanted a mellow horse I could train
and trust; a sensible one that wouldn't hurt me. That's what I got. I've
seen too many unsuspecting owners buy hot, ill-tempered, potentially

dangerous horses they end up fearing. The phrase is "overhorsed" (I once owned such a beast). Although the technology may seem tempting in the beginning, don't allow yourself to get overhorsed. Salespeople often get excited about the frills, so redirect them back to the basics instead. After all, you're the one spending the money.

Think about how you intend to use a computer before you buy it. Word processing? Graphics? Video? Sound? Internet? Think basic. This will help your decision making. Resist buying a fancy piece of software or hardware just because the salesperson loves it. You're the consumer. You're paying the bill. If your home computer will be used by the entire family at varying levels of skill, keep that in mind. Do your research together. Talk to friends before you make your choice. Avoid unnecessary complexity. The easier it is to operate, the more likely you'll use it.

Share the Wealth

Many households have one computer for everyone in the family to share, which can be a source of tension for all involved. Mom wants to catch up on her E-mail, Dad wants to check an Internet site, the kids want to play computer games or surf the Net, and there's only so much time. Things get complicated when one computer must meet the needs of so many individual preferences, perceptions, and personalities (some of us get possessive and resent having to share).

If everyone uses the same screen name, there may be issues of privacy. Just like traditional correspondence, most of us consider our on-line "conversations" personal. If you all love the Internet you'll have to discuss time lines and turn taking. Sit down as a family and establish guidelines and a schedule. If everyone enjoys the Internet, one way to keep computer sessions short could be to maintain only one phone line in your home; the kids will recognize that time on-line ties up the phone and they'll be cut off from their friends during that period. If you end up with clashes over computer use refer to the conflict guidelines in chapter 4.

CRANKY QUIZ ITEM # 5:
VIRTUAL FRIENDSHIPS

> 5. ___Are you more inclined to stay in touch with friends who have
> E-mail than those who don't?

Technological Ties That Bind

"This is my new friend. I don't like you anymore!" Those were crushing words when I was ten years old. I still remember how much it hurt,
being rejected for someone different, someone new. Those are still
crushing words today, yet this is what some of us do without saying
anything, as we link up and play with our new exciting cyber friends
while old, real friendships fade into the sunset. Before I go any further,
please know I have two on-line (cyber) friends I've never met. Both are
dressage riders and that's our bond, but our exchanges go beyond
horses and riding lessons. I consider each of these women friends
although I could walk past them on the street without realizing it.

Virtual relationships transcend physical attributes; we get only the
essence of the individual. I like that. Of course, in this cranky world,
this can be, and often is, abused. There's a lot of sex on the Internet yet
someone who *appears* to be an attractive, sensual sex kitten might actually be a foul-smelling, heavy-breathing pervert; you just never know!
Bizarre incidents occur as a result of interludes on the Internet: love
affairs (real and virtual), stalking, murder, and cultism, to name a few.

But let's venture back to the root of this discussion, which is this:
Don't trade long-standing friends who aren't on-line for the novelty of
new cyber friends. Can you have both? Of course. You just need to
make sure you're giving time to those who matter.

Anti-Cranky Alternatives for Cranky Quiz Item # 5:
Virtual Relationships
Ask Why You Go Where You Go

Communications technology has given us the impression that we
should freely express our opinion on every social issue, trivial or substantive. When I log on to AOL I'm intrigued with the constant invita-
tions to "talk about" whatever scandal or news item draws the latest
buzz. I can't imagine why I'd want to spout off on a chat line with

strangers who don't know any more about the situation than I do. But there must be some appeal because people do it.

The few times I've visited message boards to research a health or social issue, most of the comments reflected people's honest attempts to discuss an issue intelligently, but I've found my share of cranky tirades, too. Websites and special interest groups are one thing (book clubs, garden enthusiasts, bird-watching groups, and the like), but in a world where time is such a precious commodity, if you're drawn to open chat rooms or bulletin boards so you can vent your spleen (or read someone else's mental droppings), ask yourself why.

Invest in Real Friendships

Some people say they can be more open with their cyber friends than "real" ones because of the anonymity. This is a symptom of dis-Connectedness. Why depend on a virtual stranger to confide in, when you have real people in your life? If you feel you can't be yourself, or can't comfortably reveal yourself to your spouse or a good friend, consider finding a good counselor. Don't get me wrong; on-line pals can be fun when they share an interest, and you do get pretty well acquainted as your exchanges broaden in scope. But remind yourself that you have a life off-line and a collection of loved ones and friends who deserve priority attention.

Real-life loved ones always get first dibs! If you find you're putting more time in with cyber people (or computer games) than your own family, take a Quick Stop! Evaluate what's going on. Push the off button on your computer. Swap the on-line chat chums for real people: Write a note. Make a phone call. Take your partner out on a date. Do something before you make someone you care about really cranky.

CRANKY QUIZ ITEM # 6:
ON THE LINE

> 6. ___ Do you spend an hour or more on-line each day?

Help! I'm Logged On and I Can't Get Off

There are self-help support groups in our country for just about every behavioral problem or condition you can think of: substance abuse, grieving, ADD, dyslexia, pre-divorce, post-divorce, cancer, eating disorders, arthritis. Support groups provide a great forum and should I ever need one I'll certainly join. But as with all good ideas, once in a while they go over the top.

The *on-line support group for the computer addicted* tickled me, and no, I'm not joking. I love the irony of using the source of addiction as part of the cure! Maybe they limit the amount of time you can spend with your support group. Maybe you get cut off after only a few minutes and can't call back. Maybe they let you stay logged on for unlimited periods as long as you don't enjoy it.

Humor aside, people *do* get addicted to computers, from E-mail or chat lines and Internet sites to just plain old computer games. Maybe their lives just don't hold up to the fantasy they find on the screen, but computer addictions are real and can mean trouble (sexual mischief, affairs, and fraud, for example).

Anti-Cranky Alternatives for Cranky Quiz Item # 6: On the Line

Clock Yourself

A woman in one of my seminars said her husband got so hung up on computer games for a while he would ignore their son. The little boy would stand next to his dad, pull on his pant leg, and beg for attention while his dad kept saying, "In a minute. In a minute." If not addictive, computers, chat rooms, the Internet, and even games can be serious time wasters. If your spouse, family, or roommate thinks you're spending too much time with your computer and not enough with them, either go cold turkey or put yourself on a very strict program. Just because you read an E-mail doesn't mean you have to respond immediately, or even at all. Let it hover in cyberspace till you get around to answering it. Then go spend time with your loved ones.

If computer time has caused (legitimate) crankiness in your family, make an agreement about how much time you will spend on your computer each day. Use a timer. Get up when it goes off. Calculate exactly how much time you spend sitting in front of your screen in lieu of loved ones before your spouse hides your modem.

In case you're curious, I average around forty minutes a day online and most of this is sending or answering E-mail. If I go to the Internet I can easily spend an hour or two, but this is rare for me. Sometimes

I wonder what I did with the time I now spend on-line and what I'd be doing if I hadn't decided to take the plunge.

Control Your Techno Craze

Technology is only a tool and you don't need to elevate it to any higher plane than it deserves. Once again, the word is *perspective*. Yes, I love my Macintosh but it's only a machine. When the *bigger, better, faster, more, now* upgrade bug makes me itch, I remind myself that based on my needs (mostly word processing) I don't really require anything more powerful or faster. Resist the commercial pressure designed to entice you into buying every high-tech contrivance or upgrade that comes along. This could be a good time for me to tell you about the scanner I bought a couple of years ago and still haven't plugged in, but maybe I'll just forget it.

Before you buy something, ask yourself:

- Is this a want or a need?
- How often would I use this if I had it?
- Can I afford it?
- Is there anything legitimately wrong with what I already own?
- Have I gotten sucked into a *bigger, better, faster, more, now* frame of mind?

Computers can be costly in many ways. Revisit your priorities so you don't go overboard in terms of time, money, or relationships; it's deceptively easy to do. My friend Terry Brock, a technology expert, is quick to say, "Love people and use machines, not the other way around."

CRANKY QUIZ ITEM # 7:
TO HECK WITH HIGH TECH

> 7. ___ Given the choice, are you more likely to do a task in a high-tech manner (machine, power tool, or appliance) rather than low-tech (by hand)?

Was There Life before Technology?

Last winter we experienced a severe ice storm and went without power for three days. We have a generator but it was still quite an adventure, plugging or unplugging one appliance to run another and reverting to conservative water use. With a warm fire burning in the fireplace we played Scrabble by candlelight and huddled together under our non-functioning electric blanket and a sleeping bag. When we periodically turned off the generator it was pleasant and strangely peaceful without the usual household motors humming. We ate simple foods and in the evening we read by lantern light. Just about the time we'd gotten used to this scaled-back existence the power came back on, punctuated with beeps, blinks, and hums as we bounced back into our world of refrigerators, running water, computers, answering machines, and push-button energy. It was both a relief and a disappointment.

A Blast from the Past

Maybe you've occasionally wondered how our ancestors handled weather, maintained their homes, fed their families, or traveled. Imagine the expectation level of pioneers who set out for the West, knowing it would literally take months, and that they might never arrive (a skeptic might say that it sounds like air travel today). Despite occasional inconveniences, technology makes our lives much easier, but not without a cost.

Technology insulates us from the real world. Middle class kids can't imagine living in a house or riding in a car without air-conditioning. They can't fathom walking a long distance to school or cutting grass with a push mower (maybe they haven't even *seen* a push mower). Kids wonder what people did for entertainment before TV and computers, or how anyone could possibly have gotten by without a pair of hundred-dollar, high-tech sport shoes.

One Step Removed

Review your history and the technological changes you've experienced in your lifetime. Evaluate how you've become more insulated as a result. Here's what I mean by insulation: Our food is raised by farmers, processed and prepared by corporations, sold to us in attractive packages. We don't have to kill or dress an animal for meat; milk our cow; sow, harvest, or mill our grains; or grow our own vegetables (unless we garden). Once these edibles get inside our doors, we have stoves, food processors, bread makers, microwaves, blenders, juicers, and pasta machines—tools that can help us prepare a formal dinner for twelve without getting our hands dirty.

We're also insulated from having to chop our own wood, fix our own car, make our own furniture, or build our own house unless we want to. Many of our homes, cars, and workplaces are air-conditioned so our temperature and humidity are monitored. We might spend more time indoors than outside, so we don't get much exposure to the elements. Some of us have never seen, let alone tasted, warm, raw milk, or eaten a vegetable fresh from the soil.

Frankly, we sweat a lot less as a result of technology. We've become unaccustomed to the natural smell of our own bodies and consider it a turnoff. We're powdered, perfumed, sprayed, splashed, cologned, and deodorized, yet we don't even work up a sweat as long as we're within reach of a battery, electric outlet, or fuel pump (this is one of the reasons it's so easy to put on weight). Insulation from the elements isn't inherently evil, but it can cause us to lose the essence of what being alive is all about. Being one step removed from so many basic life functions warps our perspective and helps contribute to a crankiness that spikes at the slightest imposition.

Anti-Cranky Alternatives for Cranky Quiz Item # 7:
To Heck With High Tech
Take Things into Your Own Hands

Take a moment to tally up the technology that insulates you, first in your home and then at work. Then think about the noise it produces. Consider the insult to your ears and mind when you use this equipment, and its inherent hazards, compared to a low-tech approach. Now, cranky people would be put off by the silence of working by hand; they might also argue that they don't have time to do a task this way. I contend that this is part of the problem. Some people complain they don't have time to exercise yet they spend half a day sitting on a riding mower clipping acres of grass (more on this topic in chapter 11).

Avoid the Vast Waist Land

Rather than insulating yourself with technology, make room for more first-hand experience. This will mean less noise, more exercise, more exposure to tactile experiences, and usually less expense, too. Of course, use judgment. If you're a couch potato and unaccustomed to heavy work, don't go out and hand shovel your long driveway or chop a cord of wood! But if you surround yourself with things that beep, blink, whir, hum, or roar, here are four suggestions for adding a quieter, simpler dimension to your life:

- Write by hand more. Between computers, pocket planners, and other high-tech tools, some of us literally forget how to write (I mean the actual motions, not the content). Make notes. Let your hand move. Start a journal and write one page a day. Send notes to friends or family. Writing is good for your brain. In the introduction to this book I invited you to keep a special notebook of insights and ideas. I hope you're doing that.
- Regularly engage in low-tech methods (such as dicing vegetables for a special meal or raking leaves). Pay attention to what you're doing. Stay *in the moment* with every step and consciously let the sensations, sounds, or smells of the repetitive motions fill your senses. In your busy life you seldom have a chance to get fully engrossed in an activity, so take advantage.
- Monitor what thoughts are generated as a result of what you're doing—childhood memories, for example. Raking leaves in the fall evokes a sense of timelessness in me. The feel of the rake against the ground, the sound of leaves crunching, and the combined smell of the dry leaves and crisp fall air create a sense of suspended time. It's as if I'm swept into a space where I can experience every fall of my life in this one moment. The sensation doesn't last the whole time I'm raking; it comes and goes, but it's an utterly delicious feeling.
- Do something every day that raises a sweat. In our modern, appliance-saturated world, our bodies don't work as hard as they used to. That's why exercise is so necessary; it provides repetitive motions that build strength and endurance. So can hard physical work. Sweating is a natural, normal process and it's *good* for us, not something to avoid.

Handy Thoughts

The presence of appliances and machines interferes with our ability to keep mind and body connected. Ask yourself how you might enrich your existence by reintroducing some pleasurable low-tech processes back into your life. Whether handwriting a letter to someone you care about, hand washing and ironing a favorite garment, mending a broken chair, cutting vegetables, trimming hedges, waxing your car, washing dishes, or raking leaves, *fully engage* in what you're doing, as if it's a meditation. Allow yourself to get fully immersed. Maybe your *muscle memory* will kick in and, as happens with my raking experience, you'll recall good times from your past.

We're usually so preoccupied with our "to do" list we seldom give ourselves over to everyday chores; yet the direct, full engagement changes the nature of the task. This is why so many people enjoy gardening. Compare your low-tech experiences with when you use power appliances or tools. Think about how disappointed or cranky you feel when someone else's power equipment shatters your solitude. Maybe you'll agree there's a personal cost in using too much technology, too unconsciously, too often.

Practice Safe Specs

Buy a power tool or complicated appliance and the specifications often include a cautionary note implying or outright telling you that using this piece of equipment could be hazardous to your health. Many consumers blow off this advice and end up injuring themselves or an innocent bystander, and then to add insult to injury, they tie up the legal system with frivolous lawsuits. If you must use power technology:

- Know how to use it properly and safely! Don't just assume you know.
- Do something unique: actually read the directions!
- Wear ear protection even if you think you don't need it.
- Keep small children away from the area you're working in.

Cranky people would read this, thinking, "Yada, yada . . ." and then put the book down and go out and hurt themselves. This is because sometimes when we engage a motor, we disengage our brain. Stay aware: Don't let the drone of power tools lull you into a trance. Operating powerful machinery can incite a "slash-and-burn" mentality. It's easy to get careless because you can just run over, chew up, and spit out whatever lies in your path. Go for finesse in your life rather than force.

CRANKY QUIZ ITEM # 8:
THE TECHNOLOGY TRAP

> 8. ___ Are you ever inconvenienced by constant product changes, improvements, or upgrades?

Intelligent Products, Perplexed Owners

Sometimes the same technology that makes things easier also makes life more complex. A man I met on a flight once complained that his fancy "do everything" watch was two hours off and he'd lost the instructions. All the calculating and counting was making him cranky. I suggested he move to that time zone.

At a horse show, one of my friends wanted to have his last ride videotaped. It was one of those hazy Michigan midsummer days with both temperature and humidity hovering in the high eighties. When Fred turned on his fancy new videocam to test it, he got an "alert" message that read, "Dew Detected!" and the camera shut itself off, refusing to operate under the existing conditions. We teased Fred about his videocam's union contract exempting it from having to work on hot, humid days.

How do you feel about products that are programmed to make decisions for you? I'm all for a seat belt alert, as a die-hard user for decades, but I'd rather lock my own car doors than have them lock *for* me every time I take off. I'd like to have the capability to disarm my car's air bag if necessary (I've read about small children being killed when air bags deployed upon low-speed impact). What product do you use that dictates how you operate it instead of giving you choice?

My friend Carol once had a car whose doors locked whenever they were closed, even if the motor was running! Imagine stopping at the mailbox, or jumping out of the car to grab something and hearing that fateful *"click!"* Convenience is one thing, and an attempt to outfox human error has virtue, but when products exhibit their own sense of entitlement, we've gone too far.

Upgrade Hell: When Bigger Isn't Better

I loved my first Ford Explorer. After tooling around in a little Mazda R-X7 for six years in rain, snow, sleet, and gloom of night, the four-wheel drive and increased visibility were quite a treat. Five years later, when I replaced my first Explorer with another, I didn't realize that Ford had "upgraded" this model by increasing its size. I noticed the new height but the rest of the changes escaped me. One week after getting my new car I began having lower back pain, a rarity for me. With my new car the only recent change in my life, I did some investigating. My sore back was the result of an expanded and now too-large driver's seat. Rob performed liposuction on it and my backaches disappeared. I can't believe Ford just introduced yet another SUV (Supremely Ubiquitous Vehicle): the nine passenger Excursion. Shades of the sixties and the mobile fortresses people drove: The *bigger, better, faster, more, now* is rolling in high gear these days!

It's not just the automobile industry that feels compelled to upgrade whenever anyone sneezes. The computer industry lives on upgrades, and in fact builds its future on them! Now, at last, we've arrived at the area that really raises my Cranky Quotient! Whether customers need them or not, new models and upgrades relentlessly roll off the line like donuts in a Dunkin' Donuts factory. And every time we upgrade there's a chance of losing some (or all) of our old data. Think duplicates. Think backup. Think double or triple backup, just in case. New or upgraded computer software devours memory like I eat M&M's. Every time I've (reluctantly) undergone a significant software or AOL upgrade I've had to buy new memory for my computer.

As a no frills minimalist kind of user, after software upgrades I find my new system bulked up with irksome visuals, unusable options, and unnecessary features. I confess to being a fiercely loyal Macintosh fan, but I'm so far behind in hardware and system upgrades that Mac literature now reads like foreign publications. Call me backward, reactionary; I sidestep upgrade hell when I can and wish there were a low-end upgrade kit for slackers like me who only want to play in the shallow end of the pool. Maybe there are others out there who feel the same way. E-mail me.

Anti-Cranky Alternatives for Quiz Item # 8:
The Technology Trap
Buy the Best Match

Just as in a marriage, look for a good match between what you bring to the desktop and what the technology brings to you. Many people tell me they wanted to buy a Macintosh because they loved its user friendly nature but they ended up buying an IBM clone because it was cheaper. You'll have your computer for a long time. Why settle for less than what you want just to save a few dollars? For me, sitting in front of my computer for hours a day has to be enjoyable, and my Mac makes it so.

If I had another kind of computer I'd be cranky for sure! People tell me they're worried that Apple will fold and then they'll never be able to buy new software, but this concern has been voiced for well over a decade now! In fact, it's been almost that long since I bought any new software. If you're timid about computers; if you're artistic or intuitive, buy the hardware that pleases you, whatever system or style it is.

Put a Lid on Your Techno Lust

If you're a high-end user and your skills are "way out there," you have a different challenge. You have to avoid buying every upgrade or new feature that comes along or you'll break the bank. Every week there's a new techno gizmo, and contrary to what the ad says, you *can* live without it. It's tough knowing that the minute you buy new hardware or software there's already something better in the pipeline. Live with what you have and enjoy it. In the computer world, *bigger, better, faster, more, now* is a way of life. Control your lust for more because it's a losing game in time, money, and energy. Yes, techno toys are fun, but if they're taking up a lot of your time and energy, isn't there an actual person (or little ones) in your life who might benefit from some nice low-tech attention?

CRANKY QUIZ ITEM # 9:
AT THE SPEED OF BLIGHT

> 9. ___ Do unexpected electronic breakdowns make you impatient or cranky?

Breakdown: When Bad Things Happen to Good Computer Chips

"Sorry. The computer's down." These four simple words are enough to stop the staunchest heart, as visions of wasted time and money and an explosion of errors dance in one's head. With our global connections, sometimes the exhalations of a computer burp in the Big Apple can be felt in the Outback.

But often, for the average person like you or me, it merely means inconvenience: a long wait, a return visit, or reconstructing a paper trail. Chips fail. Satellites go out of orbit. Batteries corrode or die. Software corrupts. Viruses invade and take over. Programmers blunder. Technology is fallible. Some breakdowns or slowdowns will directly affect you; some won't. But let's keep this issue in the controllable realm so you have a few options for handling techno emergencies.

Anti-Cranky Alternatives for Cranky Quiz # 9: At the Speed of Blight

Program Yourself for More Patience

Pretend you've never heard anything like this before: Moments of inconvenience caused by technological breakdowns offer you the perfect opportunity to practice many of the good ideas offered in this book. The next time a teller, clerk, or technician informs you that their computer has just bit the Big One, take a deep, relaxing breath and smile. There's nothing you can do. You don't know how bad it's going to be. All you know right now is that you're going to have to wait to complete your transaction. Yes, you will be inconvenienced. But why get hung up over a complete uncontrollable?

After having read seven other chapters in this book, you should be well prepared for such an event. Simply decide that the universe has given you a test and you're an A+ student! Laugh. Go have a cappuccino or an herbal tea. And while you're sipping, remind yourself that you are only one person and the universe is not dumping on you, trying to ruin your day or your life. In the scheme of things you are just one of umpty-ump people who will be inconvenienced today. Why should you take it personally?

Sort Out What You Should Take Personally

I feel compelled to take a momentary side trip to cover this whole issue of not taking things personally because under certain conditions the concept can come back to bite you. It's one thing to tell *yourself* to not take things personally and quite another when someone else says it. Here's what I mean:

- When you remind yourself to not take things personally you're making a rational choice. You recognize the folly of thinking this incident (or person) is out to get *you and you alone* (let's face it, some people are nasty to everyone!), and when some company's computer gets a flat tire it has nothing to do with you.
- When others suggest that you not take things personally it can be a different matter. Your boss, for example, may be telling you to tolerate a coworker's crankiness to avoid having to confront the person. Sometimes instead of resolving differences people try to sidestep the matter by telling you to not take it personally. Some may, in effect, be telling you to not *feel*.

Here's a rule of thumb: when *things* happen (technological break-downs, mistakes, equipment failures) don't take it personally. When *people* issues happen, think about how to best approach the situation. Sometimes people *do* say things to compete with you or express their displeasure; other times they simply speak without the luxury of having engaged their brain beforehand. Some issues *should* be taken personally. Use your combined logic and intuition to guide you toward what you think will be the most appropriate response.

Get Real

Our high-speed, high-tech world of constant upgrades has quite an effect on our expectations, and this brings me to one of my favorite oxymorons: slow microwaves. Yes, we feed on speed. Every time I buy a faster modem I feel a twinge of embarrassment as I remember the times I sat and sat while my little 512k Mac hummed its way from one function to another. Yes, it was slow, but I was still blown away by what it could do.

These days, as I switch between my office Mac (an ancient 1993 Centris 650) and my PowerBook (an ancient 1994 PB-520), I have to adjust. My PowerBook is slower than my big computer. That extra five to ten seconds can feel very long. Most of the time I'm able to pop a Reality Bite and remind myself that this is a good time for me to entrain to a slower pace and go with the flow. It's a choice. You have that choice, too.

Could you instead view that slow printer or plotter as some kind of technological miracle, not because of its speed, but because it exists at all? Could you remind yourself that machines, like people, occasionally break down and there's nothing you can do about it? Glitch happens. Just because technology usually travels at the speed of light doesn't mean it always will. Your flexibility and sense of humor will help make the time pass when you get stopped by a techno hitch.

CRANKY QUIZ ITEM # 10: PRERECORDED PEOPLE

> 10. ___ When calling an organization do you get irked at having to interact with electronic voices instead of live human beings?

I'll Have My Voice Mail Talk to Your Voice Mail

What does it say about our society that you're surprised when a living, breathing human being answers the phone? Now you have to talk! Of course, stumbling over your words in real time is still less embarrassing than knowing that your poorly chosen words have been memorialized on someone's answering machine or voice mail.

I was initially resistant to voice mail but now I like it, provided the system is user friendly and efficient. I appreciate machines and depend on mine to record messages in my absence or to "phone sit" for me when I don't want to be interrupted. But recorded messages and voice mail can be grating for the uninitiated and the impatient.

Voice mail is a mixed bag. Whether it works depends on what you need when you call, and how well the system is set up. I once called Northwest Airlines and changed flight reservations using *only* voice mail prompts. The process was both efficient and effective. I was able to change my flight time without ever consulting a human being. The system worked!

On the other hand, I've phoned client organizations and found it impossible to reach my party, who had not left an extension number, so I got caught in a techno loop that left me in limbo. From a customer service perspective you'd think organizations would look for simplicity when they select or design a voice-mail system, but sadly they often don't.

And then there's phone tag. Just a few years ago this phrase didn't even exist; now it's standard operating procedure.

Anti-Cranky Alternatives for Cranky Quiz Item # 10: Prerecorded People

Let Technology Work for You at Work

Some employees are asked to review various voice-mail technologies before a company purchases a system. If you're this fortunate, look for simplicity of operation to keep callers from getting cranky:

- Present the menu of caller options in the most expeditious order so that the most frequent response is first on the list and the most obscure at the end.
- If many options exist, use a sequence of short prompts rather than one long, complicated list.
- If your prerecorded message offers a menu of options with a series of follow-up recordings, keep the secondary greeting very short.
- If you use a time-sensitive greeting ("Today is Monday, July . . .") keep it current.
- Make sure that ending the call, disengaging from the system, or contacting a real human being is an easy step for the caller.

The same rule of simplicity applies to pagers and any other message devices. You may be a technological whiz but your callers may not be (I'm still never sure what I'm expected to do with a pager). But keep the caller in mind and you'll probably choose the right technology for your communications needs.

Tips for Winning at Phone Tag

By the third call, phone tag starts making us all just a little cranky. In one instance, the game went on long enough that a client was so impressed with my persistence he hired me. Other times I've been able to successfully give or receive requested information from another party while never actually speaking with the person. But there have also been times when one or both of us gave up. I hope the following ideas will help you shorten the game of telephone tag.

It helps to leave enough information so someone can take some kind of action if you miss each other. Assuming you know the basics of telephone communication (leave the day, date, time, your name and number, and brief message), here are some additional strategies.

- If your message is too complicated to leave on voice mail, tell the person you will follow up with a fax explaining the details.
- If you need the person's fax number, let it be known in your initial call.
- Give a time window (days, dates, times) when the person can reach you.
- If you unexpectedly end up in your office call or fax the person to announce your availability.
- If you'll be away from the office for a few days let the person know. State your return date.

Use your fax machine creatively if phone calls aren't working. I once made a "fill out" form for a client who wanted to order some books; she completed it and I filled the order without talking on the phone. It helps to take the transaction one step closer to the result you desire.

Prioritize When You Accessorize

Telephone service now comes with almost as many accessories as a Barbie Doll. Call waiting is one such frill and there seem to be two camps. The anti-call waiting camp hates hearing that fateful click. They say it's as if the other party is saying, "Excuse me, I consider your call potentially less important than the one waiting for me. Wait just a minute while I confirm that notion." People get cranky about playing second fiddle to a new caller, *yet many of these same individuals pay for and use call waiting on their own phones!* The second camp prefers call waiting because they get cranky when they hear a busy signal. Obviously, there's no easy answer here. You'll just have to choose whichever approach makes you the least cranky: How's that for options?

A DOSE OF REALITY ABOUT COMPUTERS

Technology is embedded in our lives in ways we aren't even aware of; if you were allergic to it, even in your own home you'd probably suffer from overexposure. Computers are here to stay and if you've worked yourself into a cranky, resistant posture over what really just amounts to a clever blend of plastic, copper, and "smart sand" you just need a little attitude adjustment, that's all. Sometimes we work ourselves into a state over something we think we can't do, and only after we conquer the issue do we realize we had created a mountain out of a molehill.

MORE POWER TO YOU

You'll stay in great shape as long as you remember that computers and high-tech machines are only tools and you're the higher life-form. They're not smarter than you. They have no sense of humor. And they don't have to make you cranky (at least not too often). I encourage you to maintain your perspective about how technology fits in your life on a broader scale, what it can do for you, and what it can't. Ultimately, you're the one who makes the choice about what constitutes the best fit for the job.

Take power tools and outdoor equipment, for example. They're very effective, but depending on what you use, or for how long, the noise can intrude on your peace of mind and prevent you from connecting with the natural world. To maintain a balance in your life and preserve your peace of mind, make sure you engage in a variety of low-tech, slow-tech processes. It will also keep you from getting lazy or too insulated. Every now and then, drive with your car windows open to feel the breeze. If you have central air, don't use it for a few days during a warm spell to remind yourself of what life was like in another era. Open your windows and let your house (and your brain) air out. On the weekend, go without deodorant; let your armpits air out, too. Spend a night with candlelight instead of incandescent. In the summer, walk barefoot in the grass. Mop a floor on your hands and knees. Literally stop and smell the roses!

When we get so insulated from basic day-to-day labors, our expectations skew; we expect technology to work flawlessly (because it usually does) and we become intolerant and cranky toward inconvenience. I find that engaging in life's fundamental tasks adds a dash of "realness" to my existence. It reminds me that things weren't always so convenient and I'm less likely to get huffy when little things go wrong.

We lose a part of our humanity when we become too far removed from basic functions: walking, working, eating, engaging in a simple task with a loved one, working up a good sweat, and coming in direct contact with the earth. Think about ways you can blend your use of technology with carefully chosen hands-on labor. High-tech devices feed your desire for speed and convenience, but low-tech methods feed your spirit. Careful, conscious choices between the two can offer you the best of both worlds. You'll stay in better touch with yourself and spend more time *in the moment*. It's all a question of balance.

Change

MORE CHANGE THAN WE WANT,
LESS CHANGE THAN WE NEED

On the same day in the same physician's office, two men are given the same diagnosis; their lifestyle is slowly killing them. The advice: relax, work less, exercise more, quit smoking, eat less fat, and find something to do besides work. Three weeks later, one man is still working long hours, sneaking cigarettes and junk food, arguing that the doctor was wrong. The other man has cut back his work hours, begun a walking program, switched to a vegetarian diet, and enrolled in a yoga class. One of these men would rather die than change while the other would rather change than die.

People tell me all the time how hard it is to change. They hate it when their job assignment changes. They recoil when they hear the word *reorganization*. Whether the backdrop is work or home, change is a touchy topic. Some people use their age as an excuse, saying they're too old to handle yet one more transition or shift, but older people have gone through more change than the rest of us—they should be good at it! Change is a lot like the weather. We can complain about it, even get cranky, but it's still an *uncontrollable*.

TOO CLOSE FOR COMFORT

Our world constantly changes. Fads come and go, as do products, styles, and people. Most of us go along with exterior changes to keep pace with fashion, but the interior changes are quite another matter. Change touches on something both universal and personal. Maybe this is because some of us were taught as children to just accept things and not analyze them too deeply, that we shouldn't spend too much time "in our heads." Consequently, as adults our inclination is to keep our emotional distance from personal problems.

Even among friends, just mention something introspective ("I've been thinking lately about my resistance to change and I'm wondering if it's connected to my insecurities . . .") and watch the conversation screech to a self-conscious halt. It seems easier to stay miserable and pretend everything is okay than to go through the work of discovering what keeps us from being happy. If we ever figure it out then we have to force ourselves through a bundle of changes to make things better. Some of us will decide that this sounds like too much work, so maybe we just ought to leave things as they are.

Of course, that's short-term thinking. Sooner or later, whatever bugs us will come back and bite us in the backside if we don't take care of it up front. That's how we've become so cranky in the first place. Having to admit that we have some personal work to do is potentially embarrassing (even to ourselves) because it involves reconciling self-esteem issues, resolving the ever-present gap between illusion and reality, and accepting the cold, chilling fact that we are not perfect. It's difficult taking that long, rational look in the mirror where we're forced to admit there's some hard work to be done. But denial is even harder; our unaddressed issues eat at us until we can't stand it any longer or we lapse into a long-term case of crankiness.

BEEN THERE, DONE THAT

There was a time I feared self-knowledge. When Rob and I began our counseling, I was afraid of letting the therapist know who I really was because then I'd have to find out, too. I had to face parts of myself I didn't like, but that's what helped me change. I learned that self-improvement comes through exploration, acknowledgment, and acceptance: the ability to say, "Yes, I do this, and now that I've admitted it, I can change this behavior."

We waste tremendous amounts of energy running away from ourselves. It takes time to learn that the only real shortcut is to head straight for what hurts, to muddle through it, and come out the other side. Is the process of self-exploration easy? No, but by refusing to do our inner work, we end up feeling trapped, yearning for our lives to be different but unable to make it happen. If you're willing to work through your layers of dysfunction (we all have them) you'll have fewer reasons to be cranky. That's what this chapter is all about.

THE GOOD, THE BAD, AND THE UGLY

Maybe one of the reasons we get queasy about change is because of its uncontrollable nature. We see things happening to people (illness, accidents, traumas) and pray we'll be spared such disasters. Instead of feeling grateful for our health, freedom, or happiness while we have it, we begin to expect the negative. We brace ourselves, waiting for the other shoe to fall. Thanks to our gloomy outlook, we tend to view change as bad. No wonder so many of us are cranky, treading through life with one eye out for catastrophe and the other for woe! When changes do occur, we often have a tendency to focus on the parts we can't control rather than the options that may exist.

A MODEL FOR CHANGE

There's an irony lurking beneath this entire subject, which is that when it comes to handling work-related change most of us have a tool. We often use the standard Five-Step Model of problem solving:

1. information gathering
2. method testing
3. incorporating new approaches
4. evaluating the results
5. course correcting

Personal change requires the same process. Imagine if you constantly evaluated your *interpersonal behaviors* on their merit and efficacy, just as you might at work. Imagine continually searching for new information and approaches; when things no longer work, you start looking for a better way. When proven worthy, old behaviors are replaced by new, more effective ones. You know these steps; you do them all the time at work and with hobbies. Why not in your personal life? Think about the Five-Step Model the next time you bump up against an ineffective way of thinking or behaving. It will help you feel more confident and less cranky.

Truth be told, we live in an ever-changing world. Things will hap-

Cranky Quiz

CHANGE

Scoring the Cranky Quiz

Score 1 point for every *yes* and 0 for every *no*. Count a *sometimes* as a *yes*. Add your total: 3 points or less (Cool) means you're in good shape, 4 to 7 (Warm) indicates a need to slow down, and 8 to 10 (Hot!) indicates a raging cranky infection. You'll find anti-cranky solutions for each quiz item in this chapter.

1 ___ Do you find change bothersome, especially when you feel you have no control or choice in the situation?

2. ___ Do constant, everyday changes contribute to your stress level?

3. ___ Are you irritated by today's security systems, surveillance cameras, sign-in logs, ID verification, and other protective measures?

4. ___ Are you less likely to be thrilled, amused, or shocked than you once were?

5. ___ After a disagreement do you wait for the other person to make the first move before you're willing to talk about it?

6. ___ Do issues from your past sometimes interfere with your present peace of mind?

7. Do you think there's too much emphasis on affirmative action, cultural diversity, and the rights of minorities or protected groups?

8. When required to attend "soft skills" training at work (communication, team building, stress management) do you resent the time away from your job?

9. Do you feel that your beliefs, values, or political views are truly the way things should be?

10. When given criticism or feedback about your behavior do you feel compelled to justify or defend your actions?

Cranky Quotient _____

My change condition is (*circle one*)   Cool   Warm   Hot

pen, whether we approve or not. A negative attitude won't stop things from happening; it only stops us from enjoying or appreciating them. Thanks to increasingly fast-changing technology, the cycle of change (like time) has been compressed. The longer we live, the more change we'll experience. This is a reality we must come to accept.

As your world changes, why cling to old, outdated behaviors that no longer work for you? Many of the changes you've experienced in recent years have probably had a good side; would it help to review exactly how you've benefited? Maybe some of the changes you've experienced weren't so positive; have you let yourself accept them so you can move on? Just as you want to prosper in your work, you also want to thrive in your personal life: In both arenas, change is the gateway to insight, growth, and success, and the best news is, you're already familiar with the process that can take you there. You've done it hundreds of times.

MORE THAN SMALL CHANGE

Things Just Ain't Like They Used to Be

A couple gets into their car. After many years of marriage the woman turns to her husband and says, "We never sit close together in the car anymore, like we did when we were young." He looks at her from behind the wheel and responds, "Well, honey, I'm not the one who moved!" Sometimes we change without even realizing it. Other times we need to modify our behavior but it's the last thing we want to do.

Please Pass the Whine

Let's get the groaning over with early on in this chapter so we can get down to business. Yes, life can be hard and change can be difficult. Yes, change is inconvenient. Yes, it's constantly happening and it's a real pain when you have no choice in the matter. And as soon as you adjust to one change, another will come along right behind it. There. We got it all out. Now do you feel better?

Shift Happens

Change can be traumatic, but it helps us build new skills, alter our view of the world (and ourselves), learn, grow, and broaden our horizons.

Change helps us shift our perception of who we are and how our world works. *Actually, you're already an expert on change because it's something you've done consistently since the day you were born. You're much better at it than you think.*

Changes, good or bad, self-selected or externally imposed, bring their own set of challenges, and how we handle them is a personal choice. In the words of Christopher Reeve following his tragic riding accident, "If you want to stay in the game, you have to play the hand you're dealt." Unfortunately, some of us waste our energies whining and protesting instead of figuring how to best arrange our cards. In this chapter you'll have a chance to take an in-depth look at your attitude toward change and how you can better handle whatever life offers you.

CRANKY QUIZ ITEM # 1:
SMALL CHANGE

> 1. ___ Do you find change bothersome, especially when you feel you have no control or choice in the situation?

Here, Try This

When I upgraded my computer a few years ago it came with an enhanced keyboard, featuring a numeric keypad on the right side. As a right-handed person, this meant a farther reach to use the mouse. Watching me one day, my partner Rob said, "Why don't you put the mouse on the left side and then you won't have to reach so far." As one who is extremely right-hand dominant, I felt immediately resistant and wanted to retort, "Sure, Mr. Ambidextrous: easy for you to say!" I kept my mouth shut, but I didn't immediately take his advice, either.

A few days later he went on a trip and for some unknown reason I ended up switching the mouse to the left side of my keyboard. Rob was right. The reach *was* shorter and after a few hours my left hand began adjusting. I can now work equally well from both sides of the keyboard. This may seem like a trivial example, but I spend hours a day at my computer and this helps avoid muscle and tendon fatigue.

Anti-Cranky Alternatives for Cranky Quiz Item # 1: Small Change

Change the Size of Your Comfort Zone

If you think I'm suggesting change for its own sake, you're right. We're creatures of habit and it helps every now and then to do something new or different. Alter your morning grooming ritual; sleep on the other side of the bed; move from where you typically sit at the table. Shake yourself up a little bit. Pay attention to how it feels when you stretch your comfort zone, even with something as simple as changing the way you position a roll of toilet paper on its hanger.

All changes, large and small, feel strange or uncomfortable in the beginning. *But the more you put yourself in positions where you'll be uncomfortable, the more comfortable you'll become feeling uncomfortable.* When you stretch your comfort zone it stays stretched. You'll get used to experiencing the anxiety of the unknown.

Maybe you're wondering if I actually do this myself. The answer is yes. I'm always looking for ways to better handle situations that prompt nervousness, such as when I'm speaking to a large audience or riding my horse in the show ring. I know that confidence comes *after* performance, not before it. You can only increase your confidence by first laying it on the line. Sometimes people tell me they'll be better at handling change once they become more confident, but it doesn't work that way. Confidence is only built by operating outside of your comfort zone. Stretching your limits helps you discover your inner strength, and even if you're not 100 percent successful, you can feel good about having had the courage to try.

Take New Pathways to Change

In reading books on creativity I've learned that finding new ways to accomplish old tasks not only wakes up your nervous system, it creates fresh neural pathways in your brain, like a new scenic route off the main highway. I could almost feel new synapses firing when I switched mouse functions to my left hand. If you've ever read about brain hemispheres or whole brain learning you're aware that cross-function training enhances your mental acuity. Occasionally I consciously "teach" new skills to my less educated left hand to improve my mental flexibility.

Resist Your Resistance

Maybe it will bolster you to know that even I, a professional Change Agent, still feel an initial shot of resistance when forced to try something new. But here's the secret: I don't let it stop me. I work my way through the new territory because I know something better is on the other side. Even if, for some reason, I don't end up with a better outcome, I still end up better, and that means something to me.

When you smack up against your wall of resistance challenge it; explore it. Find out why you're so defensive. Think of your strong reaction as "emotional pay dirt." It tells you there's more to the story. Find out what it is (fear, insecurity, self-doubt) and then move ahead, in spite of it all. *Resist being influenced by your resistance!* Say to yourself, "Oh, I know this feeling. I'm resisting. What am I trying to protect or defend?" And then move on.

CRANKY QUIZ ITEM # 2:
THE STRESS MESS

> 2. ___ Do constant, everyday changes contribute to your stress level?

Yesterday, Today, and Tomorrow

Study human nature and you'll find we have an amazing capacity to prevail over seemingly insurmountable odds. When a big crisis happens, we somehow summon the strength and resources to handle it. But it's more often the buildup of life's irritating little changes that causes crankiness. Some of your daily frustrations such as traffic, weather, or long lines are uncontrollable. They represent things you *can't* change! They also represent sources of stress. Whether a change is uncontrollable, semicontrollable, or controllable, the stress that accompanies it will come in one of the following forms:

- The worry loop: anticipatory stress (stress of the future)
- The stress surge: situational anxiety (stress of the moment)
- Prolonged pressure: chronic strain (unrelieved stress over an extended period)
- Distant recall: residual distress (unresolved stress) to be covered in Quiz Item # 6

Maybe you're thinking you commonly experience all four—sometimes even in the same day! That's possible, but not necessary. Whatever your stress level, you'll appreciate the following information, because change, stress, and crankiness all tend to hang out together on the same street corner.

Anti-Cranky Alternatives for Cranky Quiz Item # 2: The Stress Mess

Shut Off the Worry Loop

Are you a worrier? If so, you need to ask yourself what good it does you. Worry prevents you from living *in the moment*, so rather than fixing on negative possibilities, force yourself to envision potential positive outcomes instead. It also helps to figure out how you'd handle things if the worst *were* to happen, and let go of your worries. You've planned; you've projected. You're prepared for all eventualities.

Worrying about a pending change and replaying your worry loop on the issue accomplishes nothing, except for ruining the moment you're supposed to be experiencing. Think of worry as "negative planning" because it points you in the opposite direction from where you want to go. Those who conquer their worry loop habit later discover that their worrying was an irrational attempt to control life's uncontrollables. Realistically, there's darned little in life you actually *can* control, including most of the changes that come your way.

Playing the worry loop doesn't work. The situation you're worried about will either happen or it won't (often, completely independent of your efforts). I used to let worry get the best of me: During the last year of my marriage, even though I was miserable, the thought of getting divorced and being on my own terrified me. For months I stressed myself out, fearing my husband would walk out on the kids and me any minute. Yet, just two weeks after he left, despite my lack of education and limited work skills, I found a job and began my new life. The lesson? Worrying about change produces stress; planning reduces it.

Steer the Stress Surge

Every day you'll have stressful moments; you cannot control or prevent every frustrating circumstance. But the *level* of stress you experience is always within your control. Wherever you are—at work, home, or traveling—when you feel a stress surge beginning to build, take an immediate Quick Stop! and marshal your mental and physical resources. Relax, breathe, release your tension. Push your Reset Button, and replace your stress-producing thoughts with calming ones.

Now add a positive mental picture of you acting calmly and competently. This is how world class athletes channel their extra energy (stress) to achieve peak performance. They steer themselves away from stress and toward success. Just like a disciplined athlete, you can face intimidating circumstances more confidently and capably by keeping your stress surge within tolerable limits.

Prevail over Prolonged Pressure Moment by Moment

Whether battling an illness, job loss, relationship problems, or some other kind of major life change, handling prolonged pressure mandates the *one day at a time* approach. Clinging to the past or getting angry will only compound your dilemma. Wishing things were different or worrying about tomorrow will deplete your much-needed energy. Each day will require your full focus so you can meet whatever challenges it brings.

When I listened to the audio version of Christopher Reeve's book, *Still Me*, I was touched by his assiduous capacity for separating each day from the next in the early days following his accident. By sheer force of will he grappled with each day's struggles, striving for one small personal victory at a time. Those who successfully battle illness, disability, or any kind of long-term challenge soon learn that the best way to minimize chronic strain is by making positive perseverance a way of life. By concentrating your focus on *now* you get through today while letting tomorrow take care of itself.

The Cranky Casualty List

Cranky people become victims of prolonged pressure because of their inability to handle common, everyday stressors. They have no tragic circumstances in their lives, no limiting physical condition, save a "hardening of the attitudes." Their only tragedy is their consistent refusal to control anxiety-imposing worry loops or stress surges. As a consequence, they rank high on the list of Cranky Casualties. Let me explain.

Some of us would rather deny that we're unhappy than go through the work of figuring out what ails us, and this gets us into trouble. The more unresolved problems we stockpile, the unhappier we get. The worse we feel, the harder it is to admit that something's wrong. This delicate framework of denial and defense gets more fragile with time.

Chronic avoidance causes us to live in a constant state of low-level grieving. We never resolve what's hurting us so we never get a chance to heal from it. We distract ourselves by overscheduling, overworking, and overspending, treating the symptoms instead of the cause. This constant state of combined denial and unrest makes us very cranky, and this is why we blow up over minor incidents and inconveniences; the magnitude of our unresolved mental burden gets the best of us.

I call this troublesome state of mind "emotional proud flesh." Proud flesh is a term veterinarians use to describe a wound that doesn't heal properly. Proud flesh heals from the outside in, rather than the inside out, consequently there's always an area that remains tender and vulnerable. Many of us suffer from "emotional proud flesh," and until we deal with the underlying issues eating away at us, the pain will always be there, no matter where we go or how fast we move. Working too much, spending too much, and moving too fast only compounds our dilemma. *We can heal our problems only from the inside out.*

CRANKY QUIZ ITEM # 3:
DON'T YOU TRUST ME?

3. ___ Are you irritated by today's security systems, surveillance cameras, sign-in logs, ID verification, and other protective measures?

This Is for Your Own Good

The first time a teller from my own bank asked for ID before cashing my check, I was insulted. She could see it on my face and she quickly said, "This is just a precaution. For our protection *and* yours, we always check signatures." Even this small community bank wasn't taking any chances!

From airport security to secured buildings, I've come to realize that these minor inconveniences represent the cost of mobility. We can wake up in one state and go to sleep in another and engage in transactions all over the world. We can order just about any product we want via the phone or Internet. No longer do local stores serve only friends and neighbors, and some of them want to take every precaution. Here's the reality: Security procedures exist. There's nothing we can do about it. Why get cranky over something you can't control?

Anti-Cranky Alternatives for Cranky Quiz Item # 3: Don't You Trust Me?

Don't Worry, Be Happy

There are all kinds of people in this world. Some, driven by greed, take advantage or break the law when given the opportunity. We law-abiding citizens suffer the consequences. If you're finding yourself insulted or exasperated over precautionary measures designed to prevent crime or thwart criminals, you have two choices: keep getting cranky, or get over it.

Yes, it's inconvenient, but why go ballistic? Yes, you may have an honest face, but so do some crooks. How can an employee possibly know what a wonderful person you are when you're getting cranky over having your ID checked?

You're a stranger, an unknown. You're not being singled out. They check everyone. *You are simply paying the price of a mobile, global society where businesses no longer know all of their customers.* Check out your expectations around this issue and give yourself a break. Just sign the log book; wear the visitor's badge; show your driver's license, wait quietly. Don't sigh, grumble, mutter, or sneer. It's your chance to keep your Cranky Quotient (and your blood pressure) nice and low.

Take the Initiative

Our mobile culture puts us in contact with strangers every day. When making business calls, if you're aggravated by being asked to identify yourself or explain the nature of your call, offer your name and reason for calling *before* the person answering the phone has time to ask. Even if you're a regular caller, do not assume everyone knows your voice: There are only a few psychic secretaries in the world, and they cost too much for the average business to hire. You'll do yourself and everyone else a favor by initiating these common courtesies.

CRANKY QUIZ ITEM # 4:
THE THRILL IS GONE

> 4. ___ Are you less likely to be thrilled, amused, or shocked than
> you once were?

The Kind of Change You Want to Resist

A lot of changes sneak right by us. Sometimes I wonder, just when was the exact moment that used cars became preowned? And when were models upgraded to super status? Are there any *regular* models anymore? Drinks and food are no longer small; they've been supersized. Outdoors catalogs have become a blend of products and adventure. Things around us transform and we seldom notice the actual moment of transformation. The same thing happens to *us*, and sometimes it takes a while to catch it.

For example, when we first take up a new hobby, fall in love, or get a new job, life becomes more exciting, but the thrill lasts only so long. One day we realize the newness is gone; now it *just is*. Over time, we settle into conditions we once held special, and unless we resist this subtle, slow turn we can become dulled to sources that once brought enjoyment and pleasure.

This happens in love, career, sports; just about every aspect of life. In time, sameness replaces novelty, and not unlike a drug addiction, it takes a higher dosage, or something new and different to get our juices flowing again. Some of us up the ante. We might change jobs, get divorced, have an affair (actual or virtual), increase the risk or difficulty in our sport of choice, or find a new, exotic diversion. Anything to avoid boredom.

Maybe this explains the popularity of risk venture sports, from mindless thrills requiring no skill such as bungee jumping or tandem sky diving, to Heli-skiing and Eco Challenges—extreme activities that summon an adrenaline rush to revitalize sluggish spirits. This may also explain the allure of movies featuring explicit sex scenes, brilliant special effects, and almost nonstop crashes, explosions, and violence.

The End of Privacy: Can We Talk?

We're accustomed to scandal and startling disclosure because we're knee deep in it. We've survived severe lapses in a president's judgment, widespread impropriety by business figureheads, and nonstop sexual innuendo in ads. These are changes we didn't need as a culture.

No *wonder* we have to keep upping the ante to feel thrilled! It's as if we've ingested a massive overdose of mental MSG, fried our palates, and from here on out, everything tastes bland.

Our minds are body-slammed with sensationalism day after day. In writing this book I've watched a few segments of each TV talk show so I could understand their angle and appeal. It only took a few minutes to realize that Jerry Springer may consider his show to hold no more import than a dust mote, but a lot of people take it to heart, including teenagers. The same applies to the other talk shows as well.

Anti-Cranky Alternatives for Cranky Quiz Item # 4: The Thrill Is Gone

Dismiss the Dysfunctional

You're not one of those people who watches sensational talk shows so you can bolster your sense of superiority and feel smug because you're not as screwed up as those dysfunctional guests, are you? What's to learn from people dredging out their soiled emotional laundry for all to see? If you want to be healthy and happy and make positive changes in your life, focus on what you're doing, not on what others are doing. There's little to be learned from negative examples. Why put pessimistic, unhealthy pictures in your head when what you want to do is make positive, thriving ones? Read an inspirational book instead. Write in your journal. Do some yoga. Walk the dog. Why focus on dysfunction when what you really want for your life is betterment?

Banish Your Boredom

The people who complain about being too busy and overloaded are usually the same ones who feed on scandal and dysfunction. They defend their talk show watching or tabloid reading by saying it breaks their boredom. Often, boredom sets in when we numb ourselves with trivial distractions instead of wholesome stimulation.

Quick thrills treat the symptoms, but not the causes. If the pleasure has drained out of your life, go inward to treat it, not outward. Boredom is a state of mind. Don't live as if you're tranquilized.

If you have to keep upping the ante to stay in the game, revisit your priorities and values so you can refresh your outlook and add the right kind of excitement to your life. This could be a good time for you to make a change! Learn a new skill or take up that hobby you've dreamed about. Find a therapist and discover who you really are. Explore your skills, attitudes, and capabilities. There's a world of potential within you, and the thrill of self-discovery is one that will last a lifetime.

Retrieve Your Wonder

A great book hit the shelves in 1998 about a giraffe who, in the nineteenth century, held the people of France spellbound as she was carted across the countryside on display for all to see. Michael Alleghenie's *Zarafa* documents the enchanting story. People stood in line for hours to see this exotic creature; whole towns came out to greet her as she passed through. After petting her and feeding her, they walked away with a sense of awe. In today's media-saturated society, think what it would take to duplicate that sense of wonder.

In a way, you don't have to go all that far. Just spend an hour with a toddler. Watch his eyes, his openness, his lack of expectation. Listen to her laugh, and feel her complete trust and comfort. When you leave, take some of that spirit with you.

If your sensibilities have been dulled by a society that "tells all and bares all," discipline yourself to view the world with a fresh mind. Let yourself be surprised. Take it all in. Look at the sky more often. Pay more attention to the natural world. Hold an everyday object in your hand and study it as if you've never seen anything like it before. Give up that numbed attitude of "been there, done that" and replace it with "try this, try that." It's sad that we get our sense of wonder trained out of us as we grow up, but you can revive it if you choose.

CRANKY QUIZ ITEM # 5:
I WILL IF YOU WILL

> 5. ___ After a disagreement do you wait for the other person to make the first move before you're willing to talk about it?

Dare to Make a Move

My older brother, Bob, invented a multitude of games in childhood that resulted in his getting to slug me, and in my desperation to gain his approval, I went along. One of the games was called Flinch. The object was to be as still as possible, without moving *anything*. Even blinking was considered a flinch. Inevitably, I would move, and he'd get to clobber me. Sometimes I think about that game when I see two people locked in a standstill over an issue, their only common ground being a mutual resolve to *not* resolve the problem. Nobody makes a move; no one dares to flinch. The fiber of many a relationship has been strained by one or both party's perverse refusal to budge.

Anti-Cranky Alternatives for Cranky Quiz Item # 5: I Will if You Will

Check Your Baggage

When it comes to initiating discussions in relationships, are you more inclined to settle things or stage a standoff; that is, would you rather wait than initiate? If you wait for the other party to make the first move, you potentially endanger the relationship by accumulating a significant load of mental baggage. Better to flinch and initiate a fight (using the guidelines from chapter 4) and empty those mental bags than risk disconnectedness! Relationships suffer when no one is willing to take the first step.

Consider the feelings that fill your heart and mind. Crankiness, anger, and resentment crowd out love, appreciation, and respect. Don't carry an active load of unresolved conflict around with you! Keep the air clear. Keep your mental baggage light.

I'm suggesting that *you* flinch: Take the initiative. Sometimes people complain, "I'm *always* the one who initiates." Great. Keep it up. You're doing a wonderful service for your relationship. It doesn't matter *who* initiates; what matters is that *someone* does. It's irrational to think this would be an equally shared responsibility (that's the influence of the Expectation Machine). Keep up the good work, and quit keeping score.

Go for Visible Change

It's hard to change when someone is watching. Remember my story of switching the computer mouse operations to my left hand? I didn't try it until Rob was gone. Let's face it: Changing your behavior as the result of a suggestion or even argument (at home) or a disciplinary discussion (at work) makes it appear that the other person was right. Well, maybe he or she was. And maybe you'll profit from making this change. At least give it a try. Yes, it may take a few days for your ego to recover, but focus on the potential for improving your relationship, or yourself. If, on the other hand, you're the one suggesting or requesting the change, back off and give people adequate time and space to take action in their own way.

CRANKY QUIZ ITEM # 6:
I HAVEN'T GOT TIME FOR THE PAIN

> 6. ___ Do issues from your past sometimes interfere with your present peace of mind?

You Can Run but You Can't Hide

Have you ever been so immersed in a physical activity that only later did you discover you had hurt yourself—a scratch, bruise, or bit of blood being the clue? You didn't sense anything at the time, but later, undistracted, you feel the hurt. Emotional wounds surface in much the same way. Preoccupation with busyness can mask our mental pain, and that's why we often wrap ourselves in it. I've already described the condition of "emotional proud flesh" and how a good share of our crankiness comes from prolonged denial and an unwillingness to resolve what bugs us. Dealing with our issues means work. It means self-exploration. It means change.

It takes time to work through our hurt and feelings of loss, so we put it off. But long-term pain causes our spirit to fray at the edges, leaving us cranky and overly sensitive to the slightest imposition. Minor irritants become major incidents. Our mood goes from cranky to combative; we go ballistic because we just can't handle any more.

Anti-Cranky Alternatives for Cranky Quiz Item # 6:
I Haven't Got Time for the Pain
Detach from Distant Recall

How many times have you heard someone say, "If that hadn't happened to me, my life would have been so different!" We all have a past. Intellectually, we know we can't change what's happened to us, but that doesn't stop us from irrationally wishing we could. It also doesn't stop us from hitting the mental "redial" button where we call up a past, painful memory again and again.

Residual stress results when we keep an old pain current; I call it "distant recall." We replay an old, sad incident and all its variations instead of leaving it behind. There's no learning and no change, only regret. Getting rid of old hurt requires letting go, so we can put that piece of our history where it rightfully belongs.

This may sound harsh, but some people lose themselves in grief, making mourning their raison d'être. They wallow in their grief, getting so caught up in their loss that they're unable to give *in the moment* presence to surviving family and friends. I like to imagine that if a dead loved one could come back for a moment that he or she would implore, "I am gone. Please put me to rest so you can rest. I would rather you remember me with pleasure than have my memory cause you such pain." Surely this is what we would want had we been the one who died.

Rewrite Your History

If you're still struggling with the residue of a change from your past you need to stop now and address it. The longer you wait the more complicated it will get. The more you try to avoid it, the more persistently it will pursue you. You can only free yourself from inner conflict by moving toward it, exploring it, resolving it.

Some years ago I attended a personal growth workshop and one of the attendees wore a T-shirt that read, "It's Never Too Late to Have a Happy Childhood." I agree. At some point we need to put our bad memories to bed for good.

Plan Your Next Transition

Getting real—facing yourself with brutal honesty—is quite a process. It takes courage and sometimes a little bit of guidance. But the more comfortable you become with who you are, the greater your capacity for initiating and engineering positive change. The benefits are endless. Getting there can be a bit rocky at times, but think of the rewards. On the other hand, constant resistance to personal growth dooms you to continue repeating the very behaviors that caused you trouble in the first place. I once heard a psychologist state that *what we resist persists*. I couldn't agree more. Facilitate change, don't fight it. The discomfort you initially experience is only temporary. But the discomfort you experience from not making the change is *permanent*!

CRANKY QUIZ ITEM # 7:
HOW ABOUT MY RIGHTS?

> 7. ___ Do you think there's too much emphasis on affirmative action, cultural diversity, and the rights of minorities or protected groups?

Entitlement for More Than the Elite

Those who have power hate to give it up, or even share it. And those who lack power often have to expend tremendous effort to get it, witness the Civil Rights and Feminist Movements. Even now, as we jump over a significant time line into a new millennium, we're still battling age-old issues of bias and intolerance over superficial differences, unwilling to acknowledge how similar we all are. Change is seldom a smooth or pretty process, but what's important is that we arrive at our destination intact, together.

The phrase "Cultural Diversity" is now embedded in our language—it's a phrase that means different things to different people. I conducted a series of diversity courses for a city and some participants came into class asking me, "Is this the program where you're gonna teach me to like gays?" I certainly got to practice my tolerance skills with this group!

But there was another audience: a room full of municipal building inspectors, mostly white males over the age of fifty. As diligently as I try not to judge my audiences, as I walked into the room I braced myself, thinking this was going to be a *long* afternoon. I couldn't have been more wrong. By the end of our session I'm certain that if I had asked, everyone would have stood up and joined hands and sang "We Are the World."

Something magical happened that day. People *got* it. They got the point that we all share in our humanity, that there are enough obstacles in life without putting up more. That session turned out to be one of the most extraordinary experiences I've had as a trainer and speaker. I think my group left with an expanded view of their world, and I know I did.

Anti-Cranky Alternatives for Cranky Quiz Item # 7:
How about My Rights?
Explore Your Attitude of Entitlement

We all know the biblical phrase "The meek shall inherit the earth," and in our huffy, cranky society, a dose of meekness would be a welcome relief. Let's face it: Some of us are quite full of ourselves. Feelings of entitlement foster dis-connectedness, but it goes way beyond that. *An unchecked sense of entitlement leads to out-and-out hostility, harassment, even murder.*

Entitlement causes us to pull away from one another, creating a rift in our society, workplaces, and communities; even in our families. To what extent are you infected by a social Expectation Machine that encourages you to think you have an edge? The character Archie Bunker on the old TV show *All in the Family* was a near-perfect portrayal of social superiority, but not all of us learned from Archie's example. Bias still thrives in the heart of many individuals, but as a society we no longer tolerate intolerance. It's the most serious form of handicap, and it's self-imposed.

Where are your social hot buttons? I suggest you examine them because feelings of entitlement, bias, and intolerance limit your scope and growth potential as a human being. They interfere with your ability to work as a team player.

One overt display of intolerance can result in your being labeled as a bigot and put the skids on your career. If, in the past, you have found yourself judging or holding back from someone who is obviously different than you, make an honest effort to discover what you hold in common with the person, not how you might be better than him or her! Feeling superior to someone because of differences in race, gender, age, sexual orientation, or physical capability is an empty, meaningless act that exceeds even the most extreme expressions of crankiness. If you think of yourself as a contemporary person who likes to stay current, update your perceptions of our changing, diverse world and you'll stay at the head of the line, for all the right reasons.

Stretch Your Social Comfort Zone

One reason we hold on to our biases (even mild ones) is because we don't give ourselves an opportunity to refute what we think we know about certain types of people.

A manager I once worked with hired a young woman who was hearing impaired. He was embarrassed in her presence and avoided her because there was no way for the two of them to communicate, but his secretary took a different approach. She took a signing class so she could interact with the new employee. Though she had never been exposed to anyone who was hearing impaired, it didn't stop her from stretching her social comfort zone.

You can do the same. If there's a person at work or at a social gathering who is physically disabled, initiate a conversation (our most common instinct is to avoid) and get to know him or her as a person. Go to a house of worship that practices a religion you know nothing about. Force yourself to get acquainted with people who are "different" from you. Find out how they look at the world (and at you). While it's easier to dislike groups of people, it's hard working up the same level of scorn toward an individual. Get to know those who are different from you, one by one. Get over your biases, one by one.

CRANKY QUIZ ITEM # 8:
I'D RATHER BE WORKING

> 8. ___ When required to attend "soft skills" training at work (communication, team building, stress management) do you resent the time away from your job?

Learning While Earning

Work has always involved on-the-job training, but work-based classroom training has become commonplace over the last two decades. The American Society for Training and Development describes employee development as a $50 million industry. The number of conferences and educational meetings held each year continues to increase. Delivering presentations that help adults learn, grow, and change is what I do for a living when I'm not writing. Of course, not everyone is as excited about learning as I am. People have actually told me to my face that they think my course is worthless, a waste of time, or that it's fluff. Others tell me it interferes with getting "real" work done. What they don't realize is that their work world has changed and learning is now a part of work. This is hard for employees who thought their formal education ended when they graduated: They weren't crazy about the classroom then, and here they are, staring at a chalkboard and a "teacher" once again!

After twenty years of teaching adults, I would conclude that some people are uncomfortable with topics of an interpersonal nature and it's common for people to resist or dispute information that invites or requires personal change. I recognize that my asking someone to self-examine or modify their behaviors can be threatening. I also recognize that I'm an outsider and sometimes people are reluctant to accept my presence. This is understandable, and it's exactly why I arrive early, to get acquainted and "prove myself" before the program begins.

I once offered a customer service program for the entire nursing staff of a conservative community hospital. One attendee said to me in a slightly cranky tone, "Well, they certainly did invest a lot of money in you, didn't they?" I replied, "Actually, they see it as an investment in *you*!" Then I explained that while the training was sponsored and paid for by the hospital, what she got out of it belonged entirely to her.

Please Don't Make Me Learn Anything!

Teaching seminars exposes me to an array of fascinating human behavior, from the fear of the classroom to the joy of insight. I'm both amused and troubled by the creativity people employ in their efforts to resist new information. Their arguments range from cranky denial ("That would never work for me!") to clever distortion ("But you can be too_____!") I call this diversionary tactic "the extreme exception."

Protesting that one can be "too" positive, disciplined, creative (you fill in the adjective) tells me the person has flatly rejected my suggestions and isn't even *considering* making any kind of change. The extreme exception ploy is an argument that cancels out rather than considers an issue. It doesn't just happen in a classroom, either. You'll hear these words coming out of a friend or loved one's mouth on occasion. Of course, with that kind of resistant attitude, people are 100 percent right: It *won't* work for them, whatever *it* is!

But I have tactful ways of turning resistance around. I understand that the best form of learning is self-discovery and my job is to help people get in touch with what they already know. After all, adult learners don't need my answers. What they do need is to be guided toward thoughtful questions.

Anti-Cranky Alternatives for Cranky Quiz Item # 8: I'd Rather Be Working

Become a Better Learner

It took me a while to discover that learning comes from questions, not answers. It seems backward at first, but it isn't. This is how Socrates taught. Asking good questions turns us inward, where the answers already lie. Once participants discover they already know much of what I'm saying they don't resist so strenuously.

You can become a better learner by asking questions. If you're struggling with an issue, look for the right questions to ask rather than answers. Instead of thinking, "This doesn't apply to me" (which is a defense mechanism), from now on, ask, "How does this apply to me?"

Avoid Invoking the Extreme Exception

Do you use the the extreme exception as a defense? Instead of being worried about being "too" (relaxed) (happy) (balanced), ask yourself, "Where is my defensiveness coming from—why am I rejecting this idea?" Just for fun, stretch your concept of what you think you're capable of to how you might benefit from a new idea. It's easy to *reject* something that's unfamiliar. It takes imagination and vision to instead *project*—to embrace new ideas and envision possibilities.

Perhaps you saw Jim Carrey's interview with Barbara Walters when he talked about creating a fake $10 million check and carrying it in his wallet. Six years later that's exactly what he was paid for the lead in *The Mask*. What if he had told himself, "Whoa! I'm getting too (confident) (extreme) in my visualization here: I'd better tone it down!"

From now on, when presented with new ideas, resist invoking the extreme exception. Rather than rejecting a behavior that, when practiced to the extreme, might be impractical, work on it in stages to maintain a balance. Try a little, then a little more. Stretch your comfort zone so you can achieve the outcomes you want without going overboard.

Embrace Lifelong Learning

Most of my program participants regularly attend workshops and classes, but I remember a General Motors employee who arrived early, hesitating at the door, his eyes conveying uncertainty. I sat down and chatted with him before the others arrived, explaining what the class would be like and suggesting he'd enjoy the experience. The attention put him at ease and as the day progressed he settled in and even volunteered a few comments.

This man's discomfort reminded me that what some people really fear is not learning, but that they won't understand right away and/or will appear stupid. Others worry that new information will shake the foundations of their belief system, and sometimes it does! If you're ever asked to teach any kind of class in your organization, keep this in mind. It will help you and your participants enjoy the process more.

Learning and changing are two activities you can do your entire life. I urge you to take advantage of whatever classes are offered, even if they take you away from your work for a while. *Sadly, the cranky people among us bypass countless learning opportunities because they're too busy trying to teach someone else a lesson.* Learning invites change. Change invites learning. How could you turn down such a tempting invitation?

CRANKY QUIZ ITEM # 9:
THE WAY THINGS SHOULD BE

> 9. ___Do you feel that your beliefs, values, or political views are
> truly the way things should be?

An Ever-Changing, Never-Changing World

Though two decades have passed since the landmark *Roe vs. Wade* case, the question of abortion and reproductive rights is still hotly debated. This hasn't changed. But the tactics of fringe groups in the antichoice movement have, with extremists choosing death and destruction over debate. We now openly discuss gay and lesbian rights, and many organizations offer marriage and spousal benefits for same sex couples; this is a change. But the issue of sexual orientation is still capable of splitting a family unit right down the middle. This hasn't changed. Nor has the prevalence of sexual harassment and hostile work environments. Some things are ever changing, others never changing.

As the social pendulum swings, some people moan that everything has turned upside down. Maybe it has, but a culture can't stand still. Socially and technologically we've experienced dramatic changes in the past few decades. Am I suggesting that all changes are good? No. They just *are*. What makes the difference is the meaning we attach to the change, and why.

Sex represents one of the conflicting areas in our lives where illusion often overshadows reality. In a society that still doggedly clings to its Puritanical roots, it's hard to not get cranky over this issue, regardless of our stand. We incessantly tease ourselves with the fantasy of sex but run like hell from its reality. Last night I saw the perfect example of our ever-changing, never-changing culture: a Victoria's Secret commercial. Between the scantily dressed models, provocative poses, and seductive faces, this commercial bore all the trappings of a girlie nightclub ad. I thought of my granddaughters who watch these commercials. They're growing up in a doublespeak, schitzy society where one minute they see a "be sexy" message on TV, while later, they get counseled to abstain. Meanwhile, no doubt, our boys are getting turned on watching the same commercial. I can appreciate how parents get cranky toward the media when they have little control over what their kids are exposed to!

Anti-Cranky Alternative for Cranky Quiz Item # 9: The Way Things Should Be
Revisit What You Believe in, and Why

Insanity has been described as repeating the same behavior over and over again while expecting different results. There was a time in my life I would have been the perfect inspiration for those words. I was stuck in the same old patterns, unable to grasp that this was by choice. I believed I was destined for a harsh life of struggle and misery. Changing my belief system changed me. I had to closely examine who I was, what I believed and valued, and why. I let go of old beliefs that no longer served me. I embraced new values. As I changed, my life changed, more than I could have dreamed.

Are you willing to plumb the depths of your belief system to figure out what needs to change? Or is your refusal to do so something that won't change? Take the time to find out what attitudes drive your behavior, in how you treat others, and yourself. Let go of the beliefs that limit your scope and take on new ones that lead you toward realizing your full potential.

CRANKY QUIZ ITEM # 10:
THAT'S NOT WHAT I MEANT

> 10. ___ When given criticism or feedback about your behavior do you feel compelled to justify or defend your actions?

I Can't Believe I Said That!

In our overly sensitive, often cranky society, communication breakdowns happen. People can take offense at the slightest inference. And to be fair, sometimes their reaction is justified. You know the feeling: You're engaged in this great conversation and all of a sudden a wild, unchecked sentence comes out of your mouth, and you've unintentionally destroyed all rapport. You wonder where in the hell those words could possibly have come from and how you're going to salvage the conversation.

Communication is like that: We don't always say what we mean, and we don't always mean what we say. Sometimes an apology is enough, but other times we deserve to be held responsible. When someone challenges you or criticizes your behavior, instead of putting up a wall, listen and consider what is being said. Don't make excuses or offer long-winded explanations; just listen. Remind yourself that the words *listen* and *silent* both have the same letters.

I am *Not* Defensive!

The writer Richard Bach once said, "Argue for your limitations, and sure enough, they're yours." Too often, we explain away our shortcomings and make excuses rather than try to improve them. We dismiss the issue with a huffy, "Well, that's the way I am." Defending your behavior or dismissing another person's observations about you ensures only one thing: You're certain to repeat the offense some time in the future. Yes, there are times you will legitimately misspeak, but when you're off base, admit it. Or when someone else feels your behavior was inappropriate, listen up. They could be right, you know.

Keep in mind that there's a difference between *intentions* and *results*. You may not have intended to offend or put off, but you did. Don't waste time defending your intent; think about the *results* of your behavior instead. A person can't even *begin* to grasp your intent if it failed to come across. When someone gives you feedback on what it's like to live or work with you, just pay attention. Stifle your ego and consider a more effective way to behave. Then swallow your pride and do it.

Anti-Cranky Alternatives for Cranky Quiz Item # 10: That's Not What I Meant

Do a Quick Flip

You'll learn a lot about yourself by listening to people who know you well and will tell you what they really think. Think of feedback as a radar system where signals are delivered, received, and sent back. Yes, it stings when someone misinterprets your words, questions your intent, or challenges your opinion. *But the message behind their message is that you failed to communicate effectively.* When you sense this has happened, flip the situation around. Think about how *you* would have felt if you had received the message you just delivered and how you might have reacted.

Doing a "quick flip" helps you grasp the impact of what you did or said and how you might revise your initial statement for a better response. Be objective enough to identify when you've legitimately stepped on someone's toes and be prepared to buff out the scuff marks.

When you get negative feedback, remind yourself that, while you may have had the best of intent, something went haywire along the way. The person giving the feedback sees you as capable of choosing a more effective behavior: How could you want to disappoint them? By viewing such comments in a positive vein it will make changing all that much easier.

You're better off apologizing than wasting your energy trying to justify your actions (I've heard people tell elaborate fibs because they just couldn't admit they had made a mistake). Lying to others makes lying to yourself all that much easier. Remember the words of Mark

Twain: "Always tell the truth; that way you don't have to remember as much."

I'll confess, there was a time when my version of the truth suffered visible stretch marks. I'm much happier now that I've lowered my resistance to change and heightened my capacity for accepting feedback. Of course, I still suffer a shot of disappointment at not being perfect, but now I can usually listen with little defensiveness. Often, the feedback is dead on and I consider better ways to behave. If I do feel any defensiveness, I try to figure out why.

I've discovered that although I'm a teacher, I learn an incredible amount from others. Much of this comes from accepting their feedback. Review how *you've* profited from constructive (and not so constructive) criticism. You'll probably be able to identify several ways you've grown, or how your behavior has changed. That's what it's all about.

Accept Positives, Too

I encourage you to also internalize the *positive feedback* you receive, too. Other people see you differently than you do. Take their positive perceptions to heart. If others consistently see you in a particular way, then that's probably how you are. Internalize it. Let their encouraging comments be a source of motivation.

A DOSE OF REALITY ABOUT CHANGE

My change management workshops usually begin with the question, "What do you know about this subject?" Participants usually come up with their own variations of the following statements:

- Change is a constant.
- Change can be positive or negative.
- Some changes are self-selected.
- Some changes are forced upon us.
- You can benefit from change.

This exercise illustrates that we know more about change than we think. But knowing is only the beginning. If I could wish for one change in our culture it would be that we'd actually live what we know instead of searching for the shortcut. In our cranky, self-absorbed society, we want the reward without having to put in the work. But change *is* work, and we all have a lot of work ahead of us if we want to replace crankiness with peace of mind. This requires ongoing learning, self-examination, and feedback; the process used in any kind of skill development.

There are skills we work hard to improve, like a golf swing or tennis backhand, and we're not afraid to invest our money in a pro who can help us. But this fervor is often restricted to physical pursuits. I once realized I was spending $60 a month on riding lessons: I was putting time and money into learning how to ride a horse better but wasn't putting equal effort into learning how to live life better!

This prompted me to start buying self-help books and take self-improvement classes, and this soon became a way of life. While I still take riding lessons to improve my technique, I'm also constantly working on my own personal self-improvement program, as well. Think about how quickly our cranky society would transform if more of us engaged in weekly lessons on effective techniques for the Game of Life! I am convinced we'd live in a better world if we all believed that graduation is the *beginning*, not the end, of our education.

That you've chosen to read this book tells me you're interested in self-improvement. Let me remind you of an absurdly simple concept just in case I glossed over it on previous pages. *It's one thing to know something and quite another to act on it.* You know the steps involved in achieving peace of mind and personal success.

But knowledge isn't enough. Even desire isn't enough. *You must act on what you know, persistently and consistently.* Perceiving changes and transitions as life lessons will help you embrace whatever comes your way. Expecting that you'll experience some initial resistance will help you push through your inertia. Cataloging your progress will help you persist through the tough times. And celebrating your success will prepare you for the next transition. Life is a process. Imagine how dull it would be with no change. It's all in how you look at it. The best part is, the more change you initiate (instead of merely waiting for things to happen) the more control you take over the course of your life. That one factor alone will reduce your Cranky Quotient significantly!

If any of this begins to feel overwhelming, remind yourself that *you know*. Rather than clinging to old beliefs that no longer apply because you (or your circumstances) have changed, challenge yourself to explore the depths of what you value today, and why. Instead of justifying or defending your resistance, rise above it all and let yourself evolve into who you really are (not who you think you should be).

Small Change

To help you remember the underlying message of this chapter, carry two coins (any denomination) in your pocket for the next two months. Let them represent *small change*. Whenever you feel a wave of resistance or defensiveness coming on, put your hand in your pocket and jingle the coins. Let them be a positive reminder that the secret to achieving a composed, peaceful life (instead of a cranky one) comes from *small change*.

Coming of Age

OLD YOUTHS AND YOUNG ELDERS

Mick Jagger is a grandfather. Does the image of a small child crawling onto the thin lap of the ample-lipped, long-lasting rock star strike you as odd? It does me. Yet, middle age rocks. Ask Willie Nelson, Bonnie Raitt, Tina Turner, Bruce Springsteen, Billy Joel, and the like. They aren't kids anymore, but who can tell? As for the "real" youngsters, some of them move with a knowing gait and glint in their eye, as if they've seen it all and done it all, and it's all downhill from here. It reminds me of a sign I've seen (and enjoyed) that reads: "Attention, kids! Act now. Leave home and get out on your own right now, while you still know everything!"

Age. It's one of our few universal experiences. We are each born, we live, we die, and what we do in between defines who we are. But numbers also define us. As I see it, the significant ages in our culture include: one, five, thirteen, sixteen, twenty-one, thirty, forty, fifty, and one hundred. Each of these birthdays represent a personal rite of passage, but after twenty-one, enthusiasm for these events often slackens (witness the black balloons and banners prevalent at fortieth birthday parties). After that, a lot of us quit counting because in a youth-fixated culture such as ours it's easy to forget that age is only a number and what really matters is the amount of *life* it signifies.

BY THE NUMBERS

Most of us view aging with ambivalence and our lack of resolution on this issue is enough to make anyone cranky. That we're growing older is good news; it means we're still alive. But the bad news is that in our culture, young is cool: The older you get the less cool you are, and who wants to voluntarily give up being cool? A quick scan of any magazine rack confirms the fact that youth sells—and buys!

Consumers from age eighteen to thirty-five are the heaviest targeted market segment: Everyone wants their money. Could it be that those of us who outgrew this age market feel a bit resentful over having been forsaken by that commercial suitor who stalked us for years and now fawns over a younger interest?

You can confirm the intended buyers with a quick scan of all those fresh, young celebrity faces on the covers (the few older faces won't look it). By the time most celebrity professions (actors, models, and sports figures, for example) reach the early thirties their careers have peaked and they're placed on the endangered species list. They become the subject of articles entitled "Aging stars who still seem to have it." Maybe these articles are intended to comfort the rest of us, but the opposite can occur. As we read about these "elders" those of us who consider them kids shift uneasily in our seats, hoping no one will notice the telltale lines on our faces (or how far away we have to hold the magazine so we can read it). No one is immune: Even people in their midtwenties fear life will pass them by if they don't hurry up and jump on the treadmill!

What's the message being hammered out about age in the celebrity world? Young is good. Old is bad. Thirty is *old*. Any sports fan will tell you how athletes start talking about retirement as they near the fateful age of thirty. Our cultural infatuation with youth inspired a screenwriter in her early thirties to pawn herself off as a teen prodigy; she didn't consider herself over the hill, but those hiring her did, and she laid her career on the line to fight a coming-of-age pressure that was being imposed on her. While the system is hard on the rich and famous it's not so easy on the rest of us, either. Our cultural age bias spreads like a virus, and the older we get, the crankier some of us get about being pushed off to the side before our time. It's not easy being gleaned!

Let's face it. Age is a complicated subject. We know life is a one-way journey, and like the old joke says, no one gets out alive. Consequently, we all have issues about our own coming of age. At the core lies the question of our own mortality and that's the Big One, for sure.

It would appear that many of the boomers would rather deal with their age issues later. That same generation who ran the gamut from idealist to materialist seems to be hedging on the coming-of-age issue, witnessed by the massive list of health club memberships, personal trainers, designer clothes, homes and cars, cosmetic surgery, and miracle drug megadoses. They seem bent on staying young for as long as they can and they're willing to pay the price.

Maybe some of the big boomer "stall" stems from this age group's public persona. Other than the post–World War II veterans, they were the first intact generation to be placed under a social microscope. The boomers enjoyed status and visibility; they had their own identity. Perhaps this is why they seem so determined to hang on to whatever vestiges of youth they can, as long as the money holds out (or their hair follicles). Maybe, at last, they will be the catalyst that helps us as a culture redefine what it really means to age—that we can move beyond the black and white of this complicated issue and finally accept the gray.

TURNING AGE ON ITS SIDE

A quick look tells us that the coming-of-age portrait in our society has transformed. Considering what kids are exposed to from the media alone tells us that young is older than it used to be, and with the options that exist to help us stay young longer (or at least look and feel it), old is younger than it used to be. Sometimes it's hard to tell the parents (even grandparents) from the kids, in both looks and actions.

My grandchildren are currently eighteen, fourteen (twins), and nine. The older ones casually see movies I wouldn't watch on a bet. I find it both ironic and worrisome that while Rob and I enjoy such innocent romps as *Life with Mikey* or *Princess Bride,* the girls might sit through something like *Pulp Fiction.* Age isn't what it used to be, on all sides of the spectrum. In some ways it's no big deal, but in other ways, it is. When we can't tell the players it's hard to define the game. When we can't tell what game we're playing we can't know the rules (or won't care). From time to time, the ambiguity and unpredictable behaviors can make everyone a little bit cranky. Our concept of age has been turned on its side and it's hard to discern which end is up.

THE BEST OF TIMES, THE WORST OF TIMES

I remember being told to enjoy my childhood because it would be the best period of my life. Somebody lied. As a young person I was self-conscious and rebellious, with an overwhelming need for approval. I don't tell my grandkids how easy they have it because it's just not true.

Imagine what it must be like for today's youngsters: There's a hole in the ozone layer; the air is filled with particulate matter that will pollute your lungs and shorten your life; your local water supply might be contaminated; the foods you eat could contain hormones, pesticides, or mercury; job security no longer exists, you'll probably never be as well off as your parents were; you might get shot at school (or work) or on your way there; don't plan on social security for your old age, but do plan on ending up alone in an old folks home your last few years. And by the way, sex can kill you. Have a nice life. *And we think today's youngsters have an attitude problem!*

THE TERRIBLE TOOS

Thanks to the messages we get from popular culture about what is desirable, attractive, or trendy, many of us feel out of place much of the time: too young, too old, or too in between. There's always the murky question of exactly where we fit, or how. It seems there's no one ideal age, stage, or gauge for measuring our proper place in the world. Like one of our friends, a parent of three teens, put it: "When I was a kid, adults ruled the world. Now that I'm an adult, kids rule the world." Many of us constantly feel as if we're on the outside looking in, even when we're the "right age." This mixed message is enough to make anyone cranky because there's never a good fit. As if that isn't enough, the generational myths pumped out by the Expectation Machine continually widen the gap between the young and the old.

Once we recognize how society's mixed messages play both ends against the middle we can begin to understand that we're all in this together. In this chapter you'll explore significant issues relating to old age and youth, and the anxiety we all feel as a result. The healthy decisions and choices you make about your own coming of age can come as a great relief. You'll discover workable ways to combine your innate strengths, wisdom, and energy to redefine the age issue for good.

Cranky Quiz

COMING OF AGE

Scoring the Cranky Quiz

Score 1 point for every *yes* and 0 for every *no*. Count a *sometimes* as a *yes*. Add your total: 3 points or less (Cool) means you're in good shape, 4 to 7 (Warm) indicates a need to slow down, and 8 to 10 (Hot!) indicates a raging cranky infection. You'll find anti-cranky solutions for each quiz item in this chapter.

1. ___ Are you put off by the attitudes of today's youth, yet empathetic about the complicated world they're inheriting?

2. ___ Do you feel pressured or conflicted about your age or stage of life, feeling both young and old at the same time?

3. ___ Are you at all fixated on weight, wrinkles, sags, signs of aging, and other physical imperfections?

4. ___ Do you put off your annual physical exams because you're nervous about what the doctor may find?

5. ___ Do you ever tell yourself you're too old to try something new, or if you haven't done it by now it's probably too late?

6. ___ Are you now (or soon to be) caretaking in two directions: parents and kids?

7. ___ Do you ever get cranky or confused by all of the conflicting information about diet, health, and exercise?

8. ___ Does it seem that your attention span is narrower and your ability to concentrate weaker than it used to be?

9. ___ Do you regularly take over-the-counter medications or try new supplements and cure-alls when they hit the shelves?

10. ___ Are you determined to grow old gracefully and with more finesse than many of the older people you come in contact with?

Cranky Quotient _____

My coming of age condition is (*circle one*)   Cool   Warm   Hot!

PLAYING THE NUMBERS

The Price Is Rites

After years of reading or watching *National Geographic* I've come to the simplistic conclusion that the more "civilized" we become the less ritualistic we are. I can conjure the image of a small native tribe where parents and elders gather together to ritually celebrate a small child's passing into the next stage of growth. Our communities are too big and transient to celebrate such events, and most families are too busy (or too uncreative) to pick up the slack. We've gone from group rites to individual passages, which means we may pass from one life phase to another feeling uneasy, isolated, or conflicted.

We're on our own when facing our first encounters with the markers of adulthood (smoking, sex, alcohol, or drugs). These early experimentations are scary, spooky, highly charged, and potentially dangerous. We've all had our own traumatic coming-of-age moments with a million questions, but of course, there was no elder to consult. In desperation we turned to our peers, who, of course, were equally lost, so we stumbled through the minefield together.

Even with those early hurdles behind us, as we moved toward becoming our own person we still had our issues. How old *is* old, anyway? If we're already old at thirty, what chance do we really have at career success, personal fulfillment, or happiness? If our friends don't know any more than we do, who *can* we ask about such things? Our lack of cultural rites ends up planting more seeds of self-doubt and potential crankiness than we realize. Knowing this, perhaps we could show a little more empathy for those currently suiting up for their first scrimmage in the coming-of-age game: today's youth.

CRANKY QUIZ ITEM # 1: UPPITY ADOLESCENTS

> 1. ___ Are you put off by the attitudes of today's youth, yet empathetic about the complicated world they're inheriting?

What's the Matter with Kids Today?

We've traditionally used report cards to measure a child's learning and conformity to the rules and rigors of school, but report cards no longer measure a student's commitment to good citizenship or ability to get along with peers and teachers. In schools today, educators complain of widespread rudeness and belligerence beginning in grade school. While violent incidents (thankfully) are relatively rare, incivility and back talk have reached alarming proportions. Have we raised a nation of brats, and if so, who's responsible? Teachers point their finger at parents and parents point back. Who or what is contributing to this crankiness?

Here are some possibilities. Most kids, supervised or not, spend an inordinate time in front of the television—more than twenty-four hours per week. While you wouldn't invite murderers, rapists, adulterers, and thieves into your home, they do sneak in, through your TV. Then there's what happens off screen: in real life some overloaded parents snap at each other and the kids, openly gripe about the idiocy of our nation's leaders, whine about the jerks they work with, and harp about their (bleeping) bosses.

Kids often watch their parents ignore speed limits, run red lights, or park illegally. Parents tell their youngsters it's bad to drink or smoke while they light one up and pop the tab on a brewski. Some parents shave a few years off their kids' ages so they don't have to pay full-price admission for movies, meals, or theme parks. Others encourage their kids to "Tell the caller I'm not home" without considering the repercussions. Back at school, some teachers violate policy by grabbing a quick smoke when and where they can. Given all this, are we surprised there's so much cynicism and so little civility in our schools and homes?

Old before Their Time

Maybe you could use an update on what today's adolescents and teens are reading. Besides the virginal Nancy Drew or innocent Hardy Boys kids are exposed to some heavy material depicting protagonists who grapple with such issues as murder, drugs, violence, and suicide. This is almost enough to make you long for the days when all you had to worry about was sex! In some books today (as in many TV commercials), parents are depicted as infantile or incompetent, and while "reality-based" stories do make some attempt at a socially redeeming message, I worry that the positive points take a backseat to the vivid story lines.

Anti-Cranky Alternatives for Cranky Quiz Item # 1: Uppity Adolescents
Know What's Going on with Your Kids
If you're a parent, do you know what your kids are thinking or worrying about? If you want to be an "askable" parent your kids need to perceive you as open-minded and trustworthy. Ask permission to scan their books or magazines so you're familiar with what they're taking in. Don't panic or restrict their exposure if you run across something that alarms you; talk about it instead. Engage your kids in conversations about what happens in school every day by asking questions that can't be answered with a simple yes or no ("What was your reaction to that?"). Respect the answers you get, even if they seem naïve or you disagree.

If you must challenge a teenager's perceptions, use questions that encourage thought and consideration of consequences ("And what do you suppose would be the result if you were to . . . "). If things seem too intense when you "talk," add an activity to reduce the intensity (doing dishes, raking leaves, taking the dog for a walk). At the end of a TV show, spend a few minutes discussing your various reactions just to maintain a connection. Remember to listen rather than judge. If you're not a parent, all of the above applies when you're in the company of someone else's kids. You can sometimes be even more of an influence because you're not a parent.

Partner with Educators
There used to be a bumper sticker that read, "If you can read this, thank a teacher." There *are* many teachers who deserve to be thanked and parents, too. There are others (of both) who aren't so great. What's happening with our youngsters today is a many-tiered, multifaceted problem, some of which is out of your hands, but not all. One thing you can do is help support your local school system, and in particular the exceptional teachers.

It's in your interest to do so because the best ones often quit as a result of the constant, unrelenting crankiness they face from students or parents and the lack of support from administrators with a political agenda. Ironically, it's often the mediocre teachers who are willing to stay and put up with the hassle. Kids bring home what they learn at school, and vice versa. Rather than getting into an argument over who is most responsible for today's cranky kids, you and your children's teachers need to work together. Ask how you can help and then do it.

Be Uncommon: Practice Common Courtesy

If you're a parent, instill manners, morals, and courtesy in your kids through the most effective channel: your example. Let them observe you respecting the space and property of others, including theirs. Let them witness you obeying laws and treating others with consideration. Practice common courtesy; meals are a perfect time for exchanging *please* and *thank you*. Be conscious of the opinions you express. Monitor what you say about others, and how you say it. In writing this I realize I've sometimes been too blasé with my own self-expression, assuming too much sophistication on the part of my grandkids. There's an old saying that we teach what we most need to learn. I think I just learned a lesson.

CRANKY QUIZ ITEM # 2:
AGE EXPECTATIONS

> 2. ___ Do you feel pressured or conflicted about your age or stage of life, feeling both young and old at the same time?

Through the Ages

I've already mentioned that it's often not the big traumas in life that make us cranky; it's the accumulation of little irritants and anxieties that get to us. Well, many coming-of-age issues might seem minor to those on the sidelines, but at the time, they represent a thorny issue for the person involved. After having experienced and witnessed more of these incidents than I care to count, I've learned to not judge, but empathize, because every age brings with it a potential Cranky Zone.

Even preschoolers exhibit anxiety about their first coming-of-age transition as they make the shift from the safety of home to the social world of day care. While we might consider some kids who misbehave in the classroom as discourteous or cranky, if we took the time, we'd probably discover that they, too, are dealing with personal issues and the bumpy process of growing up.

As a high school senior, my granddaughter Elissa got depressed over the prospect of attending community college rather than a four-year school like some of her friends were doing. Hurdles such as grades or having no specific field of study in mind didn't stop her from protesting. That she could later transfer to a four-year school didn't matter, either. It took months before she came to peace with this issue. Meanwhile, the daughter of a friend came home after a year away at school because the campus was too big, she missed her family, and decided community college would be the best vehicle for helping her stretch the cord.

A woman of twenty-five who just graduated with a business degree is experiencing her own pressures, too. Right now, she's working as a temp and enjoying the freedom a part-time job brings (time to relax, visit her family, and reflect on her future). But most of her college peers have merged onto the fast track and they're urging her to step on the gas. She's feeling pressure to not just find a job, but a *career*; that having (or not having) a title is important because it affects how people treat her. As if that's not enough, there's also the issue of actively looking for Mr. Right, or risk being left in the romantic dust.

Career. Money. Spouse. Kids. Time. The Expectation Machine hovering over her age group is in rare form, screaming that it's time to take your place in the world before someone else fills the slot. Thirty was once considered the critical age where we let go of our youth and became a full-fledged, overburdened adult. This moment of reckoning is now coming sooner: twenty-five (rather than thirty) is fast becoming the new turning point, the age equivalent of *bigger, better, faster, more, now*.

A professional couple nearing forty is deliberating over the issue of whether they should have a child, adopt one, or opt out of parenthood entirely. With the warm breath of middle age closing in, both of them recognize they must make a decision soon or the battery on that loudly ticking biological clock will run out for good.

A woman in her early sixties is beginning to think it's time to sell the horse she loves so much. She's been experiencing some health problems and because there will be a day when she's too old to ride, she wonders if maybe she should just do it now. She and her husband, who loves to travel, could travel more if she gave up her horse.

None of these instances may seem like a particularly big deal to observers. Neither might the onset of menopause, a period of midlife uncertainty, or a divorce between two people who qualify for Social Security. But to the one who's going through it, these situations can be tough. I'm sure you've spent time rooting through your own sticky issues while your friends kept telling you they were no big deal. Given that we all have our age-related life conflicts, it's easy to grasp why we have our cranky days.

Counting on Age

Depending on your age, you may be facing issues similar to those above. You may feel torn between what you think you should do and what you want to do. Cheer up; this could be the wake-up call you've been needing. There's nothing like a little bit of interpersonal trauma to help you clear the mental decks. What do you really care about? What if the foundation of your life were threatened; what would surface as critically important? Life is filled with chances to learn what really matters and there are tremendous benefits when we take advantage of them. When the opportunity presents itself, welcome the lesson.

Anti-Cranky Alternatives for Cranky Quiz Item # 2: Age Expectations

Live Your Life, Let Others Live Theirs

In my mind, one of the saddest phrases a person can utter is "If only . . ." These regret-filled words are often the result of our living to the tune of other people's expectations, instead of listening to our own. In our attempts to please (or appease) significant people in our lives, we might give up our dreams and even sometimes sacrifice a part of our identity. This happens to more of us than we might like to think. Our collective Cranky Quotient would probably drop if we listened to others less and ourselves more.

Whatever age you are, enjoy it. Instead of feeling pressured about what someone else thinks you should be doing, follow your values. Remember the suggestion from chapter 2 about living each day with your life principles and purpose in mind? Once you clarify these issues, your life will be less frantic and more focused. You'll feel more in control and less conflicted about what you're doing because it's all part of a plan.

Your clarity will guide you toward making choices that are right for you. What you want for yourself may not conform to what others want for you: Resist their pressure and remind yourself that each time you positively affirm your age, values, and principles, you move away from crankiness and closer to happiness. A meaningful life is built from the inside out, not the outside in. Instead of thinking that there's only one ideal age, just act on your personal *ideals* instead.

Listen to Your Internal Voice

There's a wise part of you that knows when you're off course. Consider this an encouraging word if you've been plagued by a sense that there's got to be something different out there for you. Look for it. If you're aching for a different kind of life it's no wonder you're cranky! Think about what you really want, and why, and how you might move closer to it. Yes, it's risky creating your own way, and it takes courage to accept whatever you get, with a minimum of whining. If you want to take the first steps toward carving out a new direction, review your goals and priorities. Revisit your dreams. Let your inner wisdom clarify what's right for you and slowly move in that direction.

Defuse the Excuses

There will always be excuses for why you shouldn't follow your own path. You can't afford it. It's too risky. What will people think? You'll never be able to pull it off. You're too young. You're too old. You're crazy to even think about it. You're not qualified (one literary agent told me I could never sell this book because I'm not a Ph.D.). Listen to all of the excuses (yours and everyone else's), and sort through them. Maybe you can't afford it. Under what circumstances could you, and what exactly does "afford" mean? Examine each excuse and challenge its premises. Think, "Why not?"

Here's your pivotal question: Are you willing to take the risk and accept the outcome? Maybe you can pull this off: Craziness and genius often travel in the same harness. So what if you're too young or too old, or not qualified? A lot of people, particularly in high-tech industries, lack formal qualifications but possess the chutzpah and passion to do what they love and get paid for it. They even end up with imaginative job titles such as *Supreme Commander of Creative Juices* or something equally kinky. You're the one who determines whether you can or cannot do something. If your spouse is terrified at this prospect consider a series of counseling sessions to work through the issue so you can take the plunge together.

CRANKY QUIZ ITEM # 3:
MIRACLE MAKEOVERS

> 3. ___ Are you at all fixated on weight, wrinkles, sags, signs of aging, and other physical imperfections?

The Pressures, Promise, and Perils of Perfection

I once walked into a women's restroom during a conference break and came upon a bizarre scene. Four great-looking women in their midthirties were holding hand mirrors while bending over so they could see their faces sag. Once wasn't enough: Screaming and laughing with horror, they repeated the ordeal, then shrieked some more. One of them proclaimed she would never again "do it on top" after seeing what her face looked like in this position. I was intrigued by this perverse display of insecurity, but with all of the emphasis on image, how could these women not suffer from sagging self-esteem? Popular magazines may offer endless articles on self-improvement, but who can escape the messages on the cover, both overt and subconscious, long enough to internalize what's inside?

I'll Take One

Maybe I lead a sheltered life, but it blows me away that we can walk into a plastic surgery factory and order up our feature of choice, like going to a parts warehouse that charges outrageous installment fees. Lips. Cheeks. Eyes. Chins. Lines. Noses. Lifts. Tucks. Liposuction. Peels. Breasts. Buns. Veins. I've read articles about teenage girls getting augmentations and implants as birthday gifts. I've seen women, who after multiple face lifts, appear as if they're wearing masks. *Cosmetic surgery has its place, but altering what's on the outside is no replacement for what's missing on the inside.*

When a well-known singer on a talk show was asked how he stayed so trim he confessed to surgical fat removal as his secret. We *expect* the beautiful people to stay beautiful, and they do. But we often end up comparing our aging self with the perpetual youth of celebrities, or people with deluxe genetic packages, not realizing how self-defeating this is. Maybe cosmetic surgery is God's way of telling us we have too much money and too little self-acceptance.

Anti-Cranky Alternatives for Cranky Quiz Item # 3: Miracle Makeovers

Work from the Inside Out

If you have hang-ups about age, review everything you know about handling uncontrollables. Instead of neurotically tracking your daily downfall, keep a running tally of what aging has done for you. Every time you note a new line on your face, a gray strand of hair (or one that's just fallen out), identify one gift age has given you. If you exercise regularly, maybe you're actually stronger or healthier. You're certainly more intelligent, have far more intellectual scope, and possess more depth of character. Is that worth something? Occasionally, when my gaze fixes on the backs of my hands, rather than thinking about how much they've aged, I focus on the many wonderful things these hands of mine are capable of doing.

Yes, we change as we age. Yes, I see lines and sags on my face when I look in the mirror, and parts of my body have been heading south for years! Some people say we trade eyesight for *vision* as we age. To me, vision means refusing to get hysterical about aging. Think of who profits from your insecurity: corporations whose products promise to conceal signs of age, or the doctors who remove them. Maybe we all need a sign on the wall that reads, "IT'S THE UNCONTROLLABLES, STUPID!"

Accept the aging issue and you don't have to spend the rest of your life disliking yourself. Why get cranky over an uncontrollable? Do your inner work. That way, if you do have some outer work done, you can enjoy it. Otherwise, it's just one more desperate attempt to keep up appearances.

Quit Playing the Age Game

There was a time when women refused to admit their age. I disclose mine because I want younger people to see that there's life, a lot of it, after menopause. I choose to welcome my birthdays rather than dread them, because they mean I'm alive! When I turned fifty, I celebrated the entire year, told everyone I knew, and kept fresh flowers in my home as a festive reminder. Why commiserate when you can celebrate? It's your life. It's your *choice*.

Think of yourself as a special ambassador for your age, whatever the number may be, because others are watching and following your lead. Like crankiness, fear of aging is an unfortunate emotional condition. Don't be a carrier! Don't be pressured into wanting a well-pressed, unwrinkled face looking like it just came back from the dry cleaners. You've earned those lines. Think of the wisdom attached to them! Yes, parts of you may be softer, but think of how firm and in shape your brain has become! Quit playing the age game and just go out and play instead.

Help Yourself to the Vital Ingredient

Two people the same age and relative state of health walk by. One appears upbeat, the other beaten. You would never guess they were the same age. Even though their physical features are comparable, it takes only a few moments to discern that one brims with vitality while the other has none. The only real difference between these two people is state of mind.

The word *vital* means crucial, alive, active. *Vitality comes from your spirit, which never knows how old you are or what kind of physical state you're in.* I know people who are old, overweight, physically disabled, and even seriously ill who exude vitality. It has to do with how they express their enjoyment of life. How much vitality do you exude? The more you have, the less cranky you'll be. Keep in mind that your face and posture visibly reflect how you view yourself and your world: Keep your spirit vital, and you'll feel (and look) uncommonly alive at any age.

CRANKY QUIZ ITEM # 4:
CHECK IT OUT

> 4. ___ Do you put off your annual physical exams because you're nervous about what the doctor may find?

Let's Play Doctor

A man called his mother after her annual checkup, asking if she told her doctor the symptoms she'd been experiencing. She retorted, "Of course not. That's *his job* to find out!" There was a time we expected our physician to call the shots in our health maintenance, but today we have to share the responsibility. The food we eat, the beverages we drink, the quantity and quality of each, our attitude, and how much we exercise all contribute to our states of well-being. Health maintenance is a critical factor in coming of age and we are literally the first generation who gets to take such an active role in keeping ourselves well. From alternative medicine to standard clinical procedures, we now have a say in what happens to our bodies. All of this latitude makes some people cranky; they just want the doctor to fix what ails them. But that's no longer the way it works. Your health is indeed in your hands.

Since the eighties, research has cited up to 70 percent of cancers as lifestyle related. We know that cardiovascular disease (the number one killer), lung cancer, and strokes are linked to smoking. High-fat diets are linked to colon cancer, heart disease, breast cancer, and more. Diabetes affects one in four Americans; some control their condition, some do not. *Healthy or ill, until we accept that we are major players in the daily maintenance of our health none of this data will make a difference.*

Anti-Cranky Alternatives for Cranky Quiz Item # 4:
Check It Out
Live for the Health of It

Our genetic profiles can make us susceptible to certain diseases, but our lifestyles are major contributors, too. Just as car owners know when their cars are running well or not, we know our bodies. Sometimes the reason we're cranky is because we hurt, and we often hurt because we're not taking good care of ourselves. Pay attention to what your body is telling you, and you'll know when you need a tune up.

Maybe those tight shoulders are telling you to release that tension; your bouncing leg is a reminder to come back and be *in the moment*, and if you've been sighing a lot maybe you're not breathing properly. Lower back pain? Your body may be complaining that you haven't stretched enough lately, or your abdominal muscles need strengthening. Your body tells you what it needs: pay attention. Think twice before you start popping pills or potions. You want to treat the cause and not just the symptoms. With the right preventive maintenance plan your body might be able to go an extra 100,000 miles, even on its original tires!

Partner with Your Health Practitioner

When you visit your doctor keep the following in mind. You know what your body feels like, ill and well. You don't want to become a hypochondriac, but you want to monitor bodily changes closely so you can stay healthy. You often know what you need to do (exercise more and eat less is a good start for most of us), and it helps to hear a doctor reinforce it. But medical science doesn't have all the answers and pills aren't always the solution. Partnering is a two-way proposition: It's your job to pick up the slack.

Fight for Your Health if You Need To

A friend of ours combated his crippling arthritis by relentlessly fighting for his health. An active college professor, Don became so incapacitated he could barely get in and out of his car. It took two years of personal research in libraries and on the Internet, numerous visits to clinics and physicians, participation in support groups, and involvement in a clinical drug trial before he found relief. Today he's active and virtually pain free, thanks to his relentless effort to take charge of his health.

When your health is at stake, explore all avenues. Make sure you're being heard. If you don't like the way you're treated by one doctor, find another. You have that right as a consumer. With HMOs and Managed Care complicating our health system, you may have fewer options, but persist. It's worth the trouble, considering that your long-term health (perhaps even your life) could be at stake.

CRANKY QUIZ ITEM # 5:
THE OLDEST EXCUSE

> 5. ___ Do you ever tell yourself you're too old to try something new
> or if you haven't done it by now it's probably too late?

Age-Old Expressions

When Chuck Yeager, lifelong test pilot and the first man to break the sound barrier, was asked what he would do when he got too old to fly, he replied, "I'll probably sneak out the back door and go fly Ultra Lites." Then he said, "You do what you can for as long as you can, and when you finally can't, you do the next best thing. You back up, but you don't give up."

Katharine Hepburn has long been my model of one who carved her own path and thumbed her nose at those who dared to judge her for it. The day my friend Hilda turned seventy-five she celebrated her birthday by riding a horse, and I got to videotape her ride. Some of her friends told her she was *too old* to do that. They also told her she was too old to ice skate but she did it anyway. There will always be people who have opinions about your coming of age. Listen to those who encourage you. When Sharyl, one of my dressage friends, turned fifty, her mother told her, "Fifty is the old age of youth, and the youth of old age." Old. Young. Your choice.

Anti-Cranky Alternatives for Cranky Quiz Item # 5:
The Oldest Excuse
Make No Excuse

Older adults are everywhere and they're doing things they're not supposed to be able to do. They are the perfect models of "no excuse." I got passed by a man more than ten years my senior while hiking the Grand Canyon: I still remember his strong stride. When I used to run 10K races I got lapped by adults old enough to have peers barely capable of navigating a thick shag carpet, but there they were, leaving me in the dust.

Yes, sometimes we see cranky old grouches here and there, but forget them. When you see an older adult who is simply kicking butt, solidly put his or her image into your memory bank. There's your model. You've seen the *No Fear* bumper stickers and T-shirts? Well, from now on, take this slogan to heart: *No Excuse*. Simply opt for style instead of speed, technique instead of power, and creative application instead of a conventional approach.

Just Say Yes

Instead of using your age as an excuse about why you can't do something, use it as a reason for why you should. When the opportunity presents itself, say *yes*. After a day-long conference, a man approached me saying, "I'd love to have a copy of your book, *Stick to It!* I'm a professional juggler; how about trading a book for a juggling lesson?" I was tired and hungry. My feet hurt. I said yes.

Learning to juggle had been a secret fantasy of mine, but I was intimidated at the prospect, worried I couldn't learn, and embarrassed at the thought of people watching. Stifling my inhibitions and saying yes gave me an hour of fun and a new skill I can show off to my friends. What is it you've been wanting to do, and is it time for you to get started? If you have to wait for the opportunity to present itself you'll jump at it, won't you? Use your age as an excuse to say yes!

CRANKY QUIZ ITEM # 6:
THE SANDWICH GENERATION

> 6. ___ Are you now (or soon to be) caretaking in two directions: parents and kids?

My Parents Won't Die and My Kids Won't Grow Up

Those same smiling young adults you lovingly sent off into the world to seek their fortunes are dolefully knocking on your door. Your parents, once models of independence, now need your constant attention. Meeting the needs of the elderly and the young at the same time puts a new spin on the term "extended family." When I talk with those who are playing both ends against the middle I hear a mix of determination, frustration, and near exhaustion. This is one of the costs of coming of age.

Anti-Cranky Alternatives for Cranky Quiz Item # 6:
The Sandwich Generation
Make Each Day a Mission

If you've added the role of caregiver to your many other duties, you may have to change jobs, cut back, or even move to accommodate all facets of your life. Fortify yourself with available resources—your spouse, siblings, friends, church members, community agencies, or volunteers—so you can stay focused on your commitment and fight off the cranky blues.

Do all you can to separate one day from the next. Your capacity to operate *in the moment* will be invaluable. Accept whatever help people offer. Take breaks from your responsibilities so you still have a life. Indulge yourself if you can afford it: Get a weekly massage, find someone to clean your house, go to a movie, or do whatever renews you. Surround yourself with inspirational reading material. Join a support group. Visit the Silent Sp-ah! regularly. Activate your sense of humor: Laughter always provides relief and pushes us a healthy distance away from what hurts. As you live one day at a time give yourself a daily dose of encouragement. Revisit your purpose and cling to the words that have brought comfort to so many: *This, too, shall pass.*

Ease the Strain

The return of adult children can be a test for even the least cranky among us, especially if there are issues (drugs, sex, law breaking, and the like) that prompt us to pray people won't ask, "And how are the kids?" Many experts discourage parents from allowing adult children to return home, perhaps in part because they're no longer fully subject to your rules. It's like trying to get a new sleeping bag back into its stuff sack; somehow, the fit is never quite the same. If you agree to your adult child's return, clearly explain that this is a temporary measure and there are standards that will have to be met or all bets are off.

If grandkids will be in your home for a while it raises the issue of who will discipline them. It may be wise to put any prized possessions away for the duration rather than risking an incident. If you start getting cranky over little impositions, or you feel taken advantage of, consider this a sign that you've gone too far in your attempts to help and maybe you need to consider other alternatives. This may sound harsh, but your first obligation is to yourself, and your personal rights far exceed the bounds of obligation and guilt.

CRANKY QUIZ ITEM # 7:
WHO'S TO KNOW?

7. ___ Do you ever get cranky or confused by all of the conflicting information about diet, health, and exercise?

Changing Theories and Conflicting Data

Now that we're in the era of personal health maintainance, we need to figure out the best approach for staying healthy. This means exposing ourselves to a potentially troublesome condition—communication overload—and its side effect—crankiness! Here's what I mean: Almost every magazine you pick up features an article on health, fitness, or nutrition. Try to find two that agree! Take dieting for example: The protein diet, the carbohydrate diet, the eat-all-you-want-diet, the only-eat-food-you-don't-like-diet, the eat-everything-you-want-only-don't-swallow-any-of-it-diet. All this, plus a gazillion weight-loss powders, liquids, programs, and pills. Some people spend their entire lives on diets, losing and gaining back enough weight to approximate a small town. Others give up in despair.

The topic of exercise is almost as confusing. Every few months there's a rollout of new machines and videos for cardiovascular training, muscle strengthening, toning, stretching, and spot reducing. Isometrics. Isotonics. Aerobics. Buns. Abs. Biceps. Legs.

Here we are, overloaded, underexercised, and overconfident that we can actually benefit by a machine or video through osmosis (buy the product, bring it home, let it sit, wait for your body to firm up). When the magic doesn't happen we get cranky.

Anti-Cranky Alternatives for Quiz Item # 7:
Who's to Know?
Take Some Food for Thought

Some of us eat to live and some of us live to eat: Consequently, we might end up more upholstered than we should be. Food can serve as nourishment, celebration, commiseration, sedation, or punishment. Instead of looking for the miracle diet that guarantees you'll lose ten pounds overnight, let the process of *gradualism* work for you. If you'd like to drop a few pounds, eat just a little bit less at every meal. Whenever you start eating for any reason other than hunger, do a Quick Stop! Put your fork down. Now, make a fist. That's the approximate size of your stomach: eat accordingly.

I know a man who lost (and kept off) twenty pounds simply by eating *half* of his usual portions. This wasn't a diet; it was a *lifestyle change*, and that's the secret. Start thinking of the word *diet* as a noun, not a verb. The better your eating habits, the better you'll feel about yourself. The better you feel about yourself, the better you'll treat yourself. The better you treat yourself, the less cranky you'll get. The less cranky you feel, the less you might eat, and so on. See? Sometimes less *is* more!

Make the First Move

It's morning. You flip on the TV. The screen is filled with a bevy of bouncing bodies in tights, inviting you to jump up and join their early workout on the beach. You haven't had your coffee. Your back hurts. You haven't even brushed your teeth. You exercise your right to flip off the TV! Maybe this isn't the perfect time or place, nor the perfect exercise, but your body needs it.

Both your body and your brain benefit when you work out. Exercise is a stress reliever; it helps your metabolism, circulation, muscles, bones, attitude, and yes, even your pores. If you've heard the phrase, "No pain, no gain," forget it. Think "No strain, no gain" instead. You want to push yourself a little but you don't want to make it hurt. Start out slowly and taper off (just kidding). Gradually increase your effort.

Use It or Lose It

Remember the beautiful people in their tights on TV? That's why a lot of us don't "do" gyms. We're embarrassed. We're intimidated.

We're flabby. We don't own tights and wouldn't wear them if we did (my friend Diana Grinwis likes to say that friends don't let friends wear Spandex). Be comforted, though. You have a lot of exercise options but you need to choose something you'll stay with. If you hate structure, venture out on your own. If you need structure, sign up for a class or join the Y. Make an exercise pact with a friend. Walking is a great exercise for just about anyone and it can range from a semi-stroll to a smoldering power walk. Maybe you can find a walking partner so you have someone who counts on you to show up every day.

If your body generally feels stiff and cramped (which is guaranteed to make you cranky), learn the basics of stretching or yoga. Don't buy a piece of equipment unless you know you'll use it; otherwise you'll end up with an expensive, inefficient clothes rack. Here are some tips on getting started:

1. Check with your physician before beginning a regular exercise routine.
2. Find something that appeals to you and start out slowly.
3. Do it.
4. Be consistent. Three days a week is better than six days one week and none the next.
5. Gradually increase your exercise time and level of difficulty or challenge.
6. Include stretching, warm-up time, and cool-down time in your exercise routine to prevent injuries and help you feel relaxed and refreshed when you finish.
7. Quit weighing yourself and focus on overall fitness rather than weight.

The older we get, the more we need to exercise. Bodies are amazingly resilient and receptive even to mild activity. If you follow these steps you'll feel better and have more energy, whatever your age. If exercising is something you've been putting off because you thought you were too busy or it wouldn't make a difference, start now. Even couch potatoes can be whipped into shape!

CRANKY QUIZ ITEM # 8:
A NATIONAL DEFICIT

> 8. ___ Does it seem that your attention span is narrower and your ability to concentrate weaker than it used to be?

Screen Savers

While attending Michigan State University as a communication major, I was involved in a mass media research project. It was 1980. We found that people enjoyed watching shows featuring extensive visual action: the more movement on the screen, the higher the interest. These findings were the harbinger of today's entertainment standards: fast action, blinding special effects, and high-speed sequences. From sixty-second commercials to six-second ones, we've traded steady pans and concentrated content for image flashes and sound bites.

Even PBS interview programs now interject unnecessary scene changes and new poses every few seconds. We've teleported from *Mr. Rogers' Neighborhood* to the launch pad of *Bill Nye the Science Guy* (just so you know, I love them both). But I can't help but wonder if this fast-food approach to edutainment has corrupted our capacity for sustained attention.

Excuse Me, What Was I Saying?

In my seminars when I talk about focus and concentration, several people in the room will declare they have ADD (Attention Deficit Disorder), citing their inability to focus, the tendency to drift from one distraction to another, and a bad case of the fidgets. Who wouldn't fit this description on occasion? I feel like that every time I sit down to write! Our time-compressed, warp-speed lifestyle fosters ADD-like behaviors in all of us. Even half-hour TV shows offer two or three story tracks rather than one, offering electronic multitasking for our brains.

Ritalin: A New Rite of Passage

In the nineties, ADD and all its offspring went forth and multiplied. Adults have ADD, kids have ADHD, and elementary school offices are beginning to house more drugs than the local Rite-Aid. No other country comes close to us in Ritalin use. Maybe like me, you're thinking, "We didn't put kids on drugs when I was in school." Yet the ADHD indicators were there: short attention span, easily distracted, unfocused. I remember two boys in my sixth grade class being periodically assailed by the nuns because they couldn't sit still like the rest of us and didn't learn their lessons as easily. Was it ADD? Is it ADD? Is it our fast-paced, screen-changing, scene-flashing, ever-present media influence? Is it all of the above?

Anti-Cranky Alternatives for Cranky Quiz Item # 8:
A NATIONAL DEFICIT
Question the Approach
I've watched my daughter Cathy struggle over the Ritalin issue with my grandkids and she's gone from one side to the other. It's tough deciding whether you want to put your child on a medication. But why, all of a sudden, in this decade and no other, are millions of kids showing up at school with their prescription bottle? What's changed? Given the infinite variations in children's personalities and emotional expression, can one drug be the solution? Who really benefits from this diagnosis and treatment? Are the ADD and ADHD diagnoses an indicator of a larger issue no one has the time or desire to explore?

Draw an Informed Conclusion
If ADD or Ritalin are part of your reality, ask these questions and more, if you haven't already done so. Get informed. Read books, request brochures and fact sheets, or go on-line and discuss the issue. Join a support group. As you weigh information from both sides of the issue make sure you know who produced a particular document (a good lesson we learned from the tobacco industry). Keep an eye out for the roots of self-interest. Eventually you'll be able to draw your own conclusions, and once you do, forward your questions and ideas to the proper channels: letters to the editor, school systems, parent support groups, psychological and educational associations, community centers. Keep the subject in front of those who make the decisions.

Mind Your Mind
We joke a lot about aging and forgetfulness, but some of it has more to do with being too busy than too old. Maybe you don't really have ADD but you've created your own self-inflicted ADD-like state by being too busy, preoccupied, and doing too much multitasking. Shades of com-

pressed time, overload, and all the other Ten Trends! Here's a reminder on how to make the most of your mind. Instead of scattering your mental resources in a thousand directions, write down everything you need to do. Make this standard operating procedure. Revisit your To Do list often.

You've heard this before: multitasking divides your attention. Help your mind out. Only do one thing at a time. Make notes when important thoughts pop into your mind (remember the incubator?). Retrain your mind to concentrate on one thing at a time and not flit from one item to another. Visit the Silent Sp-ah! regularly.

Make a conscious choice to slow down your thinking. Relax; breathe. Pace yourself. Listen to Public Radio shows that offer extended helpings of information and entertainment instead of bite-size, disjointed portions. *Fresh Air* offers half-hour-long interviews and in-depth discussions. *A Prairie Home Companion* or *This American Life* will delight you with their imagination and humor. These and other radio shows will remind you that you can be informed and entertained in a nonfrantic manner.

CRANKY QUIZ ITEM # 9:
MAGIC BULLETS

> 9. ___ Do you regularly take over-the-counter medications or try
>   new supplements and cure-alls when they hit the shelves?

Oh Magic Bullet on the Shelf, Where's the Cure-All for Myself?

We know we won't live forever, but like the song in the movie *Fame,* it sounds great and we'll take whatever pill or potion promises to stave off aging. Enter the magic bullets: Phen fen, melatonin, fish oil, garlic, ginkgo biloba, St. John's wort. Add your favorites to the list. There is a lot we don't know about biology but if there's the promise of an easy way to better health or to postpone the aging process, we flock to the pharmacy or health-food store. Miracle diets and magic bullets appeal to our time-compressed desire for fast, easy results. Oh, if it were only that simple!

Anti-Cranky Alternatives for Cranky Quiz Item # 9:
Magic Bullets
Expect No Miracles

Maybe we'd be less inclined to jump on and off the magic bullet bandwagon if the media weren't so diligent about reporting the latest scientific findings. What we forget is that each report only reflects a moment in time: Research continues, and when follow-up reports inform us that the latest miracle cure wasn't so miraculous after all, we get cranky because those doggone scientists can't make up their minds. This is exactly what makes them good scientists!

Here's the problem: We, the public, expect (there's that word again) science to be an exact, invariable process. Well, it isn't. *By its very nature, scientific inquiry is unpredictable and findings are subject to change, depending on what is being studied or measured.* When presented with news of a medical breakthrough, remember that this isn't the last word. Let your expectations work *for* you for once: From now on, *expect* conflicting results and you won't get cranky when conflicting data hit the air waves. And the next time a supposed magic bullet pops up, wait for the second or third round of confirming research before you load up on it.

Give Up Your Dedication to Medication

While at a friend's house, her daughter fell down, suffering a mild knee scrape. The child then requested, and received, a Tylenol. At age three, this toddler was self-medicating. There's an abundance of self-treatment available today, but we can misdiagnose, or improperly treat, what we might consider a minor ailment.

This happened to a man who popped a package of Tums every day for a decade until his doctor discovered a bleeding ulcer. OTC (over the counter) medications are *drugs*. Exceeding recommended dosages or extending treatment over time can mask symptoms of a serious illness. The longer a condition goes untreated, the crankier we can get, because we hurt and our body is out of balance.

You're probably aware of the toxic side effects many elderly people suffer when they fail to inform their physicians about preexisting conditions and the medicines they already take. We need look no further than the spate of deaths following the introduction of the drug Viagra. If you take any kind of drugs, prescription or OTC, you need to know how they interact with other medicines, foods, or alcohol. A good resource for such information is *The People's Pharmacy* by Joe Graedon and Teresa Graedon, who host a public radio show by the same name. Another good reference is *The Complete Drug Reference* copublished by Consumers Union and the U.S. Pharmacopeia.

CRANKY QUIZ ITEM # 10:
THE VINTAGE VANTAGE

> 10. ___ Are you determined to grow old gracefully and with more finesse than many of the older people you come in contact with?

Back to the Future
There are things to both love and hate about people who are a different age from you. Yet, you too were once a kid and you have a good chance of growing old. If you're determined to age gracefully there are a few things you can do to enjoy the trip more. For example, you can talk to both younger and older people, instead of ignoring them. You can look into their eyes, connect, and listen with interest instead of blowing them off. You can laugh with them and appreciate their experience, or lack of it. You can think about the complex, changing world you all share and the importance of living with an open mind and warm heart. By truly connecting with others you improve your chances of never turning into the old-age stereotype we all deplore: that of a cranky, crotchety, finger-pointing, complaining old codger. You want to grow old in style, right? You can do your part in helping stamp out old-age crankiness.

Just Shoot Me
Some friends and I recently had a conversation along these lines. It was one of those *Johnny Carson* moments ("how bad was it?"), only in this case, we were talking about old age. With the intellectual distance reserved for those who have not yet "walked the walk" we pledged never (let me repeat), *never* to let ourselves get so old that

we'd stoop to classic, cranky, nightmarish old age caricatures. We laughed and whooped over this, figuring if we did slip over the edge into Old Age Hell, it would mean we had lived too long and we'd be better off if someone would please just shoot us and put us out of our misery.

To avoid Old Age Hell, we pledged to wear our teeth at all times when out in public, not to yell at little kids because they are laughing or playing too loud, not to dress our dogs in doll clothes or call them "our baby," never to call our spouse "mother" or "father," never to wear plastic rain bonnets, never to drive a car so big that we can't see over the steering wheel, and absolutely not to bore everyone to tears with stories of how much rougher we had it when we were kids.

Yes, we'd all like to think it will somehow be different when it's our turn to be the oldsters, and maybe this time it will. Perhaps those recalcitrant boomers *will* help us redefine the age issue for good; I certainly wish someone would! As we live longer we deserve to find joy and peace of mind, to be taken seriously, and contribute in meaningful ways wherever we can. In the meantime, we can shape and finesse the images of how we want to age so we don't have to break our pledge about avoiding Old Age Hell.

Anti-Cranky Alternatives for Cranky Quiz Item # 10: The Vintage Vantage

Keep on Learning

When he was in his sixties my dad, a natural, untrained musician, took guitar lessons from my brother Steve. But the guitar ended up being too difficult and Dad had the good sense to give it up before it made him cranky.

At the age of seventy-three Dad tried again. He took up the keyboard this time, and everything clicked. He spends hours every week practicing and playing. He and Steve gig together, and my father has even sat in and played with a local band! Whenever I visit, I get to hear the latest piece he's perfected. While the complicated chords he contrives are quite impressive, I'm even more impressed that he always has a list of the songs he still wants to learn.

Thanks to technology and our increased knowledge about health and aging, the possibility of enjoying a long, fulfilling life is better than it's ever been. If you take good care of yourself and hail from a line of long-lived kin, you might end up with more options than you know what to do with, a problem all of us would love to be saddled with.

Use All of Your Senses

As we age our senses change a bit (seeing, tasting, smelling, hearing, and touching), but the two special senses that don't have to fade with age include our common sense and most of all, our sense of humor. Being able to smile and laugh helps you stay vital. In her book *Simple Encounters*, Chris Clarke-Epstein states that "laughing adults make teenagers nervous." How intriguing to think you can gain a psychological edge over an entire age group just by exercising your smile muscles!

When I was facing major surgery a few years ago I got hung up about the idea that I would be under general anesthesia for the first time. I told a friend about my fear of not waking up. She quipped, "Look at it this way. If you don't wake up, it's somebody else's problem!" I almost fell down laughing. It was exactly what I needed! A man I knew said his wife gave him a good chuckle after his serious heart attack. The doctor told her, "We're not sure about the extent of his condition; there could be brain damage." She looked at the doctor, paused, and then said, "How will we tell?"

If I were to fault older people in general, it would be that too many of them let their sense of humor get flabby. Keep that special sense of yours well exercised (and your common sense along with it) and there's no telling how long you might last!

Plan for Your Retirement

What do you want to be when you grow up? Write your wish list and then look around. Whatever your interest, there probably exists a community reflecting it: RV settlements, golf, travel, art, technology—you name it. Retirement isn't what it used to be and if you have the resources (and your health) it could literally be the best years of your life. The hardest part may be nailing it down (but don't get cranky over this). Explore areas you may only have dreamed of, or simply more of what you have now.

My brother Bob is now retired and working part time, and he's really enjoying his new lifestyle. I'm still in the midst of my career: There are many books I have yet to write and when I reach the age where clients will no longer hire me as a speaker, I plan to trundle off toward the nearest nursing home clad in my leotard (despite what my pal Diana says about Spandex), where I will lead the residents through a series of stretching and strengthening exercises and talk about the importance of attitude. What's your vision?

A DOSE OF REALITY ABOUT COMING OF AGE

Despite the universality of the aging process, our journey through life is an individual one. We benefit by resisting cultural or media pressures and instead setting our own standards about the significance of aging. We can create our own rites of passage by using each birthday as a marker of where we've been and where we want to go; a healthy alternative to obsessing over what we think is expected at a given time or by a certain age.

Our coming of age represents a series of singular, solitary encounters with ourselves. Much as we try, it's hard to internalize the experiences of others, even those ever-present boomers we've watched for a lifetime. How we handle aging is an individual choice. We can listen, empathize, and identify with other people's experiences; yet at some point each of us is alone with our unique feelings, perceptions, and encounters.

Maybe you remember your parents trying to prepare you for adulthood. If you were a rebellious kid like me you may have rejected their advice because it sounded so trite. In the great circularity of life, you may now be trying to pass on similar advice to those coming behind you. While some of the insightful ones may take your words to heart, the ones who most need it probably won't.

Whatever your age, I hope you'll agree that age is less a number and more a point of view—that the real essence of who you are is internal and it makes no sense to get cranky over the uncontrollable aspects of aging. That you will age is out of your hands, but how you age is entirely up to you. *What really counts is not as much the quantity of days in your life, but the quality of life in your days.*

We all experience loss and one day each of us will die. Living with that knowledge can either cast a pall over our entire existence or it can deepen our commitment to make every day count. When you approach your life with clarity and passion (there's that purpose thing again), this is when your coming of age becomes the backdrop, and not the focus of your existence.

Complexity

NEW WAYS, OLD RULES,
MULTIPLE ROLES

THE FUTURE AIN'T WHAT IT USED TO BE

Honk if you find yourself in a complex world. We're surrounded by issues with social implications we couldn't have imagined even a short time ago: cloning, genetic engineering, surrogate mothers, in vitro fertilization, and frozen embryo ownership come to mind. The question of assisted suicide and the "right to die," stretches our ethics to the max. These emotional issues divide us and eat away at our social connectedness, leaving all sides feeling unheard, misunderstood, and just plain ornery. Our personal Expectation Machines didn't account for such blurry, convoluted issues: We'd rather have easy answers and simple solutions. It's unsettling to have so many controversial, infinitely complicated issues hovering above our heads. This alone is enough to cause a low-grade cultural crankiness.

We may crave simplicity, but we get just the opposite a good share of the time. How we live is constantly being changed, transformed, and upgraded, whether we like it or not. Every day we casually use appliances and equipment that were once the stuff of sci fi: cell phones, microwaves, and computer technology, for example. Their common use changes our concept of "normal" living, but doesn't make it seamless, by any means. Our constantly changing, technologically advanced world forces us to continually redefine who we are and what we hold dear.

Between this combined social and personal evolution, our cultural landscape has become infinitely complex and some of us are cracking under the strain. As a society, we struggle with issues of poverty and welfare, hunger, domestic violence, crime, personal safety, and hopelessness. As individuals we earnestly try to balance family, health, work, social and community involvement, leisure time, and self-fulfillment. If that's not enough for you, just try to grasp what happens in our *world* each day: war, human rights abuse, famine, natural disasters, an erratic world economy, political unrest, and environmental issues.

In this chapter we'll look at ways you can lighten up some of the interpersonal complexity these issues cause, without having to undergo a full "Lifestyle Transplant" (unless that's what you want) to achieve more balance and keep your crankiness in tow.

WHAT WAS I THINKING?

We've all had our moments of faulty judgment; the straw that broke the camel's back in terms of time, energy, and money. Why did a time-compressed two-career couple impulsively buy an old house they had to gut and rebuild from the inside out? Why did another couple buy a home on a wooded lot and then spend a year cutting down over one hundred trees because they missed the sunshine? Why did a couple who admittedly had a troubled relationship decide to have another child? Why did I agree to let my son Ron, at age thirteen, get a puppy when we both knew that in four months he'd be moving to his dad's house and probably wouldn't take the dog with him? Big decisions or small, we all have momentary lapses. We can laugh at some of the small ones, but all humor ceases when we're forced to live with the consequences from the big ones. If you're still kicking yourself over a bad choice you made years ago this is a good time to let it die a natural death. Maybe the following will help you feel better about the decisions you make that complicate, instead of simplify, your life.

WHAT WERE THEY THINKING?

In my car one day, I tuned into a call-in show and Jack Hannah, the acclaimed animal expert, was the guest. A woman called with a question. She owned two chow dogs who fought constantly. In fact, it was so bad that she once fractured her arm trying to break up one of their battles. However, her question wasn't about ways to reduce the animosity between her two dogs; it was to ask if she should get a third chow because a friend had one for sale!

A young couple with two small children were featured on a TV news magazine show, depicting their struggles with time and money demands. After observing them, a consultant advised that between the expenses of commuting and child care, the couple would actually save money if the lower wage earner (in this case, the woman) quit her job and stayed home. During a follow-up segment the couple was asked if they'd reached a decision based on this expert's advice. The man and woman both decided to keep their jobs and to have another child instead. Rather than launch into a tirade about good or bad decision making, let me quietly back out of the room and leave a simple question in my place. Did the above decisions complicate or simplify these people's lives?

A SIMPLY COMPLEX SOCIETY

This chapter will help you put the finishing touches on creating a more peaceful life in a cranky society. Of course, managing complexity doesn't just involve decisions like those above: It has far more scope than that. Complexity includes everything you read about, hear about, and think about. Those knotty social and moral issues in headlines you can't easily discard add more pressure to your life than you may think. Who among us doesn't still carry images of Oklahoma City in our heads? Every now and then we have to clear our mental decks or the excess will get to us. In the previous chapters we've cleaned the floors and now we'll meticulously sweep into the corners to help you clear out some of those last stubborn motes of crankiness.

WHEN POSSIBILITY OUTSTRIPS PRACTICALITY

The Simple Truth about Life in Today's Complex Society

George Leigh Mallory's acerbic "Because it's there" explanation about why he climbed Mount Everest may have been a sarcastic retort to a dumb question, but it also reflects something innate about human nature. Sometimes we do things simply because we can. Roger Bannister, a medical student, was the first person to break the four-minute mile, despite medical theories that stated it was humanly impossible.

Cranky Quiz

COMPLEXITY

Scoring the Cranky Quiz

Score 1 point for every *yes* and 0 for every *no*. Count a *sometimes* as a *yes*. Add your total: 3 points or less (Cool) means you're in good shape, 4 to 7 (Warm) indicates a need to slow down, and 8 to 10 (Hot!) indicates a raging cranky infection. You'll find anti-cranky solutions for each quiz item in this chapter.

1. ___ Between the demands of your career and personal life do you feel overburdened and underrewarded?

2. ___ Do you ever make decisions that actually complicate instead of simplify your life?

3. ___ Would you describe yourself as disgruntled or disillusioned with our political system or its leaders?

4. ___ Are you concerned or confused over issues such as global warming, endangered species, habitat loss, and what impact human beings are having on the earth?

5. ___ Do you generally find people's language (and your own) more negative, judgmental, or profane than it once was?

6. ___ Are you bothered by the frequency of frivolous, deep-pocket lawsuits in our society?

7. ___ Do you often venture outside of your immediate community for shopping, entertainment, or health-care needs?

8. ___ When trying to make a simple, everyday purchase are you ever overwhelmed at all the choices available?

9. ___ Do you ever wonder why we human beings are so much better at putting out fires than planning ahead and preventing them?

10. ___ Do you have the nagging sensation that something is missing in your life, like the old song, "Is That All There Is?"

Cranky Quotient _____

My complexity condition is *(circle one)* Cool Warm Hot

Pushing available technology to the limits, John Kennedy's vision of landing a man on the moon inspired the reality. *Sometimes we do things simply because we can. And sometimes, just because we can, we think we must.* I urge you to burnish this concept into your brain, and from now on, when you get hell-bent to do something, stop and figure out if it's *really* what you want, or if the pressure of the Expectation Machine has morphed a simple option into a personal obsession.

Despite our complex culture and its attending challenges, I love being alive in a world where so many things once considered dreams are now commonplace. The strides of technology and medicine alone have revolutionized how we live, even how *long* we live. In the twentieth century we advanced from horsepower on the hoof to cars with computers; from the Wright brothers' *Kitty Hawk* to supersonic flight and the space shuttle; from crude surgical procedures to organ transplants. Technology has outpaced our ethical and social boundaries, and we have our work cut out for us in breaking new ground, legally and philosophically. While the issues range in scope and social significance, one characteristic they have in common is in making our everyday life more complex and our decision making far more intricate than we might like. For some of us, that's about all we can agree on when it comes to these almost impossible subjects, and the disparity is enough to make even the most mellow among us just a little bit cranky.

CRANKY QUIZ ITEM # 1:
MULTIPLE ROLES, MANY DEMANDS

> 1. ___ Between the demands of your career and personal life do you feel overburdened and underrewarded?

Me, Myself, and I

In a recent stress management program I was talking about the many demands in our lives. A man said he had recently told his doctor, "I know I'm burning my candle at both ends but I don't want to stop. All I need are more candles!" Like the character in the Michael Keaton film *Multiplicity*, if your inner flame is flickering because you're trying to balance more multiple roles and complicated demands than any one human being can possibly do, it's time to simplify your life before you run out of wick!

Anti-Cranky Alternatives for Quiz Item # 1:
Multiple Roles, Many Demands
Reduce Complexity and Increase Simplicity

You may not be able to simplify society, but you have choices about how complex you want your own life to be. *Look for complexity in any decision you make.* Want to get married and have a big wedding? Think about cost in time, energy, and dollars. Want a new pet? If you travel, who will take care of it in your absence? If you choose a dog, will it be housebroken when you bring it home? If it's a cat, where will you put the litter box and are you willing to change it regularly? Want another child? Have you considered financial costs and questions of long-term commitment? Want a new, fancier home or thinking about remodeling what you have? Think about payments, new furniture, additional insurance, and time, even if you hire a contractor.

What aspect of your lifestyle weighs you down? Do you live in a large, costly, high-maintenance home? Consider a smaller, less expensive place to live. Are you a devotee of teddy bears, Beanie Babies, Star Wars, or some other collectible? Decide on a limit. Are you surrounded by clutter? Thin it out. Do you own a seldom used, high-maintenance item (boat, RV, second home) that drains energy and resources? Sell it. Is your life all work and no play? Put a limit on how many hours you work per day or per week.

Some of us don't realize the complexity we create in our lives. Figure out what's complicating your life before your Cranky Quotient reaches a crisis point.

Weigh the Pros and Cons

Containing complexity is a value-clarifying activity. In my case, I recognize that owning a horse adds a complex dimension to my life, in both money and time. I board my horse so she's well taken care of in my absence, but Ladiebug still needs exercise and attention. Sometimes my trainer, Maryanne, baby-sits my horse (for a fee) when I travel, but owning a horse keeps me from going on extended trips unless I take her with me (which I've done). You can probably imagine that temporarily relocating a horse adds considerable complexity to an already complicated situation! But riding is my only hobby; I'm crazy about my horse and I ride several times a week. I'm willing to pay a cost for my passion. And most important, I have boundaries: I limit myself to one horse. I don't plan to breed her and have no desire to build a farm. These limits allow me to have fun and avoid unwanted complications. Here are three rules I follow:

1. Be clear on your values.
2. Make sure the rewards are in proportion to all of the costs (not just money).
3. Set boundaries and strictly honor those limits.

CRANKY QUIZ ITEM # 2:
SIMPLY TOO COMPLEX

> 2. ___ Do you ever make decisions that actually complicate instead of simplify your life?

A Little Bit of More

During a long plane trip I had a conversation with a young man who is married and the father of two children; a successful sales manager who confesses to traveling more than he would like. He tries to spend quality time with his family when he's home, but admits that because of his demanding work schedule, he feels conflicted most of the time.

His wife had complained for some time about their not spending enough time together so they started taking weekly dance lessons on one of the few nights he's home. While he says this is enjoyable, it's also one more thing to learn, one more item to schedule, and one more commitment to balance along with everything else. This couple's situation isn't unique. Like so many others, in trying to address a problem, they unknowingly added to the complexity of their lives instead of reducing it.

Anti-Cranky Alternatives for Quiz Item # 2:
Simply Too Complex
Take off before You Take On

Maybe you are in a position similar to the young man I just described. Rather than making a decision that requires more energy and commitment, find an option that requires less. Here's what I mean: if you're trying to limber up your body, instead of signing up for a class in yoga or stretching, buy a video and schedule the learning at your convenience.

For couples, I suggest "together time" as an escape from the clutches of complexity: unstructured one-on-one at home time for partners to sit, talk, smooch, cuddle, rub, and get reacquainted. It's nonsexual intimate time: no TV, no kids, no activity, no agenda to interfere. Some couples are so unaccustomed to simply *being together* they find this intimidating and uncomfortable (which, as you know by now, is a sign that this is probably exactly what they need)!

Now, some might argue that this doesn't qualify as a *date* and isn't fair for a homebound spouse, that she (or he) needs to get out. Yes, maybe so, but let's revisit the point of this discussion. Simplicity brings balance to your life; complexity confounds it. *If, as a couple, you are already spread too thin, taking on yet another commitment without giving up something else won't achieve new levels of closeness, intimacy, or relief for either of you.*

Refuse the Temptation

I was very impressed with my daughter, Cathy, recently. As she and the twins and I pulled into their drive on a Saturday afternoon after playing with horses, we were greeted by four Labrador puppies and their mother; happy dogs who had escaped from a neighbor's pen. The puppies were irresistible. Ashley and Samantha each scooped one up begging, "Mom! Can we have one? They're *so* cute!" Cathy said, "No!" (they already have two cats and a dog) and that was that. With four kids and three pets in their home, Cathy recognized that another responsibility would have added far more work than pleasure; more complication to an already complex family unit.

Start Your Personal Simplification Program Today

As we attempt to make our lives less complex, we once again face multiple options, and this is why understanding our values is so important. When you're clear on what you value, decisions are easier, and that's why you need to define exactly what simplifying your life means. For some, it has meant moving from a big city to a small community, buying a scaled-down home, and living with fewer physical possessions. For others it has meant dropping out of the rat race entirely and living at a subsistence level. But even with the more extreme approach, complexity still doesn't completely disappear from our lives, and in a way, we trade one kind of pressure for another.

If you feel as if you're being pulled in a thousand directions at once, thanks to a too-complicated lifestyle, keep cycling back to the question posed in the beginning of this chapter: Will it simplify or complicate your life? Ask yourself:

- Is this a simple addition to my life or a complicated one?
- Will this enhance the quality of my life?
- Will this be a drain on my resources?
- Will this decision give me freedom and enjoyment, or obligation and duty?
- If I truly want this, what can I give up to make room for it?
- Is there something else I'd rather do, something that's more important to me?
- How will my life be better by my taking this on?

Stay conscious of where your time and energy go and pay particular attention to the areas that incite crankiness. After a while, this evaluation process will become second nature and you'll be able to stay a step ahead of the complexity game.

CRANKY QUIZ ITEM # 3:
VOTER VEXATION

> 3. ___ Would you describe yourself as disgruntled or disillusioned with our political system or its leaders?

Political Action or Inaction?

I vote in every national election but it's less fun than it used to be. Many voters feel the same way; maybe you do, too. Michael Moore describes the quandary as deciding whether to cast our ballot for Tweedledum or Tweedledumber. At least Ross Perot livened things up in 1992 with his spicy sound bites and visual aids. That he garnered the number of votes he did reflects the American people's desire for a different kind of politician.

Part of our dilemma as voters is that it's hard to decipher what politicians are actually telling us. Between their carefully crafted speeches, spin-doctored phrases, and rancorous rehashings, it's hard to know who's saying what. If we truly want to know what's going on we have to go out of our way to read the arguments from both sides including material from media watchdogs whom we *hope* are giving us a straight answer (if indeed, one exists). All of this weighing, searching, and second-guessing can make a voter cranky!

Following the Clinton impeachment proceedings and the fallout of bad faith on both sides of the aisle, there now exists a partisan fault line that threatens the bedrock of our political system. We watched the fractures etch their way, inch by inch, for more than a year, and as the dirt flew, our nation's leaders scurried for their self-constructed moral high ground.

If crankiness were our goal we'd have to go no further than our nation's capital for our role models. Do I sound like a disillusioned voter? I am. The whole Clinton calamity was disheartening for me, both in our president's embarrassingly unpresidential behavior and the righteous backlash that ensued. In time we'll unearth the long-term repercussions of this rift. Regardless of personal opinion or party affiliation, we all pay the price when the good of our nation takes a backseat to flat-out partisanship and reprisal.

Part of the Problem or Part of the Solution?

In recent years, when I've heard the rumblings of election reform, I perk up. Let's face it, we no longer view public office as the noble pursuit it once was, nor does the press. Part of what made Colin Powell so attractive as a presidential candidate was knowing he would never run! That someone *wants to be* president almost makes him or her suspect. It's like the old Groucho Marx line about not wanting to be a member of any club that would accept him as a member. This says a lot about national pride, doesn't it?

Campaigns have become such an expensive proposition, I wonder how any aspiring candidates, particularly new ones, can pursue their dream. Our current political system benefits the incumbents and handicaps the neophytes. It makes elected office first and foremost a money game. Meanwhile, campaign costs skyrocket.

Revitalizing Voting

In a world where some people literally risk their lives to cast a ballot, I find it discouraging that 60 percent of us don't even bother. Is it apathy, anger, all of the above? I've always loved voting and go to the polls even when I feel there's little choice between candidates. In writing this, I realize it's been a few years since I volunteered for my party and it's time to do it again.

Rather than simply complaining that "someone should do something" you and I need to raise our voices. We need to ask thoughtful questions and get beyond the headlines so we can figure out what's really going on. We also need to resist the partisan projectiles of self-proclaimed media pundits and make up our own minds, for our own reasons, for our own good.

Anti-Cranky Alternatives for Cranky Quiz Item # 3: Voter Vexation

Ask Some Questions, Look for Answers

To help us all avoid becoming permanently cranky citizens we need to question the underlying assumptions of our political system and both parties, as well as ourselves. What exactly does each party stand for anymore? Who influences whom in Washington, D.C.? How do our votes stand up to special interest groups and lobbies? What if the campaign process was revamped so candidates could get their message across to voters without having to pray they pull the winning Lotto number? What if a certain amount of political advertising were free and all candidates could enjoy equal access to voters?

What if there were a lower cap on how much corporations or lobbies could donate to a specific candidate or how much that candidate could spend on a campaign? If politics is a big money game, how can we, as voters, help change it? Ask these questions. Make up your own. If we take our case to our legislators and rally our family and friends (instead of merely complaining), then maybe we can make a difference.

Get Involved, Do Something

Even though our society is imperfect we can still go to the polls and exercise our rights as citizens. Vote. Get more informed. Give feedback. Write letters to your local paper asking intelligent, in-depth questions about campaign reform, special interests, and what's *really* happening in our nation's capital. Get acquainted with your national and local legislators. Send letters or E-mails to the White House. Request government documents or get access to them through the Internet. Somebody *should* do something. And that somebody is us.

CRANKY QUIZ ITEM # 4:
UNEARTHING OUR CONCERNS

> 4. ___ Are you concerned or confused over issues such as global warming, endangered species, habitat loss, and what impact human beings are having on the earth?

The Nature of Things

What good is sea grass? The first three words of this question are often asked, although the particular *object* varies. We've become so disconnected from our natural environment we don't realize the intricate balance of all that is nature. Florida sea grass, for example, feeds many fish and marine species near the Gulf. It prevents soil from washing into waterways. Without it, the land would erode and many living creatures would die, including those that eat pesky, biting insects.

In nature, everything is connected. Introduce one local variable and witness the global aftermath: We all end up breathing particulate matter from unfiltered coal power plants on the other side of our planet. We're all threatened by the hole in the ozone layer or melting polar ice caps. We are only beginning to comprehend the connection between isolated local actions and global consequences.

In spite of all the controversies and political battles about the environment, people turn to nature for solitude, quiet time, or to rejuvenate their spirits. Going for a walk in the woods or watching a sunset cuts through the complexity of our existence and for a few precious moments our concerns get put on hold. Yet the issue of preserving natural areas for our enjoyment and appreciation (even our survival) is anything but simple. These subjects have been hotly debated for years and the specifics get very complex, very quickly.

With environmental issues (just as with politics), our cranky culture often resorts to distortion, debasement, and deceptive statistics.

The next time you hear a so-called debate on the topic, ask yourself about the experts: Are they political figures, corporate spokespersons, or media personalities (all of whom may have a personal agenda). Are they scientists specializing in a particular field of study? If so, find out who funded the study. You might be surprised.

In chapter 10 I mentioned our inherent suspicion of scientists. This may be in part because many of them are introverts who prefer being left alone with their work. True to the nature of science, they don't all agree, but they know far more than the average person, politician, or pundit! Speaking of expertise, I can't give you all the answers on the complicated environmental issues of our day; that's not my job. But I can tell you that human population has doubled in my lifetime and it's impossible for us to *not* have an effect on the earth! I encourage you to study the issues for yourself, not to add to your overload, but to help you better understand how to do your part in a complex system.

Separating the Good from the Bad

There exists a paradox in reporting environmental matters, and it's a real gem. We clearly have two camps on this topic:

- The "good news" side assures us that we have nothing to worry about. We will always have enough food and fossil fuel for everyone, today and in the future, regardless of population numbers.
- The "bad news" side says there are already serious shortages; that we're hovering on the edge of resource bankruptcy and our promissory note is already past due.

The next time you watch or hear a debate on environmental issues, notice that *both sides are treated differently*. The messengers who deliver the good news remain *independent* of their message. We hear their statistics, absorb their facts, and promptly forget who said what.

But for some reason, the messengers who deliver the bad news get *linked* to their message! While their sobering statistics and gloomy facts get thrown by the wayside, these individuals are branded as alarmists, tree huggers, or doomsayers. Instead of arguing the facts, they end up forced to wade through an undertow of labels, name-calling, and demonizing.

Once again, we end up victimized by our cultural inability to carry on a fair, two-sided discourse. *Be on guard for these tactics: Labeling and branding are cunning methods of controlling your perceptions and dismissing an important issue.* The upshot is, the person or group representing the unpopular side ends up discredited, even when they're right! We all pay a cost when people don't get a fair chance to explain their positions.

Anti-Cranky Alternatives for Cranky Quiz Item # 4: Unearthing Our Concerns

Explore the Nature of the Argument

Media hosts are not experts on the topics they feature: They don't even know all the best sources to invite, particularly on gnarly issues such as environmental matters. If you really want to know what's going on investigate all sides and always be on the lookout for the telltale signs of self-interest. That way, the next time you hear someone ask, "What good is a salamander?" you'll have an informed answer.

If reading is one of the ways you feed your spirit, spend some time browsing classics by Edward Abbey, Henry David Thoreau, or Aldo Leopold. Read the works of Barry Lopez, Bill McKibben, or Annie Dillard along with magazines such as *Audubon* and *Natural History*.

Use Resources Wisely

We waste so much in this culture, throwing away food, clothing, and furniture that people in other societies would risk their lives for. Instead of getting swept away with whining about what we want, we need to recognize how rich we are in resources and take better care of what we have.

You can do your part by picking up after yourself, buying less, repairing more, recycling, reusing. When the bagger at the grocery store asks, "Paper or plastic?" hand over your sturdy cloth bags (I carry several in my car). Think twice before you buy something, especially if it comes in plastic or Styrofoam. These materials will outlast you by centuries! Less wanting on your part equals less waste. Rather than buying more possessions maybe you could spend your money on an *adventure* instead.

Tread Lightly

What goes through you mind when you catch someone littering? From cigarette butts on the sidewalk to old furniture and appliances dumped on the side of the road, our cranky culture has brought with it a lack of respect for property and space. I can't imagine what inspires people to dump old possessions on the roadside. Even more incomprehensible are the morally bankrupt individuals who cruelly dump dogs and cats on rural roads, leaving them to fend for themselves.

Every time I walk the gravel road near our home I pass the remnants of an old couch somebody dumped years ago. A turtle pond near the railroad tracks is filled with debris. Rob and I routinely pick up trash on the road near our property—our contribution to maintaining a nice neighborhood.

Even on the home front we try to honor the camper's rule, "If you pack it in: pack it out." Imagine arriving at a frequently used campsite that shows no visible evidence of heavy use. Visitors leave it cleaner than they found it. Let's elevate this idea to the metaphysical level: Imagine what a different world it would be if we all attempted to leave our interpersonal camp a better place for our having passed through!

Share Your World with "The Others"

Farley Mowat, author of *Never Cry Wolf*, has a deep love for nature and his respect for wildlife is evident. He refers to them as "the Others." As the dominant species on this earth we've severely encroached on the Others' habitat. Our sense of entitlement leads us to abuse natural space rather than treat it with respect. Although we are only temporary visitors on this earth, the scars we leave can last for ages. Some of us successfully coexist, and some of us unthinkingly destroy the homes of many creatures. If the Others were capable of speaking to us, I suspect many of them would be pretty cranky! For the past fifteen years I've watched new houses pop up along our countryside, many on ten-acre plots as city people move to the country. The problem is, these people bring city values with them, expecting to construct a yard and a lifestyle like they had in town, leaving no room for the original inhabitants, the Others.

People first put up a big yard light. It wouldn't occur to them that this blocks out their view of the stars, something they never saw in town. They do what they couldn't do in the city: burn their trash and let their dogs bark all night or run at will. Then these busy people spend hours each week mowing every inch of their ten acres so it will be as neat as a city plot. Only a few leave a respectable chunk of wild habitat for The Others, mowing only a small patch around the house. When lawns span several acres, birds and mammals have nowhere to go, no safe place to raise their young. Just as people who emigrate to another country need to embrace new customs, those who emigrate to rural areas need to make a similar shift.

Consider that when we're sad, depressed, or in need of spiritual solace, we look for an isolated spot of habitat where we can commune with nature. These little havens of solitude are getting farther away and fewer in number. We're systematically eradicating the same precious resource that feeds our senses and renews us. If this strikes a chord in you, discover how you can better coexist with the Others. Encourage the presence of wildlife. Feed the birds. Watch the deer. Even New York City boasts red-tailed hawks and peregrine falcons, much to the delight of residents and visitors who now spend more time looking toward the sky. Mow less, sow more.

CRANKY QUIZ ITEM # 5: IT'S ONLY WORDS

> 5. ___ Do you generally find people's language (and your own) more negative, judgmental, or profane than it once was?

Something to Talk About
In the communication program at Michigan State University, the first concept students learn is the Whorf-Sapir Hypothesis:

- Without language we cannot think.
- Language influences perceptions.

It's no accident that politicians rely on speechwriters, spokespersons, and spin doctors whose job it is to shape people's perceptions. They know that creating the right mental picture will inspire the right action.

Words, Words, Words
How many times have you been in a discussion with a friend and in your desire to understand you asked your friend to clarify something. This ended up being interpreted as a challenge and your friend put

the brakes on the exchange with a dismissive, "Whatever—it's only words!"

I hear the same response when, in my programs, I suggest that positive phrases ("I have a *challenge* with this person.") are more encouraging, than negative ones ("I have a *problem* with this person."). Someone invariably says, "What's the big deal? It's only words!" I say, "You're right. It is only words. And words *are* a big deal!" What you say affects how you perceive it because of the mental pictures it creates.

A Whole New Way of Speaking

I'm pretty good with language as long as I stick to my mother tongue. One day, on my beach walk, I saw a man and woman walking together. His shirt was open and I noticed his chest and torso were badly sunburned. Ever the helper, I wanted to say something. But they were speaking Spanish. Based on my pitifully limited Spanish, I can only communicate at toddler level, unable to produce a full sentence, barely capable of a linguistic *point and shoot*. I wondered what I could say to him: maybe "Rojo!" and point to his chest; or "Caliente!" I knew this was a stretch, but these two words were the best I could do, so I said nothing.

It did occur to me as I walked on, that there is a language of interpersonal commerce, and some people (think "couples" here) are as limited in that realm as I am in Spanish. Some of us are profoundly incapable of expressing our feelings; we were never taught how. And because we don't try, we don't learn how to do it any better. I know of what I speak. I was once married to a man who used to exclaim, "Don't get into my head!" whenever I wanted to talk about our relationship.

Though some of us possess sophisticated, technological skills, our own "interpersonal technology" hails from a Dark Age, only capable of self-expression at primitive levels. Think of an emotional cave person who knows only the basics: sad, mad, glad, scared. (Okay, Og; nice start. Next week we'll try two-syllable words!) It doesn't have to be this way.

Dumb and Dumber

In the early nineties I read an insightful book entitled *Dumbth* by the perceptive and prolific Steve Allen. The book is as relevant today as when it was written. Our society is besieged with an alarmingly high number of people who are functionally illiterate and intellectually deprived, and the number is on the rise. If there's a social cause you've been looking for, volunteering in a local literacy program could be it. Instead of directing contempt toward those so lacking in reading skills or self-expression, we need to reach out and help them develop these critical skills. I'm convinced that my ability to read and comprehend was the pivotal component that enabled me to change my life.

Right now we're on the backside of a literary zenith; we're dumbing down and we don't even have the decency to apologize for it. Okay, the computer book *DOS for Dummies* was great. It met a need for people like me who find technology daunting. But a *series?* The rollout of titles that followed this successful book seems as unstoppable as the Terminator. And we've lost all self-consciousness with the *Complete Idiot's Guides*. For years we've accepted dumbed down commercials where real people interact with animated characters and apparitions in their homes, but *books?* I sound cranky over this, don't I?

Okay, so maybe you're thinking I need to lighten up. But pictorial keyboards on adding machines, TV shows that portray educated fools or glorify just plain fools, and schools that engage in social promotion (passing a child on age, not ability) indicate we're headed down an intellectual cul de sac and we don't even know it. What this means to the rest of us is that in our complex, high-tech culture there's a large and growing subculture who can't even begin to comprehend it, let alone effectively live or work in it.

There's also a significant percentage of our population that could be described as *media illiterate*. By this I mean people who are unable to discern between what's real and what isn't on television (shades of *Murphy Brown*!) and in the movies. Soap opera actors routinely receive fan mail addressed to the characters they play, and each year thousands of people visit the Iowa cornfield turned ball diamond featured in the movie *Field of Dreams*, fully expecting to catch a glimpse of Kevin Costner. You've caught the sad irony, haven't you: Some of us have trouble reading more than the words. The inability to distinguish reality from fantasy is one of the key indicators of mental illness, let alone crankiness.

Anti-Cranky Alternatives for Cranky Quiz Item # 5:
It's Only Words
Change Your Language, Change Your Life

If you want to change your life, change your language. This is so important I'm going to repeat it: *If you want to change your life, change your language.* The last two chapters will give you the basics for doing so. Changing your language does change your perceptions: you'll end up looking at the world, and yourself, differently. *How* different is up to you.

If you've ever wondered whether the words truly matter, ask yourself why it is we *fall* in love? How can someone *make* us cranky? How does a person have the power to *hurt* our feelings if they don't lay a hand on us? Why do we say we *need* something when it's really a want? What happens to our mood when we say things such as this weather *depresses* me. I *can't* stand this. This *breaks* my heart. Had enough?

Pay attention to what comes out of your mouth. Negative words have a negative effect on you and too much profanity can sour your mood. Consciously use language that implies self-responsibility and emotional composure. I *love* you. I *choose* to be cranky about that. I *chose* to feel hurt about what you said. I *want* that. I *depress* myself over this kind of weather. I *don't like* this, but I can stand it. These examples are a different way of expressing yourself. They inspire a different way of thinking. Think about how you might be affected by changing the way you speak. Understanding how my language affected my perceptions inspired me to give up my helpless, victim-oriented language and trade it for the vocabulary of a confident, thriving person. Eventually, I grew into it.

Expand Your Interpersonal Vocabulary

Self-expression is a skill that must be taught, just like playing golf or guitar. I remember those early counseling sessions where Rob and I both struggled through a maze of feelings, fears, and internal conflicts. I still remember seeing the strain on Rob's face as he struggled for what he wanted to say. And I, the extrovert, felt as verbally disabled as he. It was tough finding the right words. It was difficult formulating those first awkward phrases our counselor was trying to teach us and actually releasing them from our lips. We, too, were interpersonal cave people when we started.

Give yourself permission to stumble through this new interpersonal language. Read books about feelings. Pick a few words and then browse through a list of synonyms in a book or software spell checker. Notice the words you come across that seem to fit. Stretch yourself and start using them. Get beyond *sad, mad, glad, scared*. Learn to distinguish between irked and cranky, happy and elated, confused and ambiguous.

Be prepared: you will revert to whatever is familiar. When my friend Carol Mase worked in Germany for three years, she had to learn the language. When she traveled to Italy and Spain, she found herself using the only *foreign* language she knew, German, to communicate, fully knowing she wasn't in Germany anymore. But Carol found herself doing what we all do anyway, speaking louder and slower, repeating the same words, hoping that somehow, someone would understand what she was trying to say.

If you've resorted to the same tactics in the past when trying to express yourself, you can do better. Don't limit your emotional vocabulary. Take in the whole range of what you feel. Be willing to risk trying new words on for size, and like with a new language, don't worry about whether or not you speak perfectly in the beginning. That will come later. So will the rewards.

CRANKY QUIZ ITEM # 6:
LITIGATION NATION

6. ___ Are you bothered by the frequency of frivolous, deep-pocket lawsuits in our society?

You Just Can't Be too Careful

My new *Yoga for Beginners* tape sits in the VCR. Clad in comfortable clothing, I stand in Ready position for two minutes and read eleven warnings, disclaimers, and cautionary notes before the session begins. After reading so many alerts and advisories I begin thinking maybe yoga is too dangerous for me and perhaps I should just sit down and rest instead.

Most products we buy carry messages of dismissal, caution, or usage warnings, from toothpaste (do not swallow) to microwave packages (caution: hot!) to power tools (do not touch moving parts while unit is on). Yet accidents happen.

Daily, we're hit with abundant reminders that we live in a complex world where the word *sue* is more often a verb than proper noun. The looming presence of warnings, disclaimers, and tort cases may seem like no big deal, but let's be reminded that crankiness doesn't come from big deals. It comes from small things that keep adding up. Just the *existence* of so many red flags puts us on guard! Consider how often you're reminded that you live in a litigious society and add it to the rest of the concerns you customarily carry.

dis-Connected Consumers

Frivolous lawsuits and deep-pocket tort cases reflect the dis-Connectedness we feel as consumers, with many cranky citizens cocked and ready for the opportunity to nail a big company for a mistake. Resentful passengers who spent eight hours trapped on an aircraft in blizzard conditions at Detroit Metro weren't about to tolerate what they considered a consumer hostage situation. They filed suit! Let's face it; lawsuits are a communication modality that get the point across. But in the end, we all pay a dear cost—emotionally, socially, and economically. Years ago I remember Tom Peters talking about how Japanese families didn't sue JAL (Japanese Air Lines) after a major crash because the president of the company wept with the bereaved in their homes. Can you even *imagine* such an event happening in the United States?

Anti-Cranky Alternative for Cranky Quiz Item # 6: Litigation Nation
Entrust Yourself

Your options are limited on this one because you can't control other people's behavior. On your own you can't stop or even dissuade the wave of lawsuits that have no business tying up our legal system, unless you want to become an advocate. You can, however, spend time clarifying your own lines of accountability, responsibility, and liability to keep greed and blame at a minimum.

Determine what vestiges of greed (or its bratty cousin, blame) lurk within your heart and how you can rid yourself of these self-defeating attitudes. Greed directly opposes peace of mind: The two cannot coexist. Greed also fosters ongoing crankiness, suspicion, and discontent. As you look around you can probably appreciate that our cultural mood would immediately take a turn for the better if we all suddenly become accountable for our actions instead of pointing our collective finger.

CRANKY QUIZ ITEM # 7:
CRANKINESS OVER COMMUNITIES

> 7. ___ Do you often venture outside of your immediate community for shopping, entertainment, and health-care needs?

The Grass Looks Greener
Communities within two hours of a large metropolitan area suffer because local citizens head for the city when they want "good" shopping, entertainment, or medical care. We've already discussed how mobility has changed the face of neighborhoods; communities are similarly affected as some residents emotionally disconnect and head for greener grass. People say they snub local commerce because they can get it cheaper in the city, and besides, local resources (such as medical care) just don't compare. Some of this may be true, but can it be done without an *attitude*?

What happens to a community when home base is simply a place where we sleep and mow our lawn? When where we live isn't "good enough," indifference edges out identification. As people disconnect, a low level contempt often surfaces. People have actually told me they live in a cranky community, with local officials, citizens, and business owners at one another's throats instead of working together. Such local hotbeds of disharmony and competition seep into the larger culture and we witness the cranky results every day.

Anti-Cranky Alternatives for Quiz Item # 7:
Crankiness over Communities
Reject the Double Standard
We often choose to live in smaller communities because they're safe, convenient, and a nice place to raise children. Consider the conse-

quences if you (and others) don't support the area you deem so appealing; it may languish. If you make disparaging remarks about local officials, merchants, or schools, you're living by a double standard: Think of this as a form of social self-rejection. You're a part of your community. Emotionally disconnecting from where you live affects commerce, the quality of education, local services, and even *community self-esteem*. If this is your home, take pride in where you live. Or move somewhere you can.

Just a reminder, you benefit by helping sustain your local community. Why contribute to its decline? Join local service groups and support local commerce. Take part in local activities or holiday celebrations. Smaller communities need citizen involvement and if you look you'll notice an upswing of interest in *community* all across the United States. Join in. The law of opposites reminds us that when we most need to get involved we will be our most disconnected. Rather than locking ourselves in our homes and copping an attitude of superiority we need to open our doors, our minds, and our wallets. Support your local businesses. Stay invested in your community. You're a part of it; it's a part of you.

Join the Club

Of course, things aren't perfect where you live, but how can circumstances improve without your insight and energy? A lack of local pride isn't just a politician's problem, or a teacher's, clergy's, or business leader's. It's all of us. It's you. If you want things to be different, you need to help, and if you're wondering what you can do, the answer is closer than you may think.

Everything that inspired you to open this book is in the answer: It's about leading a life where you want to wake up in the morning. It means spending time with your loved ones while enjoying solitary time, too. Professionally, it means making a significant contribution to your work team and employer. Socially, it means identifying with where you live. It means voting and raising your voice or taking action when you feel the need. It means supporting your schools and community and respecting your natural resources. These are all the simple things that comprise a thriving life. We used to call this being a good citizen. Maybe we still do. Based on the grumbling that goes on out there, we could certainly use a few more.

CRANKY QUIZ ITEM # 8:
TOO MUCH, TOO MANY

---

8. ___ When trying to make a simple, everyday purchase are you
ever overwhelmed at all the choices available?

That's Not What I Wanted!

I used my last adhesive strip bandage and figured I'd better go buy a package to have on hand just in case. I drove to a Wal-Mart Super Store and figured I'd make a quick trip. I can't recall the last time I was so wrong! As I stood facing four shelves of product my brain went on overload. Here's what I found: nine separate brands, including Band-Aid and Curad, the two major players. Besides a litany of shapes, sizes, and designs too complex to record, I found ten different styles of strips ranging from sports models to sensitive skin, plus two special antibiotic concoctions—one with aloe, one without. There were designer strips, including Star Trek, Sesame Street, Loony Tunes, Barbie, Mickey Mouse, and Pooh, plus NASCAR and Safari themes.

Then there were color considerations: I had my choice of Sports Colors, Extreme Colors, Neon, and Crayon. My quick visit turned into an extended stay as I stared at four shelves of bandage products, dumbfounded by the variety greeting me. I flashed back on how simple life once was when the only decision I had to make about a bandage was whether I wanted a patch, strip, or spot!

With my mind still reeling, I paid for my purchase and told the cashier I wouldn't have imagined so many choices. She looked at me with one of those long gazes indicating a serious appraisal going on, and then said, "It's been a while since you bought any, eh?" In case you're curious, I bought Crayon bandages (bright blue, red, and yellow) and I can't wait to cut myself. After I told a friend my experience he looked at me like I was from Jupiter. He has small kids. He knows about such things. But it isn't just bandages.

The Burden of Choices

Many supposedly simple errands turn into complicated, troublesome ordeals because of the variety available. I had walked by the bandage shelves many times, but they never registered. You, too, pass by shelves of product, and because you have no need at the moment, you don't even notice the multitude of choices.

Try buying cough drops, toothpaste, over-the-counter medications, shampoo, or hair rinse when you're in a hurry. No way! Small wonder we're time compressed; we spend half of our time reading packages, and thanks to the complex design of kid-proof caps, we spend the other half trying to get them open!

Some people think the variety of products on the shelves is a ruse to keep us in the store. Market analysts know that the more choices offered, the more a customer is likely to buy. The momentary confusion over so many choices can undermine our confidence and this indecision can make us prone toward impulse purchases. It's also easy to *internalize* this confusion: "If I can't make a simple choice like what kind of toothpaste is best for my family how can I make a complex decision like whether or not I should change jobs or buy that new house?" You can appreciate how momentary overload such as this makes you susceptible to the influences of the rest of the Ten Trends.

If this seems simplistic, keep in mind that the simplest event can yield grave consequences. Some time-compressed parents have dashed into a store in the middle of summer, cracking a window and locking the car doors while leaving their sleeping child in the car seat. After wandering the bountiful aisles, first trying to locate what they need, and then deciphering labels to make the right choice, while getting distracted by the tempting assortment of products on the shelves, and then waiting in a line that never seems to end, these hapless, unsuspecting parents return to find their child lifeless, suffocated.

Anti-Cranky Alternatives for Cranky Quiz Item # 8:
Too Much, Too Many
Start Small
When in doubt, think simple. When time is limited, or you need only one or two items, stay away from the megastores. Bite the cost bullet, head for a smaller one, pay a little more, and you'll save on your other currency: time. If that's not possible and a big store is your only choice, resort to Plan B: ask a helpful clerk, if you can find one. Let this person help narrow your options so you don't have to waste time deliberating.

Remember the goal: simplicity over complexity. *And never, ever leave a small child alone in a locked car, regardless of the season!*

Simplify Your Life

Do you ever wish you could persuade the government to embrace simplicity? A quick look at a tax form tells us what a dream this is! You can't change the tax system, but you can lower the complexity quotient in other areas of your life. As a consumer, simplify the buying process. As suggested in chapter 5, make more cash purchases and fewer credit card transactions. For everyday maintenance products, know what brands you like and stick to them. When you run out of something, take a long look at the package before throwing it away so you can remember what it looks like. Keep a record of items that involve a special size or complicated dimension. In short, buy products that are easy to use, maintain, or repair although that's easier said than done.

Look for the places in your life where complexity has added an element of convenience, but where you pay the price in noise and nuisance. In chapter 8 we discussed low-tech chores such as trimming weeds by hand and enjoying the tactile feedback and clean sounds of the blade instead of letting a motor's incessant whine invade your consciousness. After riding my horse and cleaning her stall, I sweep an aisle the length of my home with a regular broom. The repetition of movement almost makes it a meditation. You may be surrounded by a complex, consumptive world, but you can still keep things simpler, tidier, and cozier at home, maybe even at work.

CRANKY QUIZ ITEM # 9: NO FORETHOUGHT

> 9. ___ Do you ever wonder why we human beings are so much better at putting out fires than planning ahead and preventing them?

Unintended Consequences: It Seemed Like Such a Good Idea at the Time

As a child, I loved going to the shoe store because they had an X-ray machine you could stand on and see the bones in your feet. I just couldn't get enough of it. Only years later did we learn about the dangers of radiation. The Florida condo where I wrote most of this book got a new roof last winter. Now, after a hard rain, the stairs and parking lot are strewn with coarse white grains of unknown composition. No one expected a roof repair to have a messy consequence like that.

After the movie *101 Dalmatians*, families flocked to the pet stores, buying irresistible Dalmatian puppies for their kids, later on discovering that this breed is ill-suited for small children and limited spaces. Each winter in large inner cities, small children die from smoke inhalation in home fires because they couldn't escape through the barred windows that had been installed for safety reasons. Air bags in cars, designed to save lives, have actually taken them.

The very same computer technology that revolutionized how we live and work also brought with it viruses, hacker heists, and uncertainty over the Y2K bug. When you started hearing about the Y2K bug, perhaps a nagging little question surfaced from the remote reaches of your mind—one that asked, "So why didn't someone think about this and plan for it twenty years ago when computers were coming into their own?" Action, reaction. Cause, effect. Unintended consequences.

It's easier to catch someone else's pending mistake before your own. Sometimes we're just too close and can't detect all those nasty potential snafus lining up to take us out. But there's a much larger reason, and it's biological. The vestiges of our ancestors' survival skills still flow through our veins: We're programmed to catch the small, the quick, the urgent, but not the distant, obscure, or theoretical. We're hard-wired to respond to *immediate* threats or opportunities, not *long-term* consequences.

This is why we make decisions that offer instant gratification but don't favor us down the road, such as eating fat-laden foods or not exercising regularly. *New World, New Mind*, by Robert Ornstein and Paul Erlich, offers an explanation of why we human beings appear to be so shortsighted. Understanding your nature may help you endure one less embarrassing moment when you slap your brow in consternation, muttering to yourself, "Who woulda thunk it?"

Anti-Cranky Alternative for Cranky Quiz Item # 9:
No Forethought
Know Your Limits, Stretch Your Limits

All our lives we've heard the saying that two heads are better than one. I heartily agree. Certainly, this book is the culmination of observations and analysis Rob and I have made for years about what we see in our society and ourselves. If you're facing a big decision, find a trusted soul with whom you can discuss your issue in depth. Someone else can give you insights about potential consequences because that person's view of the situation is so much different from yours. The same applies to a goal: If there's something you want to accomplish, talk about it and reach out, again, to someone you trust.

Discuss your vision; let those whose opinions you respect help you design your strategy. Their insights may help you avoid a costly mistake. In other words, now that you understand that this thing called The Future can be a dicey concept, stack the cards in your favor. With your friends (or even a counselor), try to imagine all of the possible unintended consequences, and then do some positive planning to avoid them.

CRANKY QUIZ ITEM # 10:
SOMETHING'S AMISS

> 10. ___ Do you have the nagging sensation that something is missing in your life, like the old song, "Is That All There Is?"

Therein Lies the Rub

Commercial indicators say all is well, unemployment is low, the economy is humming, but our culture is still cranky. What's wrong? If things are so good, why aren't we happier? What's the problem? What's missing?

The other day while on my walk, I ended up with a tiny stone in my shoe. All of a sudden I felt a little twinge every time I took a step. I was busy exercising and I didn't want to stop and take care of this little irritation. I wanted to keep going and wished the pesky twinge would go away. The stone shifted, as I hoped it would, but the discomfort got worse. Finally I had to interrupt my walk to stop and remove the stone. This required sitting down, unlacing my shoe, taking off my sock, and inspecting it. How the stone got there, I don't know, but I could see a red spot on my foot where the stone had pressed and rubbed. I was surprised anything so small could have created so much distress.

Stones in Our Souls

I suggest that the reason so many of us are so unhappy is that we're going through life with stones in our *souls*. We feel the irritation, we know something is rubbing us raw, but we're too busy, too distracted, or too afraid to search for it. So we live with it. Meanwhile, it shifts, irritating other areas, refusing to go away as long as we keep moving.

Finding the stones in your soul requires that you stop and conduct a thorough personal search, going as far as you have to, and as deeply as you must. In this book, you've been given the tools to pursue this process on your own. Imagine how liberating it will be when you find those stones and remove them. You won't hurt anymore.

Many people find the search threatening. They'd rather limp along, constantly wounding themselves as they go. They'd rather endure the pain than remove the irritant. I see the results every day and so do you. Call it mild depression, anger, or just plain crankiness, our bad moods are the wounds that result from choosing to live with aggravation instead of removing it from our lives. Untreated, these wounds get larger and more compromised until they turn into a festering lesion.

Of course, there's usually more than one "soul stone," and that complicates the picture. It's a slow, meticulous process, finding and removing them, but the rewards last a lifetime. You see, the more small stones that exist in your soul, the greater your feelings of discontent, anger, or dissatisfaction. You can't outrun them. You can't wish them away. You either endure them or you remove them. How can you possibly be happy when you're slowly wearing holes in your spirit?

Anti-Cranky Alternative for Cranky Quiz Item # 10: Something's Amiss
Remove the Stones
Here are five steps for removing stones from your soul before they leave a permanent scar on your spirit:

1. Increase your self-awareness. Pay attention to the little grains of emotional discomfort you face throughout your day: small spikes of defensiveness, jealousy, anger, resentment, or guilt. Instead of ignoring your discomfort, go to the spot that hurts before it gets rubbed raw.

2. Stop whatever you're doing, just as you would have to interrupt your walk to remove a stone, and make this small irritation a priority before it turns into an open wound. Take whatever time you need to figure out what's wrong. *You'd remove the stone if it were in your shoe; why should you let your spirit suffer?* At the end of chapter 2 we discussed elevating our lifestyle from the physical level to the metaphysical. You do this by visiting your soul and healing the spots that hurt.

3. Search the area. Explore your perceptions, feelings, and expectations. Identify the feelings that are causing your discomfort. Investigate the situation. Track your behavior; reflect on how you may have helped contribute to your dilemma. Take responsibility for your actions. Look at the situation from every possible viewpoint to identify the contributing factors. Clarify where you want to go from here and how to achieve the most desirable outcome.

4. Remove the pain source and treat the wound. Just like a foot injury, a bruise on your soul needs care. It doesn't matter how tough you are or how adept you are at denial. Pain is pain. You can pretend all you want, but your soul knows when it hurts. Heal yourself before complications set in. Maybe you need to apologize to someone or ask for forgiveness. There may be someone you need to forgive. Trust yourself. If you get this close to the pain, you'll figure out the most appropriate course of action.

5. Repeat this process as needed. Expect to find many stones once you get sensitized to the symptoms, but the steps get easier with practice. The fewer stones you carry in your soul, the less heartache or conflict you'll have. Get rid of the hurts that cause you pain and hold you back. Unburden your spirit so you can live the happy life you've been wanting. What better time than now?

A DOSE OF REALITY ABOUT COMPLEXITY

It's impossible to escape complexity in today's world, but effective choice management can help you sort through the controllables and uncontrollables. As social issues become more knotty and complex, keep your own life simple. As you clarify your life purpose and major priorities, you'll naturally turn away from inconsequential matters and move toward what you value. These are the core ingredients in your personal life prescription.

In the beginning, learning to live in a reflective, contemplative manner is a demanding process. It takes time to question what you're doing and why, and if what you're doing right now is the best alternative. It's hard defining what's important, or why, and ranking priorities can be quite a task. But on the other hand, once you get a sense of who you are and what your life is all about, decisions get easier and day-to-day living becomes far less complicated because you've already done the groundwork. In other words, it's worth the price of the trip: Why aimlessly drift along when you can consciously chart your course and head directly toward what you want?

In our complex, hurried, disconnected world we need to substantially link with each other as we've never done before, at an interpersonal level with our loved ones and in our communities. It's a perfect time to put meaning behind our choices and value in front of them. Loyalty needs to find a more prominent place in our lives. So does selectivity. We can't do it all, but we can do a lot. We can't have it all, but then we don't need everything. We just need to know what really matters and how to make it a part of our existence. Life gets simpler when we learn how to shift our focus like a video camera, from zoom to pan and back again. This way we sift through the noise, cut out the media clutter, consumptive pressure, and social expectations, and stay riveted on what really counts: our life, our health, our loved ones. What could be more simple than that?

Getting a Life

THE QUIZZES ARE OVER, GET READY FOR THE FINAL

You've taken ten quizzes while reading this book, now it's time for the final. It isn't a pencil and paper test; it's a take-home final. But don't feel pressured, you can take your time to finish. In addition, you get to grade yourself, you can use whatever resources you want, and if you have trouble with any of the problems you come across, you can ask for help, no questions asked.

We often say a problem is half solved once we understand it. Gaining a perspective requires reviewing the past, assessing the present, and projecting the future. As you've worked your way through these pages I hope you have a clearer view of the Ten Trends infiltrating our culture and how they've infected you. I'd guess you've already made some changes as a result of what you've read and hope you'll keep on going. This chapter will give you additional tools and encouragement to continue in your quest to lower your Cranky Quotient and help fight off the cranky virus.

You may wonder how much good your efforts will do; after all, you're only one person. Please remember that every flood begins with a single raindrop and massive social changes have taken place because of one person's passion. Imagine the contribution you can make to your community while changing the course of your life!

AT LAST: A NEW DIRECTION

When people hear my story they ask what it was exactly that turned my attitude around. While there's not one single answer to that question, I can remember some insights and experiences that turned me toward a new direction and helped me become who I am today. The incidents I'll highlight will probably remind you of similar moments in your own life. And they may also serve as a source of inspiration the next time you face a personal challenge. If I can do it, you can do it.

I DON'T WANT THIS ANYMORE

My first significant insight came two years after my divorce. I was working full time in a low-wage job. Every day was a struggle. I felt resentful, miserable, and though I was only twenty-seven I felt very old and tired. One night, in the middle of an Olympic-size bout of feeling sorry for myself I had a moment of clarity. I realized that unless I did something, I could spend the rest of my life feeling angry, inadequate, and resentful. At that moment I didn't realize my misery was self-imposed, but I did recognize there was no emotional rescue squad that was going to swoop in and save me. If any changes were going to occur they would have to come from me. I found this overwhelming! I asked myself what I wanted and I couldn't answer the question. I didn't know what I wanted but I knew I didn't want to feel so lousy anymore. The only thing I knew for sure was that I wanted to finish high school and get an education. This insight spurred me to take my GED, quit my low-paying job, and sign up for welfare so I could attend community college and get a degree—something I desperately desired.

SO NEAR AND YET SO FAR

My dream of finally getting an education seriously wavered as I stood at one of the registration tables at Lansing Community College. The woman at the table informed me that I was in the wrong building and had to go back two stations before she would be able to help me. As she spoke I felt panic surge inside me, beginning at my feet and working its way up to my throat. This was the second time that day I had had to go back and retrace my steps; to go back and do it *right*. I vividly remember my self-talk: A continuous loop that replayed the same self-damning statement, "If you can't even sign up for a class, if you're too stupid to get through registration, how do you expect to take a course and pass it?" I got out of line, wanting to disappear and never come back.

I thought, "Who am I to think I could actually go to school, that I'm *good* enough to get a college education?" After dropping out of high school not once, but twice, here I was, so close to the only thing I knew I wanted, but self-doubt was quickly overtaking me. What a fool I was to believe I could actually pull this off! Maybe I was destined to be miserable my whole life and I shouldn't try to fight it.

Despite my panic, I noticed a young woman off on the sidelines with tears in her eyes. For a moment I forgot about myself and asked her what was wrong. She, too, was having trouble registering. We went through the rest of the process together. I made two significant discoveries from this defining moment in my life:

1. Fear doesn't have to be a stopper. Still shaky and anxious, I managed to get through registration. I learned from this experience that I can control my fear rather than let it control me; I can take action anyway. It doesn't mean my fear magically disappears; it just means I'll be temporarily uncomfortable. When fear and self-doubt raise their ugly little heads, I've disciplined myself to move forward in spite of them.

2. Helping this young woman helped me discover that when I reach out to assist someone else, I forget about myself. That's how I learned the secret of customer service: that reaching out, being of service to another person, serves something inside me. I, the giver, benefit as much, if not more, than the receiver. It helped me understand the essence of *community*—that all of us are connected in a very comprehensible way, and we stay connected through cooperation.

FOLLOW THE EXAMPLES OF THOSE YOU ADMIRE

Another defining moment happened years later during a relationship crisis. Rob and I were fighting a lot and trying to resolve some core issues that would either bring us to resolution or cause us to go our separate ways. We began reading books, seeing a counselor, and paying close attention to our best friends, a couple who were several steps ahead of us in the relationship management process, including seeing the same counselor. One day I was sitting on the sofa, crying and feeling very sorry for myself. I'd been browsing through the three books sitting next to me and I could see their blurry titles through my tears:

On Becoming a Person by Carl Rogers; *A New Guide to Rational Living* by Albert Ellis; *The Intimate Enemy* by George Bach. And then I had a most astounding experience.

A ray of sunshine came through the window and swept across me. As I watched the books momentarily illuminate, a ray of thought passed through my mind: What would these wise, respected authors do if they were in my position? How would *they* handle this crisis? Would they be crying? I decided to approach the situation as they would, rationally and responsibly. Something shifted inside me and as I stood up I knew I was a different person. I had come to peace with this issue. It was a life-changing moment.

You probably caught on that all three of my major insights (taking responsibility, facing my fear, and choosing rationalism) were born from moments of panic or self-pity; I'd had years of practice in perfecting both of these emotions and could have qualified for an honorary degree. But, I finally learned how to cultivate life-affirming skills. After years of reading, reflecting, and persistently practicing the skills that control crankiness, I've created a life for myself that far surpasses any dream I ever had. Despite my losses and hardships, I'm happy with my life. I've learned to subdue my fears and summon my courage through conscious choice, self-discipline, and the repetition of self-affirming statements such as those listed in chapter 13. If I can do it, so can you.

ARE YOU WILLING TO WORK?

Getting a life, creating the life you once only dreamed of, takes work. But it's a gradual process and doesn't demand herculean effort. It requires only a series of small changes, consistently practiced over time. You don't have to jump off a cliff or take a dramatic plunge. *You just need to put conscious thought into what you want and how you plan to make it happen.*

Like watching a baby learn to walk, your entire life consists of little steps, moments in time where you make decisions that change who you are. These decisions will either take you a step closer to a desired destination, or away from your dream. You must first become conscious of those decisive moments because not all of them are obvious, and only a few are momentous. Most of them will be as simple as consciously deciding to drive the speed limit, declining a fatty food when you're trying to lose weight, or listening when a loved one talks to you, even if you don't feel like it.

Creating the life you want revolves around the core skills of self-awareness and conscious decision making. It means making the kinds of choices that you know take you a step closer to where you want to be or who you want to become. It means resisting the naysayers and negative thinkers who discourage you from being different, and by subduing your "old mental tapes" of self-damning or immobilizing messages.

If you have a moment of panic or crisis, remind yourself of successful defining moments from your life and the courage you possess. Think back on an extremely challenging moment when you prevailed; that's how strong you are. Sometimes just *surviving* a difficult circumstance is a real accomplishment! Through positive review, visualization, and self-affirming statements you can stifle your insecurities and summon the strength to stay on course. This kind of self-discipline keeps you pointed in the right direction. You'll occasionally get stalled or veer off course, but compassionately remind yourself that you have the capacity to get back on track. Treat yourself as nicely as you would a best friend.

PUTTING LIFE'S LESSONS TO WORK

In my speeches, I outline three memorable lessons learned during my twelve-year transformation; I hope they'll be as insightful to you as they were to me. Just so you know, they're still a part of my life today. I often find myself repeating these truths in a moment of doubt or denial:

- I am responsible for the decision I make.
- I have choices; even if they're difficult or limited, choices do exist.
- I need to take action because no one else will do it for me.

Constantly reminding myself that I am responsible, I have choices, and I need to take action has helped me engineer massive change and growth. I do my best to face myself honestly, to ferret out the intent behind my actions, and to assess whatever I find. I now recognize that defensiveness or excuses only perpetuate my misery. But acknowledgment and acceptance (or confrontation) of my flaws, hidden thoughts, and secret fears help move me toward the person I want to become.

I try to not blame others for my misery and instead shoulder my rightful accountability. I discipline myself to move toward my emotional pain and explore what's there (and why) rather than denying or defending it. I respectfully express my feelings and perceptions even when my viewpoint is unpopular. And I do my best to listen when someone I love or respect needs to criticize me. I may feel defensive, but I usually manage to control it and then I consider the truth in what he or she says.

I now realize that if I want to be a better person I have to take interpersonal and professional risks, consistently and persistently. Of course, it's uncomfortable, threatening, and scary. But my willingness to endure temporary discomfort yields long-term stability and inner fulfillment. I've become comfortable with the discomfort of personal change. My life is all about learning and improving as a human being, and I'm still working at it. My goal is to continue growing, changing, and evolving. The more I explore, the better I get. The better I get, the more I thrive. When I stumble, I get back up, even if I sit there awhile first and dust myself off or dress my wounds. I now understand that the "valleys" I've experienced in my life have helped my "peaks" reach new heights. I can't have one without the other.

—Ten Principles That Keep Your Cranky Quotient in the Cool Zone—

1. Live with purpose. Have a sense of who you are and what your life stands for. If this is something you've only thought about, but not taken to its full conclusion, writing your life mission statement will help you clarify the steps. Connect your sense of purpose with your everyday behavior to keep your life meaningful and congruent.

2. Enhance your self-awareness. When you self-monitor by using the Quick Stop!, Reset Button, Reality Bites, or EIS several times a day, you learn how to act as your own life coach. You encourage yourself, you don't allow yourself to get carried away with excuses, and you stay focused on your purpose. Awareness helps you prevent cranky behaviors before they take hold: Don't leave home without it.

3. Quit judging others. Take the energy you put into criticizing, judging, or sniping at others and channel it toward behaviors you can actually do something about: your own. Give up trying to mind other people's business and focus on what you need to do so you can become the person you want to be.

4. Capitalize on your innate wisdom. You're already familiar with much of what you've read in this book. Trust what you know and start practicing the good habits and healthy behaviors that will enhance your existence. Pursue them with a passion. It's like taking the good advice you'd give to a close friend.

5. Make conscious choices. Recognize when you've made the choice to get upset or angry. Although you can credit someone else for being the source of your bad mood, you're the one who's picked up the cranky baton. Accept that you're really not a victim of circumstances, you're the victim of a poor choice: letting someone else ruin your mood.

6. Think of yourself as a winner in the game of life: celebrate the positives. Study the negatives so you can prevent their recurrence. Live a healthy, vital life and share your bounty with others. Your winning attitude will generate its own energy field and people of like mind will be attracted to you.

7. Surround yourself with support. Spend your time with people who care about you, like to hear about your successes, and openly allow you to share your "boast moments." Avoid the naysayers; leave them in the dust because you no longer have time for pessimism in your life.

8. Replace negative emotions with positive ones. Quit worrying about trivial matters or running your life by fear. Laugh as much as you want; make smiling a habit. When a potential crisis raises its head, refrain from needlessly pushing the panic button. Assume good news unless you know better. If it's bad news, accept, adapt, or take what you consider to be the most appropriate action.

9. Stay connected. Invest in your relationships; enrich them. Let the people you care about know they're important in your life through little acts of appreciation. Be generous with compliments. Take a moment every day to cultivate one of your connections. Make a quick phone call, write a short note, give a few moments of attention. The

better your connections with others, the better your connection with yourself.

10. Choose compassion over crankiness. Instead of getting mad at some ill-mannered person who treats you rudely, think about how miserable he or she must be; think about what it would feel like to be that person at that moment. If a self-conscious, fumbling employee wearing the Trainee badge takes a long time to wait on you, say something encouraging. Your heart can't hold both contempt and kindness at the same time: choose the one that best serves *you*.

THE TEST IS IN WHAT YOU MANIFEST

There are examples all around you of people who consciously choose to live a life of harmony, inner peace, and happiness. There are also those who unconsciously create a life filled with chaos. You can see the visible consequences of the different kinds of choices people make. Those who create harmony and inner peace live with a sense of optimism and an open heart. Their decisions are based on trust. They feel in sync with their universe. Their confidence is evident in the risks they take and their willingness to accept responsibility. Their life isn't perfect, but they shrug off small annoyances and bless the little gifts that come their way. When bad things happen they work toward acceptance and ultimately recover. Sometimes these composed, centered people make it all look extremely easy.

The cranky ones approach their days almost as if they were in a battle; they compete, struggle, react. They keep an eye out for anyone who might try to take advantage while attempting to protect their backside. They play their cards close to their chest in fear they might disclose too much; after all, it might be used against them. Their world is filled with little annoyances and flaws that push their Cranky Quotient into the Hot Zone. And while they keep waiting for the one big break that will make things better—the Lotto, retirement, their stock splitting—they are convinced the other shoe is about to drop at any moment. When something bad does happen, they see it as confirmation of how hard life can be. Cranky people make life look very difficult indeed.

IT'S ALL IN YOUR MIND

I've been both of these types; maybe you have, too. These descriptions are a good reminder that the true test of life is all in your mind: what you believe affects what you expect, and what you expect, you manifest. Whether you're visualizing a goal or scheming to get ahead, your brain creates images around your dominant thoughts. This is an unconscious process; you don't actually feel these images, but they're there. Whether you realize it or not, you'll tend to gravitate toward the pictures you hold in your mind, like a moth drawn to a flame. Remember the times you've watched the Olympics and seen athletes close their eyes and make small movements before their event? They're consciously visualizing, and they've also done thousands of unconscious practices, too. Conversely, cranky people unconsciously focus on negative visualizations and that's why they end up with unlimited reasons to be cranky.

Chapter 13 offers over 100 examples of positive statements to help you visualize and manifest the life you want. But it's not just saying them, or seeing them, it's believing them with conviction. Before you can get the life you want you'll need to clear out the obstacles that limit your beliefs and foster a cranky lifestyle.

BEWARE OF THE BIG FOUR

Like a mirror, the external world will reflect your inner one. If you've been struggling to be happier and not succeeding, maybe it's because you're fighting the influences of what I call the Big Four. As long as I allowed them to shape my perceptions, I made little progress. In case you're wondering if I still experience the Big Four, I do, but they don't have the hold on me they once did. They might stage a visit, but they aren't allowed to spend the night.

Comprehending and Combating the Big Four

What you're about to read can help you change the course of your life. You'll need to ratchet up your self-awareness and honesty but if you remove these four negative influences from your life, things will change. Slowly, subtly, and gradually, you'll become more relaxed, less on guard, and more optimistic. You'll feel lighter; less burdened, and more open to possibility. You'll have more peace of mind. That's what it takes to "get a life." Here are the Big Four barriers to your happiness:

- insecurity
- fear
- blame
- greed

The Ins and Outs of Insecurity

Insecurity is a shroud that prevents you from feeling comfortable with who you are. As the linchpin of the Big Four, it inspires self-doubt rather than self-exploration. Insecurity feeds on fear, inspires blame, and incites greed. Insecurity binds you to inaction and blocks you from visioning positive outcomes. Before you can achieve a goal you need to have the vision, but insecurity keeps you from even thinking about what you want. When you allow insecurity to dominate, it will cause you to question yourself and your capabilities. You'll want to give up instead of try because you figure it won't make a difference anyway. Insecurity is all about trust.

You can liberate yourself from the cloak of insecurity by changing the way you think. You'll need to summon your inner resources and manufacture some temporary confidence until you build a permanent faith in your ability. This will come with practice, but if you need a refresher, go back and read the section in chapter 7 about *as if* thinking. Practice it as if your life depended on it, beginning with small behaviors in which you have no emotional investment, just to build the routine. As you get more comfortable, up the emotional ante. This approach will help you systematically replace your insecurity with confidence and self-assurance.

The Folly of Fear

Think of fear as a closed gate—a barrier that stops you in your tracks because you have no idea what's on the other side. Some people define FEAR as False Evidence Appearing Real. Your fear will conjure up all kinds of negative possibilities about what lies ahead, making it impossible for you to think of rewards or benefits; only potential loss. Yes, there are risks involved in facing an unknown and if you project massively negative outcomes and give them a life of their own, these grim scenarios will take over and immobilize you. Use your fertile imagination to project positive outcomes instead. Understand that there are many ways of traversing that closed gate. You can crawl under it, maybe even unlock it. But check it first, it might not even be locked at all: sometimes the biggest stoppers are in your mind.

If you conquer your fear you can find a chink and sneak through. On a good day, maybe you can jump the fence, or get a boost from someone else. In other words, the same energy you put into immobilizing yourself can be put into encouragement and action. Many of us make the mistake of thinking our fear will subside on its own. Don't wait; that may never happen. In all likelihood you'll need to take those first steps with fear following in your tracks, but it won't be able to keep up with you. Susan Jeffers gives similar encouragement in her book, *Feel the Fear and Do It Anyway*. Moving forward in spite of your fear is a powerful affirmation of trust in yourself and the perfect way to shrug off insecurity.

The Bane of Blame

Blame is a convenient scapegoat, and it's also a trap. It's always more tempting to think someone else "made" you feel cranky than take responsibility for your actions. But the truth is, you're making a choice. As long as you blame (your parents, spouse, kids, the world, God), you can't do anything to change the situation. Blame sits on the opposite side of the same continuum as responsibility. Once you quit blaming and start owning your accountability, you assume full control of your attitude and behavior. By flatly refusing to be ensnared by the clutches of blame you make an adult choice and place yourself in a position where you can freely and forcibly influence your world.

Take Heed of Greed

Greed is a virus that triggers feelings of unwarranted entitlement and contempt. Greed brings out the worst kind of competition, leaving no room for trust. It chews away at your spirit, breeding dishonesty and destroying integrity. When you get infected with greed, or contaminated by its cousin, jealousy, you sink to your lowest instincts. Greed will tempt you to throw away your principles to get something that rightfully belongs to someone else. When you let greed overtake you, even if you profit, you lose a part of yourself. Whatever you gain through greed (money, status, power, ego) will be contaminated. Ultimately, you'll end up the big loser. If you want to make a giant leap forward, dump your greed by the wayside and never look back.

There you have it. You can imagine how the Big Four cultivate chronic crankiness. In writing this, I remember that releasing myself from their clutches was a slow, methodical, yet infinitely rewarding process. I'm not suggesting you'll never experience insecurity, fear, blame, or greed again. You'll experience them momentarily but they won't have a grip on you as they once did: a short spike and you're done. If you've already conquered these barriers you know exactly what I'm saying. If you haven't, please know there are great things in store for you!

The Life You Want

Many of us spend our lives searching for happiness but never finding it. This is because looking for happiness chases it away. Happiness comes to us when we quit searching for it and just start *being* it. The life we want comes to us when we just start living it instead of waiting for it. This sounds very simple and in a way, it is.

Maybe it's time you quit *looking* for happiness and fulfillment and instead welcome and affirm what you have of both right now. If you want more, practice the principles in this book and incorporate the good ideas you've read or heard elsewhere. Start being the person you want to be, even if you have to force it in the beginning. If you keep waiting for the right time or circumstances you could end up waiting the rest of your life. Start now.

Habits Are the Stuff of Which Life Is Made

There's one big difference between cranky people and those who are composed and centered. It's the habits they practice. If you want to change your life, then change your habits. Do you want to be a more relaxed, less cranky person? Practice the habits that let you slow your pace and enjoy yourself, such as taking deep relaxing breaths and smiling more. Would you like to feel better about yourself? Develop new thinking habits; repeatedly tell yourself you're capable and worthwhile. Do you want to feel happier? Work on the habits of feeling appreciative and seeing abundance in your life. If you want to feel healthier, work on your eating and exercising habits. Regardless of the question, the answer is the same. Habits.

My everyday habits are completely different today from what they were during the years when I was cranky. I now enjoy getting up in the morning and at night I go to bed with a sense of appreciation and accomplishment. I can laugh at myself when I screw up and admit my flaws. I eat better. I exercise. My habits support the lifestyle I've come to love.

Cranky people engage in habits that support their crankiness while composed, calm, centered people engage in habits that support their connectedness. Pay attention to your habits: they'll tell you what you need to know about yourself.

One Last Hurdle to Jump

In reading this book maybe you've occasionally stopped and thought, "Wow. There's a lot of information here." You're right. I can't tell you how many times I've said the same thing. You only had to read it: I had to write it! Yet I wrote only one idea at a time; one word at a time. We live life the same way, one decision at a time, one day at a time. That's how we change, too: one behavior at a time. Think big, but keep the steps small and doable. Just as the old saying goes: Inch by inch life's a cinch. Yard by yard it's hard.

Sometimes, in a program, when I talk about practicing anti-cranky strategies such as the Quick Stop!, Reset Button, or Reality Bites, people say, "But that's a lot of work." Of course it is; initially. Change takes a certain amount of work. But overall, making positive changes is a whole lot less work than staying unhappy.

People also complain that it's too hard, they've already tried it, or it will take too long. They don't always realize these are just excuses. Some people use "advanced degree" rationalizations and detailed, logical sounding justifications, but when you strip them down, they too, are just excuses. It all gets down to this: If you don't like what's happening in your life, change. You can either change the situation or change yourself.

Just in case you're feeling a little short on time and you still have a few doubts about your ability to apply the ideas in this book, I thought I'd list some of the excuses that may pop into your head:

It's too complicated.
It's too hard.
I'll never be able to stick with it.
I don't have time.
My life really isn't all that bad.
I tried it once but it didn't work.
I don't know where to begin.
This sounds too simple. There has to be a catch.
It wouldn't work anyway.
I'm too busy.
I'm too miserable to try.
I'm too tired.
I'm too full.
I'm allergic.
Change is incompatible with my astrological sign.

Now you'll have to come up with some better excuses on your own. Of course, you'll be further ahead by putting your energy into positive outlets such as formulating your affirmations and personal life prescription so you can permanently immunize yourself against crankiness. That's what chapter 13 is all about.

The Emergency Department

WHERE TO GO WHEN
ALL ELSE FAILS

We live in a complex, contradictory society where the complications of everyday life can take their toll. This section is your personal emergency department—a private place you can visit in times of crisis to quickly restore your sense of well-being, revive your self-esteem, and cleanse your spirit. Here, you can liberally treat what ails you with an abundance of affirming ideas, positive images, and encouraging thoughts.

In keeping with the theme that it's the accumulation of little things in life that make us cranky, it's also the little adjustments and improvements that steer us toward a more positive direction. That's what you'll find here. Small, simple ideas with huge payoffs, if you take them to heart. They're yours to accept, internalize, and practice.

HELP WHEN YOU NEED IT

This material on positive affirmations has a dual purpose. My first intent is simply to provide you with a source of motivation. Reading these statements can serve as a quick pick-me-up whenever you need it. Just scan any page, either by category or random order, and welcome the encouraging nature of what you find. That's all you have to do. For your convenience, the affirmations for chapters 2 through 11 coincide with each Cranky Quiz item featured in that chapter. If there's a particular topic area in which you need a quick dose of comfort, go to the affirmations from that chapter.

The second purpose is deeper and longer lasting. All of these affirming statements represent important ingredients for your life mission and long-term personal life prescription, should you choose to take on this challenging assignment. You pick the specific item, and then put it to work. Just choose a particular behavior you want to work on and write the corresponding affirmation on a small piece of paper or the back of your business card. Carry it with you and read it often. Whether you use the positive statements in this chapter or create your own affirmations, here are four important considerations that will contribute to success:

1. Note that all of these statements are written in present tense, as if you've already accomplished them. It's important to express an affirmation as if you've already accomplished it so you can *internalize* the message. A phrase stated in the future tense will stay out there in the future as something you *want*, but don't yet have. While it's true that the behavior you're working on is still part of your future, phrasing it in present tense will eventually bring it into a *now* state. The more you repeat it, the more your subconscious begins to believe it.

2. Each statement is expressed in positive terms. Avoid using words such as *no, not, don't, won't, can't*. In writing your own encouraging statements, just think about the result—the way you want to feel and behave (rather than what you don't want) and choose your words accordingly.

3. Carry your statement with you and look at it every day. Memorize your affirmation so you can privately repeat it, regardless of where you are or what you're doing. Recite it several times a day.

4. Add to the impact by connecting positive images with your affirmation. See yourself engaging in the desired behavior. Feel yourself doing it exactly the way you want. The more vividly you can imagine this, the more effective your visualization will be. If you have trouble with the image, imagine sounds or feelings instead. Don't worry; it'll come. Work and rework your visualization as you repeat your affirmation.

Practice these simple steps over and over again until you've internalized the message. It takes a while for things to gravitate from your brain to your body, but be patient. In the beginning it could take anywhere from three weeks to three months; maybe more. Don't worry about the time. Just stay focused. Your consistent, persistent repetition will pay off. The more you practice these steps the better you'll get. The better you get, the faster you'll see the results.

Without fully realizing what's happening you'll gain in confidence and notice your behavior evolving toward your vision. This is why you need to be selective about the behavior you choose. Only by working on one item at a time can you exploit its full power. If you try to make too many changes at once you'll dilute the process and end up more frustrated and cranky than when you began. You don't need that. What you do need is to temporarily "put all your eggs in one basket," contrary to what most people tell us.

As you choose your area of focus, keep it to yourself in the beginning. The last thing you need is someone to tell you it won't work, or that you're crazy to try. I'm living proof that it does work and there are other good examples all around you. Athletes are a super example and *most serious athletes use this approach with great success*. They know that when they think vividly and repeat the process, nerves and fibers in their brains and bodies mobilize to make the picture happen, *even if they're not physically moving at the time*.

Think about the potential in this technique and envision what you can do with concentrated effort. Just remember, this intensely personal endeavor blends conscious desire with unconscious process. As you consciously focus on what you want, your subconscious will file it away. It may feel as if nothing is happening, but one day you'll catch it: You're different! You got it. Then you can move on to another area. Yes, this is exactly how I live my life, one small improvement at a time, and I absolutely love it! I'm a different person as a result of my affirmations, visualizations, and daily application of the strategies in this book.

THE POWER OF POSITIVE LIES

When I talk about positive lies in my speeches some people look at me with a raised eyebrow. They ask, "You *lie* to yourself?" I respond with an energetic "Yes!" and then explain what I mean. I'm convinced we lie to ourselves all of the time, only usually it's negative. We say we can't. We say we could never. We say we're not like that, but in truth, these are lies because we don't know what we're capable of until we try. Imagine how many times you've made statements like these and later disproved them.

You probably have no idea of your real potential. I certainly didn't. I'm a long way from the insecure, cranky, two-time high school dropout I once was, and there's still more potential inside me, waiting to be tapped. You have the capacity to connect with what's inside you. It's never too late. There's a reason you chose to pick up this book and maybe this is it. When you systematically work toward bringing out your best, something incredible happens, and I'll bet you're ready for such a miracle.

THE ART OF POSITIVE AFFIRMATIONS

I like to think of affirmations (and visualization) as positive lies. You may look at many of the statements in this section and think, "Well, it's a nice thought, but it certainly doesn't describe me!" You're right, it doesn't. At least not yet. But think of these statements as something you'll grow into.

I've positively lied to myself for years, and these encouraging falsehoods have contributed to my interpersonal growth and business success. I encourage you to try this clever form of positive self-programming. Here's how it works: Because your brain is unable to discriminate between fantasy and reality it accepts your positive lies, no questions asked. Your mind constructs images based on your words and that's why you want to think positive thoughts. Whether or not you know it, you will tend to gravitate toward whatever images you put into your head. You can imagine the negative pictures cranky people produce as a result of their constant griping and general mistrust of others and how it creates a self-perpetuating cycle of chronic crankiness!

In a way, positive affirmations are an adult form of *pretending*. People in my programs initially scoff at this notion. They say they're too old to pretend, but they don't realize how much of it they do. The most common form of adult pretending is that of self-deception (I'll pretend I didn't see that; I'll pretend I didn't eat that dessert; I'll pretend that salesclerk didn't give me back too much money). It makes all kinds of sense to direct this energy toward positive outcomes (I'll pretend I'm confident; I'll pretend it's easy for me to introduce myself to strangers) just like *as if* thinking encourages. I'll freely admit I'm all for employing this remnant from childhood to make me a better adult, especially since it works! I hope the following affirmations inspire you to begin an active self-improvement program that will last for the rest of your life.

—2. Compressed Time—

I live with a sense of inner peace and effective control over my time.

I take little inconveniences and time-consuming delays in stride.

I take time to exercise, eat properly, and maintain a healthy balance in my life.

I adapt to other people's paces rather than expecting them to adapt to mine.

I practice healthy sleep habits and awake rested and ready for my day.

On the road, I easily and consistently shrug off other people's aggressive behaviors.

I always drive the speed limit and avoid speeding to keep my stress low.

When communicating with others I slow my mind down so I can effectively listen.

I like to give whatever I am doing my full attention and focus.

I respect my time and perceive it as the precious commodity it is.

—3. Communication Overload—

I am a selective TV viewer, watching by choice instead of boredom or default.

I limit my exposure to daily news.

I am comfortable with silence and give myself quiet time each day.

I resist my curiosity about other people's business and concentrate on my own.

I talk with others about substantive issues that directly relate to us and our lives.

I consciously limit my exposure to ads and commercials to stay free of their influence.

I make up my own mind about substantive social or political issues.

I avoid graphic, violent images and keep positive pictures in my head instead.

I keep my backlog of paperwork and reading material trim and manageable.

I have a system for managing all of the information I'm exposed to every day.

—4. dis-Connectedness—

I successfully blend romanticism and rationalism for a healthy outlook on relationships.

I maintain interest and spontaneity in my primary relationship.

I keep agenda issues out in the open so my loved ones and friends know where I stand.

I constructively handle conflict and bring up sensitive issues with my partner.

I consciously keep myself enthusiastic and actively "tuned in" to my life.

I do all I can to support responsible parenthood.

I fully accept the choices I have made in the past and release old regrets.

I capably handle relationship challenges, past and present.

I accept family relationships for what they are, not what I wish they were.

I support quality connections and avoid crankiness in my relationships.

—5. Cost—

I handle my money in a balanced fashion, saving and spending with equal comfort.

I refuse to buy on price alone, and always consider quality, service, convenience, etc.

I think about the long-term effects of how I spend my money.

I recognize the folly of fighting over money or lying about how it's spent.

I recognize that there is far more to a job than salary and I live accordingly.

I honor social traditions and resist social pressures or expectations to go all out.

I buy gifts in line with what I can afford to keep the gift-giving process enjoyable.

I maintain a healthy outlook toward money and what it means to me.

I invest with my values in mind, placing my personal priorities over profit potential.

I maintain a lifestyle that enriches my spirit.

—6. Competition—

I accept that working conditions must change so my employer can stay competitive.

I accept the uncontrollable aspects of organizational change caused by market competition.

I adapt when market competition necessitates a change in my work responsibilities.

I help keep my workplace friendly and courteous.

I take time off from work, confident that my job will be there for me when I return.

I am free of competitive interpersonal pressures in my relationships.

I accept the inconveniences that come with attending events that involve crowds.

I take the everyday presence of social competition in my stride.

I embrace my competitive nature and apply it appropriately in all areas of my life.

—7. Customer Contact—

I let other people's discourteous behaviors roll off my back.

I handle self-serve systems or limited service personnel in a calm manner.

I accept the reality of occasional customer inconveniences.

I respect the position of support staff and treat them accordingly.

I give both compliments and constructive criticism on the service I receive.

I prevail in the face of workplace inconsistencies and challenging situations.

I skillfully resist the negative influence of cranky customers.

I treat my internal customers as well as I do my external ones.

I serve my family by bringing home the best of me, even after a bad day.

I actively involve myself in community service.

—8. Computers—

I embrace new technological tools and accept them as just another aspect of my life.

I use technological tools wisely to avoid needless interruptions.

I plan and execute projects on time, meeting deadlines with ease.

I match my abilities with technological tools so I can enjoy and benefit from them.

I value my long standing, low-tech relationships.

I consciously monitor and limit the time I spend on-line.

I intentionally engage in low-tech systems to maintain a balance in my life.

I use technology for my benefit and accept its limitations.

I take inconveniences and electronic breakdowns in stride.

I use voice mail systems and electronic communications to their full advantage.

—9. Change—

I am by nature flexible and open to change.

I shrug off the daily stress of changes, big and small.

I accept the inconvenience of security systems as a part of our mobile, global society.

I maintain my sense of wonder and awe.

I initiate communication so issues and conflicts can be quickly resolved.

I free myself from the burdens and traumas of my past so I can fully enjoy my present.

I support diversity and the rights of all people to flourish and prosper.

I consider learning as an important part of my work.

I periodically examine my beliefs and values as I grow and change.

I accept negative feedback and use it to measure how I come across to others.

—10. Coming of Age—

I have empathy for today's youth and the complex world in which they live.

I face the various phases and stages of my life openly and peacefully.

I accept and embrace the various options and choices I have in my life.

I accept myself, mentally and physically, and resist social "image" pressures.

I engage in an annual exam and periodic checkups as needed.

I lovingly take responsibility for my parents and/or children as they need me.

I sort through conflicting information on health and choose what's best for me.

I have an ability to maintain a strong focus and intense concentration.

I take good basic care of myself without relying on magic bullets or regular use of OTC medicines.

I accept what aging has to offer me with an open heart and mind.

—11. Complexity—

I keep my life balanced and rewarding.

I make decisions that simplify rather than complicate my life.

I pride myself on being a good citizen and I raise my voice about issues that matter.

I do my best to understand the natural world that surrounds me and how I fit into it.

I choose my thoughts and language carefully because I know they have an impact on my behavior.

I take full responsibility for the choices I make without holding others accountable.

I take a sense of pride in my community and contribute to its success.

I keep my consumer purchases simple and uncomplicated.

I do my best to think ahead and consider potential consequences
of my actions.

I live a full, satisfying life and celebrate my existence.

AT LAST, THE ANSWER!

After reading through these affirmations maybe you're beginning to
realize that at last, we've stumbled onto the condensed answer to the
question posed on this book's cover. The reason why everyone is so
cranky is because of *what is in their minds*. Thoreau said, "It's not what
you look at, but what you see." What's in your mind is the key to what
you see—in your world and in yourself.

WHY EVERYONE IS SO CRANKY

We're overwhelmed, overworked, overscheduled, and overspent. We
look for what's wrong instead of what's right. We snivel about what we
want instead of enjoying what we have. And we think we should get
what we want without having to work for it because we're entitled.
These negative, self-centered viewpoints cause us to bypass the simple
truth that happiness is already ours and it's always available, regardless
of what happens to us along the way. But happiness is impossible to
find when it's buried under greed, entitlement, and arrogance.

Perception equals reality. What we see out there in the world is
merely a reflection of what's inside. If you don't like the world you see,
adjust your internal mirror. Affirmations and positive visualizations
help you shift the angle so you get a better sense of yourself. When you
perceive yourself differently you see your world in a different light. A
year from now, maybe even just a few months, you'll be a different person for having read this book and put these ideas into practice. You'll
be happier. You won't feel cranky anymore.

THE MEANING OF LIFE

Rob has a sign posted above his desk that reads, "Life is not a meaning;
it's an opportunity." Life is here for us to do with as we will. We're the
ones who put the meaning into it. When I felt victimized by circumstance, my life felt devoid of meaning. But once I began making proac-

tive, conscious choices, things changed radically. Slowly, surely, they just kept getting better and better. They still are! It's as if the positive energy I've put into living a creative life continues collecting and multiplying on its own.

THE ANNUAL PERSONAL PROJECT

You might remember reading about my patience project in chapter 2 and how I worked on that behavior for an entire year. Within a few weeks I was struck by how many times a day I got to practice this skill (instead of getting cranky or impatient as I had done in the past). Patience was never one of my virtues but it is now, and every day I benefit from the 365 days I worked on it. Because this personal project was so successful it's now an annual endeavor, with a different behavioral focus each year.

The most exciting part was discovering the cumulative effect; that is, any behavior I work on for such a long time stays with me and continues to improve, year after year. For example, I'm even more patient now than I was at the end of the year I spent working on it, and the same goes for the other targeted behaviors I've chosen. It makes sense that twelve months of practice is enough to make a behavior habitual. It becomes me and I become it. How do I decide what I want to work on? I don't know. Ideas just sort of come to me. I figure they're a gift from the universe, and the work I put in throughout the year is my gift back to the universe.

YOU GOTTA HAVE A THEME

In 1995 I felt a professional growth spurt coming on. I had written one book, begun another, and had been invited to deliver a keynote speech at a National Speakers Association meeting. This is always an honor for someone in my profession. Rob and I had survived two very tough years in our relationship and we were back in sync with each other. Things were going so well, and I had an ongoing sense of positive anticipation that wonderful things were waiting in the wings.

I told Rob about my emerging professional growth spurt and we somehow conjured the idea of creating a theme for a year that brimmed with the promise of positive change. We called it the Year of Transition, imagining that we were moving to a new level, personally and professionally. In actuality, it was a special year, though not as spectacular or momentous as the ones that would follow. What actually made it most special was that we had created a purposeful focus with our "annual theme" idea.

We decided to continue this practice and created a ritual around it. Each year now on the Winter Solstice we light a candle, munch on appetizers, share some wine, and hold a ritual. We take turns reviewing our year, month by month, as well as we can remember, choosing to highlight only the positives. On New Year's Eve we hold another ceremony to celebrate the new theme we've selected and to project our vision of the year ahead. This seemingly simple practice has changed our lives. All together, we have now celebrated:

the Year of Transition
the Year of Celebration
the Year of Exploration
the Year of Adventure
the Year of Lightness

It wasn't until the second year that we realized our themes were creating a kind of synergy. In late spring Rob and I were talking about something good that had recently happened and one of us said, "Of *course* it would happen: This is our Year of Celebration!" When something bad occurred, we found ourselves saying, "Hey, we don't want to waste time thinking about negatives. After all, this is our Year of Celebration!" That's when we realized we were onto something.

Choosing a theme has given us a special way in which to view our world—a shared lens that gives us a unique perspective and way of interpreting events. The results are just short of astounding. This book is the direct product of two annual themes. I doubt I would have conceived the idea, taken the necessary steps, or embarked on such a daunting project without the inspiration that our annual themes have given us. It was during the Year of Exploration that I began researching this topic and exploring my potential as writer. I made a series of good decisions and they paid off. It was during the Year of Adventure I finished the proposal, sold the book to Hyperion, and began writing it.

Rob and I are completely taken with this process and we plan to continue it for the rest of our lives. People ask us how we come up with our themes. At some time during the last quarter of the year an idea comes to us and often, in the beginning, we're not even sure what it means. The word often pops up during a conversation and if it resonates for both of us, we take it. As the year unfolds, so does the theme. We commission a colleague of mine, Marta Varee Pearson, to design a colorful poster for us each year so we have a celebratory reminder of our focus.

Many of our friends have adopted the practice of annual themes, both couples and singles. Program participants are intrigued by the idea and many of them, too, have followed suit. Focusing on an annual theme has added meaning to Rob's and my life in more ways than we could express.

SOMETHING TO TALK ABOUT

It's probably occurred to you that sharing a common theme and having a personal annual project gives a couple something personal to talk about besides work or family hassles and the news. And there's another practice that's very much a part of the life Rob and I share. We call it "processing." Every day we sit down and process (talk, share, closely interact) our day. We call it processing because of our focus on the *process* of events rather than content. We discuss in depth how we felt, what we perceived, and how we interpreted our experiences of the day. We spend little time on the *content*; that is, what we did, who we talked with, or what we accomplished. We take turns talking, we both listen. Processing has become a precious daily ritual.

When I write a book, I need a lot of uninterrupted time to myself so I end up going away for a few months on retreat. I miss Rob a lot during that time, and he me. Processing over the phone is far less satisfying than face to face, but we try anyway. For us, being separated is one of life's non-monetary cost factors and right now we're willing to pay the price. But our ability to process—to talk openly, honestly, and in depth about what's happening with both of us at an interpersonal level—helps keep us connected, even across the country. It also makes Rob's visits during my time away very special and celebratory.

THE POWER OF PURPOSE

Finding a way to put meaning in your life directly connects to having a sense of purpose. When you have a purpose and base your behavior on it, things make sense. Somehow, purpose always pierces through the clutter and gives you a clear bearing on what you're doing, and why— maybe even how to do it better.

In 1990 I took myself on a two-day business retreat to rewrite my business mission statement and update my business plan. I came back from that retreat with a personal life mission statement, too, and I've used it as my "foundation of purpose" ever since. Rather than explain what I wrote, or how, below you'll find my current version in its entirety. I print it out on rainbow paper, encase it in a plastic sleeve, and display it. It's been a wonderful addition to my life. In moments of self-doubt or when I need to make a decision I can consult my mission statement to remind me about my purpose.

—My Life Mission Statement—

1. *My personal mission in life is to* . . .

nurture my emotional, physical, and spiritual self; to sustain healthy, supportive relationships with my loved ones and friends; to consciously experience, affirm, and celebrate my existence; and honor the natural world.

2. *I accomplish this through* . . .

- continual self-exploration and conscious self-monitoring
- self-confrontation and acceptance of feedback from others
- maintaining and contributing to supportive relationships
- scheduling my time, energy, and activities in an appropriate manner and level

3. *My values and philosophy include the following* . . .

- I believe that I am worthwhile and deserving of inner peace, personal fulfillment, and professional achievement
- I have the capacity to learn, grow, change, and improve, and prosper from every experience, should I so choose

- I value the human spirit and potential, and dedicate my efforts to seeking and celebrating that potential
- I value honesty, integrity, openness, and unconditional support in my close relationships

4. *Based on all of the above, I commit to . . .*

- creating an annual goal structure in the following areas: personal, professional, physical, family, spiritual, and financial
- scheduling and participating in an annual physical exam with recommended follow-up
- periodically reflecting on things I feel grateful about, and to resist taking what I appreciate for granted
- reminding myself that the choices I make can be conscious or unconscious, and choosing to make conscious ones
- engaging in regular, rigorous exercise (strength, endurance, flexibility), maintaining a healthy diet, and relaxation time
- choosing activities that feed my spirit, enhance my being, challenge my psyche, and let me laugh, let go, and have fun
- making rational rather than irrational choices, confronting and coming to terms with my mistakes, and letting them go
- limiting my exposure to TV, negative media images, and other potentially undermining or distracting influences
- exercising prudence in my purchases, avoiding wasteful packaging and excessive consumption, and monitoring my personal level of impact on the environment
- investing in my future by creating quality products for clients and establishing a consistent, long-term savings plan

Frequently Asked Questions about Mission Statements

1. *Do you practice your mission statement to the letter?* There's always room for improvement. But it gives me an overall sense of why I'm on this earth and how I want to conduct myself while I'm here. I keep a copy in my office posted next to my computer where I can see it. I carry a copy with me when I travel so I can look over it before I go to bed if I like. For the first couple of years I read my life mission statement weekly; now I might read it once or a twice a quarter. Frequent

readings keep the concepts fresh and while I don't have the whole thing memorized, I have a general sense of it.

2. *Has it made a difference?* By all means. It operates like a road map, reminding me of the direction in which I'm headed. For example, I'm far more faithful about scheduling my annual physical exam and making sure I follow up with mammograms and other preventive procedures I'd rather avoid. In fact, I'm inclined to make fairly healthy lifestyle choices because I have made a statement about doing so. Sometimes I wonder if it's merely an accident that I quit reading graphic mysteries and gripping suspense novels (I never did watch the movies) just a few years after writing the statement about negative images and undermining influences.

In 1995, Rob and I had to make a decision that would involve spending a large sum of money. We both sat down to process, deciding that it might help to begin our discussion by reading our respective mission statements. After a few moments of silence we looked at each other and said, "Well, that was easy. It's all right here in front of us. Let's go for it!" and then we went off to have lunch and celebrate. It happened just like that. The decision was "easy" because we'd already done the work.

3. *How long does it take to write a mission statement?* There are many answers to this question: a few hours, a few months, a year, the rest of your life. Let me explain. Your life mission statement is a living document, so in a way it will always be a "work in progress," just as you will. My first draft took about three hours, and then I tweaked it over the next month. But that's probably an exception. I think mine came so quickly because of what I do for a living. Lofty ideas are part of my life: They're what I talk about in my presentations. Even before I had a mission statement, I was aware of, and practiced, many of these concepts. Sitting down and summoning the words was relatively easy. Rob spent nearly six months drafting his life mission statement, and that might be a more reasonable projection.

If you're thinking, "Six months? That's a long time!" Maybe. But it's only a few minutes at a time, and it's such an infinitely positive, affirming exercise, you change just a little bit every time you touch it.

4. *What if I don't know what my mission is?* Even if you did know, I would suggest that before you put pen to paper, just spend some quiet

time thinking about your existence and what's meaningful to you. As you go through your day, stop and reflect on what you're doing. Think about what brings you fulfillment, feeds your spirit, and fills your heart. Reflect on your philosophy of life and what you value. Contemplate your core beliefs and the kind of life you'd like to live. Consider the motives behind your behavior: positive motivations, that is.

You don't want your mission statement to reflect any negatives such as the Big Four: insecurity, fear, blame, or greed. You want this document to be reinforcing and celebratory. You'll be surprised what surfaces when you begin focusing on these areas: Your values, beliefs, and philosophy will begin to take form. Carry a pen and notepad with you so that when you get a thought you can write it down and add it to your draft. Let the ideas come to you rather than forcing them.

5. *What happens if you violate your principles?* This will happen; count on it, particularly in the beginning. Your mission statement is a reflection of *ideals*. Similar to the affirming statements found in this chapter, it's a collection of behaviors you aspire to and want to incorporate in your life. There will be times you don't quite make it, but you still have a positive road map of where you want to go and it helps you live more consciously.

My behavior sometimes conflicts with the principles and practices in my life mission statement. I have an occasional crisis where I temporarily lose it and throw my skills out the window. These moments are infrequent and far less intense than they once were, but they do happen. My self-awareness is such that I usually know exactly what I'm doing and this takes some of the "fun" out of my dysfunction. Like everyone else, I have expectations about how I think the world should operate and if I didn't closely monitor myself I could slip into road rage or become a customer from hell. As for other transgressions (or their potential), if it weren't for obnoxious commercials I might watch too much TV. And though I scan all the tabloid headlines while standing in the checkout lane, I have the discipline to stifle my curiosity about what's inside. No, I don't buy them. Ever.

As for value conflicts, being a horse owner causes me occasional misgivings. It's a pretty consumptive sport, what with the expense of stabling, lessons, clothing, equipment, and shows. My rationalization is that riding is my only hobby and one that brings me great pleasure and continual learning.

6. *Do you ever update your mission statement*? Yes, when I feel the need. But since writing it, I've made very few changes. Mostly the wording rather than the content. It did occur to me two years after drafting my original document that I had no line about income so I added the last item. I'm still working on my financial identity. For years now, I've recognized (and accepted) that loving what I do for a living is more important to me than how much money I make. I'm very clear on what I value, and live accordingly. This is an example of why it helps to understand your driving values.

7. *Should you tell other people*? It all depends. Just as in goal setting, in the beginning, it may be well to keep this to yourself. It's a profoundly personal exercise and the last thing you want is discouragement. I do, however, recommend that couples share their respective mission statements with each other and use these important documents as an ongoing part of the relationship.

8. *Does everything you write have to be completely true*? Your life mission statement sets a direction of how you want to live, so it's a stretch of the truth, like a positive lie. In the beginning, when I would read my mission statement in its entirety, sometimes I would think, "Wow. This is pretty lofty stuff. I'm a long way from perfect and this looks like perfection." It is lofty. It's supposed to be. I still sometimes think it's a stretch, but this document is intended to define the purpose of your existence. Your mission statement reflects your higher self, your potential, your possibilities. It gives you something to which you can aspire. Again, the more you read it and tweak it, the longer you live with it, the more your behavior will reflect your words.

9. *Does anything in your life change as a result*? It all depends on how much you internalize these principles. The more you read this document, the more you'll believe it. The more you believe it, the more you'll put it into practice. If you write your mission statement and tuck it away in a drawer and never look at it again, it may have no effect. But if you regard it as a living document and make it a part of your life, I'd say yes. It may be gradual and it will probably be subtle, but you'll feel the change. I certainly have.

After reading these questions and answers I hope you've come to the conclusion that this important exercise has nothing to do with quick fixes or instant gratification. It's a prescriptive, long-term life improvement plan. As you move away from sources of crankiness, you simultaneously shift toward a more centered space. The transition is smooth, gradual, subtle. If you expect something to happen immediately you defeat the purpose. The beauty of drafting a life mission statement is that it forces you to take in the whole while you work on the parts.

FORMULATING YOUR PERSONAL LIFE PRESCRIPTION

Creating your life mission statement gives you a big picture of the possibilities, but you're not done yet. You need a mechanism for blending the ideal with the real. That's what your "Personal Life Prescription" (PLP) is all about. It's the last step in your take-home final—a day-to-day plan that blends your innate wisdom, core values, and desire to create a better life. Your PLP reflects not what life has to offer you, but what you have to offer it. Constant focus and consistent application of these practices will stamp out crankiness and connect you with all you hold important. It's your personal challenge to achieve your personal best. Once you know what you need to do next, your PLP helps you put it into place.

All you need to do is complete all of the fill-in sentences in this chapter. As our teachers told us when taking a multiple choice test, sometimes the first answer that comes to mind is the right one. In this instance, though, you must be sure that your answer hinges on *your* behavior and your ability rather than someone else's. That's why each statement ends with an "I." It is *you* who must take control.

This exercise is best when written down. If it's convenient, make a copy of this page and fill in each item. Zero in on the one or two items that hold the most potential for producing crankiness in your life. Write them down on a small piece of paper or the back of your business card. Read them often so you can review the behaviors you've prescribed and track your progress. Your day-to-day application of these specific, prescribed behaviors is what makes your mission statement work. You know what you need to do, and if you take your own good advice you'll reap the rewards. In just a short time you'll have worked your way out of the Cranky Zone and into a state of satisfaction.

You can "recycle" this exercise innumerable times and come up with a new answer every time.

—My Personal Life Prescription: To Be Taken as Needed—

I can reduce the pressure of compressed time if I:

I can reduce my communication overload if I:

I can mend my dis-connectedness if I:

I can minimize the conflicts of cost if I:

I can be less affected by all kinds of competition if I:

I can improve both sides of customer contact if I:

I can better deal with computers and technology if I:

I can more effectively embrace change if I:

I can constructively manage my own coming of age if I:

I can simplify the complications of complexity if I:

Add a Few Supplements to Your Prescription

Every now and then we need a mood supplement to give us a boost, so for the overachievers among us I've added a self-improvement bonus round. This, too, is a fill-in exercise and worthy of being written down and kept. You might recall in chapter 3 we discussed how athletes apply the process of focus, drill, and visualization. That's what it takes to make your personal life prescription effective. It can work for you only if you work for it. I find a lot of comfort in knowing that when it gets right down to it, you already know what you need to do. I've spent many hours of my life filling in these kinds of statements and watching my program participants do the same, and I'm always impressed at our ability to produce a useful answer. *We know!*

I too knew for years what I needed to do, yet I denied and resisted my own wisdom. It seemed too hard, too impossible. Now this is how I live my life. Just so you know, I've answered all of the following questions and have them in a file. I'll bet my answers aren't all that different from what you'll come up with. Indeed, we do know. And knowing without doing is far worse than not knowing.

—Some Mood Supplements for When You Need Them—

To keep my crankiness at a minimum I need to:

To maintain my connections with others I need to:

One thing I need to do more of in my life:

One thing I need to do less of:

One way I can add more enjoyment and fulfillment to my existence:

One way I can add more levity, laughter, and lightness to my life:

One way I can increase my level of appreciation for what I have:

One way I will encourage myself to continue these positive practices:

BEGENDINGS

They say all good things must come to an end but I like to think that good things go on; they just change their form. That's why I made up the word *begendings*. The end of this book really isn't the end. It represents the beginning of new and better things for you: stronger connections, more inner calm, and a renewed sense of community. It's up to you now, to take that next step. I hope in reading this book you found what you were looking for. Maybe you've appreciated rediscovering that the most important place to search for what you want is inside you. Embrace your wisdom; let it do its work and trust that others will do the same.

THERE IS A PROBLEM AND THERE IS HOPE

Writing this book has been a wonderful test of my convictions. For years, as I watched the cranky virus take hold and spread across my nation (in fact, our world), I felt so helpless, knowing I too was being infected. When I began writing this book I sometimes found it ironic that I, such an optimistic person, had chosen to write about such an inherently negative topic.

I felt as if I were opening an interpersonal Pandora's Box for all of us. While collecting and reading various articles and books I expected at some point I might get depressed because of the somber subject matter, but this never happened. It took me a while to realize that while I was temporarily focused on a problem, I always came back with a constructive strategy or positive alternative for addressing it. Although I knew we were facing a massive predicament, there was always hope.

I still feel that way. Just like the ending of Pandora's story, ours too, ends on a positive note. In your quiet moments you might just hear a little voice that whispers, "Yes, there is hope. Yes, there is promise, and there's plenty to go around." Listen to it. Let it be your guide. That little voice is your own.

Index

About the Author

C. Leslie Charles, founder of TRAININGWORKS, a human resource development firm, provides her clients with "communication solutions for changing organizations." An award-winning speaker, she has five books in print. An active member of the National Speakers Association (and two-term director), Leslie and her life partner, wildlife photographer Rob Carr, live on a four-acre wildlife preserve near East Lansing, Michigan. Her hobbies are horseback riding, reading, and hiking.

For information about Leslie's presentations, contact her at:
C. Leslie Charles
P.O. Box 956
East Lansing, MI 48826
phone: (517) 675-7535
or visit the whyiseveryonesocranky.com website.